D1795576

A Guide to Emissions Trading

A Guide to Emissions Trading
Risk Management and Business Implications

Edited by Cyriel de Jong and Kasper Walet

RISK
B O O K S

Published by Risk Books, a Division of Incisive Financial Publishing Ltd

Haymarket House
28–29 Haymarket
London SW1Y 4RX
Tel: +44 (0)20 7484 9700
Fax: +44 (0)20 7484 9800
E-mail: books@riskwaters.com
Sites: www.riskbooks.com
www.riskwaters.com

Every effort has been made to secure the permission of individual copyright holders for inclusion.

© Incisive Media Investments Limited 2004

ISBN 1 904339 23 9

British Library Cataloguing in Publication Data
A catalogue record for this book is available from the British Library

Managing Editor: Sarah Jenkins
Copy Editor: Andrew John
Editorial Assistant: Tamsine Green

Typeset by Mizpah Publishing Services, Chennai, India

Printed and bound in Spain by Espacegrafic, Pamplona, Navarra

Conditions of sale
All rights reserved. No part of this publication may be reproduced in any material form whether by photocopying or storing in any medium by electronic means whether or not transiently or incidentally to some other use for this publication without the prior written consent of the copyright owner except in accordance with the provisions of the Copyright, Designs and Patents Act 1988 or under the terms of a licence issued by the Copyright Licensing Agency Limited of 90, Tottenham Court Road, London W1P 0LP.

Warning: the doing of any unauthorised act in relation to this work may result in both civil and criminal liability.

Every effort has been made to ensure the accuracy of the text at the time of publication. However, no responsibility for loss occasioned to any person acting or refraining from acting as a result of the material contained in this publication will be accepted by Incisive Financial Publishing Ltd.

Many of the product names contained in this publication are registered trade marks, and Risk Books has made every effort to print them with the capitalisation and punctuation used by the trademark owner. For reasons of textual clarity, it is not our house style to use symbols such as TM, ®, etc. However, the absence of such symbols should not be taken to indicate absence of trademark protection; anyone wishing to use product names in the public domain should first clear such use with the product owner.

Contents

List of Contributors

Andreas Arvanitakis is a senior analyst at Point Carbon in London. He is also a qualified journalist and has covered the political and market aspects of the Kyoto Protocol, following the Kyoto process closely from its starting phase. Andreas has published numerous features, analysis and news articles on political and corporate issues concerning the energy sector and emissions trading, climate change, the Kyoto Protocol, and other environmental issues. Andreas has an MA in international politics from the Free University of Brussels and a BA in European studies (French) from the University of Manchester.

Véronique Bovee is currently director of the Dutch office for EcoSecurities in The Netherlands. She has over 5 years of experience in the field of energy and climate change, particularly with respect to the flexibility mechanisms of the Kyoto Protocol, climate change policy, analysis of renewable energy and energy efficiency projects, and capacity building. Véronique has worked in various different developing countries and countries in Central and Eastern Europe (CEE) and has worked for clients in the private sector, national governments and international organisations including the United Nations Development Programme, the United Nations Environment Programme, the United Nations Foundation, the World Bank, the Corporación Andina de Fomento (CAF) and the International Fund for Renewable Energy and Energy Efficiency. Véronique has a masters degree in environmental studies from the University of Utrecht and a masters degree in law (specialising in environmental law), also from the University of Utrecht.

Atle Christer Christiansen co-founded Point Carbon in 2000, where he currently holds the position of director. Previously, Atle worked as a senior research fellow at the Fridtjof Nansen Institute in Norway, with particular focus on climate and energy policy. His areas of expertise include climate policy, emissions trading, flexible mechanisms, mathematical modelling, numerical simulation, technological change and innovation, and new renewable energy. Atle holds an MSc and PhD in chemical engineering from the Norwegian University of Science and Technology (NTNU). He also holds a BA in Philosophy. He has been widely published in a range of international peer-reviewed journals, and is the lead author of numerous research reports and carbon market analyses.

Jos Cozijnsen is a self-employed consulting attorney, based in Utrecht. He specialises in climate change, in particular, emissions trading and has extensive international environmental law experience. From 1993 to 1997 he worked for The Netherlands' Environment Ministry. From 2002–2004 he joined Ecofys, and on behalf of Ecofys, worked a year as intern for Shell Global Solutions on CO_2 business development. Jos has organised numerous workshops on emissions trading and climate neutral entrepreneurship. His publications include: *Survey on capacity and institutions building for the use of Joint Implementation and risks and incentives for companies in the context of the European Climate Change Programme*, published by the European Commission, and "European development on emissions trading; an analysis in the framework of the Kyoto Process", published in *Greenhouse Gas Market Perspectives: Trade and Investment Implications of the Climate Change Regime*.

Robert S. Dischel has worked in the capital markets for almost two decades. He was a quantitative analyst of fixed income securities for Paine Webber, a director of quantitative developments at MetLife, a manager of mortgage-backed securities portfolios and a managing director at Aetna, the US Insurer. Robert is a frequent speaker at weather risk, energy, and financial conferences, and has published several articles on weather risk practices, climate and forecasting. He is the consultant editor of *Climate Risk and the Weather Market*. Robert earned a PhD from New York University in 1975, is certified by the American Meteorological Society as a Consulting Meteorologist, and is a member of the National Council of Industrial Meteorologists in the US.

Steve Drummond is managing director of CO2e.com LLC, the global greenhouse gas (GHG) emissions broker. Steve founded CO2e in 2000 with his partner Carlton Bartels, and runs the global business from its headquarters in London. CO2e has a long history of being actively involved in the development of new environmental markets and Steve sits on a number of committees that are currently shaping the European Emissions Trading Scheme. Prior to CO2e, Steve was a partner at PricewaterhouseCoopers in Australia, where he led financing services to the energy sector, and the global climate change financial advisory team. Steve holds a BSc in engineering from Leeds University and an MBA from Warwick Business School.

Dirk Forrister is managing director at Natsource-Tullett Europe in London where he advises European financial and industrial clients, as well as governments, on environmental markets. He has provided advisory services to numerous European private sector clients on GHG market strategies flowing from the EU Emissions Trading Directive, and he has advised a major European bank on carbon fund design. Dirk has contributed to Natsource's consulting services on carbon market implications of policy choices to the Dutch Government, the Canadian government, the UK and the EU as well as market intelligence reports to the World Bank. Prior to joining Natsource, he was chairman of the White House Climate Change Task Force under President Clinton, and he was an assistant secretary of energy in the US. He also served as energy programme manager at Environmental Defense, a major US-based NGO, and before this, as counsel to US Congressman, Jim Cooper, of Tennessee.

Anthony Hobley is a Senior Associate with Baker & McKenzie's Global Climate Change and Clean Energy Practice Group. He now specialises in both environmental law and climate change/clean energy law. Anthony's clients include the EU Commission, World Bank, BP, DuPont and BHP Billiton. Governments, international and financial institutions regularly consult Anthony on many legal aspects relating to the Kyoto Protocol and the design of emissions trading systems. Anthony has lectured and written widely on all subjects of environmental law, particularly in relation to contaminated land, renewable energy and emissions trading under the Kyoto Protocol. Anthony has a first class honours degree in chemistry with physics and recently completed a masters degree in environmental law.

Michiel ten Hoopen joined EcoSecurities as carbon advisor in September 2003. Michiel provides analytic, economic, financial, and environmental advice for private and public sector clients to support the development of GHG reduction projects and GHG management strategies in the energy, industrial and waste management sectors. Michiel has three years of experience in the field of climate change and energy. His main research areas include climate change policy, the flexibility mechanisms of the Kyoto Protocol, the natural gas transport market and the financial analysis of sustainable energy projects and technologies. He has worked for both industry and government clients including the EU and the Dutch and UK governments. Michiel previously worked for the Foundation Joint Implementation Network and the University of Groningen.

Tim Jackson is professor of sustainable development in the Centre for Environmental Strategy at the University of Surrey, and associate of the New Economics Foundation. He has published widely on different aspects of climate policy, and has a special interest in the Kyoto mechanisms – including emissions trading, Joint Implementation and the Clean Development mechanism. He is currently employed at the University of Surrey under a research fellowship on the social psychology of "sustainable consumption". In March 2004, he was appointed to the UK Sustainable Development Commission as chair of the Economics Steering Group.

Vasco de Janeiro works as an adviser on environment and sustainable development at the Union of the Electricity Industry (EURELECTRIC) in Brussels. He deals at policy level with issues such as sustainable development, climate change and energy efficiency. Before joining EURELECTRIC, Vasco completed a traineeship at the European Commission on foreign policy and worked for a consultancy firm in Lisbon on project management. Vasco holds a BSc with honours in engineering and industrial management from the Technical University of Lisbon and an MA in international politics (with distinction) from the Free University of Brussels, where he wrote a thesis on the implications of the Kyoto Protocol in EU-US relations.

Brett Janissen is a senior manager with The Allen Consulting Group, a leading Australian economic and policy consulting firm. He has worked extensively on greenhouse and industry policy issues – including as an economist and senior policy adviser to the Australian government. Brett managed the emissions trading team within the Australian Greenhouse Office (AGO) – the lead government agency on climate change policy within Australia – from 1998 to 2003. He was principal author of the AGO's emissions trading discussion paper series, the Australian government's credit for early action initiative, and AGO advice on emissions trading issues to the Council of Australian Governments' Energy Market Review. He has written and presented widely on these issues both in Australia and overseas. Brett has an honours degree in economics from the University of Newcastle (New South Wales).

Josef Janssen is managing director of Emissions Trading Solutions St. Gallen AG (ETSG), based in Switzerland. Formerly, Josef was head of emissions trading and climate policy at the Institute for Economy and the Environment at the University of St. Gallen. In 1998, he advised the Italian Ministry of Environment on the Kyoto mechanisms and, in this capacity, was member of the Italian delegation to the international climate policy negotiations at the EU and UN level. Josef holds a masters degree in economics from the University of Konstanz (Germany) and a PhD from the University of St. Gallen (Switzerland). His PhD thesis is entitled "Risk Management of Investments in Joint Implementation and Clean Development Mechanism Projects".

Cyriel de Jong is currently a research director at Maycroft and assistant professor at the Rotterdam School of Management, Erasmus University. Cyriel graduated *cum laude* in econometrics at Maastricht University in

The Netherlands and worked for De Nationale Investeringsbank NV. He completed a PhD thesis on financial derivatives and has several years of experience as a consultant in energy markets. Recently, Cyriel de Jong published on energy risk management issues in *Energy Risk* magazine, *Commodities Now* and contributed to the third edition of *Managing Energy Price Risk*.

Curt Kaminer has completed over US$7 billion in emissions trading transactions while managing portfolios in the US and international emissions and energy markets. He is a frequent contributor to conferences and symposia in this field. Curt is a charter holder of the Institute of Chartered Financial Analysts.

Makoto Katagiri is currently representative director and president of Natsource Japan Co, heading all the Asian business activities in Natsource Group, to realise the co-habitation of economy and global environmental protection. In addition to this, Makoto is the secretary general of IBRD Prototype Carbon Fund Office inside the Mitsubishi Corporation, as well as president of Green Diamond Inc in the US state of Delaware. Makoto joined Mitsubishi Corporation in 1976, and has engaged in several overseas operations and regional coordination activities. In this capacity, he has visited more than 90 countries in the world. His most recent overseas assignment was as general manager in West & Central Africa, where he made several achievements in the fields of environment, education, medicals and telecommunications.

Andy Kruger is vice president of Cantor Fitzgerald Environmental Brokerage Services, where he is responsible for serving environmental credit buyers and sellers within the Ozone Transport Commission, SIP Call, and mid-US states. Andy is an environmental engineer and attorney, who has over 14 years of emissions trading and brokering experience. Andy co-chaired the Connecticut Department of Environmental Protection's committee for development of an emissions trading and banking regulation. Andy was elected to a three-year term on the board of directors of the Emissions Marketing Association (EMA), where he also serves as EMA's secretary. Prior to his tenure with Cantor Fitzgerald, Andy held positions as an environmental engineer for the US Environmental Protection Agency in the Office of Mobile Sources, a project engineer at AER*X and an environmental attorney at a leading Connecticut law firm.

Josh Margolis, an internationally recognised emissions trading expert, is currently managing director of Cantor Fitzgerald Environment. Since 1985 Josh has provided environmental brokerage and related consulting services to clients throughout the United States, Canada, Europe, South America, Australia, and in former Soviet Union states.

Anna McCann is an associate at Baker & McKenzie, London. She is part of the environmental law team advising on contaminated land, waste and water issues, and health and safety matters. Anna also works closely with the company's clean energy and climate change group, advising clients on issues related to climate change, renewable energy, emissions trading and emissions reduction projects under the Kyoto Protocol and other regional and domestic climate change laws. Anna is a graduate in law from the University of Melbourne where she also completed a BSc, majoring in environmental science and policy. Anna has published a number of articles in relation to climate change and the EU Emissions Trading Scheme.

Karen McClellan is currently director of investments at the Climate Investment Partnership, a not-for-profit consortium of investors seeking to provide financing for commercially attractive projects that reduce GHG emissions. She was previously a senior banker at the European Bank for Reconstruction and Development in energy project finance, and has worked in corporate finance and emerging markets for many years. She frequently speaks at conferences on climate change finance and has published a case study on investment in Eastern Europe, which is taught at Stanford Graduate School of Business. Karen holds a degree in economics from Yale University and an MBA from Stanford.

Gareth Phillips is currently the global product manager for the SGS Climate Change Programme. He works from his home in the Scottish Borders and is responsible for the development and delivery of GHG validation and verification services throughout the SGS Group. Gareth has worked increasingly in the climate change sector since 1997 and prior to that was involved in forest and environmental management certification. Gareth is actively involved in the development of verification services and the implementation of the Kyoto Protocol flexible mechanisms within a commercial setting. He was a lead author on the IPCC special report on land use, land use change and forestry, and regularly presents on validation and verification. Gareth has a masters degree in forestry and land use from the University of Oxford.

Frauke Roeser is a senior consultant within the Climate Change Policy team at Enviros Consulting, based in London. She has several years of experience, both as consultant and in-house corporate sustainability manager, in the areas of climate change policy, carbon management and the wider sustainability agenda and its implications for business. Her current work focuses on providing strategic and management advice to a range of private and public sector organisations in carbon management, international climate change policy development and the emerging global carbon market. She holds an MSc in environmental strategy from the University of Surrey and an MA in literature and political sciences from the University of Giessen, Germany.

Doug Russell is the managing director at Natsource. He has 30 years experience in the public and private sectors, dealing with international and domestic regulatory development on broad scale environmental issues. His recent work includes: development of risk assessments and covenant negotiating strategies for a variety of Canadian corporations; a study on issues arising from the establishment of a North American system for emissions trading; and a study for the Pew Center on Global Climate Change. Clients have ranged from large multinational and Canadian corporations to governments and environmental non-government organisations. Prior to joining the private sector, Doug managed policy development for the federal government on all air pollution issues, and co-headed Canada's negotiating delegation to the UN Framework Convention on Climate Change.

John Scowcroft is head of the environment and sustainable development unit at the Union of the Electricity Industry – EURELECTRIC – in Brussels. He is responsible for all aspects of environmental and sustainable development policy and has been actively involved in the groundbreaking EURELECTRIC greenhouse gas and electricity trading simulations (GETS). After a long career in the British electricity industry, where he held a number of senior posts, John joined EURELECTRIC's predecessor, – UNIPEDE – in 1991 as a senior adviser, where he was responsible for environmental matters and structural and organisation issues. John graduated with a BA from the University of Liverpool.

Camilla Taylor works in Budapest with Vertis Environmental Finance, an investment and financial advisory company that specialises in emissions trading and environmental markets, where she focuses on advisory and transaction work with attention to policy analysis and its market impact. Prior to this she worked with Battle McCarthy in London, involved in the UK Emissions Trading Scheme and managing compliance for corporate and public sector clients. She regularly contributes market analyses to sector publications, and has lectured on carbon finance and management for several postgraduate programmes and companies. Camilla graduated from Oxford University with a degree in biological sciences, and has since continued her study in the areas of economics and finance.

Kasper Walet is founder and president of Maycroft Consultancy Services in Amsterdam, The Netherlands, where he has been since 1997. Whilst with Maycroft , Kasper worked on the initiation of the Amsterdam Power

Exchange and advised many of the leading energy companies in European, CEE and Asian countries. Before founding Maycroft, Kasper was a board member of the Agricultural Futures Exchange in Amsterdam. While leading the Exchange Kasper became an expert in all aspects of commodity markets, the international sales and marketing of financial services, derivatives and risk management. Kasper holds a masters degree in law from the University of Utrecht.

Introduction

Cyriel de Jong; Kasper Walet

Erasmus University Rotterdam; Maycroft Consultancy Services

It is quite generally believed that human activities are responsible for climate change and that the costs of climate change are much higher than their mitigation costs.[1] This belief is at the basis of the Kyoto Protocol and various emissions trading schemes. However, as long as greenhouse gas (GHG) emissions are a free "good" and their costs remain a burden to society as a whole, no emissions reduction will take effect. We therefore need governments to develop policies, preferably coordinated, and make sure that individual behaviour leads to overall optimal economic outcomes.

Environmental policies in general, and emissions trading in particular, are built upon the concept of so-called negative externalities. These can be defined as negative effects caused by production or consumption of goods or services for others than the actual user and which are not included in price or costs. The existence of negative externalities in a free market can lead to inefficient outcomes, that is, outcomes that fail to maximise the net benefits to society. Negative externalities are a type of market failure. For example, a coal-burning power plant might produce and deliver electricity to the advantage of both the power plant and the buyer of its electricity. However, the production process may result in emissions of green house gases (GHGs) that negatively affect others not involved in the transaction. The interests of the third party – the people affected by the plant's emissions – are not represented in the market transaction.

In order to avoid market failure and to incorporate the negative external effects, several policy instruments are available to governments. Preferably, the incorporation of negative external effects will be the producers' responsibility as in the "polluter pays" principle.

EMISSIONS TRADING AS A POLICY CHOICE

In theory, the prevention of market failure eventually leads to an efficient allocation. In the context of emission reduction, efficiency is achieved when the marginal cost of emission restriction is equivalent to the marginal damage caused by pollution. We should promptly add that the actual level of efficiency is difficult to establish, mainly because the marginal damage curve cannot be specified in a reliable way. Since efficiency is attainable yet difficult to measure, we may prefer to choose an alternative approach.

An obvious "second best" alternative is to impose an absolute emission allowance based on other considerations such as keeping the emission effects within health and environmental safety limits, and to do so against minimal costs. For this purpose, one can speak of *cost efficiency*: achieving a certain specified emission level at minimal costs. Cost minimisation will occur only when marginal costs of emission reduction are the same for all of the discharging units.

In short, cost-effectiveness consists of two components: (i) realisation of the specified emission level and (ii) cost minimisation. We can distinguish three different policy options, all of which are in a certain way cost effective:

1. To impose an *emission norm* with an allowance for each emission source. This method, also called the "command-and-control" approach, is a form of direct regulation. Through individual emission allowances, the realisation of the fixed total emission level is guaranteed. However, cost minimisation does not occur while marginal costs of various emission sources differ.
2. To impose an *emission tax*, with a tax amount X per emission quantity. This is a market-based policy: decisions concerning emission quantity are left to "market forces" (ie, emission sources). Taxing emissions leads to cost-minimised allocation because companies will choose the level of emissions at which marginal costs and tax amount X are equal. Yet, tax on emissions does not necessarily guarantee the desired emission level. In principle,

Table 1 Cost-effectiveness of policy options

		Realisation of emission target?	
		Yes	No
Cost minimisation?	Yes	Tradable emission rights (combination)	Emission tax (market-based policy)
	No	Emission cap (direct regulation)	–

the level of emissions is directly connected to the tax level; in order to realise the desired emissions level it is merely necessary to assess the correct tax amount. Regulating authorities, however, do not have sufficient information on reduction costs of the participating companies, so the chosen tax amount most likely will not lead to the desired emissions level. Only by way of *trial and error* can the assessment of the tax amount eventually approach the desired emissions level.

3. The setting up of a system for *trading of emission rights*, in which emission rights are assigned and marketable. The number of rights that is assigned at initial allocation guarantees that the desired emission level will be achieved. Furthermore, the fact that rights can be traded will make cost minimisation possible: participants will trade rights among themselves up until the point when marginal reduction costs of all participants are equal.

Table 1 presents the degree of cost-effectiveness of the three mentioned options. It shows that a system for emissions trading unites both cost-effective factors, by combining positive aspects of the two other options: respectively, an emission norm and emission tax. So, an emissions trading system can be regarded as a mixture of direct regulation (due to the establishment of an absolute emission cap) and market-based policy (by influencing the market through allocation and trade of emission rights).

CONDITIONS FOR A SUCCESSFUL EMISSIONS MARKET

The theoretical comparison of the above policy options is based on several assumptions. First, it is implicitly assumed that emissions can be measured objectively. However, regulating authorities largely depend on information that is provided by the companies themselves, and these companies could have an interest in manipulating the information where possible. Adequate monitoring procedures, including a penalty structure, should therefore be designed to make some of the policy options viable. Second, it is assumed that with the emission rights trading system a perfectly functioning market is operational. In practice, this will not be the case, especially during the initial phase. Third, it is assumed that noncompliance can be detected and penalised effectively. This is especially problematic for an international emissions trading system where individual countries are bound by a certain emission cap. Enforcement of country-specific emission caps might turn out to be a utopia. Furthermore, in selecting the best policy instrument, transaction costs of the different options must be accounted for. Transaction costs of an emissions trading system in particular are higher than those of the other two options, because an organised market must be developed.

Consequently, emissions trading is not the better option by construction. When designing and implementing an emissions trade system, close attention must therefore be paid to the preconditions in order to let the system function properly. After all, emissions trading in itself does not reduce emissions: emissions trading merely creates incentives to find the lowest cost of achieving a given amount of emission reductions. The rules of such a trading scheme need to be transparent and broadly acceptable to all stakeholders. Other critical issues are the method of determining baseline emissions, the acceptable methods for monitoring, and the accreditation of auditors to verify the reporting of baselines. Ultimately, the trading system will work only if the participating companies are well guided by incentives to minimise their compliance costs.[2]

WHAT NEEDS TO BE DONE?

In the Kyoto Protocol, parties underlined the importance of curbing GHG emissions in an absolute manner; that explains the important role given to the concept of emissions budgets and tradability of emission units. Because not enough countries have ratified the Kyoto Protocol, truly global emissions trading is still in question. However, regional initiatives are being developed or have already been implemented, for example in the European Union (Chapter 14), United Kingdom (Chapter 15), Canada

(Chapter 16), the Australian state of New South Wales (Chapter 18), and probably others in the future. In addition, trading of other emissions (allowances) are observed in, for example, the US SO_2 and NO_x programmes (Chapters 3 and 11).

So far, the discussions about emissions trading have been dominated by policy issues: the macroeconomic effects and optimal design of emissions markets have extensively been discussed in academic research and political debates, but much less attention has been paid to the consequences for individual companies. This book aims to fill the resulting gap with a different perspective. It tries to answer the question: *how can individual companies implement emissions trading within their organisations?*

This question is relevant for all businesses facing emission caps, as well as for their financiers, policymakers, regulators and service providers. In this book, we provide business and risk managers with an overview of essential actions they have to undertake to comply with emission caps at the lowest possible cost while minimising risk. Managers need to understand the emissions trading framework (Section 1), the various implementation issues (Section 2), the impact on investment and production decisions (Section 3) and the developments in their own as well as other markets (Section 4). Good and up-to-date knowledge is the first step towards maintaining and reinforcing a competitive edge. The industry and academic experts represented in this book provide these lessons and clarify them with a multitude of practical cases. After all, the full understanding and support of the business community are imperative if the emissions markets are to work.

---

1   Chapter 20 casts some doubts on the "generality" of this belief.
2   Special attention must be paid to the fact that, by applying cost-minimisation, the value of external marginal benefits – ie, benefits for environment and society from reduction – is left aside. Apart from the mentioned problematic measurability of reduction profits, this is a consequence of the concept that companies make decisions on a purely financial basis. Environmental policies, especially emission trade, are largely based on this belief for a reason: external costs and benefits can and must be incorporated, because companies will change their attitude only when they feel it "in their wallet".

Section 1

The Emissions Framework

Introduction

Cyriel de Jong; Kasper Walet

Erasmus University Rotterdam; Maycroft Consultancy Services

On 9 May 1992 the United Nations Framework Convention on Climate Change (UNFCCC) was adopted in New York. Its main objective was "to achieve stabilization of atmospheric concentrations of greenhouse gases at levels that would prevent dangerous anthropogenic interferences with the climate system" (UNFCCC, 2002). The Convention does not specify exactly which level becomes harmful, yet states that ecosystems should be able to keep their own natural balance, food supply must not be threatened and economic growth must be continued. The UNFCCC offers principles that serve as guidelines for dealing with the climate problem in terms of implementation, responsibility and initiative:

❏ The *ownership principle* states that industrialised countries possess more means for dealing with the climate issue than the developing countries. Therefore, they are encouraged to share their financial and technical means and resources with developing countries.
❏ The *principle of shared yet differentiated responsibility* takes notice of the fact that industrialised countries are the biggest contributors to emissions worldwide and therefore have a leading role when it comes to emission reduction.
❏ Finally, *the precaution principle* states that, although there is still a great deal of uncertainty about the causes of climatic changes, there is no reason for postponing measures any longer. After all, waiting for more clarity could lead to climatic changes becoming irreversible.

Five years later, these principles have led to the creation of the Kyoto Protocol and various "local" emissions trading initiatives. As a result, individual companies around the world have to manage a new commodity: the right to emit CO_2 or CO_2 equivalents. Knowing how to deal with this new business environment starts with a full understanding of the emission policies and guidelines, the emission regulations and the legal framework.

Naturally, novices to the subject of emissions trading should read this section carefully, and so be able to appreciate the rest of the book. However, the prevailing trading systems contain a high level of complexity, and so the "experienced" reader will certainly find useful the information and critical discussions throughout the book.

This section develops as follows. The Kyoto Protocol can be regarded as the mother of all greenhouse gas emissions trading schemes, so that's our starting point in Chapter 1. All these schemes have different regulations and are embedded in different legislation, which have direct consequences for companies operating therein (Chapter 2). For example, the legal status of emission allowances is still not settled and the outcome will determine how the allowances need to be accounted for and how they are treated in case of insolvency. This issue and many others prove that it is not obvious that a particular design results in a well-functioning and liquid market, as clarified in Chapter 3. Finally, because most industrialised countries will have difficulty reaching their self-imposed emission targets at acceptable costs, large reductions will have to be realised through the so-called flexible mechanisms: Joint Implementation and Clean Development Mechanism (JI and CDM). These important mechanisms are discussed briefly in the first chapter, but more extensively in Chapter 4 and with two practical case studies in Chapter 5.

Trading frameworks are continually being reshaped, so there may have been developments since the time of writing. We are confident, however, that the pertinent discussions will remain valid for many years.

The Kyoto Protocol

Jos Cozijnsen

Cozijnsen Consulting

HISTORICAL OVERVIEW

An increasing amount of scientific studies report human interference with the climate system.[1] This has raised significant public concern, and brought global environmental issues to the forefront of political agenda in the mid-1980s. As a result, the World Meteorological Organisation (WMO) and the UN Environment Programme (UNEP) established the Intergovernmental Panel on Climate Change (IPCC) in 1988. Moreover, in 1988 the UN General Assembly took up the issue of climate change for the first time and adopted Resolution 43/53 on the "Protection of global climate for present and future generations of mankind".

In 1990, the IPCC issued its First Assessment Report, confirming that climate change was indeed a threat. This prompted the call for a global treaty to address the problem. This call was echoed by the Ministerial Declaration of the Second World Climate Conference (SWCC), held in Geneva later that year. The UN General Assembly responded to these calls in December of 1990, formally launching negotiations on a framework convention on climate. Governments adopted the United Nations Framework Convention on Climate Change (UNFCCC) on 9 May 1992 in Rio de Janeiro.

The ultimate objective of the UNFCCC (Article 2) is "to achieve stabilization of atmospheric concentrations of greenhouse gases [GHGs] at levels that would prevent dangerous anthropogenic interference with the climate system". It does not define "dangerous", but it states that ecosystems should be allowed to adapt naturally,

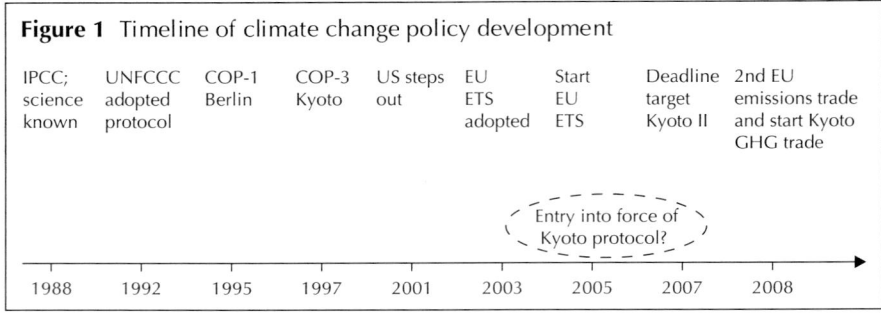

Figure 1 Timeline of climate change policy development

IPCC; science known	UNFCCC adopted protocol	COP-1 Berlin	COP-3 Kyoto	US steps out	EU ETS adopted	Start EU ETS	Deadline target Kyoto II	2nd EU emissions trade and start Kyoto GHG trade

Entry into force of Kyoto protocol?

| 1988 | 1992 | 1995 | 1997 | 2001 | 2003 | 2005 | 2007 | 2008 |

food supply should not be threatened and economic development should be able to proceed in a sustainable manner. Defining "dangerous" is a political issue, involving social and economic knowledge, perspective on what is acceptable and scientific judgement. The IPCC has been very useful in defining what GHG concentration levels in the atmosphere have a higher chance of causing the problems described above.

Industrialised country parties in the UNFCCC (Annex I Parties) agreed to make plans with the aim of stabilising GHG emissions in 2000 to 1990 levels. The EU and other countries, including the US, later offered their voluntary commitment to do so. Developing countries (listed as Non-Annex I Parties) were asked to develop in a more sustainable way, with the assistance of industrialised countries.

At the first Conference of the Parties (COP1) in Berlin in 1995, it was decided that a process would start to strengthen climate targets, mainly for industrialised countries. This process of analysis and research resulted in legally binding quantified targets through the Kyoto Protocol, adopted in 1997 at the COP3. However, at Kyoto, not all outstanding issues were resolved. The Protocol sketched the basic features of its "mechanisms" and compliance system, for example, but did not flesh out the all-important rules of how they would operate. At COP7 (Marrakech, October/ November 2001), a comprehensive package of decisions was adopted – known as the Marrakech Accords. The adoption of the Marrakech Accords thus marked the close of a major negotiating cycle and prompted all signatories to ratify the Kyoto Protocol.

Nevertheless, a major hiccup in the further implementation process of the Kyoto Protocol was the decision in 2001 of the US not to ratify. The US defended their decision on economic grounds and the absence of targets for developing countries. Not only did this decision put the ratification of the Kyoto Protocol at stake, but it also triggered a major cooling of transatlantic relations. However, in the US an increase of promising climate policies at state level have been witnessed, including a regional exchange of CO_2 allowances (see Panel 1). This programme is part of the argument for linking emissions credits of non-Kyoto states – under some conditions – to the EU emissions trade scheme.

PANEL 1 EXAMPLES OF US STATE-LEVEL CLIMATE CHANGE POLICY

❏ *Energy efficiency standards:* for residential and commercial appliances in Maryland, Connecticut, Maine, Massachusetts, New Hampshire, New Jersey, New York, Pennsylvania, Rhode Island, Vermont, Illinois and Florida.

❏ *Chicago Climate Change Exchange:* an emission reduction and trading programme with participants from six Midwest Great Lakes states, Canada and Mexico, also Brazil. At the time of writing, there were 21 participants, including large organisations such as Motorola, Dupont, WRI and Iowa University.

❏ *Cross-border GHG cap-and-trade:* planned by governors of the New England states and premiers of the five eastern provinces of Canada.

And in the following states;

❏ *Oklahoma:* Carbon Sequestration Enhancement Act;

❏ *Seattle City Light District:* achieved zero emissions through reductions purchased *via* the Climate Trust;

❏ *New Jersey:* 5% reductions in 2005 compared with 1990;

❏ *Oregon:* CO_2 standards for new power plants and reductions purchased via Oregon Climate Trust;

❏ *Portland:* 20% reduction in 2010 below 1988;

❏ *California:* adopting legislation to reduce GHG emissions from motor vehicles;

❏ *Wisconsin:* mandatory CO_2 reporting;

❏ *Massachusetts, New Hampshire and Oregon* will establish regulations to reduce CO_2 from electricity generation; and

❏ *Connecticut* will develop a comprehensive climate change action plan into legislative and administrative proposals for implementation.

Table 1 Kyoto greenhouse gases

Symbol	Name	CO_2 equivalent	Main sources
CO_2	Carbon dioxide	1	Fossil fuel combustion, forest clearing, cement production
CH_4	Methane	21	Landfills, production and distribution of natural gas and petroleum, fermentation from the digestive system of livestock, rice cultivation, fossil fuel combustion
N_2O	Nitrous oxide	310	Fossil fuel combustion, fertilisers, nylon production, manure
HFCs	Hydrofluorocarbons	$140 \sim 11,700$	Refrigeration gases, aluminium smelting, semiconductor manufacturing
PFCs	Perfluorocarbons	$6,500 \sim 9,200$	Aluminium production, semiconductor industry
SF_6	Sulphur hexafluoride	23,900	Electrical transmissions and distribution systems, circuit breakers, magnesium production

MAIN INGREDIENTS OF THE PROTOCOL

The Kyoto Protocol was adopted in 1997. The protocol requires that industrialised countries agree to limit their GHG emissions in the period 2008–2012 on average at 5.2% below their 1990 emission levels. The resulting "assigned amount" (measured in Assigned Amount Units, AAU) of emission allowances was based on six GHGs. This so-called "six-gas basket" includes carbon dioxide (CO_2), methane (CH_4), nitrous oxide (N_2O), and three fluorinated gases, HFCs, PFCs and SF_6. Each gas has a specific contribution to global warming. Table 1 contains the impact, or "global warming potential" of the other five gases compared with CO_2 and measured in CO_2 equivalents (CO_2e).

The emission targets vary from country to country, with a −8% reduction commitment for the EU as a whole, −7% for Japan and −6% for the US (Table 2). The numbers for these three economic blocs are the outcome of long, complex negotiations in Kyoto and are central to the complete package of the Kyoto agreements.

Table 2 Annex I countries and their emission targets

Country	(1990*–2008/2012) %
EU15, Bulgaria, Czech Republic, Estonia, Latvia, Liechtenstein, Lithuania, Monaco, Romania, Slovakia, Slovenia, Switzerland	−8
US**	−7
Canada, Hungary, Japan, Poland	−6
Croatia	−5
New Zealand, Russian Federation, Ukraine	0
Norway	+1
Australia	+8
Iceland	+10
Total for Annex I	−5.2

*Some economies in transition (EITs) have a baseline other than 1990.
**The US has indicated its intention not to ratify the Kyoto Protocol.

PANEL 2 COUNTRY DEFINITIONS IN THE KYOTO PROTOCOL

Annex I countries
Industrialised countries, which have historically been the biggest contributors to worldwide emissions and therefore have received in the UNFCCC and in the Kyoto Protocol (under Annex B) a leading role when it comes to emission reduction. Two subcategories can be distinguished:

❏ Annex II countries
   Members of the Organisation for Economic Cooperation and Development (OECD) as of 1992, ie, Western European countries (including the EU as a separate party), Canada, the US, Japan, Australia, New Zealand and Turkey; this category of countries has several financial contribution requirements.
❏ Other Annex I countries – Economies in Transition (EITs)
   Countries that evolve into market economies, especially former Soviet Union members as well as Central and Eastern European countries.

Non-Annex I countries
Developing countries: their emission constraints are much less strict than those for Annex I countries.

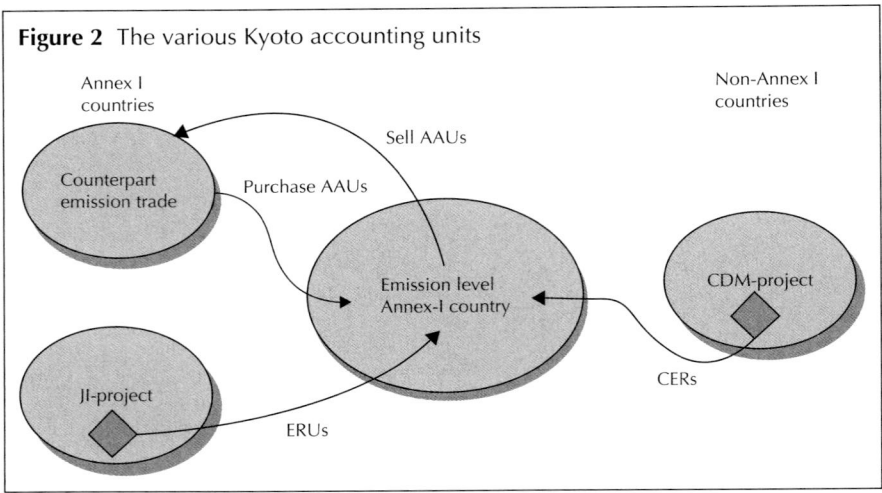

Figure 2 The various Kyoto accounting units

The EU emissions allowance according to the Kyoto Protocol is around 3,800 mt. However, predictions show that emissions in the EU will increase to 4,138 mt in 2010. To meet its target the EU will have to reduce its emissions by 1,500 mt in the period 2008–12. The EU commitment is distributed under a Burden Sharing Agreement among the member states to facilitate compliance, as shown in Figure 2.[2] This agreement allows some less developed member states tens of percentages of emissions growth. The legal significance of the treatment of the EU in the Kyoto Protocol as a Regional Economic Integrated Organisation is the following:

❑ the EU is in compliance with the protocol as long as the overall emissions of the EU as a whole meet the target of −8%, even if one member state overshoots its target; but

❑ when the EU is not in compliance, then each member state should meet its distributed national target.

THE KYOTO MECHANISMS

In order to reach their emission targets, countries can take domestic reduction measures or use the so-called Kyoto Mechanisms. These flexibility mechanisms allow countries to undertake emission reduction projects or acquire emission allowances from other countries.

The mechanisms are meant to facilitate international cooperation, to provide flexibility in the timing and location of measures and to ensure compliance with the obligations. They consist of:

❏ international emissions trading
❏ Clean Development Mechanism (CDM)
❏ Joint Implementation (JI)

Below is an overview of these measures, which will be discussed in more detail throughout this book.

International emissions trading

The Kyoto Protocol allows trading of the national AAUs by countries and by individual entities (eg, industrial sites and companies). Besides general international emissions trading, several national and cross-border trading schemes are already in place or are in development.

Very few countries have developed plans to make use of intergovernmental international emissions trading, for various reasons:

❏ the EU has already distributed its target among member states through the Burden Sharing Agreement;
❏ for political reasons countries are reluctant to buy AAUs from countries with a surplus of AAUs; and
❏ most countries are focusing instead on purchasing emission reduction credits (which can be created via JI and CDM projects) and on allocating emission allowances to individual entities that can trade on the domestic and international market.

Notwithstanding the above concerns, some countries have agreed to forward sales of AAUs; the first of such trades was announced in 2003 between the Japanese company Sumitomo and Slovakia.

Clean Development Mechanism

Under the CDM Annex I countries or authorised entities in Annex I countries can acquire Certified Emission Reductions (CERs) by investing in emissions reduction projects in a developing country.[3] CERs can be generated as soon as the CDM executive board sets the methodologies and rules (expected at some point during 2004).

CERs can be registered and saved for compliance against Kyoto commitments for 2008–12 or banked for later periods.

A CDM project can vary widely: from an operational site or a transportation system, to a clean power generation facility, but reductions must be additional to "business-as-usual". Besides reducing emissions, a CDM project should also meet broader sustainable development requirements, as set by the host country.

Countries currently undertake CDM multilaterally (eg, through the World bank) or bilaterally (eg, the Netherlands, Canada, Japan). It is foreseen that CERs will be used to meet requirements under domestic emissions trading schemes and therefore, that companies will be involved in CDM as well. Only investing Annex I countries have emission commitments; the Non-Annex I host countries do not. Therefore, requirements are to be met to prove *ex ante* (validation) and *ex post* (verification) that CDM activities lead to overall reductions of emissions compared with "business-as-usual". Methodologies to build baselines and to streamline monitoring and verification are being developed in the framework of the Climate Convention.

Currently, only a few methodologies for monitoring reductions through CDM have been approved by the executive board for CDM methodologies. A CDM methodology is needed to register CDM projects, the approval procedure questions the following.

❏ Methodologies for determining the baseline emission scenario: what emissions could be expected in the absence of such projects?
❏ What will be the emissions targets for the CDM projects and how will they be measured?

Joint Implementation

The mechanism of JI encourages the realisation of emission reductions by the implementation of projects by one Annex I country (or entity) in another Annex I country. The investor receives an agreed number of credits, so-called Emission Reduction Units (ERUs), for the investment against payment of a negotiated price. A project can, for example, comprise an industrial site, an entire municipality or an even wider region. A project can qualify for the generation of ERUs under JI only if reductions are additional to business-as-usual can only be generated from 2008.

Both participants of a JI project must be Annex I parties, and will therefore have a compliance target under Kyoto; this is what we call the zero-sum game of JI. In the EU framework, a site is eligible for a JI project only if it does not already participate in an emissions trading scheme; this is to prevent double counting. Hence, from an EU perspective, JI projects can, for example, be implemented in Eastern European countries that are not (yet) part of the EU, or by industrial sites within the EU that are too small to receive a cap under the EU ETS or that are kept from the scheme by their respective government.

It is expected that companies will be involved in JI as an accepted option to meet emission requirements under domestic cap-and-trade schemes. Since both host and investing participating (Annex I) countries have emissions commitments, requirements can be kept simpler than for CDM project approval. The main test is to prove *ex ante* and *ex post* that JI activities lead to overall reductions of emissions compared with business-as-usual.

A project under JI or CDM could also facilitate the removal of CO_2 through land use, land use change and forestry, which generates removal units. These activities are known as sink activities. A sink is a storage of carbon by means of sequestration in soils, forestation, and land use change measures.

THE KYOTO EMISSIONS BUDGET SYSTEM

Under the Kyoto Protocol each Annex I country will receive a budget of AAUs for the period 2008–12. This budget approach, instead of a numerical GHG emissions target provides the country with an element of flexibility. It can decide how it will use the budget during the commitment period, it can sell AAUs forward and it can bank within the budget years for the next commitment period. Each country is free to choose its own strategy to stay within its assigned amount. This flexibility in the timing of banking and forward selling also helps a country to cope with unexpected climatic or economic change within the period.

A country can impose the reduction burden on individual "entities" (eg, companies and industrial sites) by introducing either

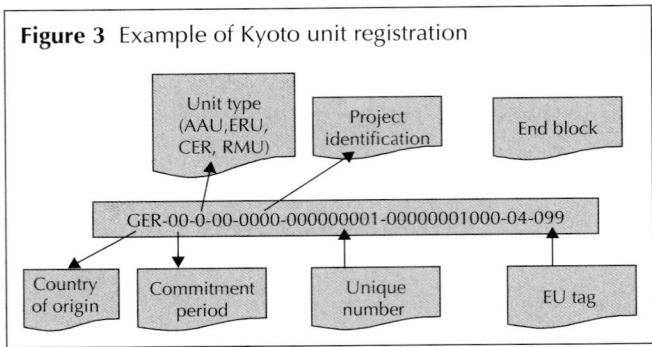

Figure 3 Example of Kyoto unit registration

a carbon-tax or a cap-and-trade system. Either way, companies are likely to be required to contribute towards the reduction of GHG emissions.

The three Kyoto flexibility mechanisms mentioned earlier operate on the basis of various accounting units. These units are tracked and recorded through national registries, established and maintained by Annex I Parties. JI projects result in ERUs; CDM projects generate CERs; and, under emissions trading, Annex I parties may exchange AAUs, that is, some of the emissions included in their assigned amounts. They may also exchange CERs and ERUs as well as RMUs. All the aforementioned units are equal to one tonne of CO_2 and each will have its own unique serial number (see Figure 3).

This is the full range of options provided for in the Kyoto Protocol. Nevertheless, parties are permitted as sovereign entities to apply stricter rules in domestic or regional legislation to the application of mechanisms. The EU, for example, has politically committed itself to achieve a minimum of 50% through domestic reductions.

Registration

A computerised system of registries will keep track of the transactions in the various accounting units of emission rights (AAUs, CERs, ERUs and RMUs). There are three components to the registry system: national registries, a CDM registry and transaction logs.

Each Annex I party must establish and maintain a national registry. This will contain accounts for any AAUs, CERs, ERUs and RMUs held by the party, as well as by any legal entity authorised by the party to hold them. The registry will also contain accounts for setting units aside to comply with emissions targets at the end of the commitment period ("retirement"), and for removing units ("cancellation"). Retirement can be used to keep the required amount of AAUs in the national registry. Cancellation can be used when a country accepts, for example, a CER for domestic reasons, but is not willing to use it to meet the country's Kyoto commitment.

The executive board of the CDM will establish and maintain a CDM registry. This will contain CER accounts for Non-Annex I parties participating in the CDM. In addition, the secretariat will establish and maintain a transaction log. This will verify transactions of AAUs, CERs, ERUs and RMUs as they are proposed, including records of their issuance, transfers and acquisitions between registries, cancellation and retirement. If any transaction is found not to be in order, the registry is required to stop the transaction.

In addition to its national registry for recording transactions in emission rights units, each Annex I party must have in place a national system to estimate its greenhouse gas emissions and removals. Prior to the start of the commitment period (by the end of 2007), each Annex I party must submit a report describing its national system and registry, as well as providing the emissions data needed to formally establish its assigned amount.

Expert review teams will assess this information. Assuming no questions are raised, the assigned amount of each Annex I party is then recorded in a compilation and accounting database. This database will record the annual emissions of parties (as reported in their annual inventories), along with their total annual transactions in AAUs, CERs, ERUs and RMUs. The transaction log maintained by the secretariat will serve as an additional monitoring tool. Every year, the secretariat will publish a compilation and accounting report for each Annex I party, based on the information contained in its database. This report will be forwarded to the COP/MOP, the Compliance Committee and the party concerned.

Figure 4 shows the network of national GHG registries that will track the transfer of Kyoto units via either: (a) domestic or regional cap-and-trade schemes (by authorised legal entities) or (b) interstate trades. A unit will be registered only once.

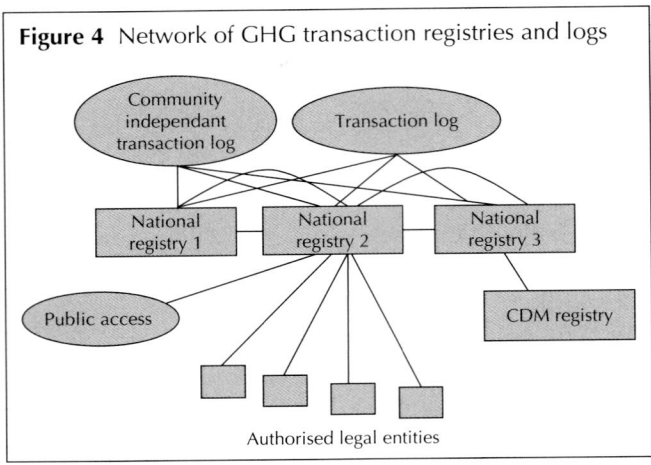

Figure 4 Network of GHG transaction registries and logs

The serialisation and digitalisation of the units and the advancement of the registries in the UK and France will ensure that most EU member states will use one of these two as their registry. The EU registry rules allow this. The transaction logs of the EU and the UNFCCC, and the CDM Registry, facilitate the oversight of the compliance with the trading rules and the overall progress.

The final secretariat report published at the end of the commitment period will form the basis for assessing whether Annex I parties have complied with their emissions targets. This will be done by comparing each party's emissions during the commitment period with the amount of the various emission credits in its national registry.

LEGAL ASPECTS AND COMPLIANCE MECHANISM

The compliance regime for the Kyoto Protocol is among the most comprehensive and rigorous in the international arena. It facilitates, promotes and enforces compliance with the Protocol's commitments. The compliance regime consists of a Compliance Committee made up of two branches: a facilitative branch and an enforcement branch.

The *facilitative branch* aims to provide advice and assistance to parties in order to promote compliance, whereas the enforcement branch has the power to apply certain consequences on parties who do not meet their commitments. Certain duties fall under the remit of one or other branch. The requirement that the use of the mechanisms be "supplemental" to domestic action (or "business-as-usual"), for example, is under the purview of the facilitative branch, as is the commitment of Annex I parties to minimise adverse impacts on developing countries. The facilitative branch also provides "early warning" of cases where a party is in danger of not complying with its emissions targets. In response to problems, the facilitative branch can make recommendations and also mobilise financial and technical resources to help parties comply.

The *enforcement branch* is responsible for determining whether an Annex I party is not complying with its emissions target or reporting requirements. It can also decide whether to adjust a party's inventory or correct the compilation and accounting database, in the event of a dispute between a party and the expert review team.

In order to address the concern that some parties could "oversell" and then be unable to meet their own targets, each Annex I party is required to hold a minimum level of emission credits. This is known as the commitment period reserve, which cannot be traded. It is calculated as 90% of the party's assigned amount. If an Annex I party goes below its commitment period reserve, it is given 30 days to restore the reserve to its required level.

This compliance reserve provision could have a hindering impact on cross-border emissions trading. For example, it is possible that a German company might not fulfil its contractual commitment to transfer an allowance to a Canadian company, because the German GHG Registry does not contain 90% of the German AAU for a certain year. Companies will have to address this risk in their purchase agreements.

In the case of noncompliance with emissions targets, Annex I parties are granted 100 days after the completion of the expert review of their final emission inventory for the commitment period to make up any shortfall in compliance (eg, by acquiring AAUs, CERs, ERUs or RMUs). If, at the end of this period, a party has still missed its emissions target, it would have to make up the difference in the second commitment period, as well as suffering a penalty of 30%. Such a party would also be barred from "selling" under emissions trading and, within three months, it would have to develop a compliance action plan detailing the action it would take to ensure that its target is met in the second commitment period.

Any party not complying with reporting requirements would have to develop a similar plan and parties that are found not to meet the criteria for participating in the mechanisms would have their eligibility withdrawn. In all cases, the enforcement branch would make a public declaration that the party is in non-compliance and would also make public the consequences to be applied.

RATIFICATION PROCESS AND THE ENTRY INTO FORCE

The entry into force of the Kyoto Protocol depends on a double threshold. First, more than 55 countries should have ratified (or approved, accepted or acceded to) the Protocol. Second, these countries together should account for more than 55% of the 1990 Annex I CO_2 emissions. To date more than 120 countries have signed and ratified the Kyoto Protocol.[4] These countries represent 42.2% of Annex I parties 1990 CO_2 emissions, which explains why the Kyoto Protocol has not yet entered into force.

These countries include most OECD countries; but many developing countries, including India and China, have also ratified. Developing countries ratify in majority, because they can benefit from CDM projects and from the adaptation and awareness funds. However, many developing countries are hesitant to negotiate on future commitments, because at a certain point emissions targets are expected from them too.

The entry into force of the Kyoto Protocol has long been anticipated. Because of the absence of the US, Russia is the only country that can lift the overall emissions of ratified countries above the 55% threshold, moving the country in a favourable position for negotiation. The current Russian president, Vladimir Putin, has stated several times that ratification would occur soon.

It will be interesting to note how the main player on the emissions market, the EU, will interact with Russia. For example, it is yet uncertain whether EU governments will purchase Russian AAUs; whether the EU ETS will be linked with Russia; and whether JI projects will happen in Russia. The general feeling of those involved is that Russia will ratify, as soon as it has become a member of the WSTO. All these factors currently influence

PANEL 3 RUSSIA'S RATIFICATION
The following issues play a role in the internal Russian deliberations on ratification:

❑ expected long term GDP growth and anticipated accompanying GHG emissions;
❑ resources needed to meet Kyoto's requirements;
❑ extra paperwork related to Kyoto;
❑ how to distribute Kyoto's revenues over government, regions and companies;
❑ possibility for Russian companies to play a role;
❑ differences between ministries' interests; and
❑ possibility of trusting the JI process.

the ratification decision by Russia and leave much room for uncertainty.

Other important countries that are reluctant to ratify the Kyoto Protocol are Australia – having large coal resources and the same concerns as the US – and some of the oil-exporting countries. Some of the oil-exporting countries, for example, want to receive compensation for every barrel of oil not sold due to climate policies. This item of compensation has been on the UNFCCC agenda for a long time, without any progress on how to handle it.

Irrespective of whether Kyoto will come into force, the EU has agreed to be bound by it, and to implement the Kyoto target of –8%.[5] The decision of 10 March 2004 constitutes how GHG emissions have to be monitored and reported in accordance with the Protocol.[6] The EU went even further in adopting a provision stating that the EU ETS can be linked with JI/CDM, even without the Kyoto Protocol being in force. That means that GHG reductions through JI and CDM are nevertheless acknowledged under the national or regional arrangement.

CONCLUSIONS
Perspectives on future developments in the Kyoto framework
The strategy at the next conference, COP10, to be hosted by Argentina in December 2004, will be to change the central focus of

the debate. On the premise that climate change is inevitable even if emissions are drastically cut, developing countries must start preparing to deal with the damages. Argentina proposes to discuss the creation of funds and mechanisms for "adapting" to global warming.

The Argentine government's initiative, which has the backing of NGOs, will focus on the question of drumming up funds that would enable developing countries to create the infrastructure – such as irrigation or canal systems – needed to deal with the associated changes provoked by global warming.

We can conclude, therefore, that the following issues will play a dominant role in the process of the further developments of the Kyoto framework:

1. How to ensure Russia's ratification and meeting of its Kyoto requirements: setting up legislation and GHG monitoring and verification systems.

2. How to involve the US and Australia again, so that overall targets will be met.

3. How to get developing country parties to contribute to emission reductions:

    a. Which of the developing countries are ready for emissions commitments? For example, it could be agreed that a developing country needs to take an emissions target when the GDP per capita exceeds a certain threshold. Various other concepts are being considered, but no official proposals have been put forward.

    b. What type of commitments can developing countries implement? Developing countries would, for example, accept more easily relative national emissions caps than absolute limits.

4. How to prepare for the negative impacts of climate change and how to mitigate climate change. The Netherlands is, for example, spending billions of euros on handling future additional flooding.

Consequently, the issue at stake is: how much would it cost to prevent the problem and how much would it cost to adapt to the problem?

1   See Chapter 20 for a critical note on this scientific evidence.
2   See Chapters 2 and 14 for more details about emission trading in the EU.
3   See the next chapter for a more extensive discussion of the CDM and JI.
4   Table 1 in Chapter 4 contains a list of Annex I countries, indicating which countries ratified and which did not.
5   Presidency Conclusions, European Council Meeting, 2004, March 25–6.
6   Decision 280/2004/EC concerning a mechanism for monitoring community greenhouse gas emissions and for implementing the Kyoto Protocol.

2

International Emissions Trading: A Legal Context

Anthony Hobley, Anna McCann

Baker & McKenzie

THE LEGAL STATUS OF THE GLOBAL ATMOSPHERE

The atmosphere is a dynamic air mass, subject to no national boundaries. It cannot be usefully regulated as if it were land or territory. The status of the "global atmosphere" under the rules of international law have yet to be settled and it is not clear whether it constitutes a shared resource, common property, common heritage or common concern or interest (see Birnie and Boyle, 2002). The 1985 Vienna Convention for the Protection of the Ozone Layer defines the ozone layer as "the layer of atmospheric ozone *above the planetary boundary* layer" (see Vienna Convention, 1985).[1] This definition recognises that the ozone layer is part of the atmosphere but does not fit into traditional models of national boundary. It provides a model for treating the atmosphere as a global unity whose problems affect all sovereign states in common and whose integrity all states are required to protect from harmful activities (see Birnie and Boyle, 2002). Similarly, in 1988 the UN General Assembly declared that global climate change was "the common concern of mankind" (see UN General Assembly, 1988). One possible interpretation of the legal effect of this resolution is that it gives all countries a legal interest or standing in the enforcement of rules concerning the protection of the global atmosphere (see Birnie and Boyle, 2002).

Whatever the status of the global atmosphere in international law, most commentators will agree that it is important to consider it as a global resource with an intrinsic value. Perhaps the best way to conceptualise this intrinsic value is to consider it in terms of the global atmosphere's ability to absorb or carry greenhouse gases (GHGs) such as carbon dioxide without undue or detrimental effects on the earth's climate (see Hobley and Blackmore, 2002).

One way in which the global community or individual sovereign states can regulate this ability is to set limits or "caps" on the total amount of GHGs that can be emitted into the atmosphere. In effect, this is what the international community has attempted to achieve through the UN Framework Convention on Climate Change (UNFCCC) and more specifically the Kyoto Protocol, which sets a quantified emission limitation or reduction for each of the developed countries listed in Annex B. Each individual country can seek to meet its national target by imposing targets on individual entities and sectors within its own economy, such as individual industrial plants and power stations or whole sectors, such as the transport sector.

CLIMATE CHANGE AND INTERNATIONAL LAW

The lawmaking process to address climate change was officially formalised at the international level in Rio in 1992, when 160 countries agreed the UNFCCC.[2] The UNFCCC has at the time of writing been ratified or acceded by 187 countries, including the US.[3] The UNFCCC is, as its title suggests, simply a framework. The necessary detail was to be settled by the governing body, the Conference of the Parties (COP) to the UNFCCC.

There are effectively three pillars to the Kyoto process: the UNFCCC, the Kyoto Protocol and the decisions of the COP.

In 1997 the COP agreed the Kyoto Protocol in what has been described as a watershed in the development of international environmental treaties. Thirty-eight developed countries (known as Annex I countries) committed themselves to legally binding targets and timetables for the reduction of GHGs. These targets are often referred to as *assigned amounts, quantified emission limitation* or *reduction commitments*, as specified in Annex B to the Protocol. Taken together for all Annex I parties they represent a global reduction of GHG emissions of at least 5% below 1990 levels. These are to be achieved in the 2008–12 commitment period, known as the Kyoto Commitment Period.

Although broadly similar, Annex I and "Annex B" countries are actually not the same, and the difference deserves some explanation.

The countries that committed themselves under the UNFCCC framework (1992) are known as Annex I countries (including economies in transition). The countries in Annex II are countries with greater commitments, notably with regard to funding and adaptation fees – basically the Annex I countries without the economies in transition. The targets that certain countries accepted under the Kyoto Protocol (1997) are defined in Annex B, and these respective countries are hence sometimes known as "Annex B countries". In this chapter, a reference to "Annex I parties" is to those sovereign states listed in Annex I of the UNFCCC who have also ratified the Kyoto Protocol and have signed up to quantified emission limitation or reduction commitments in Annex B of the Kyoto Protocol.[4]

The targeted emission reductions of the UNFCCC are acknowledged as a modest goal, yet the aggregate target represents a radical change from the still rising trend. Commentators have recently speculated that major compromises, particularly to allow greater use of sinks or land use, land use change and forestry (LULUCF), made at both Bonn (CoP6-bis) in July 2001 and at Marrakech (CoP7) in November 2001, have effectively reduced this aggregate target to somewhere between 0.5 and 1.5%. However, despite the reduction of the aggregate target at these conferences, the more detailed agreements reached there are also the bedrock for the schemes that countries and even large multinational companies are beginning to implement.

THE REGULATORY BUILDING BLOCKS: THE IMPORTANCE OF THE MARRAKECH ACCORDS

The Marrakech Accords were the result of long negotiations of the UNFCCC COP and laid down the rules for the various initiatives set up under the Kyoto framework to tackle climate change. In many respects the Accords have, in terms of detail and technicality, more in common with detailed domestic environmental regulations and guidance than the more usual examples of international treaty law. Compare it for example to earlier multinational environmental treaties containing much less detail, such as the 1997 Convention on Environmental Impact Assessment in a Transboundary Contract, the 1985 Convention for the Protection of the Ozone layer, and the 1997 Convention on the Non-National Uses of International Watercourses.

The significance of the Marrakech Accords is that they provide generic international rules or common international building blocks for implementing the obligations and mechanisms of the Kyoto Protocol, including the flexible mechanisms: international emissions trading, the Clean Development Mechanism (CDM), the Joint Implementation (JI) and LULUCF projects. This chapter focuses specifically on emissions trading.

International emissions trading allows Annex I parties who are likely to exceed their assigned amount to sell their excess allowances, known as Assigned Amount Units (AAUs), to other Annex I parties to offset their reduction targets. It also allows such parties to trade credits generated by projects under Kyoto's other flexible mechanisms.

The Marrakech Accords define a common currency based on one tonne of carbon dioxide equivalent in the form of interchangeable or "fungible" units or Kyoto units: AAUs; Emission Reduction Units (ERUs); Certified Emissions Reductions (CERs) and Removal Units (RMUs). The Marrakech Accords also complete the process of defining broad operating rules and the procedures for setting specific rules for the flexible mechanisms. These include key common elements such as:

❑ determination of baselines;
❑ monitoring;
❑ verification;
❑ design of registries; and
❑ the international carbon accounting rules.

These common building blocks make it possible for Annex I parties to design domestic emissions trading schemes that will support international emissions trading with other Annex I countries. They will also allow domestic, state or private-sector entities to consider the funding and implementation of overseas emission reduction projects, such as JI and CDM, to generate ERUs and CERs, which can potentially be brought home to use against domestically imposed emissions reduction targets or obligations.

THE US ACID RAIN PROGRAM

The principle of trading emissions has been successfully demonstrated in the USA, where markets in sulphur oxides and nitrogen oxides have been operating in some form for nearly 30 years. While not related to the issue of climate change, the experience gained under these programmes led to the introduction by the US of emissions trading during the Kyoto Protocol negotiations. Despite this and many other concessions to the US, the US stated that it would no longer ratify the Protocol.

Before the US sulphur dioxide (SO_2) Acid Rain Program (ARP) was introduced into US law in November 1990, the US already had nearly 30 years of experience of emissions allowance trading, much of which was encapsulated into the US Environmental Protection Agency's (EPA) Emissions Trading Policy of 1986. The history of the creation of the EPA's emissions trading programmes was a far cry from designing and implementing a grand blueprint for a single state. In fact, it evolved over many years as an *ad hoc* instrument to bring some flexibility into a system where the allowed level of total emissions had already been fixed by existing performance standards (see Klassen and Nentjes, 1997). Confronted with the problem that existing legislation blocked the location of new activities and even the growth of existing firms, the authorities had to do something to reduce the burden of this self-imposed scarcity by allowing specific forms of exchange. These early forms of exchange were as far from today's SO_2 emissions market as a Stone Age barter economy is from today's global financial markets.

Therefore, the early market that evolved had many restrictions on the ability to freely trade and transfer emissions rights. This is thought to largely explain why the number of trades (and hence economic efficiency) was low, albeit that the much-needed flexibility was introduced into the system and environmental integrity was largely maintained. The failure to achieve economic efficiency has been attributed to the regulatory restrictions on trade, the uncertainty over the status of the property rights and the high transaction costs. The market imperfections impairing these earlier US emissions trading programmes were largely a consequence of crafting a market onto an existing system of direct regulation in the form of emission standards. The "rules" for increasing flexibility were more a complement to, rather than a substitute for, existing "command and control"-based emissions policies.

The Clean Air Act Amendment became law in the US in 1990. Title IV of these amendments contains provisions to provide for the control of acid deposition caused by sulphur and nitrogen oxide emissions. The SO_2 ARP introduced a nationwide emissions trading scheme for electricity producers, the largest emitters of SO_2.

In contrast with the EPA's earlier emissions trading programme, the SO_2 ARP was designed with the twofold objective of reducing drastically the SO_2 emissions of the electricity sector *and* to provide from the start an institutional framework for a genuine market in emissions allowances with minimum regulatory restrictions or other market interference by the authorities (see Klassen and Nentjes, 1997). In 2002, over 11 million tonnes worth of SO_2 allowances were transferred between unrelated parties.[5] This is a substantial trading volume, considering that over 10 million tonnes of SO_2 were emitted from power plants during that same year.[6]

Some of the specific aspects of the design of the SO_2 ARP cited for its success in comparison to the earlier, less well-defined emissions trading that had been taking place in the US are as follows.

❑ Specification of allowance allocation per annum for a 30-year period allowing certainty for operators in the market as to their current and future obligations, and certainty to other players as to the continuing market for allowances.
❑ Clear definition of SO_2 allowances as the permission to emit one tonne of SO_2 during or after a specific year. This clear definition allows further liquidity and certainty. Previously the allowances were not all in a single denomination, creating barriers to trade between systems. With a defined unit it is simple to trade allowances on a one-to-one basis.
❑ Absence of restrictions in participation. Allowances can be bought by any person – not only utility representatives, but also private companies, brokers, municipalities, environmental groups, etc. This introduces an element of speculation on the market forces and increases liquidity as more players join the market.

With the exception of a set allocation for a 30-year period, these design aspects have been adopted in both the UK and EU schemes that followed.[7]

THE UK EMISSIONS TRADING SCHEME

The UK's Emissions Trading Scheme (UK ETS) (see Hobley, 2001) went live on 1 April 2002. One of the most important things to appreciate about the UK ETS is that it is contract-based rather than legislation-based, ie, companies voluntarily enter into the scheme by contracting with the government. This differs from both the US SO$_2$ ARP and the EU ETS, which are mandatory for certain operators. The second important factor to appreciate is that it is a "pilot programme" whose purpose is both to "learn by doing" and help secure London's place as a financial centre for any future international emissions trading system. The non-legislative base gives the UK ETS the flexibility to adapt as lessons are learned and so help further build expertise in this new market in the UK.

The UK ETS is designed to be a market-based policy instrument, allowing those who emit greenhouse gases to reduce their emissions in a cost-effective manner. There are four ways to voluntarily enter into the scheme:

❑ as direct participants;
❑ as agreement participants;
❑ as project participants; or
❑ by simply opening a trading account in the emissions trading registry.

Hence anyone is allowed to open an account in the registry to buy and sell allowances, similar to the US SO$_2$ system and the EU ETS. It is envisaged that, as the market in carbon matures, the trading of emissions allowances will become in practice no different from trading any other commodity. Participants may trade directly among themselves or by using third-party brokers. Participants with targets are known as target holders and those without, as non-target holders.

Direct participants must make an absolute reduction against their average annual emissions for the years 1998–2000. They will be paid a share (not to exceed 20%) of a £215 million government incentive equal to £53.37 for each tonne of carbon by which they reduce their emissions below what would otherwise have been their "business-as-usual" or baseline emissions. The share of the incentive monies and the selling of the emissions cap were determined through a government-run auction process held before the scheme commenced.[8] To be paid the incentive monies direct participants need to demonstrate that each year until

31 December 2006 they have met their annual emissions target under the UK ETS.

Companies in Climate Change Agreements (CCAs) (agreement participants) have emission targets, which they must meet so as to continue receiving an 80% Climate Change Levy (CCL) discount. The CCL is a downstream tax on all energy use whether or not such energy is derived from fossil fuel and is paid as part of energy bills. There are some 49 industry sectors – representing around 5,000 facilities – with CCAs. Agreement participants will not receive allowances upfront but receive allowances at the end of each "milestone year" in which they have targets (every second year from 2002) for the amount by which they have beaten their target. However, if they are going to emit more than their target, they will be able to buy additional allowances during a reconciliation period. This form of emissions trading is called "baseline and credit" because, unlike "cap-and-trade", agreement participants will be issued with allowances only after they have beaten their target. However, because many of the targets set through the CCAs are relative or efficiency targets – ie, relative rather than absolute emission caps – trading by these companies is subject to certain restrictions. This is because a participant's rising output, with potentially an associated rise in emissions, would still meet the target. Hence a "gateway" controls the flow of allowances from this relative sector into the rest of the trading scheme or absolute sector.

Because it does not matter where emissions reductions are made, within the geographic limitations of the scheme, direct or agreement participants have three choices: they can *meet* their cap or target by reducing their own emissions; they can *reduce* their emissions below their cap or target and sell or bank the excess allowances; or they can let their emissions *remain above* the cap or target and buy allowances from other participants, subject to the transfer of transfers through the gateway between the relative and absolute sectors. There will be no restriction on banking up until 2007 and participants with absolute emissions targets will also be able to bank any overachievement of their own target into the Kyoto Protocol commitment period starting in 2008. Therefore, companies in the UK ETS will be able to benefit from early action to reduce their greenhouse gas emissions. All reported baselines and emissions will be subject to independent third-party verification and the government has agreed a series of protocols (Reporting Guidelines) that specify in detail the methodology to be used to measure and report baselines and emissions (see DEFRA).[9,10]

THE ETS

The EU emissions trading proposal is based on Article 175 (1) of the EU Treaty and is intended to place direct emissions of the green-house gases covered by the Kyoto Protocol within a regulatory framework. Like the UK scheme, the EU ETS is designed to both protect the environment and to least impair competitiveness.[11]

An important aspect of the EU ETS is that it is compatible with, but independent of, the Kyoto Protocol, whereas the UK ETS is solely a domestic market that is independent of and structured differently from the Kyoto design. Of course, it is not completely independent of Kyoto as the UK ETS and particularly the emissions reductions it delivers will assist the UK to meet its Kyoto target. Even if the Kyoto Protocol is not ratified, multinational emissions trading via the EU ETS will already be in existence. This means that with or without the Kyoto Protocol coming into force there will be a Kyoto legacy.

The EU ETS mechanism is set out in Directive 2003/87/EC of the European Parliament and of the Council of 13 October 2003, establishing a scheme for greenhouse gas emission allowance trading within the Community and amending Council Directive 96/61/EC (the "EU ETS Directive").[12] It is due to start in January 2005 and will initially run for a first phase until end 2007. Thereafter, the scheme will run in periods of five years, the first of such a five-year period coinciding with the first Kyoto period (2008–12). It is the world's first multinational emissions trading scheme and will cover the current 15 EU member states and the 10 accession countries from the commencement. It is understood by the authors that discussions have already begun between the EU Commission and Switzerland, Norway and Canada over the possibility of linking the EU ETS to cap-and-trade schemes in those countries. Article 25 of the EU ETS gives the EU Commission the power to make such links on behalf of the EU.

The EU ETS is a mandatory system requiring all installations that undertake specific activities listed in Annex I to the Directive (not to be confused with the Annex I of the UNFCCC) to hold a greenhouse permit (or GHG permit) and comply with the rules of the scheme. The activities covered in Annex I include:

❑ energy activities including combustion installations with an aggregated rated thermal input exceeding 20 MW (approximately 6 MW aggregated output), mineral oil refineries, and coke ovens;
❑ the production and processing of ferrous metals;
❑ the mineral industry (eg, cement, glass, lime kilns or ceramic production); and
❑ pulp, paper or board production.[13]

During the first phase, only carbon dioxide (CO_2) is included in the EU ETS. However, the EU ETS Directive contemplates the addition by member states of the other five GHGs in future phases of the scheme.[14] It is also expected that installations conducting activities in other sectors such as chemicals, aluminium and transport will become obligated under the scheme in the future.

Each installation covered by the scheme will require a GHG permit. The permit will require the operators of the relevant installations to surrender, on an annual basis, sufficient allowances (known as EU allowances) to match their verified emissions of the relevant greenhouse gases for the previous calendar year. Substantial penalties will be imposed if they do not do so. In the first phase operators will incur a penalty of €40 per tonne of CO_2 that they are short, rising to €100 per tonne in the second phase. This really is a penalty and not a "buy-out" because penalised operators will also need to surrender sufficient EU allowances in the following year in order to rectify the shortfall of the previous year.

The EU allowances are allocated to individual installations by member state governments through national allocation plans (NAPs). Member states will allocate at least 95% of EU allowances to obligated installations freely in the first part of the scheme. Such allocations must be based on objective and transparent criteria. The EU Commission has published guidelines for member states in drafting their NAPs but a number of aspects of the allocation process are left up to individual member states.

In accordance with the EU ETS Directive (Annex III) and the NAP guidance, member states must allocate EU allowances in a manner that is consistent with a path towards achieving or overachieving each member state's target under Decision 2002/358/EC and the Kyoto Protocol.[15] The total quantity of EU allowances to be allocated under the NAP should not be more than what is likely to be required by the covered installations as a whole. This ensures that the scheme works towards the goal of reducing GHG emissions and ensures that competition is not distorted. It may also create a shortage and thus increase the market for EU allowances.

Each member state must inform the Commission in advance of its proposed intentions for allocation. The Commission will examine these within the framework of a Regulatory Committee. The Regulatory Committee may reject a plan if the common criteria are not observed, or where the Commission believe that the NAP falls foul of the state aid rules.[16] In accordance with the EU ETS Directive the NAPs are due to the Commission for approval by the end of March 2004 with a deadline of 1 October 2005 for the finalised allocation decision for the first phase. Only some member states actually submitted their draft NAPs by the deadline.

If member states miss these deadlines or fail to implement the EU ETS Directive correctly, they may be subject to infraction proceedings by the Commission in accordance with Article 226 of the EC Treaty as amended. In general, such proceedings take some time with negotiations pre-commencement of formal proceedings taking up to 18 months and final European Court of Justice (ECJ) judgement averaging two years following commencement of formal proceedings. If requested by the Commission, the ECJ may impose a fine on a member state following final judgement. Although the timeline for such proceedings and for any sanctions to bite may appear to be too protracted to serve as an incentive to stick to the obligations and deadlines under the Directive, member states are likely to take infraction proceedings, particularly for such a high-profile Directive, very seriously. In addition, the Commission has indicated that it will not hesitate to take infraction proceedings and has already sent a number of letters of formal notice to those member states that did not transpose the Directive into law by 31 December 2003. It is possible that there may be a staggered start to the EU ETS if a number of member states are not ready to commence on 1 January 2005.

EU allowances will exist only in electronic form and the holding and tracking of EU allowances will be effected through an electronic system of registries (see also Chapter 1). The system of registries will be governed by an EU regulation to be finalised and adopted at some stage in 2004. Before a body can hold EU allowances it must first establish an account in a national registry. One way to imagine this is to think of the registry system as the water or gas pipeline system of the EU ETS. Without these pipeline systems neither gas nor water can be stored, moved around or delivered. It is the same with the EU registry systems and the EU allowances. Similar to the US SO_2 ARP and UK ETS, third parties – such as financial institutions, banks, environmental NGOs or schools, and companies marketing carbon-neutral products – will also be able to buy EU allowances and, if they wish, cancel them, thereby increasing their scarcity. A community-independent transaction log effects communication between and reconciliation of national registries.

The national registries for the EU ETS will also be the national registries required under the Kyoto Protocol should it enter into force. In that event the UNFCCC independent transaction log will also link national registries together. This is a crucial component of the Community Monitoring Mechanism, which was established by Council Decision 93/389/EEC. The Commission states that these national registries should also provide accurate information on the emissions entitlement of the trading sectors in each member state.

LINKING CDM AND JI PROJECTS TO THE EU ETS

The EU ETS is (initially at least) based solely on government creation and allocation of EU allowances. Therefore, under the EU ETS Directive as it currently stands, obligated installations are not able to use project credits from JI and CDMs for compliance.[17] However, there is a proposal to allow credits from JI and CDM projects to be traded under the EU ETS. This will require amendments to the EU ETS Directive. The EU Commission are currently working on just such amendments in the form of a directive, which is commonly being referred to as the "Linking Directive". This differs from expansion of the EU ETS through direct links with cap-and-trade schemes in other countries, as discussed below.

The proposed Linking Directive would, as currently drafted, amend the EU ETS Directive to recognise JI/CDM credits on a limited basis and subject to certain restrictions, including a total restriction or bar on any credits from projects based on LULUCF activities or large hydro being converted into EU allowances. This is due to the uncertainty surrounding the verification of emission reductions from LULUCF projects and the perceived environmental damage associated with large hydro projects. The Commission and European environment NGOs are keen to ensure the environmental integrity of the scheme and have therefore argued against the inclusion of such projects.

The Environment Committee of the European Parliament has recently proposed a number of significant amendments to the draft Linking Directive. Most importantly:

❏ Project credits from CDM and JI projects could be used for compliance in the EU ETS even if the Kyoto Protocol does not enter into force.

❏ CDM project credits would be available from 2005 for use in the EU ETS. In accordance with Decision 16/CP.7 of the Marrakech Accords, ERUs from JI projects are unavailable until post-2008. This is because the Kyoto Rules allow for the generation of CDM project credits from 2000 but allow for the generation of JI project credits only from 2008.

There would be no quantitative "limit" on the number of project credits that could be used in the EU ETS. Instead, annual monitoring of the level of use of project credits in the EU ETS would occur to assess whether each member state is complying with the qualitative "supplementarity rule" of the Kyoto Protocol, ie, emission reductions achieved through project credits are to be supplemental to real reductions in GHG emissions achieved through abatement.

Mutual Recognition Agreements could, pursuant to Article 28 of the EU ETS Directive, be made to link the EU ETS with mandatory GHG emissions trading schemes established by regional authorities such as states within the US or Australia, even though those countries have not yet ratified the Kyoto Protocol.

These proposed amendments are consistent with one of the key objectives of the EU ETS, namely that it is compatible with, but independent of, the Kyoto Protocol. The purpose of the proposed amendments is to provide more certainty for the operation of the EU ETS.

EXPANSION OF THE EU ETS

Article 25 of the EU ETS Directive allows the option of linking the EU ETS with emission trading schemes established by other Annex I parties. Use of Article 25 might, for example, allow the emerging Canadian trading programme or a scheme in Japan to be linked to the EU ETS. The EU ETS Directive does not contemplate any link with schemes in Non-Annex I countries. However, as mentioned above, the amendments to the proposed Linking Directive could allow limited links with such schemes through Mutual Recognition Agreements.

In the absence of any federal commitment to addressing the level of GHG emissions in the US, the northeastern states have been formulating a strategy to develop their own regional cap-and-trade scheme, the Regional Greenhouse Gas Initiative (RGGI). Other states have also been researching the possibilities of introducing such schemes. In addition, many Australian states, led by New South Wales, are exploring the possibility of creating their own emissions schemes, which could potentially link together and create a *de facto* cross-nation scheme along the lines of the Kyoto model despite the fact that the federal government have refused to ratify Kyoto.

Linking with the EU ETS *via* an Article 25 route or through Mutual Recognition Agreements could in effect create a quasi-Kyoto regime covering vast expanses of the developed world without the ratification of Kyoto. However, there may be legal barriers preventing state-based schemes from linking to the EU ETS. For example, linking the US state-based schemes could be hindered by constitutional challenges.

MARKET DEVELOPMENT ISSUES

The EU ETS is essentially the creation of a legislatively based market. However, the EU ETS Directive does not address all the legal issues that will impact upon the liquidity and effectiveness of such a market. A liquid or transparent market will not evolve unless some legal certainty is provided in relation to the nature of an

EU allowance and how the trading of EU allowances fits within the existing legal regime across the EU.

The key requirement to provide certainty in the market is to legally classify the nature of an EU allowance. In the UK the decision of the Court of Appeal in *Celtic Extraction Ltd and Bluestone Chemicals v Environment Agency* (2000), is helpful in determining this issue. In that case the court was called upon to consider whether or not a waste management licence (in simple terms, a right to deposit waste material into a hole in the ground) was property for the purposes of Section 436 of the Insolvency Act 1986. The court developed three tests that need to be satisfied if such a permit can be considered to be property:

1. there must be a statutory framework conferring an entitlement on one who satisfies certain conditions even though there is some element of discretion exercisable within the framework;
2. the permit must be transferable; and
3. the exemption or licence will have value.

In the UK it is likely that an EU allowance will be regarded as a property right. But what kind of property right – eg, regulated investment, bonds, chose in action, bills of exchange, negotiable instrument, or documentary intangible – and what consequences flow from this? And will it be categorised in the same fashion across the member states?

The answer to these fundamental questions will have profound effects on other areas of business and on the liquidity of the market as a whole. For example, how will EU allowances be treated on the insolvency of a company with obligations to surrender such EU allowances at the end of the period? Should they simply be treated as normal assets of the company in which liens or charges take precedence, or should they be immediately surrendered to cover any emissions of the company up to the time of insolvency? How can banks and financial institutions take security over an EU allowance and how will they be treated under the existing financial services regimes? Will tax treatment be the same across all member states (eg, will capital gains tax be payable in some member states but not others)? The answers to these questions are beyond the scope of this chapter. However, it is clear that many of these issues can be dealt with by the implementing legislation in each member state and that a harmonised approach to these issues will improve the liquidity and certainty in the market.

At present there are no official plans to provide a harmonised approach to such issues across the EU. However, we understand that many member states have been in unofficial talks to tackle these issues in a unified manner. Both the UK government and major financial institutions are currently exploring these issues and hope to publish guidance on methods of addressing market development. This guidance could be used as the basis of a harmonised EU approach.

DEVELOPMENT OF STANDARD FORM CONTRACTS

In any large trading market standard form contracts are developed for trading to take place smoothly and with some certainty. The EU ETS and trading of JI/CDM project credits is no exception. Various entities such as the International Emissions Trading Association, the European Federation of Energy Traders and the International Swaps and Derivatives Association are working on the development of master agreements that can be used to effect trades of EU allowances under the EU ETS. Such master agreements create certainty in the product that is being traded – for both the buyer and the seller. Like all trading contracts, they must provide for the conveyance of title, payment mechanisms, trading mechanisms, events of default and termination.

The right to any CERs or ERUs created by a CDM or JI project would generally belong to the project developer or project participants depending upon the legal arrangements between the parties, unless some law exists that allocates CERs in a particular fashion. While CERs are sovereign rights in the sense that they come into existence through the host government's approval of a project and allow the creation and transfer of CERs/ERUs, they are not the sovereign property of the host government. The only exception to this is where the host government specifically implements a law or policy that places ownership of part or all of the CERs from a project in the hands of the government, in effect "politically taxing" the CERs of a project.

It is essential, therefore, to address the ownership issues in the contractual documentation of any particular project. Depending upon the way in which the project is developed and financed, and the interests of participants, CERs or ERUs may form a critical component of financing and project deliverables or may be separated out as a distinct asset.

CONCLUSIONS

The legal framework for international emissions trading is set out in the overarching UNFCCC and the Kyoto Protocol with more detail contained in the Marrakech Accords. However, while the Kyoto Protocol is not currently binding on parties (as it is not yet ratified), many industries are or will be obligated under emissions trading regimes developed on local, national and regional bases.

The largest such scheme is the EU ETS, which is set to begin on 1 January 2005. This multinational scheme is modelled on Kyoto but can continue outside the Kyoto process. The legal framework of the scheme is set out in the EU ETS Directive. However, a number of changes to the scheme are currently being considered that will bring the other flexible mechanisms under Kyoto (JI and CDM projects) within the EU scheme. In addition, there is potential to link the EU scheme with international schemes, thereby creating an even larger market. Nevertheless, there remain a number of legal uncertainties that may hinder the liquidity and effectiveness of such a market.

1 Italics are authors.
2 For more detailed overview of this process and the relevant international provisions see Hobley, A., 2002, "Is Kyoto Dead? Climate change After Bush" 5 Env. Liability, pp 167.
3 http://unfccc.int/resource/conv/ratlist.pdf, updated as at 26 February 2004.
4 See Table 1 in Chapter 4 for a list of Annex I countries that ratified the Kyoto Protocol.
5 http://www.epa.gov/airmarkets/trading/so2market/transtable.html.
6 http://www.epa.gov/newsroom/headline_091503.htm.
7 Chapter 11 discusses various market results in the US ARP, focusing particularly on investment behaviour.
8 http://www.defra.gov.uk/news/2002/02313c.htm.
9 Department of Food, Environment and Rural Affairs (DEFRA) guidelines for the measurement and reporting of emissions the UK ETS and associated protocols at htttp://www.defra.gov.uk/environment/climatechange/trading/ index.htm.
10 Chapter 15 contains an exposition of the UK experience and discusses various market results.
11 Chapter 14 discusses market results in the EU emission trading system.
12 http://europa.eu.int/eur-lex/pri/en/oj/dat/2003/l_275/l_27520031025en00320046.pdf
13 A number of thresholds apply to each category below which an installation would not be an obligated installation, see Annex I.
14 Article 24.
15 Decision 2002/358/EC is the burden-sharing agreement under which all EU member states were allocated an individual emissions cap negotiated on the basis of historic share of emissions and future projections, giving an overall reduction of emissions in the EU of 8%.

16 Article 87 (1) of the EC Treaty provides that any state aid granted by a member state or through state resources in any form whatsoever that distorts or threatens to distort competition by favouring certain undertakings or the production of certain goods shall, in so far as it affects trade between member states, be incompatible with the common market. State aid may come in a large number of different guises but has been held to include: exemption from duties and taxes; exemption from parafiscal charges; preferential interest rates; guarantees of loans on especially favourable terms; making land or buildings available either for nothing or on especially favourable terms; provision of goods, services or personnel on preferential terms; indemnities against operating losses; and the purchase of shares of a company in financial difficulties.

17 See Chapter 4 in particular for an explanation and discussion of JI and CDM.

REFERENCES

Birnie, P., and A. Boyle, 2002, *International Law and the Environment*, 2nd edn (Oxford University Press), pp. 502–3.

DEFRA, 2004, "Guidelines for the Measurement and Reporting of Emissions", URL: http://www.defra.gov.uk/ environment/climatechange/trading/index.htm.

Hobley, A., 2001, Greenhouse Gas Emissions Trading in the United Kingdom, *Environmental Law and Management* **13(2)**.

Hobley, A., and S. Blackmore, 2002, *Greenhouse Gas Emissions Trading in the United Kingdom & EU Compared: The Same Route Destination, Different Routes*, 2Env. Liability.

Klassen, G., and A. Nentjes, 1997, "Sulphur Trading under the 1990 CAAA in the US: An Assessment of First Experiences", *Journal of Institutional and Theoretical Economics* **153**.

UN General Assembly, 1988, Resolution A/RES/43/53, December.

Vienna Convention for the Protection of the Ozone Layer, 1985, Article 1.

3

Critical Elements of a Market-Based Environmental Control Programme

Josh Margolis, Andy Kruger; Curt Kaminer

Cantor Fitzgerald Brokerage, LP;
Millennium Environmental Group, Inc.

This chapter explores the critical elements of an emissions trading programme and presents a number of lessons learned by participants to these programmes. Experience garnered over the last 30 years is used to isolate those elements that are necessary for emissions trading programmes to function. The interests of industry, regulators and the breathing public demand that these lessons be heeded by those that seek to use emissions trading to accomplish environmental objectives.

You've heard the mantra time and again: emission trading saves money and generates better results. These programmes turn waste streams into profits steams, and environmental managers into profit seekers. Bureaucrats cease their Esher-like quest to write and defend regulations, and become the bankers monitoring the accounts of their industrial customers. Those that have enough emissions at the end of the year keep their good credit rating; those that don't have their accounts debited and suffer enforcement actions. Air-quality entrepreneurs compete with each other to find better and less expensive ways to extract reductions from the air and the public benefits as the air becomes cleaner in direct proportion to the value of the traded credits. At least that is the way it is supposed to work, but sometimes it does not. Poorly designed and implemented emissions trading programmes will fail, leaving one or more stakeholders short of their objectives and vowing to turn back to what they know and understand: command and control.

So what lessons have we learned from the US SO_2 Acid Rain Program?[1] What has the federal NO_x SIP call program taught us? What mistakes were made in the New Source Review offset trading and Regional Clean Air Incentives Market programmes (RECLAIM)? This chapter first highlights 16 critical elements of emissions trading programmes. The recommended elements are drawn from our participation in, and development of, emissions trading throughout the US and in selected countries around the world. The elements, or rules of thumb, are listed below and discussed in the subsequent text.

1. There must be a demand for change and environmental improvement.
2. Programme goals should be clearly defined.
3. Source category participation should be proportional to their contribution to the problem.
4. The programme should be based on a quality emissions inventory.
5. A comprehensive permit system should be in place.
6. There should be a credible enforcement threat.
7. The programme should be efficiently and effectively administered.
8. An effective emissions banking process should be included.
9. The programme should be self-supporting.
10. One regulatory entity should administer the air quality and the emissions trading programme.
11. Individuals in and outside of the administering agency should champion the programme.
12. Input from all stakeholders should be sought.
13. Allowance allocations should be fair and consistent with the programme goals.
14. The mechanics of the trading process should be simple.
15. Regulators should resist the urge to meddle with the market.
16. Economic growth will stimulate the programme.

PROTOTYPICAL ELEMENTS OF AN EFFECTIVE EMISSIONS TRADING PROGRAMME

Based on our experience, these 16 elements are critical to establishing a successful emissions trading programme. It is not necessary for each programme to have *all* of these elements, but it is necessary for each to have the right combination of elements.

Element 1: There must be a demand for change and environmental improvement

The success of a market-based programme, and all the promise that it carries with it, can be realised only if there is a real constituency that seeks change. Regulators, industry and the public must make it clear that the status quo – whatever it is – is unacceptable.

Emissions trading programmes in the US often gain favour among regulators and the public when long-standing goals (eg, clean air by a certain deadline) have not been achieved. Industry will advocate trading programmes when it understands that dirty air means that they must spend increasingly large sums of money to remove each tonne of emissions and they will soon realise that emissions trading puts them in a much better position to inexpensively extract emissions from its plants.

Element 2: Programme goals should be clearly defined

The goal of an emissions trading programme should be clearly stated. Doing so establishes the programme's objective, and defines a baseline for measuring the programme's effectiveness. Clear goals also provide the certainty necessary to facilitate investments and participation in the market.

Most emissions trading programmes are adopted to replace some or all elements of pre-existing command-and-control programmes. The primary goals of the trading programme should be to achieve environmental clean-up results better, faster, with more certainty and less expense than the programme it replaces. All stakeholders (government, industry and the public) should agree on these goals and stakeholders should also agree that the proposed emissions trading programme could achieve these goals.

Larger goals should be incrementalised and a means to judge success should be included. For example, a goal of a 10-year programme may be to reduce airshed emissions by 60%. An incremental goal may be to achieve average facility-specific reductions of 6% per year. The means by which the goals can be evaluated could include a requirement that facilities annually report their emissions. Evaluations must be made periodically to gather data that will allow programme administrators to make mid-course corrections. Timing and the process involved in making mid-course corrections should be pre-established and well known and understood by all stakeholders.

A notable emissions trading programme has been in place in the Los Angeles area. The area is about 10,743 square miles, has a population of about 16 million and has 28,000 businesses with air permits. The area, which falls under the jurisdiction of the South Coast Air Quality Management District (SCAQMD – see Panel 1), has had the longest-running regional emissions trading programme in the US. Yet it also continues to have the worst air quality. However, if measured against the programme goal to ensure that new sources do not make air quality worse, the programme can be viewed as quite a success. True air emissions reductions have occurred.

Element 3: Source category participation should be proportional to their contribution to the problem

Sources should participate in the programme in proportion to their contribution to the air quality problem.

The sources that participate in an emissions trading programme should be explicitly defined by the applicable rules, and be directly related to the goal of the programme. For example, if the goal is to ensure that the air quality does not degrade because of new and expanding facilities, setting a low threshold that triggers the need to secure air credits to mitigate air emission impacts from such facilities will help ensure the success of the programme. Alternatively, if the goal of the programme is to accomplish area-wide emission reductions, persuading a broad sector of polluting sources to participate will contribute to the success of the programme.

In the case of traditional new source review regulations, offset thresholds have historically been too high to accomplish the goal of ensuring that air quality does not degrade. Studies have indicated that most emission increases are from new and modified sources with emission changes that are considered too small, and are exempt from the need to secure offsets. Thus, those sources that are primarily responsible for the air quality problem are often exempt from the need to secure offsets.

Similar problems could arise under an allowance-based system. For example, it would be impractical to extract a 5% basin-wide emission reduction through a programme that includes only sources that contribute less than 20% of the emissions inventory. Here, targeted sources would have to reduce emissions not by 5% but by 25% to achieve the required overall improvement.

RECLAIM is a programme that has been built around the sources that contribute to the air quality problem in the SCAQMD. The programme currently includes more than 330 stationary sources that contribute air emissions. At the outset of the programme in 1994 these sources represented only 6% of the NO_x emitters and 4% of the SO_x emitters. Yet, as a group, these RECLAIM facilities contribute approximately 65% and 85% of the overall permitted stationary-source NO_x and SO_x emissions. Thus, the relatively small number of sources that are responsible for most of the stationary-source-derived problem are included in the programme. It should be noted that other emission-control programmes focus on other sectors – eg, mobile, indirect and area-wide sources. It is the goal to bring these sectors into a similar market-based programme.

Element 4: The programme should be based on a quality emissions inventory

Necessary for the success of an emission trading programme is an emission inventory that accurately represents all significant emissions sources. Regulators who seek to design and implement an emissions trading programme will find their job more difficult, and those tasked with programme evaluation will find their jobs nearly impossible to perform, without an accurate inventory to bring statistics closer to reality.

Inadequate data on the sources covered by a programme will make it difficult for regulators to assess the programme's success. If the data upon which a baseline is defined are questionable, regulators' efforts to achieve a basin-wide emission reduction goal versus the baseline will be frustrated. In addition, unless the emissions inventory is known to be complete and accurate, planning based on the baseline will be unreliable. An emissions inventory must be regularly updated. An inventory should have adequate information on its sources; be based on actual emissions rather than allowable emissions; and include both permitted and unpermitted sources.

Element 5: A comprehensive permit system should be in place

A comprehensive permit system is critical to the success of an emissions trading programme. If the permit programme is vague or only applies to a limited number of sources, the regulator loses a means of controlling the air quality problem and managing its solution. The requirement for sources covered by an emissions trading programme to obtain an air quality permit is critical. The regulator must have a means to bring sources into their system; ensure that new sources secure compensating emission offsets; and make certain that sources meet their continuing emission reduction objectives. The sources must also understand that if they meet the appropriate standards, the regulator will not hinder their operation.

A programme that requires businesses to gain advance approvals before a source is constructed, operated or modified, and that requires the maintenance of this approval during the lifetime of the facility, is critical to the success of an emissions trading programme. With such a programme the regulator can ensure that compensating emission offsets are secured prior to operation and that annual reduction targets are met. Failure to meet these requirements should result in revocation of the permit, fines, penalties or other sanctions.

Element 6: There should be a credible enforcement threat

Sources covered by a trading programme must know that there is a significant risk associated with failure to secure required offsets or allowances. The penalty should significantly exceed the cost of acquiring offsets or allowances. Sources should understand that the cost of complying with the offset or allowance requirement is significantly smaller than the penalty associated with failure to comply with the relevant rules.

The emissions trading programme must also include a means by which the regulator can determine noncompliance. Annual emissions reporting, facility inspections, source testing, emission monitoring and a comprehensive permitting system are important parts of an enforcement programme.

In the SCAQMD, the penalty for noncompliance with offset provisions is as much as US$25,000 per violation per day, the possibility of permit revocation, and potential civil or criminal penalties. Similar penalties are provided for in the San Francisco Bay Area and the San Joaquin Valley rules. Additionally, utilities that fail to secure sufficient SO_2 allowances are faced with a US$2,000 per tonne penalty (annually adjusted for the cost of inflation) and the need to cover allowances for the retroactive liability. There is also a 3:1 penalty for each missing allowance. As SO_2 allowances, for example, can be easily secured for approximately one-tenth of the US$2,000 fine, financial managers will ensure that those responsible for violations understand the economic, civil, and potential criminal consequences of their actions. In addition, penalties for failure to comply with the Acid Rain Program provisions of the Clean Air Act Amendment also include felony prosecution provisions.

Element 7: The programme should be efficiently and effectively administered

Clear and unchanging rules, consistent decisions, predictable time requirements and adherence to timeliness and schedules prescribed in the regulations will all contribute to the success of an emissions trading programme. Prompt, efficient, simple, low-cost administration of the programme is preferable, but predictable and consistent administration is essential.

In times past some California air districts took the better part of a year to process an application to bank an emission reduction credit (ERC) and six months for transfer. In recent years, this time has been shortened to months (to bank) and days (to transfer) the credits. Rightly or not, the industry believes that some air districts rarely act within the prescribed periods for processing applications and transferring credit. Furthermore, there is significant uncertainty as to the rules governing ERCs. For example, since 1976, the emissions-trading-related rules in the SCAQMD have gone through more than eight significant modifications.

A major administrative difference between RECLAIM and programmes administered by the US EPA is the allowance numbering system. Each SO_2 and NO_x allowance issued by the EPA has a separate and distinct serial number. The RECLAIM programme does not number credits. From an administrative perspective it is much easier to keep track of allowances when they have individual serial numbers.

Element 8: An effective emissions banking process should be included

An emissions banking programme will greatly contribute to the success of an emissions trading programme. An emissions bank is simply an administrative mechanism that allows sources to create, gain recognition for and store air credits for later use or sale. Having a place to put air credits once they are created will do several things: (1) provide industry with the confidence that air credits created as the result of voluntary efforts can be stored for later use if an immediate use cannot be found for them; (2) provide potential users/buyers with a means to distinguish emission reductions that have gained the mantle of certification; (3) contribute to the fluidity of the market as buyers will be willing to expend funds on an already certified commodity; and (4) alleviate concern that air credits will be confiscated by regulators anxious to meet their air quality planning objectives.

To be effective, the emissions banking programme must include the following items: (1) a clear application process; (2) a predictable review process; (3) a long shelf life for air credits; (4) protections from discounting associated with rules that are passed after an air credit is created; (5) protection from confiscation; and (6) an understandable transfer process. Failure to include these elements in an emissions bank will reduce industry's willingness to participate in an emissions trading programme.

Banking is a very important economic characteristic of emission trading programmes. The primary means of reducing the cost of emission reductions to society in general is to let the "invisible hand" of entrepreneurship lead emitters with relatively low costs of emission reductions to overcontrol (install emission controls in excess of the specific needs of the site) and then sell the excess increment of emission reduction to emitters with sites and processes more expensive to control. Since the installation of emission control equipment often entails a multi-year time horizon and companies installing controls may be reluctant to sell excess emission reductions before the equipment has been fully tested and operational, the inability to fully bank allowances over time essentially imposes a cost penalty or disincentive. Ironically, this penalises the firms that are doing the most to reduce emissions and creates programmatic disincentives to overcontrol.

The Acid Rain Program provides for banking of allowances, currently on a full-value basis. This means that emitters who have reduced emissions in one period can utilise credits at the same tonnage value in a future period. There are several examples of overcontrol of emissions that have been observed that have been facilitated by the banking provisions within this programme. First, several power plants in the US installed controls at earlier times or at greater levels than required. The architect engineering firm that designed the installation shares in the value of the excess emissions reduced by periodically selling the accumulation of allowances in excess of the site's needs. Banking facilitates this type of transaction, because it allows the site owner to know that the site's needs have first been met, before any excess or surplus allowances are sold. Second, it has become very common for utilities to allow their coal suppliers higher prices for lower-sulphur coal deliveries or penalties for higher-sulphur coal deliveries, often in the form of allowances added to or subtracted from the bill rather than cash. Coal companies are active market participants and will sometimes hedge the production of higher-sulphur seams with the acquisition of SO_2 emission allowances. Banking allows these companies to hold these allowances (either purchased or received) and more efficiently transmit the market signals that have been monetised by the trading programme into more efficient exploitation of reserves and production of coal.

The US federal NO_x programme provides for the banking of allowances within budget periods, with partial usability of prior year tonnes when large quantities are banked. Under these regulations, allowances banked will be worth not less than 50% of a future year allowance. This type of banking is not as economically efficient as the type described above for the SO_2 programme, but it is better than no banking. Additionally, NO_x controls are often less expensive and have shorter time horizons for installation, mitigating to an extent the lack of full banking in this programme. Also, the NO_x programme is in place only during the summer NO_x season, so may be disproportionately affected by unusual weather conditions. The combination of these factors with partial banking has made the NO_x market highly volatile. Price volatility trends between 50% and 75%, much of which is created by the uncertainties in the banking provisions.

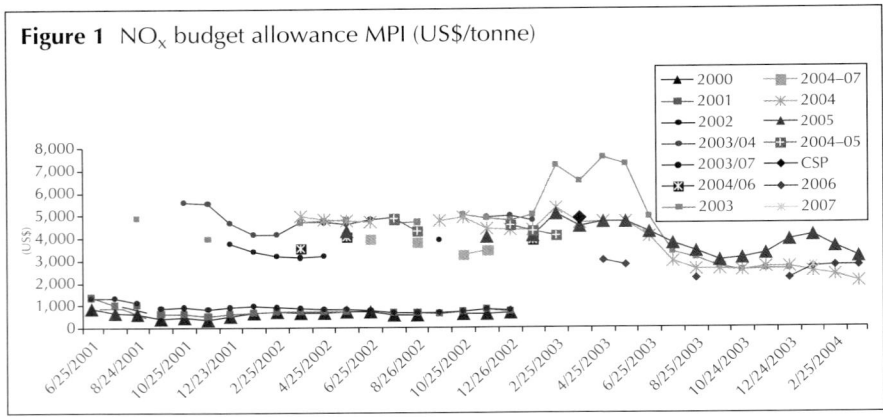

Figure 1 NO$_X$ budget allowance MPI (US\$/tonne)

The San Joaquin Valley programme highlights the value of an emissions bank. Prior to the adoption of the San Joaquin Valley bank in 1987, there were no offset trades and few sources voluntarily created emission reductions. Since then, tens of thousands of emission credits have been created, banked, sold and used.

Element 9: The programme should be self-supporting

If an emissions trading programme is to work, it must be self-supporting. A programme that lacks the resources for its implementation will fail, regardless of how elegant its design, well intentioned its regulators or enthusiastic its industry users.

An emissions trading programme should levy appropriate fees on those who wish to file for, create, bank and use air credits. Failure to set these fees at levels that allow the regulators to do their job will contribute to delays and reduce the quality of reviews. When a regulator is short of funds, problems with immediate deadlines will always take precedence over those problems that are less urgent. If the process of processing air credit-related transactions falls outside the realm of "crisis" problems, the regulator will inevitably defer air credit applications in favour of permit applications. Additionally, the regulatory body with jurisdiction should have the ability to use the fee revenue to hire support staff and support the ongoing activities of the trading programme. Such fees should not go into a general fund within the regulatory body or the government in general.

The San Diego County Air Pollution Control District and San Joaquin Valley Air Quality Management District (see Panel 1) charge hourly rates to process credit-related transactions, and staff activities are supported by these charges. Other air districts have suffered from a lack of resources in implementing their emissions trading programmes. Engineers responsible for air credit reviews are routinely pulled off these projects to process permit applications.

Element 10: One regulatory entity should administer the air quality and the emissions trading programme

The administration of both the air quality rules and the emissions trading programme should be under the control of a single regulatory entity. Multiple agencies with different levels of control can result in: (1) implementation of programmes with conflicting goals; (2) an unevenly applied permitting and offset programme; and (3) exemptions for significant air pollution contributors. The failure to account for the contribution of exempt sources and the inability to control their emissions will frustrate an emissions trading programme whose goal is to achieve an overall reduction in emissions.

In the SCAQMD, one reason why the air quality problem has persisted for so long is that major categories of emissions were outside the control of those responsible for air quality improvement. Indirect sources (eg, those that attract vehicular traffic) and area-wide sources (eg, those that use small quantities of paint) have traditionally fallen outside the scope of most air quality programmes. Industry leaders and programme administrators became more frustrated as emission controls on industry became more stringent, but pollution levels remained high. The high pollution levels were caused, in part, by the emissions contributed by excluded sources.

Element 11: Individuals inside and outside the administering agency should champion the programme

An emissions trading programme will be successfully developed and maintained only if there is a champion that supports its goals within both the entity that develops the implementing legislation and the regulatory body that must develop supporting rules and implement the programme. The champion must focus on the problems of traditional regulatory strategies and the benefits of

PANEL 1 REGIONAL EMISSION CONTROL PROGRAMMES

The 1990 Clean Air Act is the most recent version of a law first passed in 1970 and covers the entire US. Under this law, the federal Environmental Protection Agency (EPA) sets limits on how much of each pollutant can be in the air anywhere in the US. The law allows individual states to have stronger standards, but states cannot have weaker standards than those set for the entire country.

California adopted its own Clean Air Act in 1988. It sets state-wide guidelines for air districts to develop reduction strategies for air pollution. Local air pollution control districts develop plans and implement control measures in their areas. These controls primarily affect stationary sources such as factories and plants. Examples of control districts are the San Joaquin Valley Air Pollution Control District, San Diego County Air Pollution Control District and the South Coast Air Quality Management District (SCAQMD), including Los Angeles.

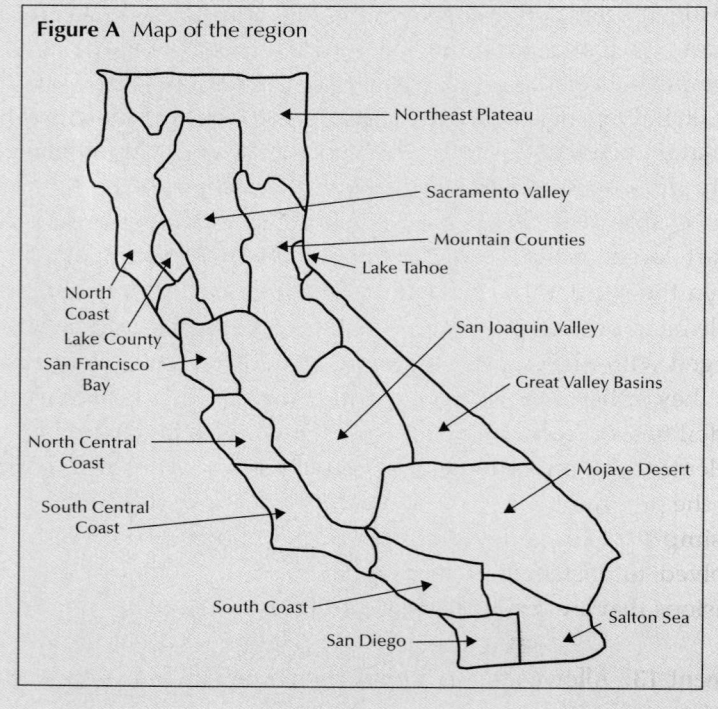

Figure A Map of the region

Northeast Plateau

Sacramento Valley

Mountain Counties

Lake Tahoe

North Coast

Lake County

San Francisco Bay

San Joaquin Valley

Great Valley Basins

North Central Coast

South Central Coast

Mojave Desert

South Coast

Salton Sea

San Diego

emissions trading to convince his/her colleagues that emission trading provides enough promise to warrant a departure from a strict command-and-control approach.

Once the emissions trading programme is in place, the champion within the regulatory agency must convince staff that industry, given proper incentives, will accomplish the air quality goals without extraordinary micromanagement by the agency. It must be made clear to staff that their roles are to ensure that industry meets the prescribed goals, to educate industry and the public on the benefits and mechanics of emissions trading and to bring enforcement against those who fail to comply. Staff must also know that senior management will support their efforts to implement the emissions trading programme.

Element 12: Input from all stakeholders should be sought

The emissions trading programme must have the support of those who are affected. Failure to gain this support will likely result in a system, no matter how well designed, that is unused, fails to accomplish its goals or does not serve its intended users.

Stakeholders of concern include those within the legislature, the regulatory agency, industry and the public. Those within the legislature develop the laws that provide for emissions trading and must ensure that their emissions trading programme does not thwart larger goals (eg, reducing basin-wide emissions). Those within the regulatory agency must manage the development and implementation of the emissions trading programme. They are charged with meeting the legislated goals. They must also ensure that they either build the programme around their resources and capabilities or secure the needed resources and capabilities to implement the programme. Industry must be involved to ensure that the programme is workable and presents a desired alternative to simple command-and-control. The public should also be involved to ensure that there are avenues for monitoring major decisions that are made as a result of the programme.

Element 13: Allowance allocations should be fair and consistent with the programme goals

One of the most troublesome aspects of designing emissions trading programmes is the need to allocate emission budgets to programme participants. Allocations must be made in a manner that protects the interests of the market and is perceived to be fair and equitable. Among the most important factors that programme designers must consider in allocating emission rights are the following:

(a) historical emission levels;
(b) the effects of economic recessions;
(c) the magnitude and speed of the reduction expected of each participant; and
(d) the effect that forthcoming rules would have had if the trading programme was not adopted.

These factors must be deliberated in the open with input from all stakeholders. Industry must be made to understand the overall cap, the total emission reduction obligation and their company's obligations. Overall, allocations must be executed in a fashion that minimises the number of "losers".

The allocation of emission rights under the SCAQMD's RECLAIM programme was perhaps the most difficult part in getting this programme going. Ultimately, it took two years of consultations with the public, industry and environmental groups to arrive at the starting allocation. Not unexpectedly, industry sought an allocation based on its theoretical permitted maximum emission levels (which were rarely achieved in practice). Regulators, environmental groups, and certain members of the public advocated the use of the most recent actual emissions, which included a time of recession when emissions were at near-term historic lows. Ultimately, a compromise was reached whereby industries were allowed to base their allocation on actual emissions that occurred during a time period that preceded the recession.

Element 14: The mechanics of the trading process should be simple

The mechanics of trading the commodity need to be clearly defined and carefully structured. Transaction costs are a clear concern here. Trading will occur only if transaction costs are minimised. If the mechanics of effecting a trade are so burdensome as to overwhelm any savings that might have been realised, companies will not trade. The steps necessary to accomplish a trade should be simple, easy to understand and replicate, and predictable.

Element 15: Resist the urge to meddle with the market

An additional concern is tempering the regulator's desire to "help" or "guide" the market. Air credit markets operate best if the regulator's role is limited to registering the transactions and maintaining information about available credits. Having said this, we are quick to add that there may be some need for the regulator to also play a role in ensuring that credits are free and clear of liens, encumbrances and pledges that may not be known to buyers.

One characteristic of emission trading markets is that new and innovative approaches to the control of emissions are implemented. These approaches are often well beyond the wildest imagination of regulators. Interestingly, regulators and stakeholders seem more often to focus on why a new and innovative way to reduce emissions is bad or how they could come up with a regulatory scheme that would have unearthed the approach rather than embracing it as a lower cost to society for achieving emission goals. An example of this has been the massive transformation of the US coal industry from producing high-sulphur coal to low-sulphur coal. Currently, more than 60% of all coal produced in the US (more than 1 billion tonnes) has less than 1% sulphur. Prior to 1990, less than 30% of all coal produced was low-sulphur. Since the low-sulphur coal is produced in the western US and displaces coal produced in the eastern Appalachian areas, a massive reallocation of society's resources has occurred over the past 15 years to meet environmental challenges monetised through the Acid Rain Program.

Over recent years emissions trading programme administrators have intervened in at least one emissions trading market to the detriment of the programme. In the early years of the RECLAIM programme NO_x RTC prices traded at or below US$1.00 per pound (US$2,000 per tonne). However, all that changed in 2001 when prices hit US$62 per pound (US$124,000 per tonne). This increase in price is generally attributed to:

1. the power plants that ran at full capacity and consumed extraordinary quantities of RTCs in their effort to supply power during the California energy crisis;
2. the lack of concern sources short on RTCs showed in the early years of RECLAIM, because they assumed they could pick up credits at inexpensive prices; and

PANEL 2 NO$_x$ TRADING

Oxides of nitrogen or NO$_x$ emissions are produced from burning fuels such as gasoline and coal at high temperatures, as in combustion processes. NO$_x$ emissions contribute to the formation of ozone or smog in the atmosphere, which impairs visibility. NO$_x$ is also a major component of acid rain.

In the US, NO$_x$ emissions trading began in 1999 on a regional basis. Regional markets for NO$_x$ allowances were created with the establishment of an emissions cap in 1994 by a group of 12 states (including Washington, DC) in the northeast, called the Ozone Transport Commission (OTC). The US Environmental Protection Agency (EPA) has expanded the markets into the Midwestern United States by way of its NO$_x$ SIP call. The OTC NO$_x$ Budget Program was designed to imitate the generally successful SO$_2$ trading programme created under the Acid Rain Program.

The emissions cap affects electricity generation units and large industrial boilers. The cap requires emitting facilities to cover their summer ozone season (1 May to 30 September) emissions with NO$_x$ allowances. Each NO$_x$ allowance equals 1 tonne of emissions. According to the EPA and the OTC, NO$_x$ ozone season emissions were reduced to approximately 60% below 1990 baseline levels in the period 1999–2002, and have been reduced by even greater amounts thereafter (still being ascertained at the time of writing).

3. the willingness of buyers to pay market price for RTCs rather than suffer noncompliance penalties.

These factors combined to create the "Perfect Storm" which caught nearly all stakeholders by surprise. The SCAQMD's reaction was swift. The power plants were removed from the programme, forced to install controls, and allowed to purchase credits from the SCAQMD. Large sources were required to submit plans that detailed how they were going to keep their emissions below their allocations. The once robust RECLAIM programme was left as a shell of its former self.

While these changes had the intended effect – prices were brought back down within a matter of months – they also had some unintended and unfortunate effects. First, power plants and large sources were deprived of the opportunity to make decisions based on their ability to buy and sell around their control cost curves. Instead, they were forced back into a command and control programme. Second, many air quality entrepreneurs that intended to put on controls to satisfy the RTC demand dropped their projects. As fast as prices dropped, so too did private efforts to extract emissions from the air that would have been funded by higher credit prices. Those that set business plans in place counting on a continued and vibrant RECLAIM programme learned a costly lesson: the government giveth and can taketh away.

We strongly urge trading programme administrators and politicians to study the RECLAIM example. We understand the need to listen to constituent demands and we do not judge the SCAQMD for responding to the clamour "to do something" to fix the RECLAIM programme. However, we caution policy makers to recognise that such actions have the effect of undermining the market and sacrificing the very goals that caused disparate stakeholders to support the programme. Quick fixes may well have long lasting and undesirable effects. Programme participants are deprived of the opportunity to make least cost decisions and therefore spend too much to remove each marginal increment of reduction and undermine the goal of a market driven programme. The public is denied the assurance that the market will promote otherwise uneconomical next generation pollution control solutions that would not be possible under a command and control situation, and society suffers as resources are inefficiently allocated.

Element 16: Economic growth will stimulate the programme

Economic growth is an important, though not necessary, success factor. New sources contribute to demand and increase the marketability of the air credits that can be sold. However, economic growth is not as critical to allowance and attainment-based programmes as it is for new-source offsetting programmes. In essence, environmental quality is a luxury good. No matter how efficient the programme in reducing emissions, consumers and producers are still faced with higher costs. When economic tides are rising, the demand for higher environmental quality rises, as does society's ability to pay, relatively painlessly, the costs from the increment of income associated with improving economic conditions.

CONCLUSIONS

The creation of a market for emission reductions allows emitters to hedge their future control requirements. In our experience, it has been evident that firms that plan compliance needs and embark on programmes of buying or selling have, in the long run, met regulators' requirements at low costs. Conversely, firms that have taken an *ad hoc* approach often seem to be "swimming upstream" relative to the market and have not achieved compliance goals at the lowest possible cost.

A fungible market eliminates a significant degree of uncertainty for emitters and thus makes decision making somewhat simpler. Emitters who anticipate high costs relative to other programme participants can embark on an allowance purchasing programme. When the price of allowances is below their cost of controls, they buy. Conversely, emitters with anticipated low costs of controls may choose to overcontrol and use the proceeds to reduce their costs of compliance.

Emissions trading programmes have resulted in cleaner air at a substantially lower cost than command-and-control programmes. If designed with the right combination of elements, trading programmes can be a powerful and cost-effective tool to realise environmental goals. The *critical elements* presented in this chapter are drawn from our review and participation in existing and developing emissions trading programmes throughout the United States. It is not necessary that each trading programme include all of these critical elements. However, each programme should include the right combination of elements to achieve the programme's intended goal. There is one last point we want to make: a market-based programme will have the greatest impact if there is a commitment to improve the environment *and* to do it in the most cost-effective fashion.

1   See Chapter 11 for a discussion of market results in the US SO_2 programme.

4

Joint Implementation and Clean Development Mechanism

Michiel ten Hoopen, Veronique Bovee

EcoSecurities

Joint Implementation (JI) and the Clean Development Mechanism (CDM) are two project-based mechanisms set up by the Kyoto Protocol. One of the principal aims of both JI and CDM is to reduce the costs of complying with the greenhouse gas (GHG) emission reduction targets outlined in the Kyoto Protocol for industrialised (Annex I) countries. These two flexibility mechanisms are also designed to contribute to sustainable development in the countries hosting the projects.

Joint Implementation

JI is established under Article 6 of the Kyoto Protocol and allows for the transfer and acquisition of Emission Reduction Units (ERUs) resulting from activities that reduce anthropogenic GHGs or enhance the removal of GHGs within Annex I parties (industrialised countries and economies in transition – see Table 1). These ERUs can be generated in the period 2008–12.[1] Projects starting as of the year 2000 may be eligible as JI projects if certain requirements are met. Investors in JI or CDM projects can be countries or private legal entities.

JI promotes investments by Annex I parties in projects undertaken in other Annex I parties. The investor country or private legal entity is able to use the resulting emission rights to meet its own target. For a project developer, one of the benefits of implementing a JI project is the ability to sell the resulting emission rights and thereby enhance the project's economic viability.

Table 1 Annex I countries

List of Annex I countries and status of ratification*

No	Country	Status	No	Country	Status
1	Australia	No	20	Lithuania	Yes
2	Austria	Yes	21	Luxembourg	Yes
3	Belgium	Yes	22	Monaco	No
4	Bulgaria	Yes	23	Netherlands	Yes
5	Canada	Yes	24	New Zealand	Yes
6	Croatia	No	25	Norway	Yes
7	Czech Republic	Yes	26	Poland	Yes
8	Denmark	Yes	27	Portugal	Yes
9	EU	Yes	28	Romania	Yes
10	Estonia	Yes	29	Russian Federation	No
11	Finland	Yes	30	Slovakia	Yes
12	France	Yes	31	Slovenia	Yes
13	Germany	Yes	32	Spain	Yes
14	Greece	Yes	33	Sweden	Yes
15	Ireland	Yes	34	Switzerland	Yes
16	Italy	Yes	35	Ukraine	Yes
17	Japan	Yes	36	UK	Yes
18	Latvia	Yes	37	USA	No
19	Liechtenstein	Yes			

*At the time of writing.

The Clean Development Mechanism

The CDM is established under Article 12 of the Kyoto Protocol. The CDM is the only flexibility mechanism in the Kyoto Protocol that involves Non-Annex I countries (developing countries). Activities that reduce emissions in Non-Annex I countries can result in Certified Emission Reductions (CERs), which may be transferred to Annex I countries.

As defined by the Protocol, the purpose of the CDM is twofold:

1. to assist Non-Annex I countries in achieving sustainable development; and
2. to help Annex I countries to achieve emission reductions that can be used to meet their emission target.

As JI does for Annex I countries, the CDM attracts investments to Non-Annex I countries, thereby leading to economic, developmental and environmental benefits.

There are two main differences between JI and the CDM. The first is that the CDM is already operational. For example, the format for the project design document for a CDM project is already available and projects can be validated and generate CERs as soon as emission reductions are verified. JI will become formally operational only after the Kyoto Protocol comes into force. This does not mean that JI projects are not possible yet; in fact quite a number of JI projects have already been developed. However, the fact that JI is not yet formally operational does lead to some risks for the project developers and buyers of the ERUs.

Another crucial difference between JI and CDM is that JI is effectively a zero-sum game. A JI project concerns parties that both have an emission reduction obligation. When a JI host party transfers ERUs from a JI project, it is transferring part of its assigned amount under Kyoto to another Annex I party. When CERs are generated, they come from a party without a reduction obligation under Kyoto and thus emission rights are created *ex nihilo*. This means that validation and verification requirements for the CDM have to be stricter. When a JI host party is not (yet) in compliance with its Kyoto obligations, JI and CDM actually become rather identical. In that situation the procedures for JI are similar to those of the CDM.

Advantages of using JI and CDM

For the countries (or businesses) buying the emission rights, using the mechanisms offers a clear advantage. When the price of the emission rights is lower than the costs associated with internal or on-site emission reductions, buying credits lowers the overall costs of compliance. This is similar to the benefits of the other flexibility mechanism: emissions trading. But JI and CDM provide more direct benefits for the host countries.

Perhaps the most important benefit provided by JI and CDM for host countries is that they serve to attract foreign investments in low-emission technologies. Both the direct investments and the resulting improvements in efficiency have a positive contribution to the economy and can lead to more employment.

Another benefit is that JI and CDM projects often also reduce other pollution in the host country besides GHG emissions, such as local air pollution. For example, a waste-management project reduces methane emissions, but also reduces odours around the landfill and reduces ground water pollution.

To the investor in JI and CDM projects, the opportunity to sell credits offers an extra source of revenue above the normal project revenues, eg, for selling electricity. This will increase the financial viability of the project. What is often very important for investments in developing countries is that part of the revenue from the project will come in hard currency and from a buyer with a good reputation (such as the World Bank, a European government or a private-sector company). The prospect of this revenue source can help to promote other financing for the project. For most project types, like renewable energy projects, the carbon revenues will cover only 5 to 15% of the investment costs (see Chapter 8). For methane emission reduction projects, the carbon revenues can cover more than half the costs of the project. This difference in extra return can have an effect on the types of project that are developed under JI and CDM. (See the end of this chapter for more on the CDM market.)

JI, THE TWO TRACK APPROACH

The international climate change agreements provide two sets of JI procedures commonly referred to as the "Two Track" approach. The two tracks refer to alternative procedures and project cycles for JI projects. The appropriate track depends on the status of the host party in meeting the eligibility requirements as set out by the Marrakech Accords (see COP7, 2001). Under both tracks the parties are required to establish a designated focal point for approving projects. Furthermore, they need to have in place national guidelines and procedures for approving JI projects.

First Track: The First Track procedures for JI apply when a host party meets all the eligibility criteria related to the transfer and acquisition of emission rights (see Table 2). In this situation, Annex I host parties are allowed to apply their own procedures for assessing projects emissions additionality. The party is then able to issue and transfer ERUs to the investing party, without recourse to any international body for approval. Therefore, the eligibility requirements that allow an Annex I host party to participate in JI First Track are stricter than the requirements applying to the Second Track.

Second Track: Under the Second Track procedure for JI, an Annex I host party can also participate in JI if it is a party to the Kyoto Protocol, and has established both its assigned amount and a registry. Under the Second Track the host party has to follow

Table 2 Overview of JI First Track and Second Track participation requirements and procedures

	JI First Track	JI Second Track
A. Process Requirements for a host party to participate	❏ It is a party to the Kyoto Protocol. ❏ Its assigned amounts have been calculated and recorded. ❏ It has in place a national system for the estimation of GHG emissions. ❏ It has in place a national registry to record the acquisition and transfer of the various emission rights (AAUs, ERUs, CERs, and RMUs). ❏ It has submitted annually a GHG inventory report. ❏ It has submitted the supplementary information on the assigned amounts.	❏ It is a party to the Kyoto Protocol. ❏ Its assigned amounts have been calculated and recorded. ❏ It has in place a national registry for recording the acquisition and transfer of the various emission rights (AAUs, ERUs, CERs, and RMUs).
B. Documentation Project requirements for generating and transferring ERUs	❏ The host party is free to decide upon and define the rules for verification of ERUs from a JI project.	❏ The host party has to follow the verificationprocedure under the Article 6 Supervisory Committee, which includes the development of a project design document (PDD). ❏ An independent entity, accredited by the Article 6 Supervisory Committee, needs to validate the PDD.
C. Issuance of ERUs	❏ The host party can issue ERUs. No approval is required from the JI Supervisory Committee.	❏ If the JI Supervisory Committee does not call the independent entity's verification report into a review procedure then the host party can issue ERUs.

Source: BASREC, 2003

the project determination and verification procedure under the Article 6 Supervisory Committee, a body that serves to regulate JI activities. The project developer has to prepare a PDD and have this approved by an independent entity accredited by the Supervisory Committee.

Because there are no specific requirements for verification of ERUs under the First Track JI, the JI project cycle under the First Track could vary from host party to host party, and could differ from Second Track JI procedures. It is likely that the First Track project procedures adopted will be more straightforward and simple than those established for the JI Second Track. It should be noted that a party meeting the First Track JI requirements may at any time opt for using the JI Second Track procedure. At the current stage it is safest for JI project developers to try to develop their project under the Second Track procedures. Institutions and procedures under the First Track have not been developed yet and it is difficult to predict if and when host parties will meet the First Track criteria. For some parties the requirements may not be met until just before the start of the commitment period (parties have until 2007 to meet some of the requirements).[2]

A key criterion for operationalising Track 2 JI is the establishment of the JI Supervisory Committee. The JI Supervisory Committee will be established at the meeting of the first Conference of the Parties/Meeting of the Parties (COP/MOP).[3] It should be able to draw on the experience of the CDM Executive Board (which performs a similar function for the CDM), which should accelerate the readiness of the Supervisory Committee. Because JI Track 2 resembles the CDM, the best way to develop a JI project now is to follow the existing CDM rules and if possible use the methodologies that exist for CDM projects. Of course a project developer should also consult closely with the host party and develop projects according to the rules that already exist in the host country.

DEVELOPING A CDM PROJECT

As indicated above, the CDM is formally operational and the rules for CDM have been established. The CDM Executive Board, the CDM equivalent of the JI Supervisory Committee, is already operational and there is a Methodologies Panel that reviews CDM baseline and monitoring methodologies.

PANEL 1 THE CDM EXECUTIVE BOARD AND THE METHODOLOGIES PANEL

The Executive Board supervises the CDM. It has ten members, all from parties to the Kyoto Protocol. Some of the main tasks of the Executive Board are approving new methodologies, accrediting Designated Operational Entities (see main chapter for explanation), developing and maintaining the CDM registry and making recommendations to the COP/MOP on procedures for the CDM.

To assist in its tasks, the Executive Board established the Panel on Baseline and Monitoring Methodologies (Meth Panel). The Meth Panel reviews the proposed new methodologies for baseline and monitoring plans and develops recommendations to the Executive Board.

In order to be eligible for the CDM, a project has to be assessed against the following criteria:

❑ requirements for CDM as included in Article 12 of the Kyoto Protocol;
❑ the guidelines and requirements for CDM as included in the Marrakech Accords;
❑ guidelines and requirements adopted by the CDM Executive Board;
❑ host country climate policy, laws and regulations; and
❑ regulations of the country in which the emission reductions are registered or into which they are sold.

Before developing a CDM project, it is recommended that project proponents conduct a quick check to determine whether it is worthwhile to start the CDM process. This will include a preliminary assessment of the amount of GHG emission reductions that the proposed project could generate and the incremental costs of developing the project. Of course, project developers need to evaluate whether the transaction costs specifically related to developing a project as a CDM project justify the investment, but they should also recognise that, generally speaking, transaction costs tend to be rather small compared with the additional revenue streams provided by the sale of CERs. (See Panels 2 and 3 for costs and benefits associated with developing a project under the CDM.)

PANEL 2 TRANSACTION COSTS OF DEVELOPING A CDM PROJECT

Table A presents indicative transaction costs for the various cost elements outlined above, as these relate specifically to the preparation phase of a CDM project. Those developing Track 2 JI projects would face similar costs but would not incur the registration fee. Costs are expressed in ranges because they are not exact and will depend on several factors, including the type of project, the size of the project, location and the costs of consultants and intermediaries involved. The upper range of these figures coincides with estimates made by large multilateral institutions regarding the costs associated with developing CDM/JI projects. Cost estimates are also included for small-scale projects. These estimates are lower since the CDM Executive Board has established streamlined procedures for these projects (see Panel 5).

Table A Estimated transaction costs

CDM Project preparation activities	Estimated costs	Small scale
Project assessment	£5,000–£15,000	£3,000– £4,000
Completion of project documentation	£15,000–£55,000	£6,500–£12,500
Validation	£5,000–£17,000	£2,700–£5,500
Development of carbon credits sales agreement	£5,000–£35,000	£1,500–£5,000
Registration fee (see box)	£2,700–£16,000	£2,700–£8,000
Total – Project development costs (CDM)	£32,700–£138,000	£16,400–£35,000

Source: EcoSecurities, 2004

The steps in the CDM project cycle are very similar to the ones for a project without a CDM component. Figure 1 presents a general project timeline.

The feasibility assessment includes an assessment of the relevant international and national regulations and policies to find out whether the project would be eligible as a CDM project. If a project passes the screening phase, the project developer can start collecting more detailed information on the project and can start preparing the project design document (see Panel 4).

Once the project developer completes the project design document and receives approval from the host country, it submits all

PANEL 3 ADDITIONAL RETURN OF DEVELOPING A CDM OR JI PROJECT

Project developers will have to calculate the return on the investment of preparing and implementing climate change projects to determine whether developing them within the framework of the CDM or JI is economically justified. In practice, that means offsetting the carbon transaction costs against the financial benefits (ie, the revenue from the sale of the carbon credits) and calculating the internal rate of return of the investment.

Table B provides summary data using the averages of the ranges presented above and using conservative figures where possible (eg, using a US$4 value per tonne of CO_2e, crediting the emission reduction for only 10 years, and assuming audits are conducted yearly). Specifically, the table presents, for a series of projects generating different amounts of carbon credits, the net present value (NPV) of the projected cashflows and the internal rate of return of the investment in carbon transaction costs. The final column in the table divides the NPV of the cashflow (excluding the project preparation costs) by the project preparation costs, thereby providing an indicator of how the risks and benefits of developing CDM or JI projects compare with each other.

As the analysis in the table suggests, the costs associated with developing climate change projects under the CDM or JI (Second Track) can represent good investments. Due to reduced transaction costs associated with JI First Track projects, their development will likely lead to even better financial results. Clearly, larger projects can more readily absorb the transaction costs, and should there be a higher price for carbon credits, then the threshold for making the investment in developing projects viable will be reduced to even lower values. As project developers consider developing JI Second Track or CDM projects, they will need to weigh the financial benefits of doing so against the risks associated with these activities.

Table B Returns on transaction costs

Tonnes of CO_2e Generated	NPV of Investment (discount rate 10%)	IRR of Investment	Risk Indicator
10,000	£15,507	15%	1.98
25,000	£168,776	53%	5.34
35,000	£272,602	76%	7.62
50,000	£428,341	110%	11.04
100,000	£945,002	217%	21.73
200,000	£1,980,793	424%	42.45

Source: EcoSecurities, 2004

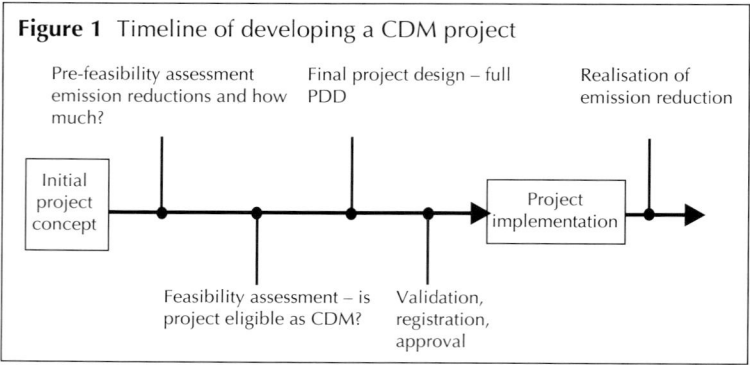

Figure 1 Timeline of developing a CDM project

PANEL 4 THE CDM PROJECT DESIGN DOCUMENT

If the feasibility assessment indicates that it is possible to develop the project as a CDM project, a PDD has to be written. Once completed, the document is made available for public comment and it has to be approved by the host country.

The PDD should contain the following information:

❑ general description of project activity;
❑ baseline methodology;
❑ duration of the project activity/crediting period;
❑ monitoring methodology and plan;
❑ calculations of GHG emissions by sources;
❑ environmental impacts; and
❑ stakeholders' comments.

The baseline is the scenario that describes the situation that would occur in the absence of the proposed project activity. Once this is known, the reductions attributable to the project can be determined. In other words, the emission reductions represent the difference between the emissions without the project (baseline) and the emissions from the project over the period for which emission reductions may be claimed. The baseline must be derived using the baseline methodology that is officially approved by the CDM Executive Board.

---

documents to a Designated Operational Entity (DOE) for validation. Validation is the process of evaluation of all relevant documents for a CDM project activity against the requirements for CDM. Validation occurs once all of the project documentation is completed, and is distinct from *verification*, which occurs during

PANEL 5 SMALL-SCALE PROJECTS (SSC) PROCEDURES AND COST IMPLICATIONS

To reduce the transaction costs associated with preparing CDM projects, the CDM Executive Board has approved streamlined procedures and standardised baselines for small-scale projects, which are defined as:

❑ renewable energy projects with an installed capacity under 15 MW;
❑ energy-efficiency projects that reduce energy consumption by up to 15 GWh per year; and
❑ activities that emit less than 15,000 tonnes of CO_2 equivalent per year.

The simplified procedures are as follows:

❑ projects can be bundled at various stages of the CDM project cycle;
❑ drafting of the PDD is simplified;
❑ standard procedures exist for baseline calculation;
❑ the monitoring plan is simplified; and
❑ the same operational entity can oversee validation, verification and certification.

the operation of the project. In effect, the validation process confirms that all the information conveyed and assumptions made within the PDD are accurate and reasonable. The DOE will check data on GHG emissions, as well as data and assumptions regarding technical, social, political, regulatory and economic impacts of the project activity.

It is the responsibility of the project developer to arrange for validation and to contract, and pay for, the services of a DOE.

The DOE submits the validation report and host country approval to the Executive Board for registration. After registration, the project is formally accepted. However, it is possible that the Executive Board will conduct an additional review (beyond the one done by the DOE). This review must be related to issues associated with the validation requirements for CDM projects. Until this review is finalised, the decision for validation is not final and thus the project cannot be registered.

THE BASELINE AND MONITORING METHODOLOGY

In order for a project to be acceptable as a CDM or JI project, the baseline scenario for the project must be established and it must be demonstrated that the project scenario is additional compared with that baseline scenario. The baseline scenario must be established with a specific methodology.

The methodology stipulates the general approach to establish a specific baseline, the key parameters and assumptions to be considered and the data sources to be used. The methodology should also provide a definition on the project boundary and explain how to deal with uncertainties and leakage (indirect emissions that could be emitted due to project activities and that need to be accounted for). A separate methodology is required for the monitoring of emission reductions.

For the CDM, a format is available that must be used to develop a methodology. There are also formal approval procedures in place for developing new methodologies. For JI those procedures are not yet in place. Because the procedure for JI Second Track will probably be similar to those for the CDM, project proponents should look at approved CDM methodologies for JI as well.

Where does developing a methodology fit in the project cycle?
Dealing with the baseline methodology is one of the first steps in the project development stage, after the feasibility of the project has been assessed. Project developers that want to validate and register a CDM project have two options:

❏ use a methodology that is approved by the Executive Board; or
❏ propose a new methodology to the Executive Board.

Option 1: Use an approved methodology
A project developer can use an existing methodology if the Executive Board approved it earlier. This is the easier and quicker option. As of April 2004, the Executive Board had approved 11 methodologies. Four of these methodologies have been redrafted to make them generic (the AM numbers in Panel 6) and are ready to be used by other project developers. A project developer can also use one of the approved methodologies that are not yet redrafted, but there is a risk that some changes will be made in the redrafting.

Option 2: Propose a new methodology
If none of the previously approved methodologies are applicable to the project, the project participants must propose a new

---

PANEL 6 APPROVED METHODOLOGIES

(as of April 2004)

AM0001: incineration of HFC23 Waste Streams

AM0002: emission reductions through landfill gas capture and flaring where the baseline is established by a public concession contract

AM0003: simplified financial analysis for landfill gas capture projects

AM0004: grid-connected biomass power generation that avoids uncontrolled burning of biomass

NM0001: emissions reductions from grid-connected bagasse cogeneration projects

NM0010: methane recovery from landfill gas used for electricity generation

NM0016: industrial fuel switching from coal and petroleum fuels to natural gas

NM0021: landfill gas recovery with electricity generation and no capture or destruction of methane in the baseline scenario

NM0023: grid-connected power generation displacing power from the operation and expansion of the electric sector

NM0026: oil-field-associated gas recovery and utilisation project

NM0032: biomethanation of municipal solid waste, using compliance with MSW rules

(*Source:* http://cdm.unfccc.int)

---

methodology to the Executive Board for consideration and approval. To propose a new methodology a draft PDD must be prepared and the new methodology has to be presented in an Annex. The methodology should be generic, so that it can be applied to projects with similar characteristics to the project for which it is proposed. The methodology should be submitted via the DOE. The project can be validated only after the methodology has been approved.

STRUCTURING CARBON TRANSACTIONS

Payment and transfer of CERs resulting from CDM projects can be structured in many ways.[4] Different structures for a theoretical project generating 25 tonnes of CO_2 emission reductions per year are outlined in the following paragraphs. Actual prices of course depend on market conditions.

Upfront payment for future stream of CERs

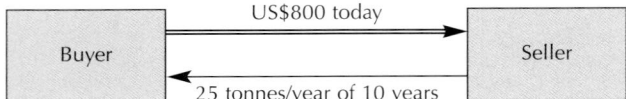

From the perspective of project developers, this upfront investment model is obviously very attractive. The opposite is the case for the buyer, who wishes to put as little upfront cash at risk as possible. Buyers prefer the forward contract/pay-on-delivery model (see below), whereby payments are made only after credits are fully validated, certified, registered and transferred.

As more credible carbon buyers enter the market and as financial markets get used to the idea of set payment structures for environmental performance, financial institutions (ie, banks) will begin to get comfortable lending to carbon credit sellers based upon the value of their Emission Reduction Purchase Agreements (ERPAs), just as banks finance power generation facilities based on Power Purchase Agreements (PPAs). This will help bridge the divide between the sellers' desire for upfront capital and buyers' risk aversion. From the perspective of developing country sellers, there is a strong potential in this path of market development, as it increases the percentage of hard currency in a domestic project financing.

Forward contract for delivery of CERs at fixed prices

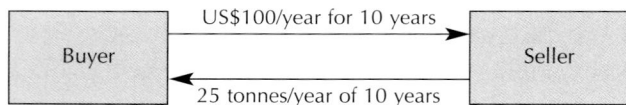

The most common structure for CDM transactions is the forward purchase agreement, whereby little – if any – cash transfers hands on contract signature, and where the price for delivery of CERs is set at the time of contract signature. These transactions are also referred to as "pay-on-delivery" structures. These forward-delivery contracts range from one year to twenty years, with a substantial number set at ten years. Most of the projects to date are ten-year structures.

The forward contract structure requires the seller to deliver a specific number of CERs, or occasionally a range of CERs, with a minimum and maximum number per year. The buyer is required to pay a fixed price for them.

Forward contract for delivery of CERs at floating prices

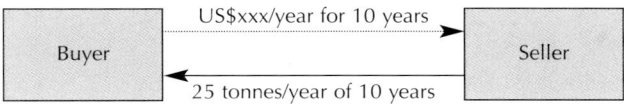

A key issue in "pay-on-delivery" contracts is whether forward prices for delivery are set firmly or are benchmarked to some outside parameter. A transaction structure with floating prices requires the seller to deliver a predetermined volume of CERs each year, but the price paid by the buyer is reset each year based on an index.

Given the immaturity of the CDM market, most buyers are insisting on fixed-price contracts, as there is a general consensus that prices will increase in the future. As the limited number of buyers currently have greater negotiating power, the fixed-price contract is currently the norm. However, while a floating-price structure appears more attractive to sellers in a market where many participants assume that carbon prices will increase, it is not without substantial risks to sellers. Specifically, a floating price makes it much more difficult for the seller to plan their future cashflows, as the total payment to be received from the buyer will be uncertain every year. Furthermore, if there is an oversupply of credits in future markets and prices fall, the seller will receive much less than they currently anticipate and could be unable to meet obligations on the project.

Option payment for future delivery of CERs

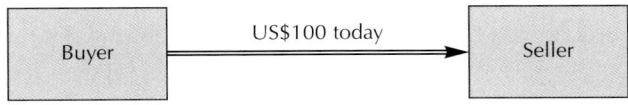

Buyers occasionally wish to structure a transaction in which they purchase an option to buy a predetermined number of CERs from the seller in the future, but are not obligated to purchase them until they exercise the option. In an option structure, the buyer must pay the seller for the option today, in return for the right to exercise the option (ie, inform the seller that the buyer wishes to enter into a contract to take delivery of the CERs) at a specific date in the future.

If the buyer exercises the option, then:

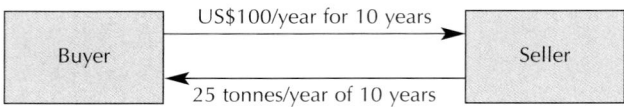

The advantage to a buyer of an option structure is that it provides him or her with a great deal of flexibility. For example, if a buyer is concerned that they may need additional CERs in the future, but is uncertain of the amount they will need, they can use an option contract to prevent the risk of rising prices for CERs in the future. For sellers, an option structure provides them with an up-front payment, and may not require them to deliver CERs in the future. However, an option structure can create additional risk for the seller if he or she is unable to deliver CERs when the option is exercised by the buyer. Therefore, sellers are usually advised to enter into option structures only when they expect to have a large number of CERs to offer, and generally then offer options only on a small proportion of their total CERs. Also, while the premium may be a valuable source of immediate capital, the question remains concerning the degree to which a project can be forward-financed based on options, since there is no certainty that the option will be exercised. Several private-sector trades have used the option structure. However, details regarding the deals are not public at this time.

Spot market

The spot market is the structure in which a seller delivers CERs from one year of emissions reductions in return for a one-time payment from the buyer. In this structure there is no forward commitment between the seller and buyer for additional delivery of CERs or payment, although there is nothing precluding the parties in a spot transaction from executing another spot transaction the following year.

The advantage of the spot market to both buyers and sellers is that it provides them with maximum flexibility for the future. However, the disadvantages for a seller include (i) the risk that he or she cannot find a buyer in subsequent years, and (ii) the risk that the price declines in the future. For the buyer there is significant risk that the price of CERs increases in subsequent years.

Another issue that must be negotiated is what happens in the event that the project activity produces additional credits. Typically, many buyers, such as CERUPT, place an option on first right of refusal. This must be negotiated, however, because the price may actually be higher, or lower, in the future, which benefits either the buyer or seller.

CONTRACTING TRANSACTIONS

The contracting of a CDM transaction is primarily designed to minimise the risk that the buyer or the seller does not perform on their obligations under the contract. In the current stage of the market, buyers are almost all large, financially stable organisations, while sellers range significantly in size and financial strength. Therefore, the contracts are mostly designed to protect the buyer. The four contractual issues that most often arise and the common solutions are as follows.[5]

1. Delivery risk

In a fixed-delivery contract, the buyer has substantial risk if the seller fails to deliver the contracted CERs on time, resulting from (a) volume risk if the buyer cannot find replacement CERs in time, and (b) price risk if the buyer can find replacement CERs only at a higher price than in the current contract with the seller.

Some buyers have contractually required substantial financial penalties (often several times the agreed purchase price from the same year) if sellers are unable to deliver CERs under the terms of the contract. This provides the seller with a significant incentive to deliver CERs on time.

Thus, sellers have a financial incentive to take on delivery risk mitigation responsibilities. This is accomplished in the following ways:

❏ committing only a percentage of a project's anticipated performance to a firm delivery contract;
❏ cross-collateralising several projects into a pooled production portfolio;
❏ purchasing delivery options from other producers – often combined with business interruption insurance to have the financial ability to exercise the options in a time of underperformance; and
❏ developing more formal insurance products (several financial institutions are currently developing such instruments through either using cash premiums or bundling many projects into a pool); however, it is expected that this kind of product will be useful only for industrial producers of CERs.

In current practice, on a project-by-project basis, sellers will often reserve 20% or more of the credits from each year's production into a non-delivery "buffer". In fact, buyers will often insist upon that type of buffering in the contract. As such, buyers will forward-contract for only 80% (or less) of the expected delivery volumes, and the seller is prohibited from selling the additional CERs until they fill the buffer. This type of contract has a dual purpose: to help ensure that each year's commitments are readily achievable; and to build up a pool of carbon credits. This pool can be tapped in case of a project failure to produce credits for a significant period of time.

2. Timing risk

Sellers face a risk that the CERs they create are sufficient in volume to fulfil the contract requirements, but that the timing of delivery varies from the contract dates. This can put the seller in a position of contractual noncompliance, thereby triggering severe financial penalties.

A mechanism that sellers can use to mitigate timing risk is the use of a multiyear delivery period. In this contract, the seller is allowed to spread out the delivery of CERs over a longer time period; for example, rather than being required to deliver

100,000 tonnes/year for 10 years, the seller is required to deliver no less than 300,000 tonnes in any three-year period, for a cumulative delivery of 1,000,000 tonnes over 10 years. Whether a seller can spread out the delivery of CERs is of course dependent on the needs of buyers.

3. Counterparty credit risk

Buyers and sellers cannot enter into long-term contractual agreements if they believe that the counterparty carries with it a substantial credit risk. Counterparty risk for buyers is often significant because the sellers are located in developing countries, and a seller cannot have a higher credit rating than the country it is based in.

The traditional manner of addressing this kind of risk is via third-party insurance, such as guarantees provided by export-import banks and the MIGA product from the World Bank Group. However, currently these facilities are not equipped to handle emission transactions, as there is no experience in assessing risk in these kinds of delivery contracts. Moreover, the types of insurance provided by international development institutions tend to be fairly narrow in that they cover only items such as political insurgencies and *force majeure* events, rather than comprehensive guarantees.

Counterparty credit risk also includes the risk of fraud by the selling party, in which the CERs purchased by the buyer do actually represent emissions reductions due to fraudulent activity by the seller. The buyer mitigates this risk through an independent verifier to confirm that the seller has created CERs prior to making payment.

On the other hand, it is unfair to consider credit risk strictly from the perspective of the seller. As energy-trading groups – particularly in the US – have undergone systemic meltdown since the collapse of Enron, one must consider the implications these developments are likely to have on the buyer's financial credibility several years down the road.

4. Country risk and currency risk

Sellers of CERs are located in countries that are generally considered to have significant country risk. As a result, corporate buyers are often concerned about entering into a contractual arrangement with a seller. However, country risk is actually relatively low for buyers because most contracts are "pay-on-delivery", in which the buyer is not obligated to make any payment until they have received verification from an independent party that the CERs have been created by the seller. The seller is also required to have host country approval for the sale of CERs, further limiting the country risk. Finally, participants in a CER transaction are almost never exposed to currency risk, because the currency flows are always from a developed (ie, hard-currency) country to a CDM country, while the flow of CERs is not affected by currency rates.

CREDIT BUYERS

There are a number of different buyers in the marketplace with a variety of diverse objectives that can be summarised as follows.[6]

Purchase of low-cost emission reductions

Most of the buyers in the market have a degree of sensitivity to the cost of emission reductions. Current market prices for CERs are quite low in comparison with forecast prices under many market studies. Buyers who purchase at a low cost today can "potentially" sell at a much higher price in the future.

Minimisation of future risk

This is a primary determinant of buyer behaviour. Buyers are concerned about the potentially large liabilities associated with not being compliant in the future.

Risk-diversification

A number of buyers are purchasing different types of credits under all of the trading mechanisms in order to spread their risk in a portfolio.

Learning by doing

Buyers are keen to undergo early "learning by doing" by engaging in comprehensive project documentation, external verification and certification of CERs, in order to improve their knowledge of the market and reduce risks and transaction costs in the future.

Good Publicity

Some buyers are purchasing credits in order to demonstrate that they are contributing to sustainable development and are concerned about the future of the global environment.

The carbon credit market still has relatively few buyers, but more are entering the market. The vast majority of the publicly known capital for purchasing emission reductions comes from various funds and multilateral buyers. The major institutional buyers include:[7]

❏ World Bank Prototype Carbon Fund: US$180 m
❏ Carboncredits.nl, the Dutch ERUPT/CERUPT: €250 m
❏ Netherlands Carbon Development Fund: €35 m/year for up to four years
❏ IFC–Netherlands Carbon Facility: €40 m
❏ Andean Development Bank: €40 m
❏ Community Development Carbon Fund: US$100 m (target)
❏ World Bank Bio-Carbon Fund: US$100 m (target)
❏ European Development Bank: €100 m
❏ Canada CDM fund: US$100 m
❏ Denmark JI/CDM Fund: €100 m (approximately over five years)
❏ Development Bank of Japan: US$100 m
❏ Japan Bank for International Cooperation: US$100 m
❏ Rabobank: €40 m
❏ Belgian government: €10 m
❏ Austrian government: €72 m
❏ Asia Carbon Fund: US$120 m
❏ Finnish government: €10 m

The two most influential institutional purchasers of carbon credits are the Prototype Carbon Fund of the World Bank (PCF) and the Carboncredits.nl (ERUPT/CERUPT) programmes. These programmes were the first to enter the market. The PCF was established by the World Bank in 1999 and has been capitalised at US$180 million. Investors include governments and the private sector. The fund invests in carbon projects that qualify under JI or the CDM. The main objectives of the fund are the procurement of high-quality emission reductions that qualify under the UNFCCC, and developing knowledge that can be shared with other market stakeholders. ERUPT/CERUPT are carbon project investment programmes from the Dutch government that are managed by Senter.

Senter buys ERUs from JI projects, through ERUPT – principally in Eastern Europe – on behalf of the Dutch Ministry of Economic Affairs and buys the CERs from CDM projects through CERUPT on behalf of the Dutch Ministry of Environment (VROM). Both programmes are implemented on a tender basis, during which interested parties are invited to submit expressions of interest over stipulated periods. Senter shortlists candidates from these expressions of interest and shortlisted parties are then invited to submit a detailed project proposal, including a full PDD.

1   Emission reductions before 2008 can also be rewarded; this is called early crediting, or early action. However, early crediting is possible only if the host country approves this and is willing to transfer its AAUs from the period 2008–12. This means that the host country transfers part of its Kyoto ceiling from the first commitment period in exchange for emission reductions during the years before the commitment period. That country thus lowers its Kyoto ceiling without equivalent emission reductions within the commitment period.

2   The Secretariat, in due course, will maintain a publicly available list of countries that meet the eligibility requirements for JI First and Second Track projects, and of those that have been suspended (Decision 16/CP.7 Annex, Section D, paragraph 27).

3   The Meeting of the Parties (MOP) to the Kyoto Protocol takes place only after the Kyoto Protocol comes into force. The Conference of the Parties to the Convention (COP) takes the role of the MOP until entry into force of the Kyoto Protocol.

4   From: United Nations Development Programme, 2003.

5   Chapter 8 discusses risks that are general to all JI and CDM projects, particularly market and political risk. Here we discuss various sources of risk typical to individual projects: delivery risk, timing risk, counterpary credit risk and country and currency risk.

6   From: United Nations Development Programme, 2003.

7   Sources: UNDP, 2003; IETA Trading Schemes Database (http://www.pointcarbon.com/schemes.php).

REFERENCES

Baltic Sea Region Energy Cooperation, 2003, *BASREC Regional Handbook on Procedures for Joint Implementation in the Baltic Sea Region.*

EcoSecurities, 2004, "Carbon transaction costs and carbon project viability, cost implications for implementing Clean Development Mechanism (CDM) or Joint Implementation (JI) projects".

COP7, 2001, "Report of the Conference of the parties on the first part of its seventh session", held in Marrakech from 29 October to 11 November.

United Nations Development Program, 2003, *The Clean Development Mechanism: A User's Guide.*

World Bank Prototype Carbon Fund, 2002, "Impact of Carbon Finance on Project Financing", PowerPoint Presentation.

5

Joint Implementation and Clean Development Mechanism: Case Studies

Michiel ten Hoopen, Veronique Bovee

EcoSecurities

The previous Chapter gave an outline of Joint Implementation (JI) and Clean Development Mechanism (CDM) projects. In this Chapter we investigate what projects have been carried out so far and present two practical cases studies, a hydropower project in Romania (JI) and a wind project in Jamaica (CDM).

CDM PROJECTS UNDER DEVELOPMENT

It is interesting to look at what kinds of project are being developed as CDM. Figure 1 shows the shares of different technologies in all CDM projects. Projects accounted in this figure are those for which a full project design document has been developed (as of end 2003). Renewable energy projects dominate with a share of 73%, including bio/landfill gas. Most projects reduce CO_2 emissions, except the projects in the bio/landfill gas category (16%), which reduce CH_4 emissions, and one project in the industrial sector, which reduces HFC gases. There are no solar energy projects and only a few geothermal energy projects (5%).

The fact that a project design document (PDD) has been written does not mean that a project will actually be implemented: many of the projects from Figure 1 have not yet started the process for official approval. A project that already has its baseline and monitoring methodology approved by the CDM Executive Board is much more likely to actually be implemented. Obtaining this approval is currently a big hurdle in CDM project development, since by April 2004 only 11 projects had received approval for their methodology.

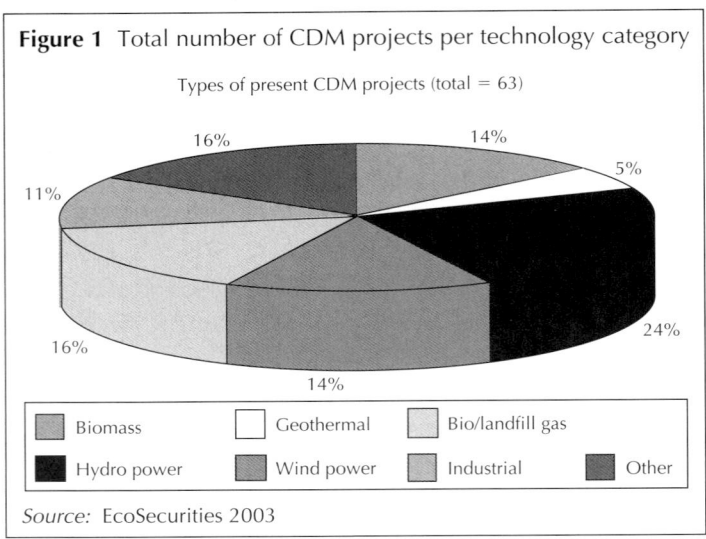

Figure 1 Total number of CDM projects per technology category

Types of present CDM projects (total = 63)

Biomass
Hydro power
Geothermal
Wind power
Bio/landfill gas
Industrial
Other

Source: EcoSecurities 2003

This approval is probably a better indicator for what projects will be successful CDM projects.

Of the 11 methodologies that are now approved by the Executive Board, five deal with landfill gas destruction. This is much more than would be expected looking at the 16% of all PDDs in Figure 1. Because landfill projects tend to generate larger amounts of Certified Emissions Reductions (CERs) than other renewable energy projects, the share of landfill CERs that will actually be supplied into the carbon market over the next couple of years may be well over 50%.

Landfill projects

So why have five methodologies for landfill gas destruction been approved? And does this mean landfill projects will be the most successful projects under the CDM? There are two factors that explain the early success of landfill projects. One is the very large amount of CERs they can generate, particularly relative to the capital expenditures required for such projects. The other is that, without the CDM, landfill projects would not be attractive at all; this makes it very easy to prove the project's additionality.

As explained in the previous chapter, the opportunity to sell credits offers an extra source of revenue above the normal project revenues. For most project types, the extra revenues from the sale of CERs could cover 5–15% of the investment costs. Projects that have a very low return without the CDM and generate only small amounts of CERs are not turned into feasible projects by the CDM; this is one reason why there are no solar energy projects in Figure 1.

Landfill projects are very different. In some situations the CER revenue can even cover all the investment costs. In itself, using landfill gas is often a very expensive way of generating electricity (although very large landfills that can easily be connected to the grid may be exceptions). These projects involve investments in systems that capture the gas from the landfills and investments in generating capacity and grid connection. Because the amount of methane produced by a landfill is small compared with other sources (eg, using natural gas from a grid) and because production of methane fluctuates, the generating capacity is usually not very large and the cost per kWh produced high.

The difference with other renewable energy CDM projects is in the methane combusted in a landfill project. In many developing countries, there is no legislation that says landfill gas has to be captured and burned. This means that, without a CDM project, these landfills emit large amounts of methane into the atmosphere. Given the global warming potential of methane of 21 times that of CO_2, landfill projects can generate very large amounts of emission reductions.

Because of the large emission reductions, CERs can cover a significant part of the investment costs: the CER revenues can even be larger than those from the sale of electricity. Another benefit is that the CERs are sold for hard currency. In fact, it can even be profitable to develop a landfill project that flares the gas and does not generate electricity at all. The CERs are then the only source of revenue.

Additionality

The internal rate of return (IRR) can be used as an indicator for the financial feasibility of a project. A project is feasible if the project IRR is higher than the IRR required by the project developer. Different technology types face different risks and therefore require different rates of return. As a consequence, the value of the IRR required by a project developer will not be the same for each technology (and project location).

Table 1 Average IRR for projects of different technologies

Technology	Average IRR including sale of CERs	Average IRR excluding sale of CERs	Number of projects on which data is based
Landfill	19	10	3
Energy efficiency	19	17	1
Wind power	15	14	3
Biomass	14	12	5
Geothermal	13	12	1
Hydropower	11	10	2

Source: World Bank Prototype Carbon Fund, 2002

The IRR can also be used to demonstrate project additionality, ie, showing the project itself is not the most likely baseline scenario without the CER revenues. The problem is that it is very difficult to prove (to a validator) what the required IRR is, since this depends on project- and company-specific circumstances. However, a large difference between the IRR with and without the sale of CERs will make it easy to prove additionality. Table 1 lists technology specific IRRs both including the sale of CERs as well as excluding these revenues.[1]

As Table 1 indicates, for most types of renewable energy projects, the sale of CERs adds only one or two percentage points to the project IRR. It is difficult to prove that a project is being implemented just because of such a small increase in IRR. Even energy efficiency projects, which usually have quite high IRRs without selling CERs, do not seem to be getting off the ground on a large scale under the CDM.[2]

For landfill projects, however, the increase in IRR for the projects in the sample is 9 percentage points. And, even though these figures are based on data from only a few projects, the impact is clear and the IRR increase can be even larger for projects that flare landfill gas, where there would be no revenue at all without the sale of CERs. These large differences in IRR make it very easy to show that landfill projects are additional. This at least partly explains why five different landfill methodologies have been approved by the Executive Board.

HFC reduction projects are similar to landfill projects in that they generate large amounts of CERs on relatively small investments

(HFC23 has a global warming potential of 11,700 times that of CO_2) and the investment would not be attractive without the CDM.[3] So far, only one methodology has been accepted for an HFC reduction project, but it was the first methodology to be accepted by the Executive Board and it is also the first methodology that has been reapplied to a second project.

Projects reducing methane and HFC emissions are likely to supply a large amount of CERs in the near future.[4] These projects reduce emissions with relatively little investment and additionality can easily be proven. However, such projects also contribute relatively little to the sustainable development in the host country, which is one of the purposes of the CDM. The introduction of landfill projects has benefits to the host country but will not transform the way Non-Annex I countries develop, and HFC-reducing projects do not have much impact outside the factory besides limiting greenhouse gas (GHG) emissions. The amount of possible projects of this type is also limited. As countries start introducing legislation that limits methane and HFC emissions, these projects will no longer be fully additional.

Other CDM project types, especially renewable energy projects, have a much larger positive impact on the sustainable development of the host countries. At the same time it is highly unlikely that many renewable energy projects would be developed in the absence of CDM in many developing countries, due to unfavourable market conditions and the existence of significant market barriers. This has been recognised, for example, in the IPCC Special Report on Technology Transfer, which mentions the slow progress of the development of renewable energy in Non-Annex I countries as a result of a number of policy, technical, financial, management, institutional and awareness barriers.

The existence of market barriers is another way to demonstrate additionality. It can be used to demonstrate that renewable energy projects would not take off on their own. Market barriers were accepted in the Marrakech Accords as a way to demonstrate additionality. Methodologies that use a barrier analysis in their additionality assessment have already been approved, but only for some project types and under specific circumstances. As more different methodologies that use a barrier analysis will be approved, other project types such as renewable energy and energy efficiency projects in various sectors can compete on the CDM market, even if they show only a small increase in IRR.

CASE STUDIES
JI: a hydro project in Romania

The development of hydro projects provides a clean, reliable, renewable and efficient source of energy, without increasing the total amount of GHGs emitted into the atmosphere. Although hydro offers a highly efficient source of new energy, in most cases the high initial capital cost makes securing investment capital and debt financing rather difficult. This forces a country to either continue generating power with the installation of relatively higher polluting fossil power plants, or resorting to the do-nothing scenario, which leaves the local population without the energy required.

This case study demonstrates how developing the environmental revenue stream of a hydropower project through carbon credits can provide the financial lift needed to successfully develop the project. The description of the case study below indicates the importance of carbon credits for the development of a hydropower project in Romania.

The Surduc-Nehoiasu hydro project

In 1998, the Romanian government invited Montgomery Watson Harza (MWH) to invest in one of a number of unfinished hydroelectric projects, which were left partially completed by the former communist government when it was overthrown in 1989. The projects available had several things in common:

❑ all had been partially completed, then abandoned due to a lack of financing;
❑ abandoned sites were characterised by abandoned buildings, construction equipment and partially completed tunnels, dams and powerhouses;
❑ all surrounding regions suffered from unemployment rates that often exceeded 70% of the adult male population; and
❑ projects had been poorly conceived, and the estimated cost to complete the works often exceeded US$3,000/kW.

Having assessed the several partially completed hydropower projects, MWH selected the Surduc-Nehoiasu hydroelectric plant for further completion. The plant is a partially built run-of-river hydro-power plant with 55 MW of capacity and 152.7 GWh/year output. The project is located in the central part of Romania, about 150 km north of Bucharest with a drainage area covering the counties of Buzau, Vrancea and Covasna. The project harnesses the hydro-electric potential of the Bâsca Mare river.

The project creates significant benefits for Romania, such as foreign investment, good-quality construction jobs to the village of Nehoiasu and a reduction in local pollution. However, the project was not financially feasible, due to the inability to achieve an energy price that could be sustainable over the long haul, and therefore the project faced abandonment. Generating value for the environmental benefits generated by the project could change this situation. Through the mechanism of JI, the environmental benefits obtained through the sales of carbon credits increased revenues of the project.

Qualifying for carbon credits. An opportunity to sell the emission reductions of the Surduc project came along with the announcement of the first Dutch ERUPT programme. ERUPT is a call for tender from the Dutch government to buy emission reductions from JI projects. MWH submitted an expression of interest as a response to the call for tender. The project was shortlisted, which implied that a detailed study had to be carried out in order to determine whether the project was eligible for JI and could generate verifiable emission reductions that could be sold as carbon credits. MWH contracted EcoSecurities to assist them in developing the carbon credits of the Surduc project. All required project documents had to be developed in a period of three months, including the validation of the undertaking as a JI project. EcoSecurities was the carbon adviser to Harza Engineering, handling the quantification, registration and transaction process. MWH did provide project specific input in the JI preparation process of the project.

The key criterion for developing carbon credits under JI (or CDM) is that the project should result in GHG emission reductions that are additional to any that would have occurred in the absence of the proposed project activity. In order to assess this, a baseline study had to be carried out presenting the situation that would have occurred in the absence of the project. For this purpose, accurate data on the power sector in Romania needed to be collected as well as information on how the sector was likely to change in the next 10 to 15 years.

It was very difficult to collect accurate data. Very general data were available and easily accessible, but it was more difficult to get data on actual fuel consumption per plant, which plants were operational, dispatch priorities, etc. The authorities with access to the baseline data initially did not want to cooperate, as they did not know what their data would be used for. In the end, with support from other government authorities the data were made available, only just before the deadline of the tender.

Based on the data provided, various different baseline scenarios were worked out, taking into account economic, policy and legal factors, the main one being that Romania is one of the accession countries for the EU. The assumptions for the selected baseline are that the project is going to displace a mix of coal, natural gas and oil fossil fuel plants, and conservatively assumes that all plants will be natural-gas-fired in 2030. This results in a decreasing baseline curve. In other words, the electricity grid is polluting today, but will become less polluting (per MWh generated) over time, and this was reflected in the emission reductions generated by the project.

In addition, it needed to be demonstrated that the project did not result in any significant environmental impacts and that it contributed to sustainable development. This could be easily demonstrated, as an environmental impact assessment had been made on the project; the project produced electricity through a clean source of energy; and it resulted in the inflow of private-sector money into the Romanian economy. Other benefits related to sustainable development were that the project resulted in an increased economic activity in the region and the country as a whole, given that most of the equipment, materials and labour would be secured within Romania.

Transaction costs and benefits. The development of a hydro project into a JI project involves upfront costs. These transaction costs are related to the costs of developing a baseline, arranging host country approval, development of a monitoring plan and arranging validation of the venture as a JI project. One of the great advantages of the Dutch ERUPT programme is that these transaction costs were partly reimbursed.[5] This implied that the project developer did not bear the risk for making upfront transaction costs in a situation in which the project is not considered to be eligible for generating carbon credits.

Apart from the costs to be made during the project design phase, costs for monitoring and verification have to be made during the project implementation. In total the transaction costs of a project are around €75,000–100,000, depending on the complexity of a project and how often verification is carried out.

The sales of JI carbon credits generated approximately €3 million extra revenues for the project. The revenues thus easily cover the transaction costs for developing the endeavour as a JI project. Taking into account the estimated project costs of US$56.9 million, carbon credits contributed to about 5% of the total project costs. These extra carbon revenues enabled the project to reduce the price of energy by US$0.5/MWh. Combined with a relief of VAT, this permits the reduction in energy price to a level that becomes sustainable on a long-term basis.

Host country approval. It was relatively easy to arrange host country approval for the project, since the Dutch government had done some capacity building activities in Romania to train people in the government on JI projects and the ERUPT guidelines and process. Moreover, Romania and the Netherlands signed a memorandum of understanding to cooperate on JI and transfer carbon credits from JI projects. It was thus already clear which ministry was responsible for JI and who would write the letter of approval. The fact that MWH had a local office in Bucharest also helped in receiving this letter on time.

Project conclusion. The main challenge of the project was to find a buyer of the carbon credits and to collect accurate information to carry out the baseline study. Paying upfront for transaction costs, without being certain that the efforts result in benefits, is also considered a barrier. However, for Surduc this was not a real issue, since ERUPT paid for a part of the total transaction costs. Overall, the project was successful as it resulted in an Emission Reduction Purchase Agreement with the Dutch government.

CDM: a wind project in Jamaica
The Wigton wind farm project

Renewable Energy Systems (RES) Ltd and the Petroleum Corporation of Jamaica (PCJ) are working together to develop the Wigton wind farm project in Jamaica. For this purpose they established a project company, Wigton Wind Farm Ltd, to own the project. The company is registered in Jamaica. RES is the leading UK developer of wind energy projects, having completed in excess of 30 wind farm projects worldwide. PCJ is owned by the government of Jamaica. It is the national oil company and has also been given the responsibility of developing renewable energy projects.

The Wigton project involves the construction of a 20.25 MW wind grid connected project in Jamaica. The project will comprise 23 turbines, with each machine having a capacity of 900 kW. The planned output is 63 GWh per year. The project will be located at Wigton, Manchester Plateau, about 15 km south-southwest of Mandeville, on land owned by the Bauxite mining company, ALCOA. The power generated will be sold to the Jamaican Public Service Company (JPSCo), which is a subsidiary of Mirant, a large US power company.

The project will be the first commercial wind farm in Jamaica and the whole Caribbean. Therefore, it is considered risky to project investors and therefore it is difficult to secure financing. Due to the various financial and other difficulties in developing it, the project proponents hired EcoSecurities to assess whether the project could generate carbon credits and thus an additional revenue stream.

Qualifying for carbon credits. The project partners RES and PCJ have been looking to develop the Wigton project as a CDM project since 2000. At that stage, the Power Purchase Agreement was not yet signed and additional revenues were needed to make the project commercially interesting. In order to assess the potential contributions of emission reductions to the financing of the project, a CDM feasibility assessment was carried out. This included an assessment of the volume of emission reductions.

The first party that was interested in buying the carbon credits was the Prototype Carbon Fund (PCF) from the World Bank. However, the negotiations never ended in a signed contract for the sales of CERs. The carbon credits will now be sold to the multilateral development bank CAF (Corporación Andina de Fomento). CAF is buying the CERs resulting from the project on behalf of the Dutch government.

The project preparation work included the development of a baseline study, a monitoring plan, development of a baseline and monitoring methodology, filling out the project design document and organising a stakeholder consultation process. The baseline and monitoring methodology have been submitted to the CDM Executive Board for approval. RES carried out the environmental impact analysis.

The baseline study indicates that the project is additional, considering the fact that wind is a new technology in the region; that it will be the first commercial wind power plant; and that CDM was taken into account from the beginning of the project. In other words, from 2000 onwards, the revenues from CERs were included in the financial analysis of the project. The data to calculate the emission reductions are provided by the electricity company, JPSCo. They do, however, have data on fuel consumption only for the state-owned plants, not for the plants operated by independent power producers. It was not possible to get hold of these data and thus general assumptions have been made to calculate the emission factors for these plants.

Transaction costs and benefits. Similar to JI, the development of an undertaking into a CDM project involves upfront transaction costs. For CDM these costs are actually slightly higher, considering the additional time and effort it takes to develop a baseline and monitoring methodology and submitting this for approval to the CDM Executive Board. This procedure does not yet exist for JI projects. Making these upfront costs is a risk for the project developer. To reduce this risk, public funding was used to cover the majority of the transaction costs. For the Wigton project the total transactions costs, including monitoring and verification, are estimated to be around €100,000.

The sales of CERs from Wigton as a CDM venture will result in approximately €2.5 million extra revenues for the project. Taking into account the estimated project costs of US$28 million, the carbon credits contributed to about 10% of the total project costs. This is higher than for the Surduc project and is partly due to the fact that the carbon credits from Surduc were sold to ERUPT for only a five-year period, since JI projects generate credits only after 2008. For Wigton, the carbon revenues could be sold over a period of 10 years.

Host country approval. One of the main barriers for developing the venture as a CDM project was the difficulty in arranging host country approval. This was due to the fact that Jamaica had not yet officially decided which government authority would act as the focal point for CDM and who could officially provide the required letter of approval for the project. Also, there was a lack of capacity to assess CDM projects. This process was facilitated in two ways:

❑ contact with the local embassies, who assisted in establishing contacts with the relevant government authorities and in arranging to get the requested letter within the required timeframe; and
❑ organising some training workshops on CDM, based on the request of the government, during which the project was presented and questions answered.

CONCLUSIONS

Both case studies indicate that carbon credits can help in overcoming barriers to implement renewable energy projects. The process of developing carbon credits involves transaction costs and is not entirely without risk for the project developer. The availability of public funding to (partly) pay for the transaction costs in developing JI and CDM projects can reduce the risks for project developers. With access to such funding, project developers are more likely to follow the route of JI and CDM, which is a process with an often uncertain end result.

The barriers that developers face when developing JI or CDM projects will vary from case to case. For example, in those countries where the host government does not have any institutional capacity for JI or CDM, it will be a more difficult process to arrange host country approval. Also the access to accurate data, which is a key to baseline development, varies from country to country.

Overall, it can be concluded that carbon credits can help to overcome barriers to implementing a project. However, carbon credits are not meant to convert a poor project into an attractive one, nor is it a source of windfall profits for developers. The case studies indi-cate that carbon credits can take a project from being marginally unattractive to one that is marginally attractive, or that the CDM or JI process can help overcome important barriers that would have otherwise prevented the project from being developed. In other words, it will have to be assessed on a case-by-case basis whether developing a project as JI and CDM indeed provides a solution to existing barriers.

1   It is important to bear in mind that many other factors also play a role in the issue of add-itionality, such as the existence of barriers, impact of CDM on the diversity of cashflow and impact of CDM on improved debt service ratio.
2   The fact remains that many potentially viable energy efficiency projects are not implemented at all. This is an indication that financial analysis is not the only way to prove additionality; a good IRR without the sale of CERs does not mean a project will actually be implemented.
3   In developing countries where there is no legislation that forbids or limits the emission of HFC gases, it makes no economic sense to reduce these emissions without the opportunity of the CDM.
4   Besides landfill projects, other methane-reducing project opportunities are in waste water treatment and agriculture.
5   Note that transaction costs were reimbursed to a maximum of €37,500.

Section 2

Implementation, Financing and Risk Management

Introduction

Cyriel de Jong; Kasper Walet

Erasmus University Rotterdam; Maycroft Consultancy Services

Many believe that policymakers and regulators are often all too keen to design complex regulations and impose all sorts of restrictions, exceptions and detailed guidelines, without being fully aware of implementation problems. The previous section contains many examples. This behaviour often draws attention and resources away from what emissions trading is eventually about: to get emission reduction projects running.

With all the information that one can find on the framework and regulations of emissions trading, much less information is available on implementation within individual companies. This is surprising, since emissions trading can become a long-lasting success only if companies are able to reduce emissions and do so in the most economical way. This section discusses the hurdles that managers have to overcome and provides lessons about measuring and monitoring emissions, financing emission reduction projects, carrying out carbon transactions and managing the risk of meeting emission targets. The analysis and valuation of emission reduction investments is strongly related to these issues and is covered in Section 3.

Direct investments in emission reduction projects are still risky due to the uncertainty surrounding various policy issues, uncertainty about implementation within individual countries (eg, the National Allocation Plans in the EU, and CDM guidelines in developing countries), long approval procedures and uncertain future price levels. Nevertheless, companies are well aware that they have to undertake certain actions, such as setting up monitoring protocols and reporting procedures (Chapter 6), as well as preparing themselves to trade carbon credits (Chapter 9). Furthermore, early action actually may be rewarding as a test for internal procedures and systems, to help spread risks, to build up good relationships in the market and to raise awareness within large parts of the whole company.

Unfortunately, uncertainty often kills the more innovative initiatives. Even if projects are expected to be profitable, upfront investments might be considerable (Chapter 7). Project finance can be an elegant solution, but high transaction costs make it attractive only for larger-sized projects. This partly explains the paradox that there are tremendous resources available on the one hand, whilst relatively little actual activity is being observed on the other, especially in Joint Implementation and Clean Development projects (Chapter 8).

Of course, we wouldn't be writing this book if there were remedies to this paradoxical situation of tremendous interest and money versus little actual activity. Many promising projects and financing structures are already implemented or under development, and much uncertainty is currently being resolved through updated regulations, the build-up of knowledge and some promising initiatives within governmental bodies and individual companies (including the Dutch Senter and UK CarbonTrust). We might just as well observe the silence before the storm – a storm that may be at full strength in just a few years' time. The many practical lessons about implementing emissions trading within individual companies presented in this section will help you to be prepared and to weather this storm.

6

Monitoring, Verification and Accounting of Emissions

Gareth Phillips*

SGS

Monitoring of activities has long been recognised as an important responsibly of management under the assumption that "it is impossible to manage what you do not measure". In the context of greenhouse gas (GHG) emissions and emission trading systems (ETSs), monitoring and verification have assumed a new level of importance. Both monitoring and verification of GHG emissions will be a new concept for many. Data that have been collected and used, or collected and not used, in the past now have a highly significant financial and compliance value. Although for many the direct costs of an ETS will be outweighed by the indirect costs of increases in energy prices, reporting of GHG emissions is becoming increasingly important. Verification likewise has taken on a new role and is now the tool of choice to ensure both financial and environmental integrity.

Société Générale de Surveillance (SGS) is an inspection, verification and testing company. Since 1997, SGS has been building experience in the GHG emission sector and since 2001 has been specifically involved in the verification of GHG emissions from participants in the UK Emission Trading Scheme (UK ETS), voluntary and potential Kyoto projects (Clean Development Mechanism, or

*The author would like to acknowledge the contributions to this chapter of Dr John Miles, measurement expert and lead assessor for the SGS Climate Change Programme.

PANEL 1 USEFUL DEFINITIONS

Measurement – specifically the means of recording an amount or a level of activity usually through the use of a meter such as a flow meter, a weighbridge or an electricity meter.

Monitoring – a systematic process of recording information from one or more meters in order to directly or indirectly determine amounts or activities over a defined time period.

Verification – review of monitored and reported data by independent third parties to qualify the reporting systems and the reported levels of activity.

These terms are not be confused with the following.

Validation – this tends to refer specifically to the assessment of project design against criteria. Even more specifically, it refers to the validation of a CDM project against the texts of the Decision 17/CP.7 or the Marrakech Accords from the 7th Conference of the Parties held in Marrakech in 2001.

Accreditation – the confirmation that a third party is independent and competent to undertake the validation and verification activities.

Certification – this is the final step where a verifier may certify annual emissions or emission reductions – except in the California Climate Action Registry, where the term "certification" replaces "verification".

CDM, and Joint Implementation, or JI) and, most recently, in the California Climate Action Registry (CCAR). This chapter is based on the experiences gained over this time period. It looks at the specific meanings of the terms "measurement", "monitoring" and "verification"; explains the key principles of monitoring and reporting; explores some of the existing protocols for monitoring and reporting; reviews the developing science of verification; and explores how these new sources of information are used for registration purposes, management decision making and the forecasting of emissions. Finally, the chapter concludes with a review of the link between verification and trading systems.

THE KEY PRINCIPLES

All monitoring and reporting protocols are built (more or less explicitly) around several key principles. Understanding the key principles (or guiding principles) is important because they will help to construct a robust and effective emission report that is more likely to fulfil the specific requirements of the ETS in question and significantly ease the verification process. For example, the UK ETS is based on the five key principles of faithful representation, completeness, accuracy, reliability and transparency. To ensure that the participants deliver on these key principles, the mandatory reporting protocols explicitly define eligibility to participate, what sources of GHGs must be included, how emissions are to be calculated, how measurements should be taken, what default values may be used, etc. In addition to this, direct participants in the UK ETS are required to have their emissions verified by accredited verifiers. The verifiers check that the participants have applied the key principles correctly.

All GHG inventories should satisfy the following:

Completeness

This refers to the inclusion of all eligible sources. The sources to be included are very specific to the ETS in question. Surprisingly, there is considerable variation in what is to be included, as shown in Panel 2. For example, the first phase of the EU ETS covers CO_2 emissions from (energy-generating) combustion facilities with input thermal capacity exceeding 20 MW and CO_2 process emissions from a specific list of industrial sectors. The UK ETS allows emissions from either CO_2 or all six Kyoto gases (CO_2, CH_4, N_2O, PFCs, HFCs and SF_6) but not from electricity generators or from transport. The CCAR allows emissions of all six gases from all activities including transport. Not only does the subject of completeness cover specific GHGs (CO_2 only or all six Kyoto GHGs) but there are also size thresholds that determine which sources *must* be included or excluded and what *may* be excluded. Generally, large sources above a certain threshold must be included and there are usually provisions for the exclusion of small sources in order to reduce the reporting burden.

For UK ETS direct participants, sources of less than 1% or 10,000 tCO_2e could be excluded. This approach allows a company with thousands of sources to effectively exclude all but the very largest. The CCAR allows the exclusion of small sources up to a total of 5%. This approach forces a company with thousands of small emissions to collect a large amount of data. Care must be taken over the optional exclusion and inclusion of sources. If total emissions reduce, or emissions from a small source assume a greater relative importance, they may cross a threshold and have to be included. Emissions excluded now may be mandated into the scheme at a later date. It is usually left to the verifier to check that the correct sources have been included in the report.

Consistency

Consistency is important because most registries and schemes wish to subtract the current year's emissions from either allocated permits or a historic datum to draw conclusions about changes in performance relative to a target. If the measurement and calculation procedures change from year to year, the result would be like comparing apples and pears. The desire for consistency can be compromised by the inevitable improvement in the quality of monitoring data. First, when historic data are used to determine the allocation of permits (as in the EU ETS, for example) it is likely that the quality of current and future data will be better than the historic data against which performance is assessed. Second, when an operator upgrades the monitoring system by, for example, installing direct flow meters rather than using a mass balance approach, they will improve the accuracy of the data but compromise consistency. The change in the methodology may work for or against the operator. One way of minimising the risk of a significant change is to run both systems in parallel for a sufficient period of time to estimate the impact of the change and then adjust the allocation of permits accordingly. The EU ETS rules require operators to improve the accuracy of their reporting as opportunities arise and verifiers are required to point out such opportunities. The "competent authorities" (the bodies responsible for implementing the EU ETS in member states) may decide to apply such methods to deal with the impacts of improvements in accuracy in an equitable and transparent manner.

Comparability

Inevitably, registries, regulators and other stakeholders are going to compare one company or facility against another, because an absolute or relative emissions figure is a benchmark of performance. There is an implicit assumption that, if the same calculation techniques have been used, performance may be relatively comparable, and hence protocols are sometimes industry- or sector-specific.

In reality, such comparisons are of value only when the product is homogeneous (eg, electricity, cement and steel) or where industries have the flexibility to do something about emissions. For example, there is little value in comparing a new plant with an older plant that uses older technology – obviously the emissions will be greater in the older plant, but, until the price of carbon is very high, both plants are likely to live out their economic lifetime.

Accuracy

The term "accuracy" or sometimes "faithful representation" refers to the freedom from consistent over- or under-estimation and the reduction of uncertainty associated with the measurement of data. Accuracy is the least well understood of the key principles. Although most protocols require accurate reporting or faithful representation, few give specific guidance on how they deliver accuracy. Uncertainty is a fact that goes along with any measurement from a meter. Even the most accurate meters cannot measure a parameter without some uncertainty. It follows that a good monitoring protocol should provide some information on acceptable levels of accuracy or uncertainty. Accuracy or uncertainty is discussed in more detail below.

Freedom from material error or omission (being "reliable")

"Materiality" is the term used to cover the controllable part of error or uncertainty. Errors commonly arise from the collection and handling of data – for example, misreading of meters, transcription errors, assigning the incorrect unit (this might be reporting tonnes as kilograms or *vice versa*). Lost data and estimated readings also contribute to measurement or controllable error. The concept of materiality allows the verifier (not the operator making the report) to consider whether an error is likely to alter the behaviour of the users of the data. If the verifier thinks the error is sufficiently small, it may be classed as "immaterial". This really means that this error makes no difference. The UK ETS and EU ETS specify guidance for the treatment of measurement errors. The threshold is 5%, but this is only guidance. Verifiers will be on the lookout for situations where a participant might be under pressure to slightly decrease emissions in order to comply with a target, and in these circumstances a smaller threshold might be applied. The verifier will also aggregate small errors, irrespective of whether they under- or over-estimate the emissions. If the aggregated errors exceed 5%, then the verifier may decline to verify the data until adjustments have been made.

Transparency

This refers to how easily the sources of data can be identified and the calculations followed. It is the opposite of a black box! Verifiers will want to check where each piece of data comes from and confirm that it is correctly used in the spreadsheet. Where spreadsheets have been developed in-house, the verifier may choose to follow the calculations through each step, checking source and dependent cells, and checking that, for example, 12 monthly totals are summed to give an annual total. Alternatively, it may be easier to simply take the raw data and reconstruct the calculation to try to achieve the same result. Another trick is to enter a huge number into the "front end" that will dwarf the rest of the entries and check that it comes out correctly at the far end. Proprietary software, once audited, can provide the verifier with a higher level of confidence without the need to check each cell exhaustively. Where programmes have been tested, the verifier may be able to confirm the data that are entered into the "model" and then trust the results.

Cost effectiveness

This is to reassure participants that they will not be forced to spend large amounts of money on state-of-the-art metering kit.

Timeliness

This is to facilitate the completion of an annual inventory shortly after the end of the accounting period and thereby help the participant manage their compliance status most effectively.

Performance improvement

This is to help participants improve their quality control procedures and generally improve the quality of their inventory data.

Monitoring protocols

Monitoring protocols have at least three general objectives: the first is to control the implementation of the scheme rules; the second is to enable the determination of an absolute level of emissions over a given period of time; and the third is to enable comparisons from year to year. When monitoring data are used internally, the absolute level of activity may be less important than the comparison from year to year and therefore less emphasis may be placed on accuracy. There is an assumption that errors in the monitoring protocol will be repeated from year to year while the differences in activity will be relatively accurate.

However, once data are taken outside the boundaries of the facility for comparison with other facilities in a benchmarking exercise, or used as the basis of an environmentally and financially sensitive ETS, for example, accuracy becomes much more important. It's again a question of apples and pears! For internal purposes, it may not be particularly important how the "apples" are defined, but the same definition should be used from year to year. In an ETS, things are different. If the ETS is to have environmental and financial credibility than monitoring, reporting and verification must adhere to some or all of the key principles described above. These principles take shape in the monitoring protocol, which defines (in more or less detail) how operators should measure specific activities, and, where appropriate, calculate GHG emissions.

There is a growing number of GHG monitoring and reporting protocols specifically designed to address the needs of specific ETSs. Despite their differences, essentially, all of the protocols are basically measuring the same things – emissions of GHGs. So, they all demonstrate some degree of overlap in the technical content.

Perhaps the most significant differences between schemes and their protocols relate to the treatment of direct and indirect emissions, process and transport emissions, as we discuss below.

Direct and indirect emissions

Direct emissions arise from the combustion of fossil fuels on site. Indirect emissions are the emissions associated with the use of electricity generated elsewhere and delivered to the site via cables. If indirect emissions are reported, the generating sector cannot be included in the scheme, or double counting will occur. This single factor radically changes the nature of the ETS. Where generators are included, caps on emissions are likely to lead to increases in electricity prices and the generators will be encouraged to generate more efficiently. Where generators are excluded and the users of the electricity are responsible for the emissions, there will be a greater awareness of the impact of emissions – and, consequently, actions – among the users. For example, the UK ETS excludes generators while the EU ETS includes them, which creates two very different schemes. The advantage of including the generators and excluding indirect emissions is that the main source of GHG emissions is captured directly in the scheme and the generators are then directly encouraged to generate more efficiently. In the UK's National Allocation Plan (NAP) for the first phase of the EU ETS, the generating sector is required to deliver the bulk of the emission reductions required. The disadvantage is that their inclusion will inevitably lead to increases in the price of electricity as they pass the costs of carbon purchases or abatements on to their users.

Process emissions

Process emissions fall into two categories: CO_2 and non-CO_2. They arise during manufacturing, mining, refining and chemical processing. CO_2 process emissions arise, for example, from the manufacture of steel, ceramics, cement and building products. Significant quantities of non-CO_2 GHGs are released during coal mining and in untreated landfill gas (CH_4, Global Warming Potential (GWP) 21), manufacture of adipic acid (N_2O, GWP 320), manufacture of HCFC22 (HFC23, GWP 11,700), aluminium smelting (PFCs, GWP 6,500–9,200). SF_6 (GWP 23,900) is used in specific manufacturing processes as an insulating gas (see also Table 1 in Chapter 1). Non-CO_2 emissions typically account for approximately 10% of an Annex I Party's GHG emissions. Due to the high global-warming potential of the gases (their environmental impact relative to 1 tonne of CO_2), and the technologies available, emissions of non-CO_2 GHGs can be substantially reduced at relatively low cost. Alternatively, process emissions can be addressed through regulation, at least in countries where regulations are effective. For example, Integrated Pollution Control regulations could be used to reduce emissions of CO_2 and non-CO_2 GHGs from industrial sources. The European Commission is preparing legislation to phase out the use of SF_6. In a similar way, the Montreal Protocol provides for the phase-out of ozone-depleting gases. The Montreal Protocol and the Kyoto Protocol provide two contrasting methods of addressing global pollution: the old style of "command and control" and the relatively new "cap-and-trade".

Transport is the real culprit. GHG emissions from transport are rising rapidly all over the world and many governments lack the means or the will to tackle them.[1] To date, only voluntary schemes offer the choice of reporting transport-related emissions and they are specifically excluded from the UK ETS and the EU ETS. Several CDM transport projects are under preparation in Non-Annex I countries and there have been signs that the European Commission and some member states may decide to include transport in the second phase of the EU ETS. Transport emissions are particularly difficult to address because of the political sensitivity and the strong links between transport (particularly international air transport) and the economy.

PANEL 2 EXAMPLES OF EMISSION TRADING SCHEMES AND REGISTRIES

Table a describes six active schemes. The EU ETS, UK ETS (agreement and direct participants) and CDM are discussed in depth elsewhere in this book. The remaining ones are briefly described below.

WRI/WBCSD is a voluntary GHG reporting protocol designed to help corporate organisations to report their GHG emissions. The protocol provides good methods of calculating emissions from specific activities and these have formed the basis of protocols used elsewhere – eg, in the CCAR. The WRI/WBCSD Protocol does not have a register to record emissions, nor a trading element. The World Economic Forum has subsequently launched a register in which to record verified emissions that may be calculated using the WRI/WBCSD Protocol.

CCAR is a register in which to record verified historic emissions. There is no trading component at this stage. Participants enter voluntarily, with the aim of protecting their baseline from early action in the event that a regulatory regime is introduced at a later stage. For example, a company has implemented its abatement options voluntarily, thereby reducing its emissions from 2002 onwards. If a regulatory regime was later introduced that awarded credits based on average emissions from 2002 onwards, the company would find itself penalised relative to its competitors, who would be rewarded for not taking any early action to reduce their emissions. The CCAR aims to protect its members against such a situation.

Table a Summary of some key features of selected GHG registries/trading schemes

	EU ETS	UK ETS agreement participants	UK ETS direct participants	WBCSD/WRI corporate reporting protocol	CCAR	CDM EB
Voluntary/ Mandatory	Mandatory	Voluntary	Voluntary	Voluntary	Voluntary	Voluntary
Level of application	Facility	Facility	Facility	Corporate	Company (CA or USA)	Project
Scope of coverage	Defined	Defined	Specific rules for including and excluding sources	Level 1 required, Levels 2 and 3 optional	Specific rules relating to ownership or management control	Defined
Gases	CO_2 (for phase 1)	CO_2 only	CO_2 only or all 6	All 6	All 6	All 6
Direct/indirect emissions	Direct and CO_2 process	Direct and indirect	Direct and indirect process	Voluntary	Direct and indirect (process in preparation)	Direct and indirect
Verification	Yes	Yes to sell	Yes	Voluntary	Yes	Yes
Comment	Prefers measurement of fuel use. Specifies levels of accuracy. Provides reporting format	Tied into Climate Change Levy Negotiated Agreements	Specific non-CO_2 protocols. Does not address uncertainty	Widely used as the basis for monitoring and reporting in other schemes, eg, CCAR, WEF, GHG Registry	Online reporting tools facilitates calculation	Each protocol (methodology) specifically deals with the definition of the baseline, proof that the project is additional to "business-as-usual" and how to monitor project emissions. Does not address uncertainty

MEASUREMENT METHODS

The core provisions within GHG protocols are basic calculation or direct measurement methods. Calculation depends on the type of emission source and can be categorised into (1) combustion of fossil fuels, (2) production processes, (3) mass balance data and (4) direct emissions.

Emissions from combustion of fossil fuels

CO_2 emissions from combustion of fossil fuels, the predominant source of GHG emissions can be calculated as follows:

> Level of CO_2 emissions = Activity level (eg, tonnes of fuel consumed) $\times$ emissions factor (tCO_2 emissions per unit of fuel) $\times$ oxidation factor (to account for carbon loss as soot, etc).

For example, a factory burns gas to provide steam and direct heat for cooking. The quantity of gas is metered at the entrance to the site and monthly invoices indicate the periodic gas consumption. The gas invoices also provide the correction factors (to account for variations in temperature and pressure) and the average calorific value of the gas. These data allow the conversion from m^3 of gas to kWh (the invoices often show energy consumption in kWh as well). In this example, the factory has consumed 11,354,221 kWh of gas during the year. The protocol specifies the emissions factor in terms of the kg CO_2 per kWh for different fuel types – the value for natural gas is 0.19 kg CO_2 per kWh. For natural gas, the oxidation factor is usually 0.995, reflecting the fact that nearly all of the carbon in the fuel is burned. If it is not burned, it is detectable as soot in the exhaust. To convert from carbon to carbon dioxide, multiply by 44/12 (the respective molecular weights of CO_2 and C). The carbon emissions are $11,354,211 \times 0.19 \times 0.995 \times 44/12 = 7,870,550$ kg of CO_2 or 7,871 tonnes of CO_2.

Emissions from production processes

CO_2 emissions from processes (eg, cement, steel and lime production) are a little more complicated and require some knowledge of the chemical processes taking place, but the same basic formula may be applied whereby the total emissions are a function of the tonnes of product or raw material used and the emissions factor associated with that product or raw material.

For example, CO_2 process emissions from the manufacture of 1 tonne of cement are approximately 0.75 tonnes (although this number depends on the particular plant, raw materials and energy source). Once the emission factor has been calculated, as long as the process does not change, CO_2 emissions may be easily determined.

Emissions from mass balance data

The same basic approach can be applied to mass balance or stock change data to account for, for example, fugitive emissions of refrigerants from air-conditioning units. Then we define activity level as follows:

Activity level = opening stock at the start of the year
+ stock purchases during the year
− closing stock at the end of the year.

And the emissions factor is the Global Warming Potential of the gas.

For example, if the opening stock of HFC-134a (a coolant used in some refrigeration units) is 100 kg at the start of the year; accounting records and stock control records confirm the purchase of 4×100-kg drums throughout the year and the closing stock is 135 kg, then 365 kg has been used to top up the system throughout the year. HFC-134a has a global warming potential of 1300, so the fugitive emissions amount to 474,500 kg or 47.5 tonnes CO_2e.

Direct emissions

For direct measurement of emissions the basic formula is:

Emissions level = flow rate × time × concentration
× global warming potential.

Flow rate is the measured flow of gas vented to atmosphere and can be sampled to estimate a mean flow rate per unit time or totalised over the year.

For a flow rate, time is the length of time the vent stream is venting to atmosphere – often taken as 365 days per year. The volume of the GHG is determined by multiplying the flow volume (flow rate $\times$ time) by the concentration of the gas as a percentage of the total gas flow. If the result is to be expressed in mass terms, the volume must be converted to mass by multiplying by the density of GHG in question. These calculations may be made automatically by sophisticated mass flow meters.

For example, a coal mine pumps huge quantities of air through the mine shafts to keep the air breathable and maintain a low concentration of methane in the ambient air. The flow rate is determined by a flow meter attached to the vacuum pumps or measured directly in the vent shaft using an anemometer. The flow rate is $70\ m^3$ per second. The vents operate 24 hours a day 365 days a year and total flow = 2,207 million m^3. The average methane concentration, by volume, is 1% = 22.07 million m^3. The density of methane at 26°C is 0.00068 tonnes per m^3; therefore the mass of methane emitted = $22,075,200 \times 0.00068 = 15,011$ tonnes. Methane has a global warming potential of 21, therefore the mine emits a total of 315,233 tonnes CO_2e.

ACCURACY AND UNCERTAINTY

Describing how to address accuracy or uncertainty is perhaps the most important role of a monitoring plan. However, it is also the most poorly understood. The term "accuracy" is a bit misleading, because it implies that the error associated with each measurement is known. It is not possible to know the error of a measurement: the uncertainty associated with it can only be estimated and "uncertainty" is therefore the better term to use. For example, if a meter measures the same known quantity a thousand times, a range of results will be achieved. A histogram of these results will show:

❑ a normal distribution centred on the true value; or
❑ a normal distribution with the mean displaced from the true value; or
❑ a skewed distribution.

If the distribution is normal, then the uncertainty can be expressed as a percentage of the mean. By convention the uncertainty range is normally defined as +2 standard deviations (σ) around the mean. Since $+2\sigma$ encompasses approximately 95% of the results, it can be said that, for this example, an uncertainty of 1% at the 95%

confidence level means that 950 of the 1,000 results will be within +1% of the true value.

If the distribution is displaced the meter will show a bias that produces a systematic under- or overestimate in the measurements. On the other hand, a skewed distribution implies that the measurements are not subject to simple random variables and the conventional uncertainty expression should be treated with caution.

It is vitally important that a monitoring protocol specifies the permitted uncertainty of a meter and that the verifier then checks (a) that the meters in question are manufactured to the required specification, (b) that the meters are installed correctly and (c) that the meter has been in calibration throughout the reporting period. Unfortunately, many protocols fail to define the acceptable limits of inaccuracy, the EU ETS being one notable exception (see Panel 3). In other instances, meters are at best required to reflect best practice, standard practice or fitness for purpose, but such requirements are open to different interpretations.

PANEL 3 ACCURACY IN THE EU ETS

Accuracy in the EU ETS is addressed through a tier structure in which levels of accuracy (or permitted inaccuracy) are described for each of the parameters used to calculate emissions. Small emitters, with less than 50,000 tCO_2 per year are required to report each parameter at a lower level of accuracy. For example, combustion facilities burning liquid or gaseous fuels releasing less than 50,000 tonnes CO_2 are required to report activity level (eg, amount of fuel consumed) to within 5% or better (tier 2a) or 4.5% if stock change is used (tier 2b); both net calorific value and the emissions factor may be the country-specific value reported by the member state to the UNFCCC in their latest national GHG inventory or better (tier 2); oxidation factor may be taken as 0.995 (tier 1). Similar facilities with emissions in the 50,000 to 500,000 tonnes CO_2 bracket are required to measure activity level at 2.5% permitted inaccuracy (tier 3a) or 2% if stock change is used (tier 3b) with the same net calorific value, emissions factor and oxidation factor. Similar facilities releasing more than 500,000 tonnes CO_2 are required to report activity level to within 1.5% (tier 4a) or 1% if stock change is used (tier 4b); they must determine their own net calorific value and emissions factor by analysing representative samples of the fuel used (tier 3) and the oxidation factor may be taken as 0.995 (tier 1).

Errors resulting from imperfect meters can never be removed completely; improving the meters is all we can aim for. For this reason, the inaccuracy or error associated with metering can be described as inherent or uncontrollable error. In approving a monitoring protocol, the authority effectively accepts the environmental liability associated with these errors. Failure to specify acceptable uncertainty limits therefore leaves the authority with an unknown level of uncertainty, threatening the environmental credibility of the scheme.

For example, in the measurement of HFC23, emissions samples are typically taken from the main vent and analysed to determine the HFC23 content. (HFC23 is a powerful GHG with a global warming potential of 11,700, released as a by-product of HCFC22 manufacture. HCFC22 is a coolant and is used in medical anaesthetics, cosmetics and flavourings.) The concentration of the stream is highly variable, depending on the levels and type of activity at the time the sample is taken. Sufficient samples must be taken to provide an accurate estimate of the mean, but this could require samples to be taken and analysed once a week or more frequently. It is practically possible – the number of samples required to provide a mean with a specified accuracy at a given confidence interval (eg, ±5% at 95% certainty) can be calculated based on the estimated variation in the raw data. Without clear guidance, operators may take fewer samples leading to more inaccurate estimates of the mean and therefore greater uncertainty in the estimate of total HFC23 emissions. The high global warming potential of HFC23 greatly exacerbates the impact of this uncertainty.

Reporting

Several monitoring protocols include reporting guidelines – for example the EU ETS and the CCAR. A reporting format greatly helps the process of reporting and verification and comparison between similar facilities and over time. The reporting format can come in the form of a written report, highlighting the items to be covered within it. This helps by ensuring participants do not neglect to include important information and discourages the inclusion of unnecessary information. Tables and summaries using consistent units will facilitate the consolidation of reports, for example within industry sectors or for comparison with top-down national inventories and projections.

The CCAR presents an optional reporting online tool (CAR-ROT). Participants define the scope of their inventory, enter the necessary activity data onto bespoke data-entry screens, and are helped to choose the appropriate emissions factors. This tool has many of the advantages listed above and also helps to demonstrate transparency during the verification process – as the tool has been extensively audited and verifiers can be confident that, if the correct data are entered, the reported emissions will be correct. This aids transparency and speeds the verification process.

In the absence of a reporting format, what should be reported? The report should be very clear on the scope of the inventory, reporting period, included sources and protocols utilised. It should show how the inventory has been constructed to address the key principles and ideally it should provide references to the internal procedures developed to control and assure the quality of the data. In a perfect world, the inventory report would be a freestanding document with annexes containing examples of raw data or reference to data sources utilised, calibration certificates and key quality assurance/quality control procedures. Such a document would greatly facilitate verification by demonstrating transparency, completeness, consistency and accuracy. Such a document would also be a useful and accessible management tool that could contribute to management decisions.

Verification

Verification is the activity that provides the financial and environmental credibility of an ETS. As Table 1 shows, the majority of the voluntary schemes require verification and even the 1605B voluntary reporting programme in the US gives participants the option of undergoing verification. Verification adds a cost to the reporting process but it is clear that the authorities in charge of the schemes feel that the benefits outweigh the costs.

The most advanced verification is currently being practised in the UK ETS and will shortly be implemented in the EU ETS, CCAR and the CDM. The current trend is for a verification process implemented by accredited third parties that delivers a verification opinion with a high level of assurance or, conversely, with a low level of risk of error.

Accreditation confirms that the verifier is competent and independent and can therefore perform the services required. Accreditation is common among verifiers whose organisations and management systems are developed to ensure competence and independence. Accreditation may be given against a specific standard or left to the verifiers to select. In the UK ETS, for example, accreditation is under ISO Guide 65 (EN45011), which describes the requirements for organisations offering product certification services. Other schemes have left the choice open, but the important characteristics are how the organisation ensures it has the capacity to do the work and that only competent staff undertake the work; how they ensure team members have no conflicts of interest (eg, current or recent involvement with the client); and how they make the final decision to issue an opinion.

Verifiers should work to provide a moderate or high level of assurance in their opinions. This reflects the amount of time, effort and expertise required to complete the work and the wording of the final verification opinion. For example, if financial accountants are going to use the opinion to calculate the financial value of GHG assets (excess permits) or liabilities (emissions), they may require a high level of assurance. Similarly, regulators may require a high level of assurance to protect the environmental integrity of the programme. Verifiers develop their own methods of ensuring an appropriate level of performance. However, it is widely accepted that verification is based on an assessment of where risks of error or omissions leading to a material mis-statement are greatest. This means that the verifier will review the sources, the data collection and handling procedures associated with them and then decide which areas present the highest risks. They will then focus the verification effort on these areas, defining sampling programmes where necessary. Most verifiers also require the lead assessor to submit a recommendation, supported by justifications, to an internal and independent decision maker. The decision maker is the one who actually makes the decision to issue the verification opinion. Such requirements are laid out in ISO Guide 65, which defines the management systems required for organisations offering product conformity certification and verification.

PANEL 4 TIMING AND COST OF VERIFICATION

The timeline for the completion of a verification engagement depends very much on three factors:

1. the complexity of the organisation and the number of point sources that are significant and need to be verified;
2. the permitted levels of inaccuracy, the detail of the protocols and whether or not the verifier has to assess compliance with the rules of the scheme – eg, eligibility to participate, identification and inclusion of mandatory sources; and
3. the preparations made by the participant.

Given these uncertainties, it is difficult to estimate time inputs. However, based on experience, the following "ball-park" scenarios may apply:

❏ In simple cases of one or two sources of delivered energy on one site, where revenue meters and invoices are present, the work can be completed within one to two days for the first engagement and possibly one day for subsequent engagements.
❏ In more complex situations, involving the import and export of energy, multiple CO_2 GHG sources, some included, some excluded and particularly where non-regulated submetering/ subdivision of energy flows is involved, the time can increase to three to five days or more for the first engagement and two to three days in future.
❏ For companies with non-CO_2 process emissions where metering, calibration, sampling testing, etc, are involved, the first engagement may take ten days and subsequent engagements five days.
❏ Where unexpected problems arise, additional time may be required.

Time and expertise input is also a reflection of the verifier's view of risk. Risk-averse verifiers will spend more time on the engagement and therefore cost more, but the verification opinion will be correspondingly stronger. In addition to time spent on site, the verification team is also required to complete document reviews and internal reporting procedures and submit its recommendation to an independent decision maker – so, during ten days of work, the team may be on site for only six.

The ability to sample sites within groups has a significant impact upon time and costs. In the UK ETS agreement participant sector, verifiers are permitted to issue verification opinions to individual sites based on a desk review of a "data verification pack" (which contains documentary evidence of the audit trail – eg, invoices to support declared fuel consumption) and site visits to a sample of the group members.

> Costs are dependent upon individual verifiers' fee rates. These fee rates will reflect the relatively specialised nature of the work, high liabilities, value of the service to the client, time restrictions (particularly in the case of mandatory schemes that have a short reporting window – like the EU ETS) and accreditation costs.

Accounting

The primary use of the data in the GHG inventory is to report it to the relevant authorities or stakeholders in the form of an "unqualified verification opinion". Such an opinion provides positive confirmation of the reported data – for example, "In the verifier's opinion, the data are considered to be complete, transparent and free of material error or omissions." Depending on the specific rules of the ETS the verifier may be required to verify emissions (UK ETS direct participants), certify emissions (CCAR), certify emission reductions (CDM), verify excess allowances (EU ETS), or verify overperformance (UK ETS agreement participants). Where verification of emission reductions is required, these are determined by comparing current emissions against historic emissions, a target or predicted business-as-usual emissions. Internally, the data may be used as a means of managing a potential compliance risk and, if necessary, trading to take advantage of market fluctuations.

In the EU ETS, monthly data may also be required for internal accounting purposes, since EU allowances are an asset. As the facility emits CO_2, these assets are destroyed. The reduction in allowances must be evaluated at the current market prices and the change in asset value shown in the company's financial accounts. Managers are likely to be very interested in the current and predicted compliance status in order to minimise the costs of compliance at the end of the year. This requirement for monthly data will influence the reporting procedures.

Most UK ETS agreement participants, on the other hand, report relative performance against negotiated targets in the form of an improvement in energy efficiency. Participants do not have allowances and therefore there is no explicit requirement to account for allowances in financial accounts or on a monthly basis.

However, predicting performance against a relative target is harder than against an absolute target because of generally complex relationships between plant utilisation, base-load energy consumption and energy efficiency. An overriding factor is that at present the cost of CO_2 on the UK market is relatively low and it may be just as easy to purchase emission permits at the end of the accounting period.

Many elements are required for an effective and efficient trading system, including:

❑ a register in which to record and track allowances and facilitate the transfer of traded allowances from one account to another;
❑ brokers and trading platforms to facilitate trade and publish current and future prices;
❑ sufficient buyers and sellers to provide liquidity in the market;
❑ a means of allocating allowances (the NAPs in the EU ETS; the late-night negotiations in Kyoto for Annex I Parties in the Kyoto Protocol; baseline methodologies for CDM projects); and
❑ mechanisms for monitoring and reporting of GHG emissions.

These requirements are being developed in parallel, and sometimes in conjunction, across at least half a dozen credible trading schemes and registries. The progress is rapid, spurred by the political will and a growing awareness of the likely environmental consequences. Much of the work has been approached in the spirit of "learning by doing", but some of the requirements, such as liquidity, can be addressed only by legislative measures. Voluntary schemes are weakened by the fact that only winners are likely to volunteer into the scheme. The EU ETS is the only scheme to date that will ensure the participation of both winners and losers and thereby create a viable market.

CONCLUSIONS

The relatively wide variety of monitoring and reporting protocols available belies the fact that, essentially, their common purpose is to report on emissions of GHGs. The technical content of these protocols should be relatively similar, but in fact most are found lacking in their treatment of uncertainty – they fail to define permissible levels of uncertainty in the measurement of the parameters used to estimate emissions. Further differences emerge in relation to the scope of what is to be reported, and how it is to be reported. There is ample scope for monitoring and reporting protocols to evolve and learn from one another.

Ultimately, the environmental and financial credibility of the scheme rests on the reliability of the reported data. Monitoring and reporting protocols provide essential instructions and guidance on how to report GHG emissions in a manner that will enable trading schemes and registries to function in a credible manner. As we have seen, verification by independent third parties is an essential means of protecting that credibility.

---

1   Figure 3 in chapter 14 shows the sharp rise in GHG emissions from the EU transport sector.

7

Financing Greenhouse Gas Abatement Measures

Josef Janssen

Emissions Trading Solutions St. Gallen AG (ETSG)

Global markets for greenhouse gas (GHG) allowances and credits are increasingly becoming a reality. From January 2005, more than 12,000 installations in the enlarged EU will participate in the EU scheme for trading in CO_2 emission allowances. Compliance may be achieved through use of a variety of instruments, including the project-based Kyoto Mechanisms Joint Implementation (JI) and in particular the Clean Development Mechanism (CDM).

The financing of GHG abatement measures will be an important issue for the companies covered by the EU emissions trading scheme, as well as for the developers of JI and CDM projects. This chapter discusses financing options for the GHG abatement projects to be realised, in industrialised as well as developing countries. We first examine the relevance of financing GHG abatement projects and discuss general options for financing GHG abatement measures. Then we study in more detail one financing instrument that appears to be particularly relevant in the context of large-scale projects, namely off-balance-sheet project financing. The last section will draw some conclusions.

THE NEED FOR FINANCING

Financing is characterised by an initial inflow of funds, which implies a cash outflow at a later stage. Financing requirements correspond to the (positive) difference between accumulated cash outflow and cash inflow of an investment project. In the context of emissions trading and the Kyoto Mechanisms, funds are required to finance GHG abatement activities.

The main methods of reducing energy-related CO_2 emissions include:

❏ energy efficiency improvement, including cogeneration and steam recovery;
❏ fuel switching; and
❏ switching to renewable energy, including biomass.

Different abatement options involve different abatement costs and different cost profiles in terms of investment costs and operation costs. This is crucial from the perspective of financing, since different cost types require different financing instruments. To give an example, switching from oil to natural gas in industrial heat and power generation may not require significant modifications of the combustion installation. However, the variable costs in terms of fuel costs may rise significantly. Associated emission abatement costs imply a permanent increase in the required working capital, which may be financed through short- to medium-term financing such as bank loans or trade credits (see below). In contrast, substituting a gas-fired combustion installation by a cogeneration biomass plant may involve relatively high investment costs that are to be financed through medium-term to long-term instruments such as project finance. Thus, it is important to keep in mind that different abatement options require different financing solutions.

The additional cash outflow associated with abatement activities needs to be covered by a corresponding amount of cash inflow. The procurement of a sufficient number of receipts to cover abatement expenditures is the basic problem of financing CDM, JI or other GHG mitigation projects under any emissions trading scheme.

In addition, a key notion in financing is time, and thus it is vital to understand the timing of cashflows associated with GHG abatement projects. In order to understand this point, it is useful to distinguish between two basic abatement options: the first causes operating expenditures, and the second investment expenditures.

In the first case, the additional cash outflow could be caused by the use of more expensive but less carbon-intense fuels. In principle, the revenues of selling emission permits should outweigh the additional costs incurred. Otherwise, the project would not be economically

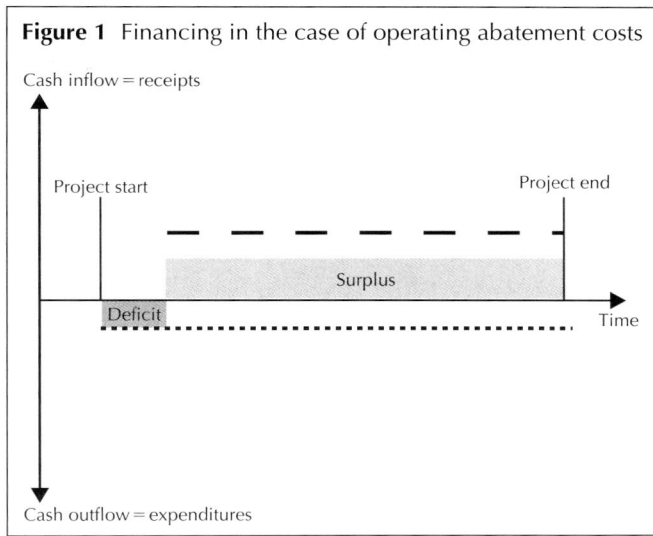

Figure 1 Financing in the case of operating abatement costs

Cash inflow = receipts

Project start

Project end

Surplus

Deficit

Time

Cash outflow = expenditures

viable, as shown in Figure 1. Due to this time lag between cash out-flow and inflow, there is a need for financing abatement activities from sources other than receipts from permit sales.

In the second case, the installation of new plants would lead to relatively large amounts of cash outflow prior to the project's oper-ation phase in order to pay the technology supplier and construc-tor (see Figure 2). Once the new equipment is in operation, the project starts to generate cash inflow from the sale of (surplus) emission permits, but in the first years of operation this cash inflow is typically not sufficient to pay back the initial investment costs. As a consequence, the accumulated net cashflow rests negative over several years, requiring long-term financing.

General options for financing GHG abatement measures

Financing instruments are usually classified according to different criteria, including the following:

❏ legal status of capital providers and liability: equity versus debt financing;

❏ origin of funds: internal versus external financing;[1]

❏ maturity of (external) funds (time horizon over which the prin-cipal amount remains outstanding): short-term (up to one year), medium-term (from one to five or seven years), and long-term

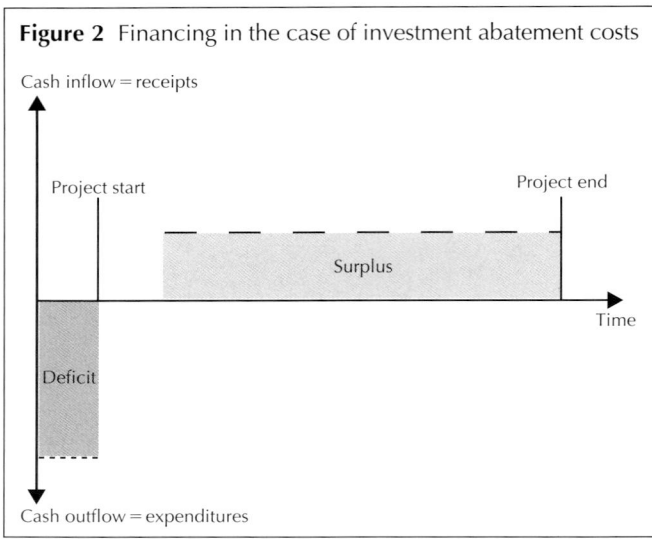

Figure 2 Financing in the case of investment abatement costs

(above five or seven years) (see Harris and Pringle, 1989).[2] Some debt is perpetual and has no specific maturity.

In the context of developing countries, an additional distinction is frequently made between:

❏ domestic versus foreign sources; and
❏ private versus official development finance.

Figure 3 shows how the financing classifications according to the first and second criteria are interrelated.

The financing patterns of companies in different countries vary to some extent (see Shapiro, 1999).[3] In Europe and the US, internal finance through retained earnings has consistently supplied the largest share of financial resource requirements. The percentage of external finance is positively correlated to the business cycle: when profits are high, companies can rely on internal financing.

Concerning external finance in developed countries, debt accounts for the largest share of external funds regardless of the country. New share issues play a small and declining role in financing investment (see Shapiro, 1999).

Sources of external financing vary widely across different countries. In some countries, such as the US and the UK, companies raise

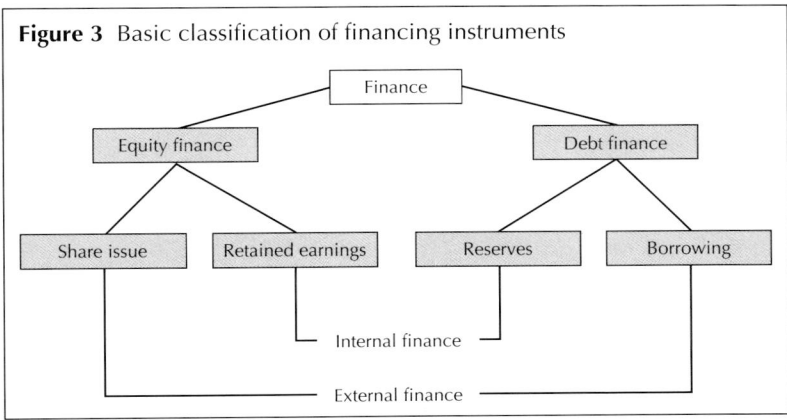

Figure 3 Basic classification of financing instruments

funds directly from financial markets through the issuance of nego-tiable securities in the public capital markets ("securitisation"). Companies in Continental Europe and Japan rely more heavily on bank borrowing or non-marketable loans provided by financial intermediaries. The choice between financial intermediation and securitisation depends on the relative costs and risks of the two alternatives.

Another important distinction in debt finance is that between "on-balance-sheet finance" and "off-balance-sheet finance". The latter is also called "project finance" or "no- or limited-recourse finance", whereas the former corresponds to conventional corporate finance. It is important to note that the notion of "project finance" should not be confused with the financing of projects in general. The two financing forms differ significantly as regards the lender's security arrangements. With limited-recourse project financing, the project borrows on a stand-alone basis. While some guarantees may be required, the loan or the lender's repayments are secured pri-marily by the project's assets and future cashflows with limited recourse to the developer or project sponsor. In on-balance-sheet financing, lenders look to general corporate assets as security for the debt as well as to other external collaterals if the company is unable to repay the debt. Figure 4 illustrates the basic difference between conventional corporate finance and project finance.

Due to the fact that project finance involves a series of complex contractual arrangements, arranging it is very costly. Therefore,

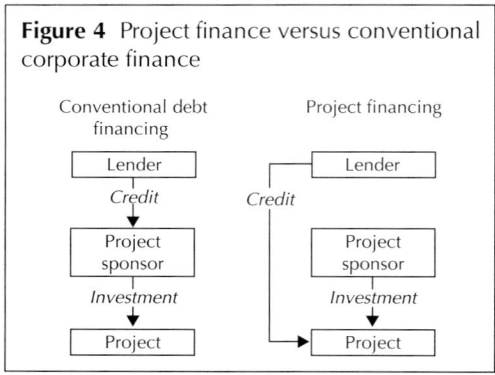

Figure 4 Project finance versus conventional corporate finance

a project is unlikely to attract the interest of project finance lenders if the debt component is less than about US$10–20 million. As a consequence, project finance is typically applied to finance large projects. This also applies to the financing of GHG abatement projects in industrialised or developing countries.

When discussing the financing of GHG abatement projects, it is important to understand how the cashflow associated with the sale of emission permits may affect the finance of the overall project. In the case of on-balance-sheet finance, the creditworthiness of the borrower is typically judged on the basis of their balance sheet and other financial statements. As a consequence, it does not matter whether the borrower uses the funds for financing a project that is or is not expected to earn surplus emission allowances or emission credits. What counts is the borrower's balance sheet. This is in contrast to project finance, where the lender scrutinises very closely the financial viability and expected cashflow of the project to be financed. Here, the future cashflow associated with the generation and sale of (surplus) emission permits might well affect the creditworthiness of the project.

This second point is most important and should be clearly understood. It implies that with on-balance-sheet finance the raising of funds for GHG abatement projects, such as JI or CDM projects, is basically independent of the question of whether or not the project earns marketable emission permits. Therefore, neither the project developer nor the lender needs to consider the emission permits in their financing analysis and arrangement. Obviously, the project developer should consider the value of emission permits in their capital budgeting decision or investment analysis. Emissions trading or the Kyoto Mechanisms do not add anything new to conventional finance, meaning that a company can arrange financing for a GHG abatement project as it would do usually without taking into account any emission permits. The financing of a GHG abatement project is separate from the fact that it is a GHG abatement project. In contrast, off-balance-sheet finance is probably the sole financing form when it makes a difference whether the project is a GHG abatement project or not. Hence, we will concentrate on project finance in the remainder of this chapter.

Short- to medium-term financing instruments

Short-term funds are often raised to finance seasonal or temporary increases in working capital, such as the build-up of inventories of seasonal goods. Such seasonal financing might be repaid with the cash generated from the sale of the goods and the resulting reduction of inventory. Short-term financiers are thus concerned with the strength of the company's balance sheet, the quality of assets and other claims against the assets. In general, short-term funds can be obtained from a variety of sources including other business companies, banks and the money market. Major financing instruments are trade credits, loans and commercial papers.

Medium-term funds are usually raised to finance permanent additions to working capital or fixed assets. Repayment usually comes from profits or cashflows generated from operations over a period of several years, rather than liquidated assets. As a consequence, providers of medium-term sources are more concerned with the income statement, looking to the company's earning power of sustained periods of time.

Nearly all companies rely to some extent on trade credit as a source of short-term funds. Trade credit is short-term credit extended by a supplier in connection with goods purchased for ultimate resale. This definition also encompasses credit extended by a supplier of raw material to a manufacturer for producing its products. The credit appears on the supplier's balance sheet as an account receivable, whereas it is an account payable on the buyer's balance sheet. Where goods are imported from abroad, trade credits are referred to as export finance. Export finance permits the payment for imports to be deferred beyond the date of shipment. Instruments of export finance are similar to those employed for domestic trade.

Trade credit arises from the company's normal operations, specifically from the time lag between receipt of goods and payment for them. The extent to which trade credit is used as a source of funds varies widely among companies. In general, manufacturer and smaller companies make extensive use of trade credits. Within certain limits, a company may use its discretion with respect to the extent to which it uses trade credit as a source of funds. By altering the payment period, a company can expand or contract its accounts payable.

Depending on the creditworthiness of the debtor, trade credits could be used to finance the achievement of emission abatements, eg, through fuel switching from oil to natural gas, without large modifications of the plant. The additional funds required to pay for a more expensive but less carbon-intense fuel could be arranged by a trade credit extended by the fuel supplier. The creditor would probably charge some implicit or explicit interest rate for the trade credit.

Bank loans provide a major source of short-term and medium-term financing.[4] To ensure that the borrower maintains an adequate degree of liquidity, restrictions may be imposed on minimum net working capital, payment of dividends and on the purchase and sale of fixed assets. Pledging assets to others is often prohibited by negative-pledge clause.

Although commercial banks are the most important of the intermediaries that finance business companies, other financial institutions (such as finance companies and insurance companies) also supply short- and medium-term funds. In many developing countries, banks are typically the only major source of formal financing for industrial investments, since capital markets are underdeveloped and do not provide alternative financial instruments (see UNIDO, 1997). In industrialised countries, banks are also a major funding source for small- and medium-sized companies. Moreover, most companies depend on banks for short-term loans.

In general, a distinction is made between unsecured and secured loans. An unsecured loan is one against which no specific assets are pledged as collateral.[5] Commercial banks are the largest supplier of unsecured loans to business companies. Short-term unsecured bank loans usually take one of the three forms: a line of credit, a revolving-credit agreement or a simple single-transaction loan.

A secured loan is one against which specific assets are pledged as collateral by the borrower. Such financial arrangements are also called asset-based financing. Accounts receivable and inventory are the most common collateral for short-term loans, since they are reasonably liquid. In the case of accounts-receivable pledging, the bank advances the funds against the pledged receivables but retains full recourse to the borrower if receivables are uncollectible. Commonly, equipment or real estate serves as collateral to secure a term loan.

How do emission allowances and credits relate to such collaterals? In principle, the equipment employed to abate GHG emissions, eg, a cogeneration plant, could be used as collateral. However, this is also true if the project does not earn marketable emission permits. As a consequence, and in this regard, emissions trading or the Kyoto Mechanisms do not change the financing aspects.

More interestingly, accounts receivable or inventories related to emissions trading and the Kyoto Mechanisms could be used as collateral to a loan. Different possibilities are conceivable. First, accounts receivable from sales of emission permits could in principle be used as collateral to a loan if the counterparty is sufficiently creditworthy. This option is interesting in cases where the GHG credits or any surplus allowances are sold in the form of a long-term contract.

Second, loans could also be secured by inventories of emission permits. In the case of JI and CDM projects, this option is not suitable because emission credits are issued only once emission reductions have been verified (and certified, as regards CDM projects). Since emission credits are not issued *ex ante*, the project operator will probably not hold any large inventories of emission credits. However, in the context of cap-and-trade systems, such as the EU emissions trading scheme, emission allowances are issued at the beginning of a year. Since actual emissions occurring in one year need to be balanced by a corresponding number of allowances at the end of the year or at the beginning of the successive year only, operators of installations covered by cap-and-trade systems do hold large inventories of allowances. For example, in the first period of the EU emissions trading system, each year Germany will allocate 499 million allowances to the approximate 2,400 installations covered by the emissions trading scheme. At an assumed market price of €10, the value of the overall inventory would correspond to roughly €5 billion. These allowances inventories could be used to secure loans. Indeed, some banks have started to explore related opportunities.

Long-term financing instruments

Long-term financing instruments include retained earnings, common stock, preferred stock, corporate debt and convertible securities. The important distinction in long-term financing is that between debt and equity, such as retained earning and stocks. In recent years, the demarcation line between debt and equity has become increasingly less distinct by the development of hybrid forms of finance such as warrants and convertibles.

Retained earnings are the profits remaining in the company after dividends are paid. Retained earnings are a dominant source of (equity) financing for an established business. Access to retained earnings depends on the profitability of companies and also the dividend polices they adopt. A possible disadvantage of financing with retained earnings is that, unless the company's earnings are very stable, they are an unreliable source of financing. Perhaps the most serious problem associated with retained earnings is that many companies treat them as essentially free capital. This gives such companies an added incentive to invest in investments of negative net present value (see Shapiro, 1990). The potential problem can be mitigated if the use of retained earnings is justified by a rigorous capital-budgeting analysis.

The array of instruments for raising debt finance is even greater than for equity finance. Apart from maturity, debt may be distinguished by its seniority. In general terms, seniority indicates preference in position over other lenders.

Since retained earnings are an important source of financing for an established business, it may be expected that to a large extent GHG abatement measures will be financed by retained earnings.

The earnings retained could originate from the operator's core business (eg, production of power or cement), or even from the sale of (surplus) emission permits generated in the past. In the latter case, emission credits or allowances could represent a source of financing. This point is quite important: emission credits or allowances *per se* are not a source of financing, but a possible source of income and, as is clearly shown by Figures 1 and 2, the financing is distinct from any income stream generated at a later stage by the investment to be financed. Thus, sources of financing and sources of income are not the same, as is frequently perceived by proponents of JI or CDM projects.

Private foreign sources for financing CDM projects

As regards financing of CDM projects, the availability of (private) foreign sources is frequently considered to be necessary for implementing GHG abatement projects. Generally, private foreign sources of financing include foreign direct investment (FDI), portfolio equity investment, commercial bank lending and portfolio debt lending. FDI is defined as an investment involving a long-term relationship and reflecting a lasting interest and control of a foreign direct investor or parent enterprise in an enterprise resident in an economy other than that of the foreign direct investor (see UNCTAD, 2000). There are three components in FDI:

❑ equity capital;
❑ reinvested earnings; and
❑ intracompany loans.

In the Kyoto community, a financing model that is based on foreign sources has been called "bilateral CDM". In contrast, in the "unilateral CDM" model, the operator or owner of a plant raises funds in the country where the GHG abatement project is realised. There has been a long and controversial debate in international CDM negotiations of whether the unilateral model should be allowed or not. The main argument advanced by proponents of the bilateral model was that, in some way or another, the bilateral model would better ensure the environmental integrity of CDM projects.

The Marrakech Accords, which govern the CDM, do not prevent operators in Non-Annex I countries from implementing CDM projects unilaterally. The decision not to exclude the unilateral CDM model is very important for the following reason. In general, the share of total investment of developing countries financed by foreign savings is relatively modest. The fact that in general a major part of capital formation in potential CDM host countries is financed through domestic sources rather than foreign sources such as FDI, implies that the largest share of CDM projects in most developing countries will be financed and implemented unilaterally. As a consequence, it would be very inefficient to require financing or co-financing of CDM projects through FDI or other foreign sources, because a significant abatement potential would not have been realised in the future.

FINANCING GHG ABATEMENT PROJECTS THROUGH PROJECT FINANCE TECHNIQUES

As previously stated, project finance should not be confused with the financing of projects in general. Rather, it is a highly specialised financing technique that may be defined by the following features (see Nevitt and Fabozzi, 2000; Pollio, 1998).

❏ Lending by a financial institution to a specific project that is legally and economically independent from the project sponsors (*off-balance-sheet financing* from the sponsors' perspective).
❏ The lenders expect to be repaid only from the cashflow generated by the particular self-liquidating projects (*cashflow-related lending*).
❏ The sole collateral for the loan is the assets and the revenues of such a project, except for very limited recourse to the equity owners or other parties interested in the project (*limited-recourse financing*). This implies that project lenders will have priority access to a project's cashflow. The shareholders may not receive much of a return on investment until the project debt is paid off.

Project finance is a very direct way of financing. There are a number of reasons to investigate project finance as an alternative for on-balance-sheet financing. It is especially popular with various developers undertaking a project, which is often the case in GHG projects. Furthermore, financiers may be interested and have confidence in only a particular project and not in all the companies developing the project. In particular, project finance reduces the risk that project developers spend money uneconomically (eg, on other projects). Also, not all companies, especially in developing countries, have easy access to capital markets, and project finance is then a good alternative. However, even very creditworthy companies often opt for project finance, for various practical reasons such as accounting treatment, restrictions on borrowing, tax benefits and the mitigation of political risk. Indeed, a GHG project may be planned for a country where the political situation does not warrant the exposure of foreign investment. In such a situation, it might be preferable to involve institutions such as the World Bank as project lenders to prevent political action against the project due to the likely need of the host country to keep lines of international credit open.

In order to judge the relevance of project financing techniques for GHG abatement projects, it is necessary to understand which economic activities are commonly financed through project financing. This is shown in Table 1.[6] As can be seen, project finance techniques are applied in a wide variety of different sectors.

In the context of project finance and GHG abatement projects, two main issues deserve particular attention. First, if the operator of an installation wants to abate GHG emissions by measures that

Table 1 Project finance sectors*

Agricultural	*Petrochemical/chemical plant*
Airport	Port
Bridge	Power
Commercial property	*Prison*
Gas distribution	*Processing plant*
Gas pipeline	*Pulp and paper*
Gas field exploration and development	*Rail-infrastructure*
Hospital	*Renewable fuel*
Hotel, resort, casino	Road
Industrial/commercial zone	School
Manufacturing	*Steel mill*
Mining	Telecommunication project
Oil refinery	Theme parks, recreational facilities
Oil pipeline	Tunnel
Oilfield exploration and development	*Urban railway, other transport infrastructure*
Other infrastructure project	*Waste*
Other downstream	*Water and sewerage*
Other upstream	

*A large number of sectors covered by project finance techniques are also relevant in the context of GHG emissions trading and the Kyoto Mechanisms. Those sectors are represented in Italics.

involve investment costs, could the GHG abatement investment be financed by means of project finance techniques? Second, how can one enhance project financing of common projects by means of emissions trading and the Kyoto Mechanisms? These two questions are quite similar, but take different perspectives. In both cases, the bankability of the project in question must be ensured.

In order to finance GHG abatement projects through project finance, they must meet certain bankability requirements. Bankability refers to the acceptability of a project's structure as the basis for project financing by banks. In other words, projects need to be creditworthy.

Creditworthiness is assessed by means of various ratios. The fundamental ratio is the debt service cover ratio (DSCR). This is defined as the cashflow in a given period divided by the debt service in that period.[7] Here, a basic difference between project finance and common corporate finance becomes evident: in the former, the creditworthiness is mainly assessed on the basis of the predicted cashflows of a project in comparison with the latter, where the balance sheet of the project sponsors serves as the main source of information to determine creditworthiness.

A basic requirement for bankability is that the DSCR should not fall below a certain threshold value at any time during the loan lifetime. Depending on the risks involved with the project, the critical DSCR is generally between 1.5 and 2.0 or even higher.

There are two basic strategies to enhance the DSCR: first, at given future cashflow, the project sponsor may inject more equity capital into the project, thus requiring less debt; second, at a given debt–equity ratio the project sponsors may try to increase the future cashflow. Exactly this may be achieved by structuring the project in such a way that it earns marketable surplus emission allowances or emission credits. As a consequence, in addition to the cashflow associated with the primary project output such as heat, power, cement or steel, the project gets a second source of income and cashflow in the form of emission permits and this second source may facilitate a bank's project financing decision. Indeed, this has been the case with a number of JI projects in which the Dutch government or the World Bank is involved as buyer of a stream of generated emission credits. Obviously, the extent to which the sale of emission permits can increase the DSCR depends on the number of credits or allowances

Table 2 Possible impact of the Kyoto mechanisms on the internal rate of return (IRR) of different projects

Country	Project type	IRR without emissions trading (%)	IRR with emissions trading (%)	IRR increase (percentage points)	IRR increase (%)
Romania	District heating	10.5	11.4	0.9	9
Costa Rica	Wind	9.7	10.6	0.9	9
Jamaica	Wind	17.0	18.0	1.0	6
Morocco	Wind	12.7	14.0	1.3	10
Chile	Hydro	9.2	10.4	1.2	13
Costa Rica	Hydro	7.1	9.7	2.6	37
Guyana	Bagasse	7.2	7.7	0.5	7
Nicaragua	Bagasse	14.6	18.2	3.6	25
Brazil	Biomass	8.3	13.5	5.2	63
Latvia	Methane	11.4	18.8	7.4	65
India	Methane	13.8	18.7	4.9	36

Assumption: Permit price at US$3 per tonne of CO_2e.
Source: World Bank, July 2001

to be sold, and on respective prices. As regards quantities, they will depend on the type of project and the country in which the project is going to be realised. There are no public figures available on the possible quantitative impact of emissions trading and the Kyoto Mechanisms on the DSCR, although the World Bank has explored the possible impact of the project-based Kyoto Mechanisms on the profitability of investments, which to some extent, is related to the DSCR (see Table 2).[8]

Banks try to limit their downside risk associated with any loan. For this reason, they will be willing to lend against future cashflows associated with the sale of emission permits only if these are not too risky. As a consequence, GHG abatement projects should be structured in such a way that downside risks are limited. That means in particular that the project company should enter into a long-term emission permit purchasing agreement with a creditworthy counterpart. Since future prices of emission permits are too uncertain, probably no bank would be willing to lend against the cashflow associated with emission permits to be sold on the spot market.

Project finance is a promising instrument to finance large-scale GHG abatement projects if project developers and sponsors succeed in allocating risks to those parties that have a comparative advantage in dealing with them. In addition, project sponsors need to persuade loan arrangers to take into account the cashflow implications of emissions trading or the Kyoto Mechanisms. This might not be an easy task since most banks will not have the required expertise related to emissions trading and the Kyoto Mechanisms, although a couple of European banks active in the field of project finance have started to explore the impact of emissions trading and the Kyoto Mechanisms on their project finance activities. By considering the potentially positive impact of emissions trading and the Kyoto Mechanisms on their project finance activities, lenders may maintain or even increase their competitive advantage, either by providing financial advice or by offering more attractive financing conditions. In any case, lenders should take into consideration any possible risks that may arise from the implementation of GHG emissions trading systems.

CONCLUSIONS

Arranging financing for GHG abatement activities is one of the major challenges for successful participation in GHG markets, in particular as regards CDM projects. A wide variety of different financing options are available, ranging from retained earnings to debt financing through bond and commercial bank loans. For established companies, internal financing from retained earnings is typically the most important source. In developing countries, the dominant sources of external (debt) financing are commercial bank loans as a consequence of less developed capital markets.

Emission credits or allowances *per se* are not a source of financing, but a possible source of income generated at a later stage by the investment in GHG abatement measures, although the earnings from the sale of emission permits in the past could be used to finance future GHG abatement measures.

As regards external debt financing, it is important to distinguish between on-balance-sheet financing and off-balance-sheet financing or project finance. This distinction is particularly relevant in the context of large-scale projects because only these projects could be financed both on-balance-sheet and off-balance-sheet.

In the case of on-balance-sheet finance, the creditworthiness of the borrower is typically judged on the basis of their balance sheet and other financial statements. As a consequence, it does not matter whether the borrower uses the funds for financing a project that is or is not expected to earn marketable emission permits. What counts is the borrower's balance sheet. This is in contrast to project finance, where the lender scrutinises very closely the financial viability and expected cashflow of the project to be financed. Here, the future cashflow associated with the generation and sale of surplus emission permits might well affect the creditworthiness of the project.

This point is most important and should be clearly understood. It implies that, with on-balance-sheet finance, the raising of funds for a JI, CDM or other GHG abatement projects is basically independent from the question of whether the project earns marketable emission permits or not. Therefore, neither the project developer nor the lender needs to consider the emission permits in their financing analysis and arrangement (obviously, the project developer should consider the value of emission permits in the investment analysis).

This is in contrast to project financing, where the bankability and creditworthiness of a project is judged on the basis of the project's future cashflow. Since emissions trading and the Kyoto Mechanisms could have a significant impact on the project's overall cashflow, these instruments may affect the financing conditions if the cashflow associated with the sale of emission permits is sufficiently secure. In most cases, the existence of a long-term emission permit purchase agreement between the project company and a creditworthy buyer will be a most important prerequisite for making the emission permit cashflow bankable. If the emission permit cashflow is large enough and sufficiently secure, banks will be interested in creating competitive advantage by offering more attractive financing conditions that reflect an increased creditworthiness. In any eventuality, banks active in the field of project finance should examine the possible risks arising from the implementation of the EU emissions trading scheme.

---

1 Internal financing comes from internally generated cashflow. It is defined as net income plus depreciation minus dividends. External financing is net new debt and new shares of equity net of buybacks (Ross, Westerfield and Jaffe, 1999). To obtain external funds, a company issues claims against its income and assets. Liabilities are contractual claims; equities are ownership claims (Harris and Pringle, 1989).
2 Sometimes a distinction is made between short-term and long-term debt only.

3   The optimal capital structure of companies has been subject to extensive economic research. For a recent contribution to the literature, see Bolton and Freixas (2000).

4   Medium-term loans by banks are also called term loans.

5   A collateral is an asset pledged to ensure payment of a debt security or loan.

6   This classification follows the classification used in the leading project finance database ProjectWare.

7   The debt service corresponds to the interest payments and the agreed repayment of the principal.

8   Also see Table 1 in Chapter 5 for return enhancement of CDM projects per technology.

REFERENCES

Bolton, P., and X. Freixas, 2000, "Equity, Bonds, and Bank Debt: Capital Structure and Financial Market Equilibrium under Asymmetric Information", *Journal of Political Economy* **108(2)**, pp. 324–51.

Harris, R., and J. Pringle, 1989, *Introductory Corporate Finance* (Glenview, Illinois: Scott, Foresman and Company), pp. 613.

Nevitt, P. K., and F. Fabozzi, 2000, *Project Financing*, Sixth Edition (London: Euromoney Publications).

Pollio, G., 1998, "Project Finance and International Energy Development", *Energy Policy* **26(9)**, pp. 687–97.

Ross, S. A., R. Westerfield and J. Jaffe, 1999, *Corporate Finance*, Fifth Edition (New Jersey: Prentice-Hall).

Shapiro, A. C., 1990, *Modern Corporate Finance* (New York and London: Macmillan).

Shapiro, A. C., 1999, *Multinational Financial Management*, Sixth Edition (New Jersey: Prentice-Hall).

UNCTAD, 2000, *World Investment Report 2000: Cross-border Mergers and Acquisitions and Development* (New York and Geneva: United Nations Conference on Trade and Development), pp. 267.

UNIDO, 1997, *Industrial Development: Global Report 1997* (Vienna: United Nations Industrial Development Organisation).

8

JI and CDM Projects – Finance in Practice

Karen McClellan

Climate Investment Partnership

The Kyoto Protocol has three mechanisms that are intended to offer some flexibility for nations seeking to meet their targets: emissions trading, Joint Implementation (JI) and the Clean Development Mechanism (CDM). These so called "flexible mechanisms" were introduced in part due to successful experience with the market for SO_x and NO_x allowances, which was developed in the US in the 1980s.

CDM and JI are both *project-based* instruments and function by creating reduction credits for the project investor when carbon emissions are displaced. Together, the two schemes enable project developers to receive a so-called "green premium" in the form of Certified Emissions Reductions (CERs) for making a climate-friendly investment. These CERs can be used to meet an investor's Kyoto or voluntary targets or sold for cash.

The two mechanisms apply to different geographic regions and are governed by somewhat different rules. JI status is applied to projects located in economies in transition, while the CDM targets developing countries. As trading-based mechanisms, JI and CDM are considered critical tools for fostering technology transfer and foreign investment in climate change projects. High expectations exist in developing countries as to their long-term benefit. Despite initial resistance, the main proponents of the Kyoto Protocol now view JI/CDM as integral to the reduction of greenhouse gases (GHGs) as well as to the affordable achievement of national commitments.

What kinds of project will benefit from these mechanisms? First, in terms of technology, projects eligible for CDM/JI status include "clean energy" generation and/or GHG mitigation. Examples include renewable energy, district and industrial heating, energy efficiency, and distributed generation; chemical decomposition, waste management, such as landfill gas capture, sewage treatment and agricultural waste management; and intermediaries that bundle such projects. New CDM technologies include the abatement of HFC23, a gas that is 11,700 times as destructive as CO_2, and the reduction of nitrous oxide, which is associated fertilizer production. Each of these investments must consistently reduce GHG emissions over a set period of time.

Perhaps most widely understood are those projects that promote "clean energy" generation, or renewable energy. Most of the world's potential for renewable energy now lies in the developing world, just as their economies have a huge need for new sources of power. Table 1 shows the existing installed base of renewable energy, indicating a large potential for new investment.

Burgeoning demand for energy in the developing world is the major driver of new investment in renewables. The US Energy Information Administration's recent long-term forecast to 2025 predicts the strongest growth in energy use from developing countries, especially China and India. Energy use in developing countries is forecasted to soar by 91% over the next two decades, while rising 33% in industrialised nations.

Table 1 Renewable energy in the developing world, installed capacity as of 2000 (MW)

Technology	World – all countries	Developing countries
Small hydro	43,000	25,000
Biomass	32,000	17,000
Wind power	18,000	1,700
Geothermal	8,500	3,900
Solar thermal	350	0
Solar PV (grid)	250	0
Total renewable power capacity	102,000	48,000
Large hydro	680,000	260,000
Total world electric power capacity	**3,400,000**	**1,500,000**

Source: Martinot *et al* (2002)

One country that has made a large commitment to renewables is China. The rapid ascent of China's economy has occurred despite the outdated and chronically failing power grid and production system. Even with the forecast 2004 expenditure of 200 billion yuan, or US$24.2 billion, to build traditional power plants, the widening gap between consumption and production means that China will become increasingly dependent on imports.

Partly as a result of this predicted energy shortage, investment in renewable energy is on the rise. China has a currently installed base of 19 GW, but estimates for commercially exploitable renewable resources approach 400 GW, with wind energy the largest expected growth area. By 2005, total renewables are expected to be around 26 GW, rising to over 30 GW by 2010. India and countries in Latin America are also actively promoting renewable energy.

Thus, while the Kyoto Protocol is not yet in force, there is sufficient impetus for investments in climate-friendly projects to make the flexible mechanisms viable if they are recognised by regional schemes. Through its proposed linking directive, the European Commission's European Trading System accepted JI and CDM based emission reductions as a means for its member states to access cheaper sources of carbon than what will be available through its own trading regime. By some estimates, the CDM will have to deliver 55 million tonnes of carbon per year between 2005 and 2007 to meet shortfalls in the European market.[1]

CDM: THE OPPORTUNITY

Theoretically, at least, the CDM market represents a significant investment opportunity. The flexible mechanism is designed to positively affect the underlying economics of a clean-energy project. This is because carbon finance is designed to make projects easier to finance. With carbon trading, an extra cash flow (in addition to that which is normally generated from project operations) is created, in proportion to the tonnes of CO_2 or equivalent that is avoided through the project. The extra cash generated from selling CERs is a "free" source of revenue, which can be used to secure debt or provide extra dividends to equity investors. In project finance, where the financial parties have no recourse to the balance sheet of a sponsoring corporation, cash flow is king, and the potential for carbon credits to improve creditworthiness and returns is an

Table 2

Technology	Extra expected return at US\$4/tCO$_2$e
Hydro, wind, geothermal	0.5–2.5%
Crop/forest residues	3–7%
Municipal solid waste	5–15%+

Source: Prototype Carbon Fund, 2003

exciting development. The size of this "green premium" is linked to the type of technology used, as well as to the underlying fuel mix of the economy in which the project is based. According to the experience of the World Bank's Prototype Carbon Fund (PCF), the impact of reduced carbon emissions at US\$4/tonne of carbon dioxide equivalent (tCO$_2$e) on project returns can be summarised in Table 2.

Not only can a carbon-derived cash stream boost internal rates of return, but it also diversifies and reduces project risk. When properly organised and when fulfilling the external validation and verification requirements, credits awarded in the form of CERs can be used to "buy down" the project risk, secure debt, mitigate currency risk or improve returns to investors.

An example of this is given in Figure 1 where carbon cashflow is used to secure a subordinated loan. SPV is a special purpose vehicle, ERs are emission reductions, ERPA is an Emission Reduction Purchase Agreement, and the buyer of the emission reductions in this example is the World Bank.

Under such a structure, the project developer is able to rely on a second source of project cashflow from its CERs. The project developer concludes an ERPA with the purchaser of the emission reductions. Such an agreement has important features that minimise many elements of country risk (including currency transfer and convertibility risk). Features of an ERPA include:

❏ it can provide a reliable source of cashflows at a fixed purchase price, denominated in US\$ or euros;
❏ it is sourced from the US or Europe;
❏ it is backed by investment grade purchasers (in this case, AAA-rated);

Figure 1

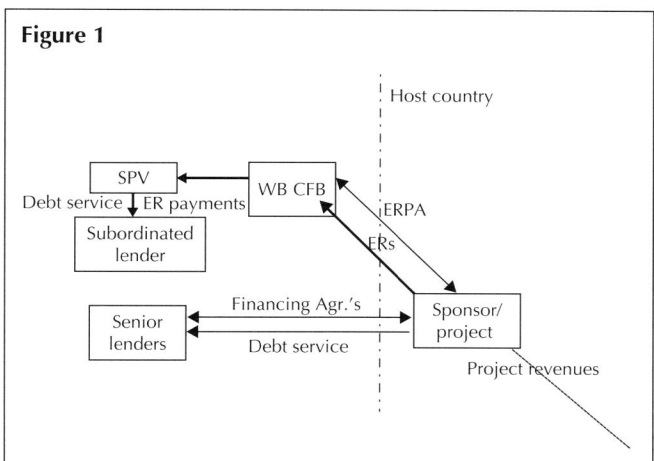

❑ it is endorsed by the host country in a letter between the host country and the purchaser; and

❑ it is assignable to creditors, so revenues may be placed in escrow for debt repayment.

As a result, carbon finance, when properly structured, has the potential to breathe new life into emerging market clean energy projects.

Due to these incentives, up until recently, many observers assumed that CDM and JI projects would deliver sufficient tonnes of carbon to swamp the international market. Sadly, this rush of investment has not happened, and, as of early 2004, the potential of the flexible mechanisms remains largely unrealised. Despite their significant potential to help achieve Kyoto Protocol targets, the real-life development of CDM- and JI-driven investments has proved laborious and speculative at best. Most projects have been encumbered by a number of risks and obstacles, in addition to the commercial uncertainties of being small and therefore relatively expensive to develop.

POLICY-RELATED OBSTACLES

What accounts for this market failure? A key obstacle is the complexity of the Kyoto rules. Carbon projects are difficult and risky to develop, in part due to the complicated eligibility requirements.

These include meeting complex and often unclear monitoring, baseline and additionality requirements; fulfilling sustainability criteria; receiving permission from the host country; and, in the case of the CDM, getting the project approved by the CDM executive board. For the average project developer, these obstacles remain formidable.

First, the project must meet the requirements set out in the Kyoto Protocol, meaning that it reduces emissions beyond levels achieved through "business-as-usual". In general, three tests exist to evaluate whether a CDM project is "additional":

❑ Test 1: an alternative exists for the project that is more economically attractive.
❑ Test 2: without the sales of carbon credits the project is not economically viable.
❑ Test 3: several significant barriers exist.

A developer must show how their project meets one of these general criteria in order to prove its "additionality".

Second, the project must have a properly established baseline, which determines how much carbon is being reduced through the investment. This will depend on the fuel mix of the economy in which the project is proposed, and can follow a number of different calculation methodologies. Later, carbon reductions must be independently verified and monitored. The project developer will have to spend capital on all of these measurements.

A project will then have to get approval from the designated national authority (DNA) of the host government. The developer can get such approval only if such an authority exists, meaning that the country will have had to make basic infrastructure preparations for the CDM, such as establishing a registry, determining qualifying criteria for a CDM project and designating an authorising body, which might combine the operating responsibilities of more than one governmental ministry. In some cases, the DNA will simply require the developer to meet local and national laws; in others, it may require consultation with local stakeholders such as unions and NGOs.

Finally, the project and its methodology for reducing carbon emissions will have to be individually approved by the CDM Executive Board, which has yet to approve a single CDM project. The Board, in fact, has yet to approve some of the most widespread

PANEL 1 FINANCIAL ADDITIONALITY

The concept of "financial additionality" is often misunderstood, and has done much to cloud consensus on what constitutes project eligibility. There is a belief among members of the NGO community, for example, that if a project is profitable for the developer, it is not eligible for the CDM. For example, if a project has an IRR of 15% before carbon returns in a country where 15% is considered adequate compensation for risk, it might be argued that that project is not additional.

In reality, the perverse result of this argument is that only bad or unprofitable projects should be eligible to sell carbon reductions (such projects would have limited commercial potential and therefore no prospects for financing, let alone successful operation). Furthermore, the concept of financial additionality, as some interpret it, leaves out basic financial principles, for example that investors in risky markets will demand higher returns. Most fundamentally, there is no business-as-usual scenario in developing countries, as most clean energy projects are simply not getting funded. This means that the return on capital required by investors for small renewables projects in emerging markets is still higher than such projects can offer, or that other market failures exist – thus any investment is additional. Carbon finance and other tools are needed to get these projects off the ground. For the sake of moving forward, therefore, most observers have discounted financial "additionality" criteria as being beyond the intentions of the Protocol. Unfortunately, the issue still casts a shadow over CDM project development.

Environmental additionality, on the other hand, is an accepted criterion, and means that the project cannot benefit from carbon reductions, which were in any case required by local legislation.

renewable-energy technologies – such as wind power. It can be assumed that these hindrances will slowly disappear as policies become clear and the governing bodies gain confidence and begin to function more efficiently.

Methodologies that have been accepted to date are shown in Figure 2.

Until recently, JI projects were thought to have tremendous potential due to the need for investment in the outdated energy infrastructures of the former Soviet bloc countries, the so-called economies in transition. To the dismay of many project developers, however, the accession of several Eastern European countries to the EU poses a disincentive for JI. This is because the most advanced accession countries, including Poland, Hungary, the Baltics and the

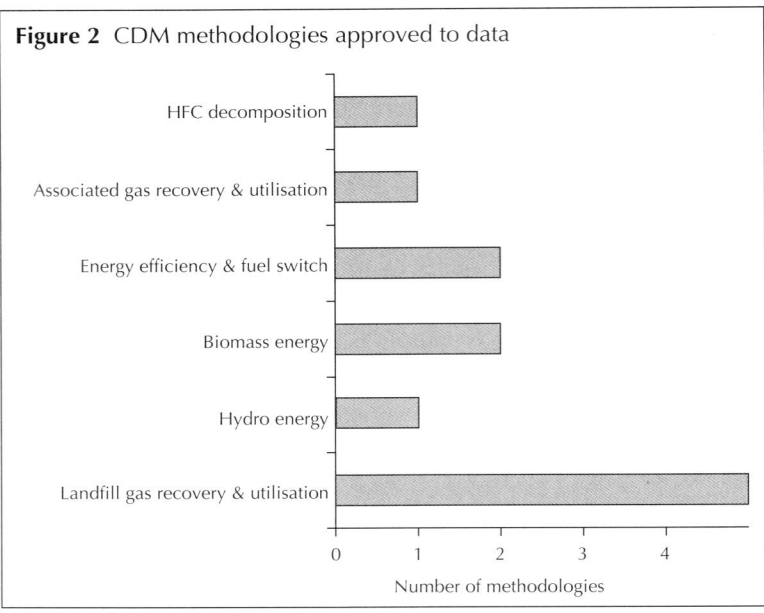

Figure 2 CDM methodologies approved to data

Czech Republic, where investors have put most of their cash, have until the end of 2004 to use their old, highly polluting baselines to calculate the net carbon reductions. After accession, even though the environmental benefit of many investments will be substantial, baselines will be redefined according to new EU emission standards. These new baselines, against which carbon emission levels are measured, will be considerably lower, leaving less room for JI credits.

In concrete terms, this means that a highly polluting coal-fired plant in Poland that switches to natural gas will, prior to EU accession, be entitled to get JI credits for the entire reduction of carbon emissions, amounting to many hundreds of thousands of tonnes of avoided carbon. Once monetised, this would mean additional project revenues of several million euros. Post-EU, the plant would get credits only for the difference between emission levels allowed under the EU and those achieved by switching fuel to natural gas, leading to a much smaller green premium.

As long as Russia's participation in the Kyoto Protocol remains undecided, JI projects will have to be sourced from relatively risky transition economies such as Romania, Bulgaria and the Ukraine, where significant uncertainty remains regarding payment history and regulatory regimes.

Although the market for JI projects is theoretically quite large, CDM projects have outstripped JI in terms of their potential and interest to investors. Eligibility criteria for CDM projects are also complex however, and we shall focus on these projects in the remainder of this chapter.

POLITICAL RISK

In addition to bureaucratic hurdles, such as those discussed above, there remains a myriad of political uncertainties related to the Kyoto Protocol. While certain national and regional carbon regulating regimes are developing (notably the European Emission Trading System, which covers 25 of the 38 Annex B countries with Kyoto targets), the Protocol – poster child of international climate change – still languishes as unratified, and ideological differences between the opponents and potential participants are large. The US almost certainly won't enter into the first commitment period, and its reluctance to ratify has weakened the resolve of its North American neighbour, Canada, and provided ammunition for opponents in Russia. The fate of the Protocol lies in the decision to be made in Moscow, where, although the treaty would bring highly needed infrastructure finance to Russia, the Kremlin continues to play a waiting game.

While some would argue that the ratification of the treaty is becoming less important, as its mechanisms and targets are being adopted by regional markets, most believe that an international system is still the most rapid, efficient and equitable way to enforce international action on climate change.

MARKET RISK

These circumstances have dampened the price available for CDM-based carbon credits, which have suffered from poor liquidity and an assigned value much below the actual cost of reducing carbon emissions in developed countries. For some time, the major buyers of carbon credits, the PCF and the Dutch government, have been offering US\$3–5 per tCO_2e. Currently, CERs are trading at US\$5 (€4.10) and EU allowances are at €7–9. Prices will remain variable and will continue to diverge until traders can be more certain how the EU trading system will allocate allowances. Many project developers and governments, notably the Chinese, have gone on record saying that the price discrepancy between CDM CERs and the projected value of carbon allowances under the EU trading system is too high. Until prices stabilise, project developers will not be able to accurately predict the actual cash amount of the CDM green premium and how it will affect the value of a potential project.

OBSTACLES TO FINANCING CARBON PROJECTS

Assuming that these policy and pricing obstacles to CDM can be overcome, the problem of finding investment for these projects remains the key obstacle to the widespread use of the trading mechanism. This is in fact the most difficult hurdle to overcome.

The main barrier to the more widespread use of CDM is the upfront financing necessary to get a clean energy project off the ground. Currently, despite the potential trading of carbon reductions from climate-friendly projects (such as project development, bridge or construction financing and long-term equity capital) continue to be, in most cases, difficult to attract.

In light of the various risks, both lenders and equity investors have reason to be timid. Large international lenders are loath to finance projects under a certain size, say, US$20 million. The risk assessment, due diligence and disbursement costs are too great to make them profitable. Moreover, these banks prefer to enter emerging markets with a co-financing partner such as a local bank, pushing up the required project size even further. Unless the project appears to have the potential to be widely replicated, large lenders have not been interested in the typical CDM project size and structure.

The perception of risk in the emerging markets has not diminished. There is strong concern with legal protection (contract enforceability), payment discipline, independence of the judiciary, rules governing exit and many other issues. In addition to these concerns, the additional security offered to a lender by a CDM carbon off-take agreement (an ERPA) is not yet taken seriously by the international financial community: banks are not yet ready to lend against the future cashflow associated with a carbon sales contract as they would against a power purchase agreement. For example, as the World Bank reports,

… current experience shows that banks generally tend to heavily dis-count carbon revenues under these ERPAs (relative to, for example, revenues from power purchase agreements), therefore limiting the capacity of greenfield clean-technology projects to use the value of the ERPA to access commercial loans. To illustrate, of more than 30 PCF projects for which there are agreed terms, only three have had access to commercial financing, and of these only one has reached financial closure.[2]

As a result, the capital that could be available though carbon finance and that is needed to kick-start new projects is frequently hard to come by unless the project developer is backed by a large equipment manufacturer, quasi-government funding or other sources of upfront cash.

Equity investors have similar concerns: emerging market risk, small deal size and the lack of a visible exit strategy to return their investment principal. Furthermore, there is a natural limit to the size of investment returns that can be expected from renewable energy, or indeed any utility. This return will not be larger just because the project is in India: as a utility competing with other forms of power generation, a wind farm in India can achieve the same return on investment as one in Italy. As fast-growing economies often offer an opportunity for much more lucrative returns than are found in the utility sector, a private equity investor will find it difficult to convince their investment committee of the merit of such an investment.

Until risk perceptions (and, indeed, real risks) change and mar-ket mechanisms are improved, CDM projects, integral to the effi-cient functioning of carbon regulatory regimes, are in real danger of not delivering the carbon reductions upon which the world's emitters have come to depend.

CARBON PROCUREMENT INITIATIVES

It is useful to review what initiatives have been taken by govern-ments and the international community to help stimulate the market for carbon purchases, a first step towards bridging the financing gap associated with the CDM. The best-known buyer of project-based carbon reductions is the World Bank's PCF, whose mission has been to catalyse the market for project-based GHG emission reductions by buying carbon emissions on behalf of governments and others.

Through its stakeholders, governments and corporations, the PCF has sought to link OECD buyers of emission reductions with projects in emerging markets, thus facilitating commercially viable, climate-friendly investment. While the PCF rarely provides upfront financing for the future delivery of carbon, and therefore still does not address the financing gap mentioned above, it is helping to monetise streams of carbon, making it more likely that the CDM projects will perform financially over time. At the time of writing (April 2004), the PCF has about US$400 million under management in five separate funds, and calculates a ~25% market share in project-based emission reductions.

The PCF buys mainly pre-Kyoto compliance reductions, ie, reductions that are expected to qualify under the Protocol's trading mechanisms. In 2003 the prices per tonne of carbon paid by the Bank ranged from US$2 (non-Kyoto-compliant) to between US$3 and US$6/tonne, depending on whether the buyer or seller takes the risk that the project will be successfully registered under the CDM or JI rules. For projects not intended for compliance with the Kyoto Protocol, a spectrum of ERs are traded, depending on the regulatory regime or voluntary scheme in which the reductions are to be used.

The PCF is also launching a credit-enhanced fund for small, development-related projects called the Community Development Carbon Fund, a carbon procurement fund designed to help address market failure in financing "small-scale" projects (as defined under the CDM). These projects face acute difficulties in finding financing due to their size and due to the fact that many proposed small-scale projects are intended to serve the rural poor in some of the most impoverished countries.

The Dutch government has also been an early pioneer in purchasing both CDM and JI allowances. Since 2000, the Dutch Senter programme has signed agreements of some €160 million with project developers around the world. Although these buyers have brought a degree of liquidity to the market, many purchase agreements remain nothing more than paper, as the underlying project has so far failed to get financed. To date, the PCF reports on its website that it has negotiated ERPAs for 13 projects, totalling nearly US$50 million, with negotiations under way for another 16, totalling US$112.5 million.

As the requirements – and mandatory nature – of the European Trading System rules became clear, several governments and private companies have launched carbon procurement funds, designed to buy allowances upon delivery. A sample of these is below.

❏ The Development Bank of Japan (DBJ) and the Japan Bank for International Cooperation (JBIC) plan to jointly establish a carbon fund in 2004. The fund is targeting a size of 10 billion yen (approximately €85 million), with the two governmental banks contributing 2 billion yen each. Japan is struggling to reach its Kyoto target, and both the Japanese government and companies have shown great interest in CDM projects as a way to cut GHG emissions.

❏ KfW, a German development agency, plans to launch a fund of €50 million using a combination of public and private resources for the purchase of carbon from CDM projects, and to improve its facility with the Kyoto mechanisms.

❏ The French bank CDC Ixis has pooled €30 million in French government money with potential private sources to launch a €100 million fund to buy and sell carbon. Fund managers plan to source the projects mainly from French multinational infrastructure developers, and invest mainly in large projects (10–12 total) in JI and CDM countries.

❏ A US$200 million "mutual fund" carbon pooling mechanism, Natsource Greenhouse Gas Credit Aggregation Pool, has been designed to standardise and spread carbon risk among its membership. These members are mainly public and private entities in Canada. The economies of scale are intended to ensure low-cost compliance for investors.

❏ The Austrian government has announced an expenditure of €350 million over 10 years on CERs, which can be used for compliance within the Kyoto Protocol and the European Emission Trading System.

Other carbon procurement funds and auctions are under way by various European governments, including Finland, Spain and Denmark. All of these buyers are seeking to acquire carbon offset through long-term forward contracts. None propose to pay project developers upfront, and this is very rare, even under the PCF. Insurance products could serve to combine and cross-collateralise a portfolio of projects under discussion. While these might serve to allow payment for some of the carbon in advance, they are still on the drawing board, as adequate mechanisms must still be found to account for project credit risk.

Thus we are left in a dilemma: CDM projects are needed to reduce carbon for the world as a whole, and are given special financial treatment through the Kyoto trading schemes. But due to the absence of upfront funding, as well as the lack of access to international capital markets and the sources of funds increasingly set aside for carbon finance, the onslaught of projects predicted by policy experts has failed to materialise. Instead, a result of this financing gap, many good CDM projects are going unfunded. Meanwhile, the window of opportunity for the CDM is closing: as most projects take one to three years to develop, the first commitment period of the Kyoto regime (2007) is fast approaching.

NEW SOLUTIONS TO THE CDM FINANCING GAP

A number of new instruments are emerging to address the lack of financing for CDM projects. First, with the advent of real regulatory regimes, carbon finance can pass on to the developer an upside in the value of their carbon as opposed to a low fixed price. With so much capital being amassed for the purchase of carbon into the European Emission Trading System, it is unlikely that the price differential between perceived marginal abatement costs in Europe and the historical CDM prices is sustainable. Indeed, we see CERs becoming a commodity that will increasingly be priced off an index.

One new development pointing to this trend is ICECAP, a financial instrument aimed at large European emitters (carbon buyers). This was launched by a team in London, backed by Investec Bank and a UK energy company, and is a floating-rate carbon fund that will be linked to an independent carbon index. Carbon emitters will be able to purchase "units" of pre-Kyoto-compliant reductions to meet obligations under the EU or another regime. The floating-rate structure allows developers to share in some of the upside expected to occur in the price for carbon. The pricing provides a "cap" and "floor" for units of carbon (other buyers have all been fixed-rate until now). The instrument will offer CERs priced off an index on a floating-rate basis. So, carbon sellers will share in the market upside (or downside) as delivery dates approach. While the ICECAP carbon units have not yet been priced, the fund managers' expectations are somewhere between US$4 and US$13/tonne. The resulting carbon index will trade close to other energy price indices as the market gains liquidity.

The point here is that there are commodity-type market mechanisms under development that have the potential to marshal a lot of capital for emission projects. The current closed-end procurement fund model as practised by the PCF and the Dutch government may soon become a thing of the past.

A second helping hand for CDM projects may come from organisations such as the newly formed Climate Investment Partnership (CIP). This not-for-profit association of public and private financial organisations has been established to help provide upfront financing for GHG and renewable-energy projects. CIP is different from other carbon purchasing funds in that it creates a network to finance the underlying project, not just purchase the carbon for delivery at a later date. The Partnership acts as an investment clearinghouse combining resources and expertise from public and private financial organisations. This helps to bring together suitable projects with investment resources, including equity, debt, grants, guarantees, insurance and specialist GHG expertise. The CDM partnership model appears in Figure 3.

The CIP is working with the PCF, the European Investment Bank and other project suppliers and financiers to get financing for suitable projects by sourcing, screening and assisting with the negotiation and structuring of these projects. The CIP is also developing various bundling structures, including equity funds, which will have risk mitigation properties, and is working with Swiss Re to develop insurance products on a portfolio basis. It is hoped that this initiative will improve the market for financing many worthy CDM projects.

A portfolio of sample CDM transactions from the CIP portfolio can be seen in Table 3, which yields some common features of CDM projects.

First, as is well known, methane-based emission reductions add the highest increase in returns, due to the relatively more

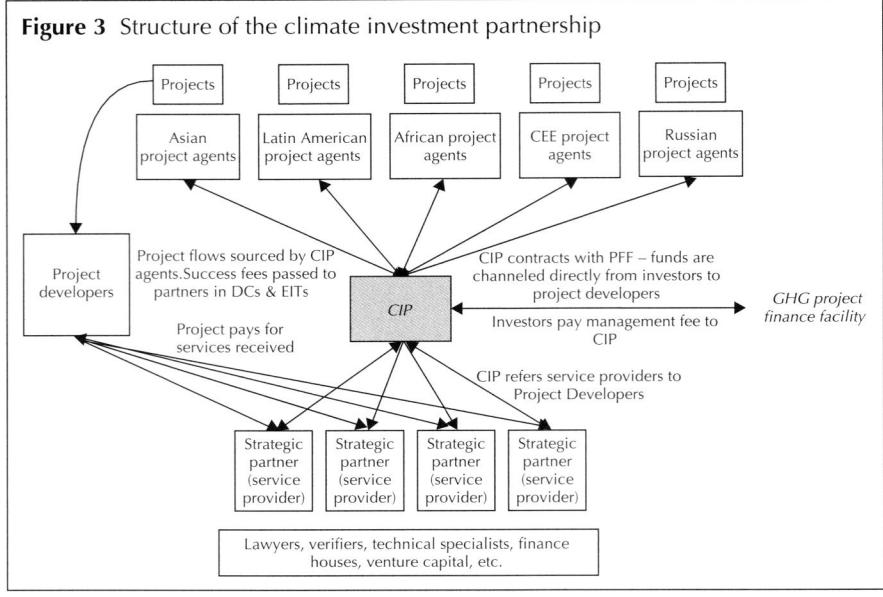

Figure 3 Structure of the climate investment partnership

destructive nature of that gas as opposed to carbon. Second, some project types, such as biomass, while small in terms of total cost, deliver a disproportionate amount of carbon, whereas others – such as wind technologies – require a high investment but produce relatively little in terms of carbon and must be highly viable on their own. Last, these projects are spread over a wide geographic area, allowing an investor to pursue diversification techniques such as spreading country risk while sticking with one or two technologies.

CONCLUSIONS

The CDM and, to a lesser extent, JI mechanisms were designed as a pioneering way to link international investment in clean energy projects with market demand for carbon reductions. As the critical tie between these two markets, they are ambitious: many obstacles and risks prevent the smooth flow of cash for carbon reductions to small project developers. For the time being, it can be said that it is much easier to finance a traditional fossil fuel plant than a CDM-based renewable-energy project. Yet the CDM/JI mechanisms may yet perform the market function

Table 3 Sample of CDM project portfolio

No of projects	Technology	Countries	Total investment (million US$)	Expected project internal rate of return	Expected carbon premium[1]	Internal rate of return including carbon	ERs until 2012 (mtCO$_2$e)
3	Biomass electricity	Dominican Republic, India	49	15%	4%	19%	1.2
2	Biomass heat	Romania, Russia	8	15%	5%	20%	0.5
1	Energy efficiency	Romania	8	16%	1%	16%	0.01
3	Hydro	India, Uganda	67	15%	3%	18%	1.1
2	Landfill gas	Brazil, Poland	63	16%	11%	27%	6.2
2	Wind	India	88	14%	2%	16%	1.6
13			283	15%	4.6%	20%	10.6

for which they were designed. Several government initiatives have helped to create liquidity in the carbon market; now more must be done to provide upfront financing for CDM projects themselves.

1   Dresdner Kleinwort Wasserstein equity research estimate, 2004.
2   See http://www.carbonfinance.org.

REFERENCES

Martinot, E., et al, 2002, "Renewable Energy Markets in Developing Countries", *Annual Review of Energy and the Environment,* **27**, pp. 309–48.

Renewable Energy Development Strategy and Market Potential in China LIU Hongpeng (WREC VI, 2000, pp. 90–6).

9

Trading Instruments and Risk Management

Steve Drummond

CO2e.com

The operator of an installation that emits greenhouse gases (GHGs) and that is caught up in an emissions trading scheme has two fundamental choices: "reduce" or "buy". The emitter may invest in new plant and equipment to reduce their emissions (or in some circumstances reduce production, at an economic cost), or they can buy compliance instruments from other emitters who have a surplus. If the "reduce" option is attractive, the emitter may even reduce emissions by more than necessary and become a seller. This chapter is concerned with the "buy" option.

An emitter who is buying emissions instruments in order to discharge a legal obligation must first ensure that what they buy will be accepted by the regulator for compliance with the emitter's obligations. This can be more difficult than may at first be expected, given that by far the greatest volumes of GHG transactions are carried out by companies in anticipation of national trading and compliance rules. They therefore need to make an educated judgement that what they are buying will be acceptable to a future regulator.

Fortunately, there is coherence between most emerging national and regional trading schemes. They are all informed by the Kyoto Protocol, and therefore all have at least some of the Kyoto-defined emissions trading instruments in common. The Kyoto Protocol specifies three instruments: the Assigned Amount Unit (AAU), the Certified Emission Reduction (CER) and the Emission Reduction Unit (ERU). Companies in the European Emissions Trading

Scheme (EU ETS) may use some CERs and ERUs for compliance, in addition to the fundamental instrument of the scheme, the European Allowance (EUA), which is a form of European AAU. Similarly, the emerging Canadian and Japanese trading schemes are expected to accept all three Kyoto instruments. Understanding these instruments is the first important step towards building a compliance strategy.

Once an emitter knows what they need, and when they need it, they will have to decide how to enter the market. There are a range of market intermediaries available to assist and provide channels to market, and there is an array of contract structures available to manage price, volume and delivery risk. In general, the emitter will have to pay for certainty, and so their use of instruments will reflect their appetite for risk. The same contract structures are of course available to the trader as well as the compliance buyer. The trader uses them to manage the same risks (price, volume and delivery), but with a different objective – that of speculating to maximise financial gain, rather than ensuring that sufficient compliance instruments are held at the end of the compliance period to discharge a legal obligation, and that this is achieved at minimum cost within a given corporate risk appetite.

This chapter presents the most common compliance instruments and discusses the principal traded markets (details of which also appear in other chapters). It introduces the standard contract structures available to the compliance buyer or trader, and discusses contractual solutions to some of the unique aspects of trading emissions. Lastly, it discusses the role of market intermediaries. The chapter uses examples to illustrate the concepts, and, where it does so, it takes the viewpoint of the compliance buyer. The same principles apply, however, to both sellers and traders.

TRADEABLE INSTRUMENTS

There are fundamentally two types of emissions instrument in use in international GHG markets:

❏ An *allowance* is a subdivision of a national or regional GHG emissions limit under a "cap-and-trade" scheme. An allowance represents the ability to emit one unit of GHG, typically one (metric) tonne of carbon dioxide equivalent (tCO_2e). The regulated entity (a country or a company) surrenders one allowance to the regulator for every unit of GHG emitted during a given compliance period.

❑ In some systems, additional emissions *credits* can be introduced into the system from sources not directly regulated by the scheme. Emission credits arise from projects that reduce emissions below "what they would otherwise have been" if the project had not occurred. An *emission reduction* represents the difference between actual emissions once the project is operational, and an agreed "business-as-usual" baseline. The reductions are independently verified. Emissions credits is created when emissions reductions are certified by an appropriate body.

In addition to the instruments listed in Panel 1, there are a number of local schemes that have issued, and are trading, GHG instruments. The instruments issued are not directly linked to the Kyoto legislation and are not currently fungible with other schemes, so these schemes exist largely in isolation from global trading activity. The three largest of such schemes, each of which has issued its own instrument, are the UK ETS, the New South Wales (NSW) state trading scheme in Australia, and the voluntary Chicago Climate Exchange (CCX) in the USA.

The UK ETS involves 6,000 companies trading UK allowances, and will run until 2007. The scheme started in 2002 and is part of the UK government's package of policies and measures to help meet its obligations under the Kyoto Protocol. The scheme mixes direct emitters and indirect emitters (large energy consumers), and companies trade against targets that are set both in terms of absolute and relative (ie, emissions per unit of output) emissions. The instrument, the UK Allowance, is either (in a small number of cases) issued by government, or, more usually, issued by a company outperforming its agreed emissions target and creating a surplus reduction. The UK Allowance is government-endorsed, and balancing actual emissions performance against target (by purchasing UK Allowances to make up any shortfall) enables the complying company to claim a rebate on payments of the Climate Change Levy, a UK energy tax.

Following the failure of an earlier voluntary system, the government of New South Wales introduced the mandatory NSW

PANEL 1 COMPLIANCE INSTRUMENTS

There are five principal greenhouse gas (GHG) instruments in global use. Each is denominated in units of one tonne of carbon dioxide equivalent (tCO_2e).

AAU An allowance representing a subdivision of the national cap of an Annex B (developed) country under the Kyoto Protocol. An AAU is the fundamental compliance instrument for governments under the Kyoto Protocol.

At the time of writing, an AAU has no compliance value for a corporation anywhere in the world because no government has made a firm commitment to allowing corporations to use them directly as compliance instruments. The Canadian government has been strongest in stating that AAUs should be compliance instruments for Canadian corporations in a national scheme to start in 2008, but details are still scarce. There are currently no plans for the use of AAUs within the European Emissions Trading Scheme (EU ETS).

EUA An allowance created by the European Commission for use as a compliance instrument in the EU ETS. Medium and large emitters in the energy, steel, cement, glass, ceramic, pulp and paper sectors in Europe are included in the EU ETS.

The exact legal nature of an EUA is not yet finalised, but for intergovernmental purposes it is an AAU. A final decision will be made within the EU registries regulation, due for completion in mid 2004.

From a corporate perspective, an EUA behaves like an AAU within the EU (eg, you cannot transfer it between national registries that are not in compliance with the terms of the Kyoto Protocol and the Marrakech Accord). An EUA may not exist anywhere other than a designated national registry, however, so it cannot be transferred outside the EU unless the European Commission establishes a formal link with the target country. At the time of writing, no such links have been established.

CER This is an emissions credit from a project in a Non-Annex B (developing) country certified under the Clean Development Mechanism (CDM) of the Kyoto Protocol. CERs may be issued on the basis of verified emission reductions (VERs) made from 2000 onwards.

ERU An emissions credit from a project in an Annex B (developed) country certified under the Joint Implementation (JI) rules of the Kyoto Protocol. ERUs may be issued on the basis of verified emission reductions made from 2008 onwards.

Track 1 JI A JI project carried out in a country that is fully in compliance with all its obligations under the Kyoto

Protocol and is therefore able to transfer Kyoto instruments to and from its national registry. Track 1 JI projects need no third-party confirmation of environmental additionality (this being left to the host government).[1]

Track 2 JI A JI project carried out in a country that is not in compliance with all its obligations under the Kyoto Protocol and is therefore unable to transfer Kyoto instruments to and from its national registry. Track 2 JI projects need endorsement by the supervisory committee, as stipulated in Article 6 of the Kyoto Protocol.

VER An emission reduction that has been verified by an independent third party but has not been certified for use within a trading scheme. VERs, which by definition have not been certified for use within a regulated emissions trading scheme, are used for voluntary action such as the voluntary offsetting of corporate emissions. The voluntary purchase of VERs by companies who wish to offset corporate emissions, emissions associated with the production of a given product or emissions associated with travel is starting to thrive, and there are many offset schemes promoted by specialist businesses and by NGOs.

GHG Abatement Scheme on 1 January 2003. Under the scheme, NSW electricity retailers and certain other parties must meet mandatory targets for reducing the emission of GHGs from the production of the electricity they supply or use. Participants may pay a penalty, or purchase credits, created by undertaking energy efficiency, forestry or other emissions-reducing activities in NSW. Credits created under the scheme are called NSW Greenhouse Abatement Certificates (NGACs). The NGAC may extend its influence to other Australian states, as a number of them are studying the scheme. It may equally have a short life, however, if changing federal government policies were to result in the ratification by Australia of the Kyoto Protocol.

The USA, where there is currently no federal- or state-endorsed traded instrument (though there are a number of state-based schemes in the making), has seen the development of the voluntary, intra-company CCX. The CCX is a members-only organisation that has brought together companies and public-sector organisations that reside in the USA, Canada and Mexico to voluntarily assume emissions caps and to trade allowances representing a subdivision of the collective cap. The traded instrument is called a CCX Carbon Financial Instrument and represents one tonne of CO_2. The CCX also includes credits from certain projects.

MARKETS

The instruments that will be of primary interest to a regulated emitter are those that can be used to comply with local obligations. For example, if the operator of an installation included in the EU ETS, may comply during Phase 1 of the scheme (2005–7) by surrendering EUAs or CERs to the regulator, and from Phase 2 onwards by surrendering EUAs, CERs and ERUs for compliance. AAUs may not be used for compliance in the EU ETS, and so they will have no value to the emitter as compliance instruments, though they may be held, and traded for speculative or other purposes.

PANEL 2

At the time of writing (April 2004), principal global carbon flows were as follows:

❑ Speculative trading of Phase 1 EUAs in Europe, in anticipation of the start of the scheme on 1 January 2005.

❑ Small quantities of CERs being bought by European companies for use in the EU ETS.

❑ Larger volumes (millions) of CERs being bought by Canadian companies for use in an anticipated Canadian domestic emissions trading scheme. The Canadian government has announced that it will have a domestic trading scheme from around 2007 and has said that emitting companies will be allowed to use AAUs, ERUs and CERs for compliance. Much larger volumes of CERs are being bought by Japanese companies for use in an anticipated Japanese domestic emissions trading scheme. Plans in Japan are less far advanced than in Canada, and are subject to a review during 2004.

❑ Purchases of tens of millions of CERs and ERUs by governments and multilateral agencies, most famously the Dutch government and the World Bank Prototype Carbon Fund (PCF).

❑ Voluntary purchases of smaller volumes (millions) of VERs by US corporations for voluntary compliance purposes.

Before September 2003, the EUA market was largely characterised by an absence of sellers, and few trades. From April to September 2003 the market traded up from the €6–7 mark to a high of €12–13. Trades were conducted by a small group of European energy and power traders.

Two key factors subsequently emerged to pull the market back down. First, as individual member states began publishing their draft National Allocation Plans it became apparent that there would be very little scarcity in the market, most having chosen to issue sufficient allowances to almost completely cover the business-as-usual requirements of affected sectors. Second, the EU announced that it would allow the use of CERs for compliance in the EU ETS from 2005 onwards.[2] CERs have been priced at about US$5 for some time, and there are potentially material volumes available.

In response to the legislated link between the EU ETS and CERs, leading players in the emerging EU carbon market have begun to move to arbitrage the perceived price differential. Typically, buyers have sought to make forward purchases of CERs from 2005 to 2012, with annual quantities in the range of 50,000–150,000 tCO_2e. Prices have remained in the range of US$4–6. Projects involving landfill gas recovery and small-scale hydro have been favoured, although

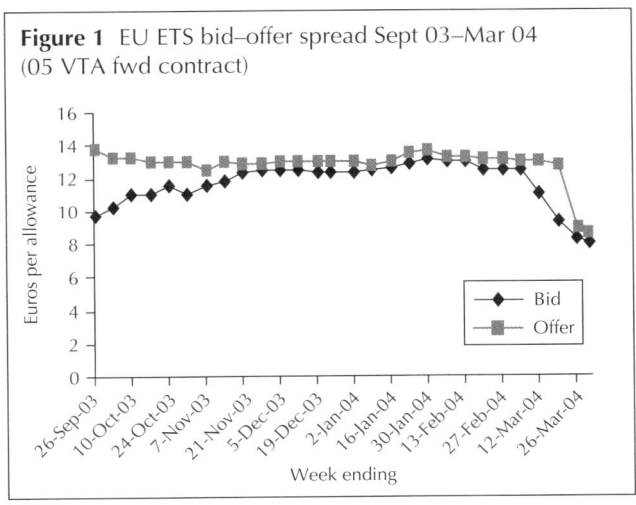

Figure 1 EU ETS bid–offer spread Sept 03–Mar 04 (05 VTA fwd contract)

larger-scale projects – in particular those connected with HFC abatement – have begun to attract attention. Overall, however, the mood remains one of caution. Although attracted by the underlying price advantage of CERs, to date only a limited number of European companies yet have the capacity to evaluate and manage (internally at least) the risks associated with contracting CERs for compliance purposes.

The EU ETS will also accept ERUs from 2008, though since this is further in the future, and the rules for issue of an ERU are less clear-cut than for a CER, there has been little activity in the nascent ERU market to date, other than some government purchasing activity.

While EU companies judge their compliance options against the financial risk of a €40/tCO$_2$ fine for noncompliance, Canadian businesses face no such regulatory restrictions until 2008. Although the Canadian scheme is likely to place strong emphasis on domestic project-based reductions, reductions achieved via the Kyoto mechanism will be eligible emission commodities, and in this sense the Canadian scheme will mirror the EU ETS. In response, leading Canadian businesses have switched from purchasing VERs to CERs in order to hedge their position.

CDM projects developed by public–private partnerships – for instance, the World Bank's PCF and government-sponsored programmes such as CERUPT – have perhaps been the most significant component in the development of the nascent private CDM market. The public mandate of these organisations has meant that they have been less subject to the conservative risk–reward dynamic that confines private-sector investment in emerging markets. This has allowed them to pursue a "learn-by-doing" approach to CDM project development against a background of considerable uncertainty, and in so doing generate a pool of local knowledge, contact and experience, upon which private-sector investors and developers have been able to capitalise. Examples of PCF purchases include the El Canada Small Hydro project in Guatemala, a run-of-river hydro plant displacing thermal power, delivering total project emission reductions of 3,887,520 tCO$_2$e; and the Pannongreen Pecs Heat and Power Project in Hungary, a coal-fired-to-biomass boiler conversion, delivering total project emission reductions of 2,645,500 tCO$_2$e. Most CERs are currently being sourced from Central and South America. There are a number of key reasons for this:

❑ previous (successful) experience of CDM project development – Latin American countries such as Chile have been at the vanguard of developments in project-based emission reductions;
❑ clear national policies/legal framework defining sustainable development;
❑ established bodies and government procedures for CDM project approval; and
❑ the underlying strength of the business environment.

Some supplies of CERs are starting to emerge from Asia. Between them Indonesia, India and China hold over 70% of the global opportunity for CDM project development, but until recently a lack of political commitment coupled with general concerns over investment climate had stalled progress. The government of India has now approved a range of CDM projects, including biomass, wind power and methane recovery. In China, the PCF is preparing to invest a total of US$21.25m in two projects: coal-bed methane and run-of-river hydro. In each of these countries considerable CDM opportunities are emerging: fuel switching, in particular from coal to gas; capture and/or use of methane, sulphur hexaflouride and other gases; and energy efficiency projects are among the favourites. In addition to the political, economic and country risks faced by conventional projects, the most significant risk associated with private investment in CDM in these regions has been an ongoing uncertainty over the application of CDM rules, as developed in the Marrakech Accords, and the ratification of the Protocol itself.

Most ERUs are being sourced from Central and Eastern Europe, but volumes are much smaller than for CERs. While CERs can be generated and used from 2000 onwards, ERUs do not come into existence until 2008. In addition, many of the Eastern European countries that had been expected to supply ERUs will now be covered under the EU ETS. Many of the businesses in these countries that could have undertaken JI projects will now be covered by the European scheme. Looking forward, pending ratification of the Protocol, the Russian Federation may well be the single source of ERUs.

In the southern hemisphere, sources of high-quality ERUs are starting to emerge from New Zealand. In December 2003 the

New Zealand government announced it had approved a total of 15 JI projects, including wind farms, hydroelectricity and industrial heat schemes.

AAUs and ERUs (being compliance instruments post-2008) and VERs (being voluntary) do not trade much at the present time. The vast majority of transactions are in CERs, with EUA activity growing fast.

CONTRACT STRUCTURES

Effective management of carbon emissions, from both a trading and a compliance prospective, is made possible through a variety of standard contract structures. As in existing commodity and financial markets, these structures allow for: trading in the underlying asset itself (spot); an obligation to buy or sell the asset at an agreed date in the future (forward); an option to buy or sell the asset at an agreed date in the future; or use of the underlying commodity as security against short term borrowing (repos).

In theory, there are a large number of contract structures that could potentially be used in carbon emissions markets. The instruments that are employed can be used in many different ways and with different motivations. The following section looks at the basic structures that have either been used or are anticipated to be used in the current carbon emissions markets, and discusses some of the basic motivations for using them.

Spot   A spot transaction has immediate delivery for immediate settlement. Spot transactions account for the vast majority of transactions in existing national schemes such as the UK ETS.

Since none of the international instruments really exist yet, there are no spot transactions in the international markets. Looking forward, once national registries exist in Europe (theoretically from September 2004), it will be possible to do spot transactions as soon as tradeable instruments are issued into registry accounts. This will be February 2005 for EUAs.

It is less clear when it will be possible to carry out spot transactions of CERs, as the CDM executive board still has to decide on how the CDM registry will operate (and, once the decision is made, it must be constructed). Transfers of

CERs between accounts in national registries are unlikely before 2008 because of national Kyoto compliance criteria set out in the Marrakech Accord (eg, a country has to have submitted its national emissions inventory to the UNFCCC and have it approved before it is able to transfer instruments in and out of its registry, something that is unlikely to happen before 2007). There is current discussion, however, seeking various ways of enabling buyers of CERs to take delivery before 2008. A legal formula to achieve this must be found if the EU ETS is to function as legislated.

Forward A forward transaction is a contractual commitment to transact in the future on terms agreed today. Forward transactions account for the vast majority of GHG transactions entered into during 2001–4. Examples of forward transactions are:

❏ the most commonly used terms for current transactions on the EU ETS, which provide for delivery in December 2005, with payment within five days of delivery; and

❏ CER transactions, where a buyer will typically pay on delivery for a stream of CERs to be delivered annually from now until December 2012.

Options A buyer of an option buys the right, but not the obligation, to either buy ("call") or sell ("put") credits or allowances at or before an agreed date in the future. The buyer of the option pays a "premium" now for this facility.

Call options have been relatively popular in the VER market, when buyers were speculating that a given VER may have compliance value in the future. Premiums have been set in the region of 15% of the exercise price of the option. However, the future that many past VER purchasers were anticipating is now getting close, and, as legislated schemes become more clearly defined, the purchase patterns are shifting towards firm purchases of known compliance instruments.

There has therefore been little option activity in either the CER or EUA markets to date. In the CER markets, sellers are looking for certainty that they will be able to sell their

Swaps   A swap is when two companies swap positions in different instruments. This may be in linked or unlinked markets. For example, there have been swaps of Danish allowances for UK allowances (the two schemes had no direct links at all).

Spreads   Two traders enter into back-to-back transactions to buy and sell linked instruments in order to exploit perceived differences in pricing. There has been some spread activity in EUAs, with traders trading pricing differences between 2005 and 2006 delivery EUAs.

Repos   Short-term secured borrowing, using tradable instruments as security. Companies in the EU ETS are expected to use repos backed by EUA allocations to reduce the cost of short-term borrowing/working capital.

CERs in order to finance the underlying projects. This will change as a secondary market starts to open up in CERs (ie, traders and banks on-selling CERs, rather than the project developer).

These contract structures provide an emitter or trader with a complete range of tools with which to manage a regulatory, voluntary, or indeed speculative "carbon" position. The extent to which they may choose to utilise them or indeed trade at all will depend largely on the current and/or future GHG trading environment in which they operate.

Let us consider an emitter operating under the EU ETS. Say the emitter wins a substantial contract and they anticipate that as a result their emissions will exceed their agreed target by 30,000 tonnes of CO_2 by the end of 2005. At some stage before the end of the reconciliation period (the end of April 2006), the emitter must therefore purchase an extra 30,000 EUAs. Depending on their view of EU ETS market pricing, the emitter could pursue a variety of trading strategies. If the emitter believes the market price for EUAs is likely to rise, they could respond to the requirement in a number of ways, as follows.

Spot purchase

The emitter makes an immediate purchase of the required number of EUAs, having decided that an equivalent purchase at any stage later is likely to cost more. Once purchased, the EUAs will be transferred into their account in the EU ETS electronic registry, and they can simply keep them there until they need to surrender them to the regulator at the end of the reconciliation period. The risk associated with this strategy is that by buying EUAs before they are actually needed the emitter has locked itself into a price (the price of EUAs may go down) and a volume (the emissions forecasts may exceed or fall below reality). It has also tied up working capital, which has an actual cost (interest payments) and an opportunity cost (scarce capital that could be used elsewhere in the business).

Forward purchase
The emitter may make a forward purchase of the required number of EUAs, agreeing to take delivery in the future, at some point prior to when they will be needed. No physical transfer takes place until the "delivery date", and hence the only upfront costs are transaction costs and there is no impact on working capital. The risk associated with this strategy is that (a) the contractual obligation to deliver or receive allowances at the agreed price will remain, regardless of how the spot price moves, and (b) if the market as a whole is confident of a price rise, the seller's forward offer will reflect this, and hence there may be little potential for "upside" gain for the buyer (and, by definition, if the market fails to make the expected gains by the agreed delivery date, the buyer will overpay for their allowances).

In addition, the emitter becomes exposed to the creditworthiness of the seller of the EUAs, who may fail to deliver as agreed and whose ability to make good or pay compensation for a breach of contract needs to be considered. Equally, the seller may question the emitter's credit status, since the seller wants to know that the emitter will be able to pay on the delivery date. If the emitter does not have a published credit rating, proving adequate creditworthiness takes time and may cost bank fees.

Option
The emitter may enter into a "call" option contract, giving them the right (but not the obligation) to buy the required number of EUAs at an agreed ("strike") price, at some point prior to the end of the reconciliation period. The emitter pays a fee for this right

(called the "premium") at the time of entering into the option contract. If the spot price moves higher than the agreed strike price, then the emitter will exercise their option and purchase the EUAs. If the spot price moves lower than the strike price, then the emitter will simply purchase on the spot market near the end of the reconciliation period.

The benefit of this structure is that it grants price certainty plus flexibility (if the expected emissions do not occur, the emitter does not need to exercise the option) and that it uses less working capital than a spot purchase. One pays for this flexibility, however. The same credit issues apply as for forward purchases.

Swap

The emitter may have another (non-EU ETS) installation that is expecting to have a surplus of UK Allowances in the UK ETS. If the emitter can find a counterparty that is expecting a surplus of EUAs and wants UK allowances, the two companies can do a swap. This is the same as if the emitter had sold UK allowances and bought EUAs, but no money has changed hands, which can reduce transaction costs. How many EUAs get swapped for each UK Allowance (or *vice versa*) depends on the market price of the instruments.

Spread

Spread activity is not primarily compliance driven, since there is no net transfer of EUAs. Entering into a spread is a speculation on the forward price of allowances (or credits). A basic spread is where one delivery date is bought, and another sold, within the same instrument. For example, the emitter may buy 2005-delivery EUAs and sell 2006-delivery EUAs. The reason for doing this would be that the emitter anticipates a profit from relative movements in price between delivery dates. This may happen when, owing to temporary supply-and-demand pressures (or, in a nascent market, different views of forward valuation), one delivery date trades at a premium to its own fair value.

Repo

Although the emitter may need 30,000 more EUAs before the end of the reconciliation period, they may already have 1,000,000 EUAs sitting in their registry account doing nothing, which they will not need until the end of the reconciliation period. By entering into a repo, the emitter can use the 1,000,000 EUAs as security on a short-term loan. Since it is secured, the loan will be at better than unsecured overdraft interest rates, and so the emitter's cost of doing business reduces.

RISK AND RISK MITIGATION

Entering into a commercial transaction incurs risk, and this is as true for buying and selling emissions instruments as it is for other goods and services. The counterparty may not pay, they may not deliver, or the transaction may fail for reasons that are no fault of either buyer or seller. These risks are managed by suitable contractual terms, and by taking precautions to understand, and possibly enhance, the counterparty's ability to perform. The principal transaction risks, and the usual approaches to mitigating them, will now be considered.

Standard contracts

Risk is dealt with in the contract. For liquidity to develop, risks need to be addressed in a standard contract and transactions need to be governed by a commonly accepted contract that has tight definitions and clear consequences if things do not go as planned.

A common approach enshrined in a standard contract is easier to achieve in a "commodity" market, where there are a minimum number of variables (beyond price, quantity, delivery) that are not common to all transactions. These conditions exist in the EU ETS, and the vast majority (if not all) of EUA transactions to date have used the International Emissions Trading Association (IETA) master trading agreement.[3] Other standard contracts are under preparation, one by the European Federation of Energy Traders (EFET), and one by the International Securities Dealers' Association (ISDA).

IETA was the first to develop a standard contract, and was motivated by a desire to help launch trading in the EU ETS. Different contracts are used because the legal departments of large trading organisations become wedded to an accepted form. For example, EFET is widely used by electricity companies for trading electricity, so the attractiveness to a large energy trader of understanding all the risks inherent in the IETA contract, when an EFET version is soon to be available, can be limited. Some energy traders have therefore simply preferred to wait until an EFET contract is available before starting to trade. Similarly, banks may prefer an ISDA version, as they use the ISDA forms in many other markets.

No such standard approach exists for CERs and other instruments, where bespoke contracts are currently the norm. This is primarily because of the large variation among the underlying projects, the greater diversity of legal jurisdiction and the generally lower credit rating of the seller (leading to different approaches to dealing with credit issues). The current state of play is that the large buyers have their own standards, and brokers also supply example contracts to clients. IETA has produced a guidance document, which describes all the pressing issues.

Credit

Credit risk is the risk that a party will not receive its expected outcome from a contract because the other party can't or won't pay. Sellers take credit risk if they transfer credits or allowances to the buyer before getting paid. Buyers take credit risk if they pay in advance of delivery, or if the seller fails to deliver and the buyer then has to replace the missing instruments from the market (at a possibly higher price).

Where both buyer and seller are investment-grade companies, or can demonstrate adequate credit, the contract will typically deal with payment and delivery clauses simply, with no constraints or additional structures imposed by credit issues. This is the circumstance anticipated in the IETA master trading agreement for EUAs. If adequate credit cannot be demonstrated – either because it does not exist or because credit checks are too expensive for what might be a small, one-off transaction – other approaches are taken.

For spot markets there are a number of simple solutions. In the UK ETS, for example, it has become common for a small buyer to electronically transfer the payment for the agreed transaction to the account of the investment-grade seller, whereupon the seller transfers the allowances to the buyer. This is a fine method if volumes (and hence value) are relatively small, and for many of these transactions the entire contract is a voice-recorded telephone agreement, followed up by a faxed confirmation showing price and volume. Some brokers offer simple clearing solutions, whereby the buyer transfers funds, and the seller transfers allowances to the broker, who forwards them to their rightful owner once both have been received.

For CERs and ERUs, the seller often has little credit. Two basic precautions are often employed to deal with this.

❑ The buyer pays cash on delivery of the CERs or ERUs.
❑ The buyer may insist that early flows of CERs or ERUs are placed into an escrow account, to be drawn down by the buyer in the event of nondelivery by the seller in later years. This creates a cost for the seller, since instead of being paid for early reductions, they are put to one side, and held available to be supplied to the buyer to replace missing CERs/ERUs if production dips in a later year. This provides the buyer with increased certainty of delivery, however, and hence provides the buyer with greater value.

Delivery

Delivery of EUAs should not be an issue. The EU member state registries do not exist yet, but they are under construction. When they exist, delivery will simply comprise an electronic transfer from the seller's account to the buyer's account.

Delivery of ERUs is in a sense not problematic, as an ERU should be able to be issued into corporate accounts in national registries (once they are in place), and so transfer should again be relatively simple. An AAU has the same characteristics.

This is not the case for CERs, however. The first CERs are expected to be issued by the CDM executive board in 2004, and are expected to be issued into a temporary CDM registry. The question is whether a buyer can hold an active account in the CDM registry or if the CERs may be transferred to the buyer's account in a national registry before 2008. There are a number of legal considerations surrounding this issue, and it is not yet resolved. Contracts need to deal with such ambiguities.

VERs are contractually delivered. Some voluntary registries exist, but these are not used for all transactions and, where used, provide visibility rather than security. Delivery is a matter of contractual transfer, with warranties provided to guard against double-selling.

Non-delivery

Nondelivery of an EUA is a default under the contract, with the seller being liable for the buyer's full replacement cost.

Typical terms for CER/ERU/VER non-delivery in the primary market (ie, direct from the project) require the seller to make good the shortfall with replacement CER/ERU/VERs of equivalent quality. Alternatively, some contracts share the price risk in the event of non-delivery by requiring the seller to pay monetary compensation at an agreed percentage of the actual replacement cost. So, for example, if the contract specified that the buyer pay cash on delivery of CERs, and the seller did not deliver, the buyer would have to go into the market and purchase replacement CERs. The contract may say that the seller is required to compensate the buyer for half of the difference between the agreed contract price and the actual market price. If the market price is greater than the contract price, therefore, the seller takes a penalty and the buyer has part-compensation for the additional cost of purchasing the required CERs.

Political risk

Political risk principally impacts Kyoto instruments, ie, AAUs, ERUs and CERs. The risk is that an instrument may not be able to be used for compliance, and therefore loses its value. This risk stems from two sets of legislation:

❏ for an AAU/ERU/CER to become a compliance instrument under the Kyoto Protocol, the Protocol must enter into force (ie, Russia or the USA must ratify it); or
❏ the CER or ERU must comply with a restricted list of technologies eligible for use within the EU ETS.[2]

Typical terms for commercial transactions cancel the contract if the CER cannot be used as a compliance instrument because the Kyoto Protocol has not entered into force, or the CER cannot be used within the EU ETS, by an agreed date (often 31 December 2006). Any monies paid are refunded upon contract cancellation. Political risk therefore rests with the seller. In a small number of commercial contracts political risk is transferred to the buyer. The usual mechanism is that the buyer pays for the VER at an agreed rate, and then pays a premium on the price when it becomes a valid compliance instrument (ie, a CER).

Most government purchase programmes, and the World Bank PCF, pay for the VER, with no further conditions. The buyer therefore takes the political risk. The rationale behind this approach is that project developers need certainty of revenue, in order to develop projects. Purchasing VERs widens the pool of project developers beyond established corporates that are financially able to speculate on the existence of a future carbon value.

The final set of risks with a CER have to do with approval by the CDM Executive Board. Typical contract terms simply cancel the contract and refund any monies paid, if the project has not received CDM Executive Board approval by an agreed date.

MARKET INTERMEDIARIES

Emitters can find and contract directly with suitable counterparties if they wish, but there are numbers of market intermediaries seeking to concentrate liquidity and provide services to ease the transaction process. There are three basic types of market intermediary that are of relevance to most emitters introducing brokers, aggregators and funds. These are explained further in Panel 3.

PANEL 3 INTRODUCING BROKERS

Brokers create liquidity by introducing buyer and seller. A broker will usually not take title to the instruments (though in some markets this is done so that buyer and seller may remain unknown to each other). Brokers are a good source of pricing and market information, and an essential resource for most market participants, especially those who are not in daily contact with the market.

If transacting through a broker, EUA transactions are typically agreed with the broker by recorded telephone conversation. The agreement is subject to the acceptability of the name of the counterparty (this is determined immediately if there is an established trading relationship between the two parties, or following credit checks if there is not). The broker will then email a confirmation note to both buyer and seller. Buyer and seller complete the transaction by signing a contract between them (or a confirmation sheet if master trading agreements are in place). The most commonly used contract is the IETA EU Allowances Emissions Trading Master Agreement.

The contracting process for CER, ERU, AAU and VER transactions is more complex. A good broker will have standard documentation available and will be actively involved in the negotiations. Typically a transaction occurs in two stages. The two parties will first agree a term sheet, which contains all the material commercial terms for the transaction. Once this is signed, the parties will draft full contracts, and carry out any necessary due diligence. The whole process usually takes a few months.

A broker should be a regulated entity under the relevant financial services authority (eg, the FSA in the UK), and will typically charge a fee upon the successful legal conclusion of the transaction.

Aggregators

An aggregator is typically a bank, large trader or energy management consultant, who provides a service to emitters to manage their allowance trading needs. The aggregator will typically become the counterparty to the transaction (buy or sell), and will aggregate orders from a number of emitters before taking the combined volume to market. This has advantages for the emitter, as an aggregator will be able to deal in odd volumes (eg, the EUA market tends to trade in minimum lots of 5,000), and may also provide some price certainty. The emitter will pay a premium over market price for this service.

Funds

There are a number of carbon "funds" in the marketplace. This is a slight misnomer, since they are in reality group purchase vehicles. These vehicles are also sometimes referred to as "buyer pools". Differences in nomenclature centre on who takes title, and the regulatory status of the manager.

If you invest in a fund, what you get really depends on the fund design, but essentially you pledge money, which is drawn down as required to purchase CERs, ERUs or VERs that are expected to become CERs or ERUs in due course. The purchased instruments are then distributed to the fund investors in proportion to their investment. Detailed issues such as whether the fund takes title to the instruments and who pursues the seller in the event of nondelivery differentiate fund offerings.

Participating in a fund outsources the requirement for an emitter to become expert in the purchase process for CERs and ERUs, and removes the requirement to differentiate between projects with different-quality attributes in the primary market. It also enables the fund participant to better establish portfolio benefits by receiving CERs and ERUs in smaller volumes from a greater number of projects than would be possible if purchasing direct in the primary market. Funds also have greater purchasing power.

The disadvantage of purchasing through funds is a loss of control over purchasing policy and cost. Also, to date, although these vehicles provide portfolio benefits, they tend not to be internally hedged against nondelivery from the underlying projects.

Brokers are the most visible and accessible section of the intermediary community. They are easily found on the Internet, know what is going on and will be happy to provide information and discuss the state of the market.

Whether or not an emitter uses a broker to transact depends on the extent to which it wants to take responsibility for its own trading strategy. If the broker is not used, then an appropriately regulated and creditworthy aggregator will be happy to provide a service whereby the aggregator thinks about when to enter the market, effectively outsourcing the management of the emitters' compliance price risk. The emitter will pay a premium for this.

Funds, or buyers' pools, offer a means of buying smaller volumes of CERs/ERUs, for emitters that are probably managing their own EUA position, but that either have small requirements for CERs/ERUs or do not want to become expert in the complex purchase process for these instruments in the primary markets.

CONCLUSIONS

The "reduce-or-buy" decision should be a pragmatic one, based on whether it is cheaper to reduce emissions through internal investment or through purchasing compliance instruments in the marketplace. The calculations underlying this decision should take into account the risks and corollary benefits of internal investment, and include a strategy for managing price risk if the "reduce" option is selected.

Transacting in carbon emissions instruments need not be complicated, and market intermediaries exist to help smooth the process of buying or selling contracts for emissions allowances or credits. It is vital that, before approaching the marketplace, an emitter has a good understanding of the cost of the alternative "reduce" options, a view as to what volume the emitter is seeking from the marketplace and when, a good understanding of their board's appetite for risk and a knowledge of the impact of different contract options on the corporate finances. As long as you know your corporate position, you will be dealing from a position of strength.

1 Environmental additionality is the concept that an emissions reduction must be additional to what would have otherwise occurred in the absence of the project. This concept is built into the CDM, and is not necessary for Track 1 JI, since a part of the host country's absolute emissions cap is being transferred. The host government therefore is deemed to have sufficient incentive to ensure that a reduction in emissions equivalent to the amount of ERUs being transferred has really taken place.

2 Companies may use CERs (from 2005) and ERUs (from 2008) for compliance in the EU ETS, subject to volume restrictions and subject to a ban on CERs and ERUs from land use, and use change and forestry until at least 2008, and a ban on the use of CERs and ERUs from nuclear and "large" hydro.

3 Available at http://www.ieta.org.

Section 3

Investment and Production Implications

Introduction

Cyriel de Jong; Kasper Walet

Erasmus University Rotterdam; Maycroft Consultancy Services

This section is about the question of "make" or "buy": whether to invest in internal emission reductions or buy allowances in the market. Investments in the right place at the right time will determine whether compliance costs are minimised and if the world is going to meet emission targets cost-effectively. Surprisingly, little has been written about this topic and we hope to make a valuable early contribution.

Investment analysis is firmly embedded in financial theory, which enables us to draw upon many useful financial references and theories. Nevertheless, the uncertainty brought about by tradable emission rights makes us believe that one particular theory should be employed: real options. Real options analysis is based upon the valuation and decision-making approaches employed in financial markets and has gained considerable acceptance in various market segments: after successful applications in the oil, gas and mining industries from the late 1980s onwards, the real options analysis tools are now being applied in energy markets, in the development of medical drugs and in the valuation of new business start-ups (Ronn, 2002).

Central to all these applications is the quantification of uncertainty and the flexibility to respond to this uncertainty in the most optimal way. This flexibility may include the option to postpone investments, switch to other projects, expand or abandon existing projects. In some ways, applications in the emissions market are not much different from applications in other markets. However, tailoring the analysis tools to the problems at hand will naturally improve their added value.

This section first provides a general investment framework for emission reduction projects (Chapter 10). Much has been written about the US SO_2 market, and, although many of its features are clearly different from those of the greenhouse gas markets, several useful investment lessons can be inferred from early trading experiences therein (Chapter 11). The last chapter takes the analysis to the most practical level with a hypothetical case study. The case study presents a particular emission reduction project and clarifies that incorporating flexibility is key to optimal decision making.

REFERENCES

Ronn, E. I. (ed), 2002, Real Options and Energy Management (London: Risk Books).

10

Emissions Trading and Investment Decisions

Cyriel de Jong; Kasper Walet

Erasmus University Rotterdam; Maycroft Consultancy Services

The Kyoto Protocol and the various trading schemes discussed in this book are all designed to reduce emissions. Ultimately, sustainable emission reductions will be achieved economically only with the right cost-effective investments in cleaner production technology, including energy savings. Therefore, emission costs deserve a central and strategic role in new investment decisions. Market trading will result in a verifiable market-wide price for reducing one unit of emissions. This common, though fluctuating, benchmark will become the yardstick by which investments are judged. It should therefore be incorporated into any investment decision that involves emissions, whether it concerns reductions or expansions.

This chapter uses financial investment theory in order to aid managers incorporate emission costs and thus help them make better investment decisions. We do this by focusing on compliance strategies and related investment policies. Step by step, it will be demonstrated how investment reduction choices are influenced by various compliance opportunities, such as internal reduction, banking, and spot and forward trading. Special consideration will be given to the presence of real options, which arise as a result of significant fluctuations in emission prices.

This chapter lays a theoretical foundation of investment decision making. The theory will be applied in the next two chapters in an analysis of the US SO_2 market and in a practical case study that focuses on the real option value of investments.

COMPLIANCE OPTIONS WITH EMISSION TRADING

Entities that are subject to an emission trade regime are free to decide in which way they will comply with their emission target. This renders the system its flexibility and its ability to channel investments to the most profitable or least costly projects. The various compliance options will be discussed below. First, we describe the choice between autonomous reduction and external trade. Next, we discuss the opportunity of banking – ie, collecting emission rights for future use – in relation to compliance decisions. Finally, we clarify the concept of real options, which assigns value to the flexibility of the various options and to the timing of making investments. It will become clear that investing in autonomous reduction capacity leads to a certain loss of flexibility, and investment decisions must include this loss.

Participants of the emission trade system are faced with the fundamental choice between autonomous reduction and external trade (buying and selling of emission rights). It's therefore useful to analyse how this decision is made in the case of a participant aiming to minimise costs.

An emission rights trade system gives an entity the right to discharge a certain maximum of pollutants, within a given time. The fact that rights can be traded leads to a realisation of emission reduction at a place where costs are lowest. A transaction between two random entities, A and B, will happen if A has reduction costs P_A that are lower than costs P_B of party B. In this case party A will (further) reduce its emissions and then sell the "released" rights to B at an agreed price P_m. Ignoring transaction costs, in order for a transaction to take place, this price P_m must be somewhere in between P_A and P_B: $P_A < P_m < P_B$. This way the transaction will guarantee an added value for both parties.

With a large number of buyers and sellers, the combined supply and demand of emission rights creates a market price P^*. Parties compare this price to their marginal reduction costs (abatement costs) and decide what kind of action should be taken: which amount of emission rights to buy or sell, and which level of emission reduction should be realised internally. Table 1 gives an overview of decision making at an individual entities' level. Decisions are made on the basis of the (expected) market price for emission rights. For now, price volatility is left out; later in this

Table 1 Decisions depending on individual circumstances

	Market price emission rights $P^* <$ marginal reduction costs P_u	Market price emission rights $P^* >$ marginal reduction costs P_u
Emission level $Q_u >$ emission target Q_t	**I** *Buy* emission rights	**II-A** *Autonomous reduction +* *Sell* emission rights (if $Q_t > Q^*$)
		II-B *Autonomous reduction +* *Buy* emission rights (if $Q_t < Q^*$)
Emission level $Q_u <$ emission target Q_t	**III** *Sell* emission rights	**IV** *Autonomous reduction +* *Sell* emission rights

chapter, the importance of volatility and its role in decision making will be demonstrated.

The different circumstances mentioned in Table 1 can be analysed further. We use the following notation:

P^* = Market price for emission rights.

P_u = Marginal reduction cost for the party concerned. This cost curve (abatement curve) is downward-sloping: at higher emission levels marginal reduction costs are lower than at lower emission levels. This is based on the assumption that costs of emission reduction increase when earlier reductions have been carried out.

Q_t = Emission target assigned at initial allocation.

Q_u = Current emission level.

Q^* = Optimal emission level. At this level marginal reduction costs P_u equals market price P^*.

Situation I (see Figure 1)

In this situation, the current emissions level Q_u is higher than target Q_t. Furthermore, marginal reduction costs P_u at emissions level Q_u are higher than the market price P^*. To achieve the emissions target, buying rights is recommended instead of internal emissions reduction. The resulting emissions level is Q_u as opposed to the optimum Q^*.

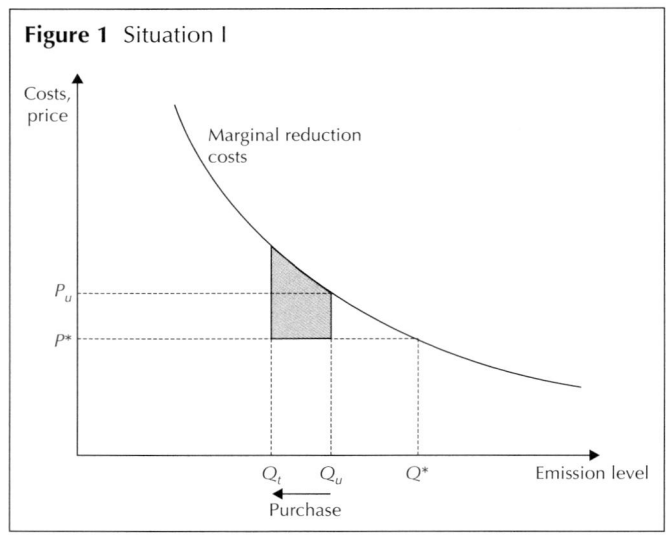

Figure 1 Situation I

This suboptimal result is based on the cost curve (abatement curve) and can be interpreted only one way: an increase in emissions does not yield additional returns. More specifically, when $P^* < P_u$ it could be possible that the entity chooses to increase emissions and therefore purchases more rights or sells fewer. In this case market price P^* must not be compared to marginal reduction costs P_u, but to marginal increase profits $P_{\hat{u}}$, which will typically not be the same. In order to keep a clear view, this option will be left out. Assuming that $P_{\hat{u}} < P_u$, this choice is justified.

Situation II-A (see Figure 2)
In this situation, marginal reduction costs P_u at the current emissions level are lower than the market price P^*. Given the fact that current level Q_u is higher than target Q_t, autonomous reduction will take place. Emissions will even be reduced below target level, because also at this target Q_t marginal reduction costs are still lower than the market price. Emissions will be reduced to Q^* and the emission rights are sold at market price.

Situation II-B (see Figure 3)
In this case the starting point is similar to Situation II-A: marginal reduction costs at current emissions level are lower than the market

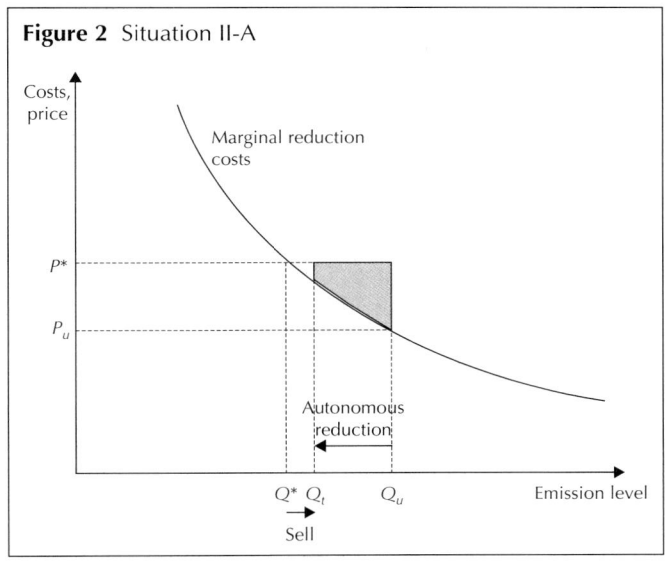

Figure 2 Situation II-A

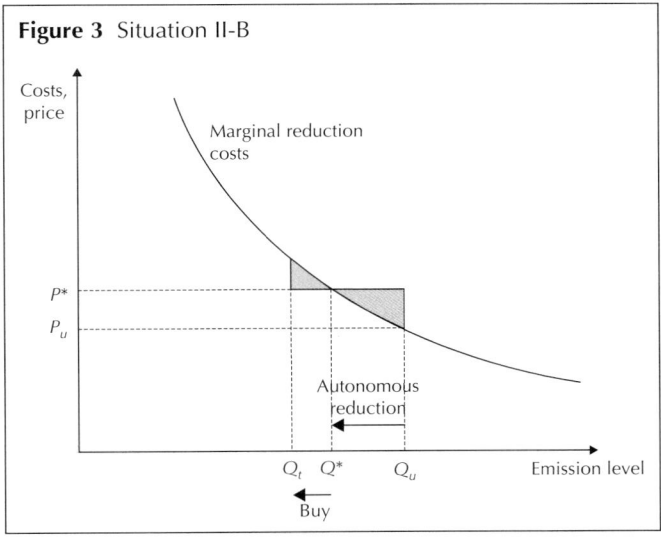

Figure 3 Situation II-B

price, and the current level is higher than the emission target. This also results in autonomous reduction, but here marginal reduction costs already reach market price level before the emission target is achieved. Emissions will be lowered to level Q^*. The resulting gap

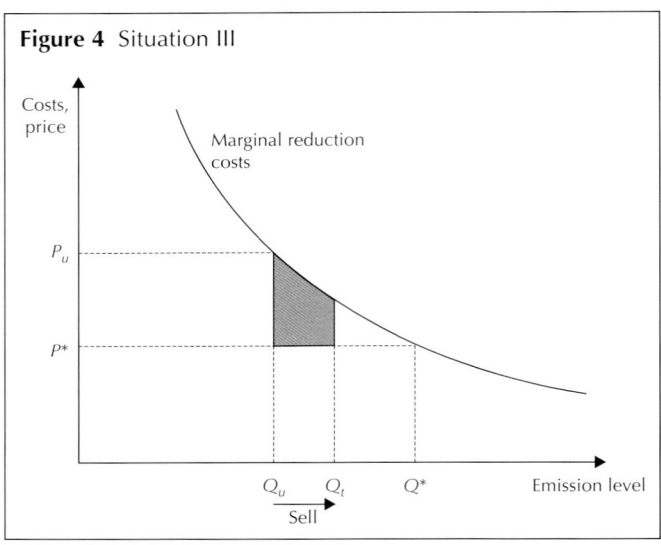

Figure 4 Situation III

between Q^* and Q_t will be closed through the purchase of emission rights in the market.

Situation III (see Figure 4)

Here the marginal reduction costs are higher than the market price. In addition to this, there is an emission rights surplus since the target level is higher than the current emissions level. The surplus emission rights can be sold on the market. Just as in Situation I, optimal emissions level Q^* is not reached in this case.

Situation IV (see Figure 5)

Now, the current emissions level is lower than the emissions target; excess emission rights can be sold at market price. Furthermore, because the market price is higher than marginal reduction costs at the current emissions level, reducing emissions until Q^* and selling the resulting rights will add value.

In short, it can be stated that in the above situations emissions level Q_u determines the starting point. At this level marginal reduction costs P_u are applicable. If $Q^* > Q_u$ emission will be maintained at level Q_u and the difference between Q_u and Q_t will either be purchased (Situation I) or sold (Situation III). If $Q^* < Q_u$ internal emission will be reduced to Q^* level. The difference between Q^* and Q_t

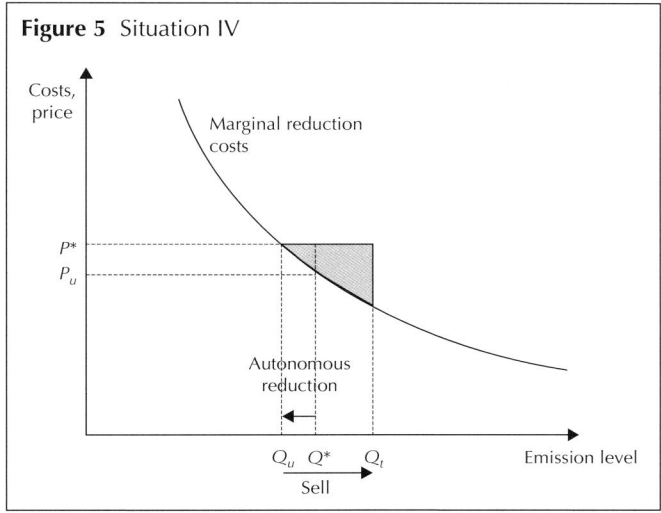

Figure 5 Situation IV

will then be purchased (Situation II-B) or sold (Situation II-A and IV) on the market.

STATIC VERSUS DYNAMIC EFFICIENCY

The examples described above show two different methods for narrowing the gap between actual emission level and emission target: autonomous reduction and external trade. In the examples, both methods are used at the same time, although in real life the timeframe for using both methods varies. After all, trading emission rights can be used as a short-term solution while autonomous reduction often requires long-term planning.[1]

The cost efficiency resulting from emission trade can be divided into *static efficiency* and *dynamic efficiency* (see Gagelmann and Hansjürgens, 2002). Static efficiency is attained when emission rights are redistributed at short notice via trade. Static efficiency is about a correction with regard to the *permitted emission level* of the participating entities. Dynamic efficiency can be achieved – or is aimed for – in the long term, when entities correct their *actual emission level*, for example in order to avoid having to buy emission rights or realising a surplus that can be sold. Static and dynamic efficiency are closely related: both methods complement each other when searching for an optimal (cost-minimising) strategy concerning the balance between actual and permitted emission levels.

When making an investment decision on reduction capacity, one needs to consider which part of the already existing static efficiency can be replaced by dynamic efficiency. The fundamental difference between these two plays a part: dynamic efficiency requires a once-only large investment, which will have a lasting effect on emission reduction. Each separate commitment period, a company reaches static efficiency by selling or buying rights. A comparison must be made between initial investment costs in dynamic efficiency and the net present value (NPV) of resulting extra benefits on the one hand, and avoided costs of static efficiency on the other.

NET PRESENT VALUE

Suppose that a company can make an investment I today, which yields emission reductions Q_t in years t ahead, and each year the reductions are *expected* to be worth the market price P_t. If the company has emissions below its allowance, then they can be sold; if the company has emissions above its allowance, they can be used to avoid the costs of buying emission rights. Therefore, each year the investment creates a future value of Q_t multiplied by P_t, which should be discounted at an appropriate risk-adjusted interest rate to obtain the present value. This risk-adjusted interest rate is preferably determined by the risk of the project under consideration, or alternatively by the cost of capital or financing costs for the whole company. Deducting the initial investment from the discounted expected revenues yields the NPV of the emission reduction. This is shown in the following calculation (where e equals the (approximate) number 2.71, used for continuous discounting):

$$\text{NPV} = \text{present value of revenues and costs avoided}$$
$$- \text{ initial investment}$$
$$= \sum_t \frac{Q_t \cdot P_t^*}{e^{r \cdot t}} - I \tag{1}$$

Standard investment theory (for example, Ross, Westerfield and Jaffe, 2002) tells us that each investment with a positive NPV should be carried out. If there are multiple competing projects to invest in, then the one with the highest NPV should be selected, or a combination of projects must be selected that produces the highest (positive) NPV. Standard investment theory is based upon this principle, rather than other popular principles such as "minimum payback period" or "maximum revenue", because the NPV represents the potential increase in total firm value.

A company can use the NPV criterion to achieve dynamic efficiency through (dis-)investments in *reduction* capacity. A change in reduction capacity can be part of an investment in *production* capacity, but this is not always necessarily the case. If it is, the initial investment does not only affect emission reduction; the present value of extra benefits and avoided costs of static efficiency should be integrated into the NPV calculation of the whole project.

This integral view on investment decisions, however, does not dismiss the comparison to be made between initial investment and resulting benefits and cost savings. In order to keep things clear, investments in reduction capacity will be regarded as autonomous, separate investment projects for the rest of this chapter. If revenues and costs of the other project components have a relation with the emission revenues, then this separate analysis will not work. This is, for example, the case in the power industry, where higher emission costs (so larger benefits of emission reductions) will go hand in hand with an increase in power prices. To complicate matters even further, fuel costs for power production also correlate with both power and emission prices. An investment in new power production should therefore take an integral view on all these project variables at the same time for a proper risk–return analysis. We discuss this further in Chapter 12.

BANKING

An important factor in an emission trade system is the possibility of banking to save up emission rights for future use. A participant who has surplus rights can – instead of selling them – keep these rights in an emission bank and use them later to comply with the target that applies at that time.

Figure 6 shows the course in time of the total emission target and the actual emission under a trade system, assuming participants are fully informed and make optimal decisions. The system is comprised of two phases and in the second phase (after time T) the emission target is more stringent than in the first phase (before

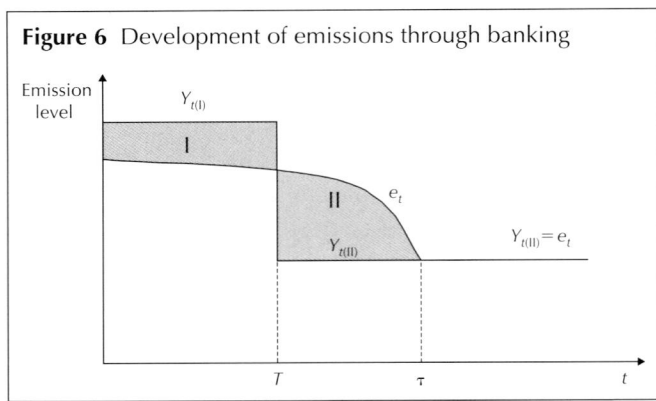

Figure 6 Development of emissions through banking

time T). In this situation banking activities can be divided into three separate terms:

1. $0 \leq t < T$: The first phase of the system is in force. Emission target $Y_{t(I)}$ is as yet relatively easy to achieve and this gives participants the opportunity to put the excess rights $(Y_{t(I)} - e_t)$ in the emission bank.
2. $T \leq t < \tau$: Start of the second phase, with more stringent emission targets. The emission bank set up earlier is now used to fulfil the emission surplus that has arisen.
3. $t \geq \tau$: At a certain moment τ in the second phase, the emission bank is emptied. From this moment onwards emission target $Y_{t(II)}$ and emission e_t are equal.

Figure 6 clearly shows the improved flexibility brought about by banking. At the transition point from first to second phase (T) the emission target is immediately sharpened, which would oblige companies to make a similar reduction of emissions without a banking option. Banking, on the other hand, gives the opportunity of gradually reducing emissions during a longer period until the second phase target. This also provides ecological benefits, because part of the reduction is achieved sooner. After all, by banking, the emission in Phase I is being reduced to below the emission target level (Field I); corresponding emission rights will be used in the second phase in order to make a gradual decrease of the emission level possible (Field II). The surfaces of I and II are equal; part of the emission reduction is transferred from Phase I to Phase II.

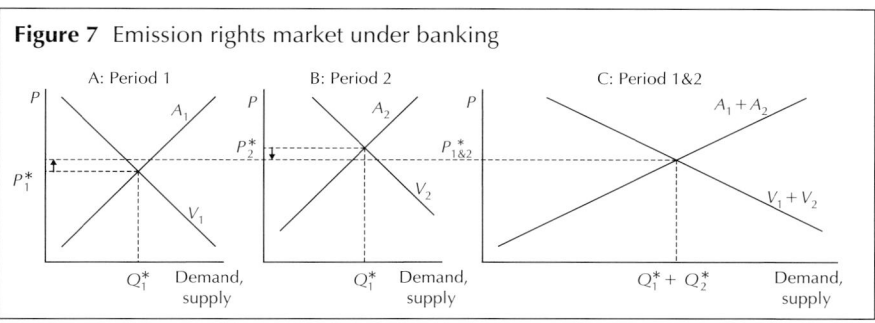

Figure 7 Emission rights market under banking

Banking can be an attractive option, for example when a lowering of the target or increase of emission rights prices is expected. Banking brings about more flexibility in the way entities cover their emission goals. More or less, it is another form of trade. Next to *spatial trading* (external trade with other participants), now there is the opportunity of *intertemporal trading* (the "transfer" of emission rights to one's own company in the future).[2]

Theoretical cost savings of both trade concepts are comparable. Spatial trading leads to a situation in which marginal reduction costs of all participants are similar: they are equal to the market price of emission rights. Trade activity will continue until this optimal situation is reached (see Tietenberg, 1996). Intertemporal trading causes a similar saving of costs; in an optimal situation the market price in different periods – discounted against the risk-free interest – will stay the same through banking (see Schennach, 1998). Figure 7 shows this dynamic market efficiency in diagrammatic form.[3]

Figure 7 shows a situation in two successive periods. In Period 1 the price of emission rights P_1 is lower than price P_2 in Period 2. As long as the price in Period 1 is still lower than in Period 2, there is an incentive for participants in Period 1 to save up emission rights in an emission bank. In this period the demand for rights V_1 increases and the supply A_1 declines, resulting in a higher price.

In Period 2 however, the demand for rights V_2 decreases and the supply A_2 increases, causing a lower price. Both periods can be seen as "communicating vessels" in which the collective demand $V_1 + V_2$ and collective supply $A_1 + A_2$ in both periods eventually give a balanced price $P_{1\&2}$. This shows that the price of emission rights in different periods – discounted at the appropriate interest rate – are equal in the resulting balanced situation. However, this result is based on the assumption that prices in Period 1 are below the prices in Period 2. If the reverse is true, then prices in the two periods will converge only if borrowing of emission rights is allowed: the higher costs in Period 1 will then be avoided and replaced by the market price in Period 2.

More generally, in a world of perfect markets where participants can make perfect forecasts on the future availability of and need for emission rights, there is a direct relation between prices in different periods. First, when both banking and borrowing of emission rights are allowed, then the prices in different periods will be equal, except for their time value. This results from the potential to bank when future prices are (expected to be) higher, and the possibility to borrow when future prices are (expected to be) lower.[4] When only banking is allowed (as is typically the case), then the result is somewhat less strong: the price in period t will not rise with more than the interest rate.[5]

This result of intertemporal price relations is formally demonstrated in Schennach (1998). He shows that the investment problem is an integral part of the optimisation problem through several periods in time (see Panel 1).[6]

PANEL 1 INTERTEMPORAL PRICE RELATION
On a general economic level, efficiency in a single period of time is attained when the emission m_t is at a level that ensures that (1) marginal costs for additional emission reduction $c'_t(m_t)$ equal the market price for emission rights P_t, and (2) the emission rights price is as low as possible. Efficiency in a multi-period framework is attained when marginal reduction costs in each period equal the market price for emission rights in that period and when the sum of all costs (discounted back to today at interest rate r) is minimised.

$$\min_{\{m_0, m_1, \ldots\}} \left\{ \sum_{t=0}^{\infty} c_t(m_t) \cdot e^{-rt} \right\}$$

With the possibility of banking, the actual emissions m must be at a level that ensures that the above-mentioned objective (overall cost

---

minimisation) is achieved. The emission levels cannot be chosen freely, however, but are subject to two logical banking constraints:

1. The emission bank account in period $t + 1$ (S_{t+1}) must equal the account in period t plus the allocated rights (Y_t) minus the emission m_t.
2. The bank account may not become negative (since borrowing is not allowed).

$$S_{t+1} = S_t + Y_t - m_t$$
$$S_{t+1} \geq 0$$

where
m_t = actual emission in period t;
$c'_t(m_t)$ = marginal costs for emission reduction in period t;
Y_t = total number of allocated rights in period t;
S_t = emission bank account in period t;
r = interest rate.

It can be shown (Schennach, 1998) that efficiency is attained when:

$$c'_{t+1}(m_{t+1}) = (c'_t(m_t) - \lambda_t) \cdot e^r$$

where
λ_t = Lagrange multiplier related to the constraint $S_{t+1} \geq 0$.

The above result states that the marginal costs of emission reduction in period $t + 1$ equal:

1. the marginal costs in period t (time value adjusted) when borrowing is not optimal ($S_{t+1} > 0$);
2. somewhat less than the marginal costs in period t (time value adjusted) when borrowing would have been optimal ($S_{t+1} = 0$ and thus $\lambda_t > 0$).

If the non-borrowing constraint is binding (2), then no emission rights will be transferred to the next period. This is a situation where market prices for emission rights increase with less than the interest rate or even decrease.

The assumption of perfect foresight about future market situations, on which the Schennach (1998) result is based, can be relaxed when we replace actual prices with expected (forward) prices, as in the case of a market for forward trading. The relation between forward prices (for emission rights in different forward periods) and spot prices is equal to the general forward price relation for storable commodities. This relation states that the forward price for delivery of the commodity in period t (F_t) equals the current spot price (S), valued forward to period t:

> Forward price relation for storable commodity:
> Forward price for delivery in period t
> $\quad$ = spot price valued forward to period t
> $$F_t = S \cdot e^{rt} \tag{2}$$

This result can be translated directly to assess the market forecasts to see whether they do accurately incorporate the banking option. For example, an expected increase from €10 in 2007 to €12 in 2008 is probably based on the assumption of stricter emission targets from 2008 onwards. However, the jump in price is not sustainable if banking is allowed, because companies will respond to this expected price increase by banking before 2008, which in turn will make prices converge. Forward arbitrageurs will drive this convergence process, as they do in all markets for storable commodities.

The possibility of banking makes an adjustment to the NPV calculation necessary, because mutations in the emission bank will alter yearly proceeds and costs:

> NPV including banking = present value of revenues and costs
> $\qquad\qquad\qquad$ avoided − initial investment
> $$= \sum_t \frac{(Q_t - \Delta S_t) \cdot P_t^*}{e^{r \cdot t}} - I \tag{3}$$

The NPV with banking, of course, is not lower than without banking. After all, banking creates extra flexibility to achieve the fixed emission target; a company can make use of this according to its own insights. Actually, the above calculation presents an optimisation problem: mutations in the emission bank through the years should be chosen in a way that maximises the total NPV.

REAL OPTIONS

Investment decisions always take place in a dynamic environment, where there is uncertainty about future market circumstances. The standard NPV method is a frequently utilised way of judging various investment projects. However, this method is based on some implicit assumptions that projects in practice do not always comply with. Especially the assumption that either an investment can be reversed free of charge, or – if the investment is final – the decision has a "now-or-never" character: if the decision not to invest has been made, the possibility of investing ends altogether, even in the coming periods (see Dixit & Pindyck, 1994).

In order to involve these shortcomings in the NPV method, an additional valuation of *real options* can be used. The surplus value of this approach lies in the fact that the degree of flexibility of projects is being valued. The presence of these options influences the value of an investment project and therefore the decisions that are to be made.

A few options deserve special attention. First is the *deferral option*, also called option to wait. A company that has an opportunity to invest in fact has an American call option.[7] The company has the right – not the obligation – to "buy" assets at any chosen time. If the company actually invests, in a way the option is claimed; the possibility is dismissed to postpone investment until more or better information is available. The resulting loss of option value – opportunity cost – needs to be incorporated in the decision, as part of the project costs.

A second option is the *abandonment option*. If a company has invested in a project, changing circumstances in time could cause the project – contrary to expectations – to make a loss. The possibility to disinvest at acceptable cost – in fact to exercise an (American) put option – increases flexibility and represents a certain value. With projects that actually have this kind of flexibility, this value needs to be part of the initial investment decision, by adding the value of the abandonment option to the NPV of the project.

Apart from the above-mentioned options, some other examples of real options can be given. They all provide flexibility in their own way and therefore represent value, particularly the *option to expand* (American call option) and the *option to switch* (combined put and call option).

Probably the two most important optionalities are those to defer and to abandon. Incorporating these two options, the NPV can be adjusted as follows:

NPV including banking and real options
= present value of revenues and costs avoided
+ abandonment option (AO)− deferral option (DO)
− initial investment

$$= \sum_t \frac{(Q_t - \Delta S_t) \cdot P_t^*}{e^{r \cdot t}} + \text{AO} - \text{DO} - I \qquad (4)$$

The project generates value – and thus should be executed – if the overall NPV is positive. The effect of incorporating real options is that projects are accepted that have a negative "standard" NPV, but that may be abandoned easily. Similarly, projects with positive "standard" NPV are not yet executed, because there is a significant option to defer (see Pike and Neale, 1999).

Real options have a significant role in the choice of strategy when it concerns achieving emission targets: an investment in autonomous reduction capacity involves both creating and losing options. The case described in Panel 2 may clarify this.

PANEL 2 CASE STUDY: INVESTMENT SELECTION WITH REAL OPTIONS

A company participates in an emissions trading scheme with an emissions target below its current level. For the time being the company fulfils its obligations through the purchase of emission rights. The company considers replacing the emission rights purchase plan with an investment in autonomous emission reduction. It analyses two potential projects, A and B.

Project A is characterised by a low initial investment, high operational costs and a reasonable emission reduction. Furthermore, Project A is highly flexible: disinvestments are relatively cheap because the machinery can easily be sold to other companies when emission rights trade at low prices.

Project B demands a higher initial investment, but requires lower operational costs. Furthermore, it achieves an emission reduction twice the size of Project A. However, Project B is not so flexible. The machinery is very user-specific, such that the investment should be treated as a sunk and irreversible cost: disinvestments will hardly ever be optimal, even at very low price levels.

Decision problem: the impact of real options

The company is faced with four opportunities: (i) investing in A, (ii) investing in B, (iii) investing in both A and B and (iv) not investing. If it decides not to invest today (iv), then the investment opportunity is not lost: investment may be postponed up to T periods ahead (T is the investment horizon). The investment horizon depends on the extent to which new technologies become available.

Both projects can be judged on the basis of expected market developments using the standard NPV method augmented with real options. The possibility to postpone the investment creates a deferral option that should be treated as an opportunity cost. In addition, Project A contains an abandonment option that increases its NPV.

In Chapter 12 we will formally analyse how real options can be valued. Here we just assign some hypothetical values to the different options, in a situation where the option values are decisive:

Table A Comparison of investment projects

	Standard NPV	Deferral option	Abandonment option	Actual NPV
Project A	−2	+2	+5	+1
Project B	+2	+4	−	−2

According to the standard NPV, investing in Project B would be optimal; investment in Project A on the other hand is not wise even if it were the only available project. The real option values radically change this situation. Due to its high and irreversible initial costs it is better not to start Project B yet, but to wait for market developments that make the investment more certain. Because of the relatively low initial investment, the option to defer (an opportunity cost!) is not so valuable for Project A. Moreover, this investment can sufficiently be recouped if markets move against it. So, Project A should be undertaken directly. Project B might be undertaken at a future period in time when market circumstances improve sufficiently.

CONCLUSIONS

When making production and consumption decisions, usually the negative external effects of emission are not taken into consideration; this is a form of market failure. Prevention of this market failure will eventually lead to a more efficient allocation, although the degree of efficiency is difficult to measure. An alternative is to aim for cost effectiveness: to be able to achieve the determined emission level against minimal costs. Theoretically, a system of emission rights trading is an excellent way to attain this cost effectiveness.

Under an emission trade regime, participants must decide how they are going to achieve their fixed emission target. Actually, companies need to take a *make-or-buy* decision: aim for autonomous reduction (make) or trade emission rights (buy). Investment decisions can be based on the NPV calculation of the various projects available. By successively adding the influence of banking and the value of real options, a more accurate NPV calculation is obtained, which serves as a guideline when making investment decisions.

In the next chapter, this augmented NPV concept (including banking and real options) will be used as a framework for judging investment in reduction capacity under the US Acid Rain Program, the SO_2 trade system in the US. Later, in Chapter 12, the real option methodology will be explained further. We will apply the methodology to a case study in which we calculate the NPV of a CO_2-reducing investment project. This will demonstrate the important role of real options within the decision making process.

1   Here it is assumed that autonomous reduction is durable. An *ad hoc* decision to temporarily lower production or to switch to another fuel could also bring autonomous reduction.
2   Theoretically, transfer from future emission rights to the present is possible. This opposite to banking, called borrowing, could present serious objections, particularly from an ecological point of view. In practice this method is not often used and will therefore not be discussed here.
3   It is implicitly assumed that spatial trading in the various periods has already fully taken place. So, marginal reduction costs of all participants and market price for emission rights are equal.
4   The explicit assumption "borrowing" may be relaxed when emission banks are sufficiently filled to meet future demand for emission rights.
5   The interest rate should be risk-adjusted to incorporate the price uncertainty about future emission rights.
6   This problem applies to all participating units together. Under the implicit assumption of complete information, optimal decisions of the individual units can be derived from this.
7   An American option can be claimed either on or before the expiry date, as opposed to European options, which can be claimed only on expiry date. (These terms do not indicate a geographic division of use of options.)

REFERENCES

Dixit, A. K., and R. S. Pindyck, 1994, *Investment Under Uncertainty* (Princeton, NJ: Princeton University Press).

Gagelmann, F., and B. Hansjürgens, 2002, "Climate Protection through Tradable Permits: the EU Proposal for a CO_2 Emissions Trading Programme in Europe", *European Environment*, **12**, pp. 185–202.

Pike, R., and B. Neale, 1999, *Corporate Finance and Investment – Decisions and Strategies* (Hertfordshire: Prentice Hall).

Ross, S. A., R. W. Westerfield, and J. Jaffe, 2001, *Corporate Finance* (New York: McGraw-Hill).

Schennach, S. M., 1998, "The Economics of Pollution Permit Banking in the Context of Title IV of the 1990 Clean Air Amendments", Working Paper no MIT-CEEPR 98-007, Cambridge, MA.

Tietenberg, T. H., 1996, *Environmental and Natural Resource Economics*, 4th edn (New York: HarperCollins College Publishers).

11

Compliance Strategies in the US Acid Rain Program

Cyriel de Jong; Kasper Walet

Erasmus University Rotterdam; Maycroft Consultancy Services

As discussed in the previous chapter, captive companies have several options available to help them achieve their emission goals. In particular, Chapter 10 discusses the fundamental difference between static and dynamic efficiency. In order to explore producers' behaviour it is useful to take a look at past experiences with the SO_2 trade system in the US, and also to analyse whether the system is comparable CO_2 trading systems. First, a short résumé of the SO_2 trade system will be given; then we discuss the observed investment behaviour under this system. Finally, we investigate the meaning of these experiences with regard to expected investment behaviour under any future CO_2 system.

CHARACTERISTICS OF THE SO_2 TRADE SYSTEM

Trading of SO_2 allowances in the US has been running since 1995, structured in two phases. Phase I began in 1995, limited to emissions from the largest, highest-emitting power-generating facilities. Phase II, which commenced in 2000, tightened the annual limits on the large plants, and set restrictions on smaller, cleaner plants and all new plants. As of 2002, the programme encompassed 3,208 electricity-generating units. Total emissions from the sources covered amounted to some 10.2 million tonnes in 2002 (almost 70% of nationwide emissions), a reduction by more than 7 million tonnes from 1980 levels. By 2010, the programme will lower the cap to 8.95 million tonnes of SO_2 emissions, a 50% reduction from 1980.

The emission trade system in the US is also known as the US Acid Rain Program, since its main goal is to reduce acid rain. The main cause of acid rain in the US is sulphur dioxide, SO_2. To deal with the SO_2 emission problem Title IV of the 1990 Clean Air Act Amendments was formulated. Policymakers developed the definitive US Acid Rain Program based on criteria mentioned in Title IV.

Gagelmann and Hansjürgens (2002) have distinguished five aspects that together determine the functioning of an emission trade system:

(i)   the range of the system;
(ii) determination of the total emission level;
(iii) primary allocation method of emission rights;
(iv) market forces; and
(v)   monitoring.

Below we explain each aspect and its function within the SO_2 trade system.

The SO_2 trade system has a "downstream" approach: the emitting entity is obliged to obtain sufficient emission rights. The alternative is an "upstream" system, which commits producers and importers of fuels to obtain emission rights, depending on the greenhouse gas emission that these fuels will eventually cause. Participation in the US Acid Rain Program is limited to electricity producers, who together are responsible for 70% of SO_2 emissions in the US in 1985. The programme is divided in two phases. In Phase I (1995–9), 263 large and most polluting units were obliged to participate. These so-called Table A units – they are mentioned in Table A of the statute – are responsible for 57% of SO_2 emission by electricity producers in 1985 (see Ellerman *et al*, 2000). In Phase II (from 2000) most remaining installations of producers were included in the programme.[1] Producers had an opt-in choice for Phase I: they could decide to let certain units participate in Phase I even though they are not mentioned in Table A. In the first three years of Phase I (1995–7), a total of 199 units made this opt-in choice, 138 of them participating in each of these three years.

With regard to the total emission level, the first choice that needs to be made is between a system with absolute allowance (cap-and-trade) and a system with a relative allowance, stipulating maximum emission levels *per production unit*. The US Acid Rain

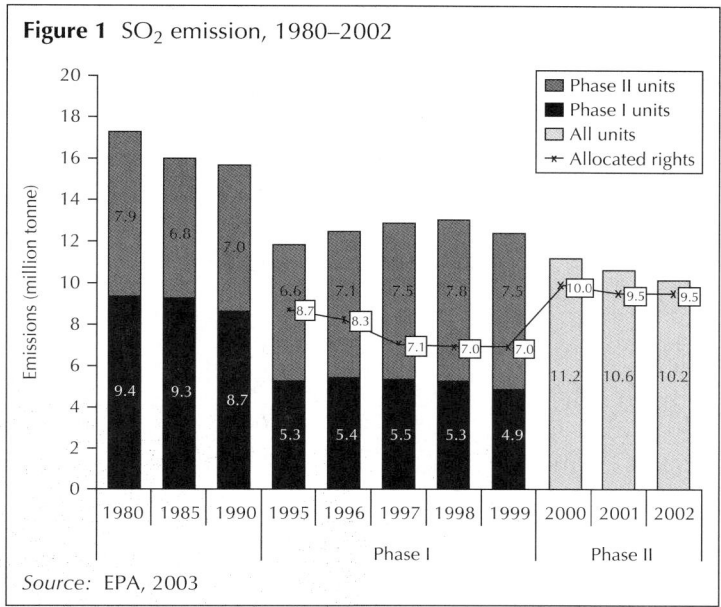

Figure 1 SO$_2$ emission, 1980–2002

Source: EPA, 2003

Program uses an absolute allowance system (cap-and-trade), which is being reviewed each year. The target is to reduce SO$_2$ emission by 50% in 2010 compared with the basis year, 1985, and to consolidate that level in the following years.

Figure 1 shows that the actual emissions in 2002 (10.2 million tonnes) is already 41% lower than emissions in 1985 (17.3 million tonnes). The amount of allocated rights in 2002 (9.5 million tonnes) is even 45% lower compared with the level in 1985. The fact that emissions in 2000, 2001 and 2002 are higher than the amount of allocated rights does not imply that participants fall short of their collective target: saved-up rights (through banking) compensate for the emission surplus.

There are two variations of the primary allocation method.[2] The first is to distribute emission rights via auction. From an economic efficiency point of view, this is the best option, as emission rights will find their way to those entities that have the highest autonomous reduction costs; these entities will be prepared to bid the highest price for rights in order to avoid autonomous reduction. The alternative is free allocation, based on, for instance, historical emission or production ("grandfathering").

Allocation of rights under Title IV mainly happens through grandfathering, free allocation based on historical production.[3] Participants in Phase I receive rights equivalent to 2.5 lbs/MMBtu multiplied by average fuel use over the years 1985–7.[4] In Phase II large, "polluting" installations receive rights equivalent to 1.2 lbs/MMBtu multiplied by average fuel use over 1985–7. "Cleaner" installations in this phase have a target below 1.2 lbs/ MMBtu, depending on size of installation, emission details over 1985 and use of fuel.

In addition to free allocation, each year an auction of a limited amount of rights takes place. This auction is intended particularly to give new installations the opportunity to obtain rights.[5] In Phase I 150,000 and in Phase II 250,000 rights per year were auctioned. This corresponds with between 1.7% and 2.6% of the total amount of allocated rights per year from 1995 to 2002 (see Figure 1). The auction method is the so-called *zero-revenue auction*: proceeds return to the participating producers in proportion with the amount of deducted rights.[6]

A functional market is first and foremost a liquid market, with the following requirements:

❑ continuous sufficient supply and demand;
❑ enough market parties; and
❑ minimal market restrictions (see Gagelmann and Hansjürgens, 2002).

In spite of the relatively small number of participants the SO_2 system has developed into a liquid market. The presence of a few hundreds of units means that there are enough market parties to create sufficient supply and demand. The market restrictions are minimal as well. Ellerman *et al* (2000) give some examples of restriction absence:

❑ international trade is possible;
❑ trade activities are not controlled by a supervisor beforehand or after;
❑ purchase and ownership of rights are possible for third parties – not limited to producers that need to reach their emission target;
❑ emission trade techniques and frequency are not restricted; and
❑ rights can be saved up for future use via banking.

Ellerman *et al* (2000) also observe that the SO_2 market is efficient, because it (increasingly) possesses the following characteristics:

❑ transparent price information for buyers and sellers;
❑ low transaction costs;
❑ quick possibility of arbitrage; and
❑ participants make optimal use of reduction possibilities via emission trade.

Rose (2000) is more conservative about this last point: he states that cost reductions are achieved via trade, but there is certainly no question of optimal use of possibilities as yet.

The final aspect of a functional emission trade system is effective monitoring, consisting of surveillance and sanctioning. Without monitoring, emission trade cannot function properly; environmental effectiveness of the system would be jeopardised and participants would lose confidence. Surveillance on emission levels is done by the obligatory installation of continuous emission monitoring (CEM) equipment. In addition, there is a database, the Allowance Tracking System, which registers the exact amount of rights per participant. Transactions between parties are processed, so that at any given time information on the ability of parties to cover their emission can be provided. When at the end of a year a party cannot show sufficient rights to cover its total emission, penalties of more than US$2,000 per tonne of SO_2 are imposed.[7] When the penalty amount is compared with the (average) rights price, it becomes clear that this is an effective way to get parties to keep within their targets. In 2001 the penalty amount (US$2,770) was already 13 to 18 times higher than the market price of emission rights, varying from US$152 to US$211.[8]

MARKET RESULTS
In this section we discuss the experiences of the SO_2 trade system from 1995 until and including 2002. Market results will be investigated, followed by an analysis of participants' strategies.

In Phase I (1995–9) and the first three years of Phase II (2000–2) of the trade programme, practically all participants reached their emission goals. Noncompliance with emission targets was sporadic: in the 2000–2 period, emitters of the equivalent of, respectively, 54, 11 and 33 emission rights were fined (EPA, 2001, 2002, 2003).

This is an encouraging result, but in principle this only means that the total emissions equal the amount of provided emission rights and that the internal and/or external reallocation of rights functions properly. It is more interesting to look at how, and to what extent, extra emission reduction (*overcompliance*) is taking place.

Overcompliance had a strong impact during the first years of the programme. While in the five years of Phase I the total amount of allocated rights was 38.1 million (equal to the same amount in tonnes of SO_2), the total emission was merely 26.5 million tonnes of SO_2. The remaining 11.6 million rights can be used to cover emissions in the following years via banking. In the first three years of Phase II overcompliance disappeared: the actual emission was higher than the amount of allocated rights. Consequently, a total of 3 million rights have been withdrawn from the emission bank.

The price of emission rights during the first years of Phase I was considerably lower than expected. In 1992 the first emission rights transactions were reported, against prices of US$300 and US$265 per tonne – as was expected at the time. Then the prices – auction prices, market prices and prices of direct transactions – show a downward trend: around US$100 per tonne in 1996 and 1997. From 1998 it has been more or less stable at US$150–200 per tonne (see Figure 2), still lower than initially expected. Only recently did prices break out above US$250 per tonne.

There are a number of explanations for these relatively low prices of emission rights and we will discuss each of them.

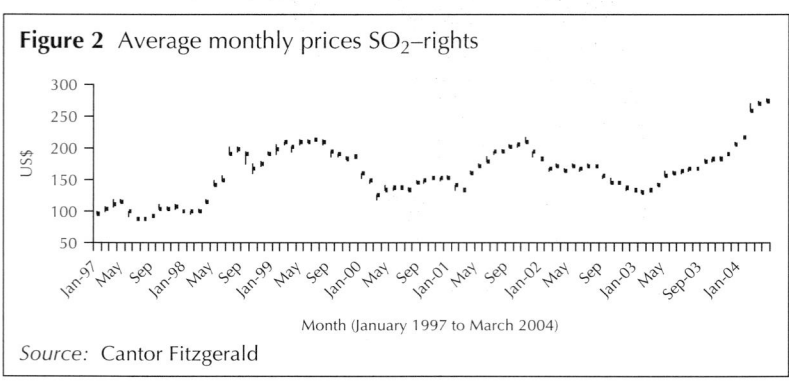

Figure 2 Average monthly prices SO_2–rights

Month (January 1997 to March 2004)

Source: Cantor Fitzgerald

1. market defects;
2. inadequate models;
3. deviating incentives;
4. market principles; and
5. irreversible investments.

1. Market defects

Ellerman *et al* (2000) mention three shortcomings of the market, suggested by third parties, which may have contributed to the low prices of emission rights:

❑ faulty design of the auction method;
❑ insecurity regarding exchange value based on rights transactions; and
❑ trade barriers and transaction costs.

However, none of these seem to be convincing statements. Schmalensee *et al* (1998) too notice that opponents of emission trade see the low price of rights as a symptom of the malfunctioning emission trade market, yet these critics are unable to give a sound basis for their statements.

2. Inadequate models

Prices of emission rights are forecast through models that represent reality, yet at the same time show a simplified version of this reality. Several researchers argue that certain aspects of the trade programme are not incorporated in the models on which prices are based, and therefore these models are inadequate. Three aspects of the programme are not included in the forecasting models: allocation of bonus rights when investing in scrubbers;[9] phasing of the trade programme – most potential sellers of rights will join in Phase I, whereas potential buyers will only join in Phase II; and substitution and compensation units that lead to a further decrease of compliance costs. The omission of these aspects means that emission rights prices based on models are being structurally overestimated.

3. Deviating incentives

Flexibility mechanisms of an emission trade system intend to give participants the opportunity to minimise their cost of compliance.

The implicit assumption is that the decisions participants make are indeed caused by an incentive to minimise costs. In practice this is not always the case. For example, for public utilities cost minimisation is certainly not the main objective.

Deviating incentives may have contributed to low emission prices. The authorities have systematically created incentives to invest in scrubbers, causing investments that are not economical to carry out. These investments further diminish the need for other compliance options (such as the purchase of rights), which leads to a lower price. Ellerman *et al* (2000) agree that political pressure and grant schemes have brought about a number of investments in scrubbers, but doubt the influence of this on emission rights prices – pointing out some intended investments that have been cancelled for economic reasons, in spite of political pressure.

4. Market principles

This concerns the changing market circumstances that have affected – in this case lowered – marginal costs of compliance. In this context Bohi and Burtraw (1997) have distinguished three possible explanations:

1. competition and innovation have lowered the costs of both scrubbing and switching;
2. the availability of inexpensive low-sulphur coals; and
3. equilibrium effects: the costs of the trade programme are included in the electricity prices → higher prices lead to less electricity demand → which in turn causes indirect emission reduction.

The pressure on prices through innovation, as mentioned in the first of these explanantions, is also acknowledged by other authors. Both Schmalensee *et al* (1998) and Ellerman *et al* (2000) recognise the influence of innovation, but they believe the difference between expected and actual prices is too big to be caused just by cost reduction through innovations.

5. Irreversible investments

Ellerman *et al* (2000) say that such arguments do not fully explain the low emission prices during the period 1995–7. Furthermore, they observe that a convincing argument should explain not only the low prices but also the difference between (low) prices on one hand and (high) long-term marginal compliance costs on the other. Theory predicts that marginal costs and emission prices are equal, but in reality this does not happen: emission rights prices in 1995–8 varied from US$70 to US$130, while long-term marginal compliance costs were around US$350 in 1995.

Both observations originate from two phenomena that influence each other:

❏ long-term investments in scrubbers and long-term coal-purchasing contracts lead to inflexibility within the compliance strategy; and
❏ the unexpected availability of cheap low-sulphur coal diminishes the required emission reduction.

We will clarify these observations below.

Compliance decisions need to be made at an early stage. In particular the decision to purchase scrubbers already required commitments back in 1992 and 1993, when price information was incomplete and uncertain. An enquiry among participants in 1996 showed that the choice for scrubbing was largely made based on the expectation that emission prices would be somewhere around US$300 and US$400 per tonne. Besides, many participants who chose fuel switching signed long-term contracts in 1992–4 to buy low-sulphur coal at premium prices. They had in mind the expected market circumstances in Phase I, especially the predicted high(er) prices of both emission rights and low-sulphur coal.

The expected higher prices of rights have led to overinvesting in reduction capacity, which resulted in lower than expected prices. After all, overinvesting enabled producers to cover their emission targets autonomously. As a result, the external demand for emission rights decreased. For example, only 13 of the 49 participating producers called for emission rights in the first three years of the programme. The paradoxical situation of high price expectations, eventually resulting in lower actual prices, is a typical example of a self-denying prophecy. Market players anticipate market developments influencing these developments at the same time. In this case, their collective behaviour leads to predictions remaining unfulfilled.

Apart from the expected high emission prices, another factor has contributed to overinvesting in valuable reduction capacity: the initially expected *high price* of low-sulphur coal combined with the sudden availability of *inexpensive* low-sulphur coal. Looking back, one can see that long-term contracts for the purchase of coal have been entered at prices that were too high.

A correcting response to these unpredicted market developments is expected. The enquiry mentioned earlier shows that certain proposed investments in scrubbers have indeed been cancelled. A third of the respondents mentioned the low emission prices as a reason and two-thirds identified the low price of low-sulphur coal in comparison with the costs of scrubbing (see Schmalensee *et al*, 1998).

COMPLIANCE STRATEGIES

In the previous section market results during the first years of the programme were discussed. This section deals with compliance strategies of the individual participants and also the coherence between strategies and market results.

The three most important options that assist the achievement of emission targets are autonomous reduction, trading and banking. Compliance strategies can contain one or more of these options. In the first place, the choice of strategy depends on price signals in the market. Swift (2001) notes that, in practice, participants do indeed quickly respond to these signals by adjusting their strategy. In Phase I of the trade programme he distinguishes three stages in which price signals are followed by participants' behaviour changes.

The first stage – even before the programme became operational in 1995 – shows overinvesting in reduction capacity. In the next stage, structurally lower emission prices become evident, resulting in proposed scrubbers' investments being cancelled. Instead, more use is made of the fuel-switching method in the third stage.

To support the basic strategy of autonomous reduction, from 1995 intra-utility trading and banking were introduced to reallocate available emission rights both in space and time. During the third and last stage, near the end of Phase I, the majority of participants were active on the external emission trade market. Nevertheless, most of the companies still believe in internal solutions, working with both autonomous reduction and banking.

Ellerman (2000) agrees with this, but emphasises the actual *shift* of compliance strategies in time, instead of the gradual appearance of various *additional* compliance options. According to Ellerman, before 1995 internal solutions dominate. After 1995, when overinvesting becomes apparent, he notices a shift towards strategies that are based on the market circumstances at that particular time. A change toward more flexible instruments is clearly apparent.

Autonomous reduction

The two major ways of reducing SO_2 emission autonomously are scrubbing and fuel switching. Scrubbing requires a substantial initial investment, followed by relatively low operational costs. Scrubbing leads to long-term emission reduction: once the scrubber is acquired SO_2 emission will be reduced against relatively low costs during a longer period.

The other method, fuel switching, requires a lower initial investment than scrubbing but extra costs result from the purchase of (more expensive) low-sulphur fuel. Fuel switching gives the producer more flexibility: when emission rights prices drop, the producer could choose to switch back to more sulphur-rich fuels. Nevertheless, long-term buying contracts could limit this flexibility.

The actual emission reduction during the years 1995–7 was achieved mainly through fuel switching. Still, a substantial part of reductions (37%) during these years was realised via scrubbing (see Table 1).

Moreover, emission reduction via scrubbing shows an upward trend. This is logical, given the long-term character of this type of investment. It is expected that, in view of the *sunk cost* component of the investment, the absolute contribution of scrubbing will not

Table 1 Emission reduction methods (million tonnes)

	1995	1996	1997	Total
Scrubbing	1.3 (32%)	1.5 (39%)	1.6 (40%)	4.4 (37%)
Fuel switching	2.8 (68%)	2.3 (61%)	2.4 (60%)	7.5 (63%)
Total	4.1 (100%)	3.8 (100%)	4.0 (100%)	11.9 (100%)

Source: Swift (2001)

diminish in the coming years. This does not apply to fuel switching: emission reduction through fuel switching dropped by 0.5 million tonnes in 1996 (2.3 tonnes) compared to 1995 (2.8 tonnes).

Scrubbing is responsible for 35% of emission reduction in the first five years of Phase I. From the early 1990s a total of 27 scrubbers have been installed, with a capacity of 16.167 MW (see Swift, 2001). This is significantly lower than expected. The other reduction method, fuel switching, soon turned out to be the less expensive alternative. Many companies decided to install a scrubber at just one of their units, then use the rights that become available to fulfil emission targets at the remaining units. This policy was followed by 16 of the 51 participating companies in Phase I.

A total of 59% of emission reduction in Phase I was achieved through fuel switching. Thirty-four of the 51 participants have based their strategy on this method. Here too, companies reduce emission with a limited number of units and then use the released emission rights to fulfil the targets of the remaining units.

Trading

At the start of the US Acid Rain Program, external emission rights trade was still in its infancy. Few participants were willing to opt for purchasing rights in an evolving, uncertain market. Uncertainty about availability of rights in itself was already a reason to opt for a safer alternative: autonomous reduction. Almost every participant in Phase I made this choice. As Ellerman (2000a) puts it, "an executive needed little imagination to realize that the consequences of not having enough allowances to cover emissions in Phase I were more serious than the consequences of having spent a little more (and reduced emissions more) from not having relied on the allowance market". Clearly, this excerpt shows that the loss of flexibility through internal investments was not well accounted for.

Inter-utility trading – the external trade of emission rights in order to cover targets – makes up for less than 3% of the total required emission rights in Phase I (1995–9): 708,372 of the total 26.5 million rights. Only three participating companies in Phase I exceeded their emission target: Illinois Power (emission surplus 503,208 tonnes), Tampa Electric (60,138) and Duquesne Power (14,237 tonnes). Twelve companies used inter-utility trading in order to exceed their target, but only during one or two years of the

Table 2 Traded rights in Phase I

Period	Number of traded rights in external market
Until March 1993	130,000
April 1993–March 1994	226,384
April 1994–March 1995	1,466,996
April 1995–March 1996	4,917,560
April 1996–March 1997	5,105,924
April 1997–March 1998	8,452,358
Total	20,299,222

five-year period of Phase I. Illinois Power is the only company whose strategy is based purely on the purchase of rights. Tampa Electric and Duquesne Power both combine purchase of rights with fuel switching (see Swift, 2001).

The low level of external trade does not imply that units do not make use of trade opportunities. On the contrary, there is a brisk trade among units, but mainly through intra-utility trading. Participants with a number of units internally reallocate their emission rights, so that each individual unit covers its target. This results in a concentration of reduction at certain particular units. For instance, if a scrubber is acquired at a large unit, enough reduction will be realised to cover the targets of other units. Nearly 60% of companies work with intra-utility trading in Phase I (see Swift, 2001). During the period 1995–7 this internal reallocation of rights covered around 75% of the demand for rights by overemitting units (see Ellerman *et al*, 2000).

As shown in Table 2, external trade activities increased as Phase I progressed (see Ellerman *et al*, 2000). This table is about transactions between non-related parties, who did not necessarily participate to Phase I. Phase II participants and third parties are also allowed to trade emission rights.

Banking
An overview of the banking activities of participants in the first few years of the programme is given in Figure 3. The emission bank gradually expands in the course of Phase I. At the end of 1999 a total of 11.6 million rights are collected through banking.

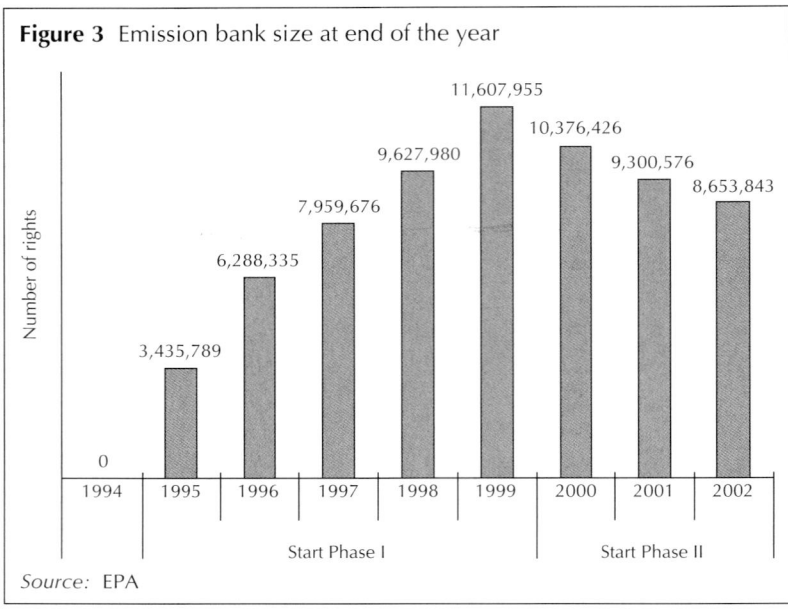

Figure 3 Emission bank size at end of the year

Source: EPA

Over the first two years of Phase II 2.3 million rights are with-drawn from the bank. This is in accordance with the theoretical concept of banking. In Phase I, when targets are still relatively flexible, the emission bank expands. Then, at the beginning of Phase II emission rights are withdrawn from the bank. This procedure ensures a gradual reduction of emission until the – now more stringent – target is covered.

Practical experience proves that, when compliance strategies are being defined, the option of banking is used in addition to autonomous reduction. Schennach (1998) recognises this as well. Phaneuf and Requate (2002) however, consider banking and investing in reduction capacity as substitutes and therefore say that banking causes investments to drop. This is partly true: banking does make it possible to postpone investments that may be necessary in the coming periods. Yet Phaneuf and Requate do not recognise that banking and investments carried out in previous periods can go together.[10] Furthermore, banking can be an extra reason to invest in reduction capacity in time, because it provides more flexibility as regards the allocation of surplus rights that are released after reduction.

CONCLUSIONS

In analysing market results of the first few years of the US Acid Rain Program, two observations can be made: (i) Phase I of the programme shows substantial overcompliance, accompanied by banking of surplus rights; and (ii) the price of emission rights is considerably lower than expected, while marginal reduction costs and the (lower) emission rights prices vary. This is caused by overinvestment in reduction capacity, which in turn is caused by an overestimation of both emission rights prices and prices of low-sulphur coal. Participants' compliance strategies are predominantly based on internal solutions, linking autonomous reduction investments to banking.

To what extent do the observations mentioned above differ from the theoretical insights as researched in the previous chapter?

Practical experiences with the trade system indicate that the choice between autonomous reduction and external trade is indeed made on the basis of expected emission prices. As observed investment behaviour shows, investments are made when prices are expected to be high; intended investments are reversed when prices turn out to be lower. In addition to this, banking is an integral part of any investment decision. The observed banking pattern is in accordance with the model of Schennach (1998). Moreover, banking has contributed to reduction investments. The banking opportunity adds to the NPV of an investment, so that more often they turn out to be cost-effective.

Overinvestment in reduction capacity could indicate that participants do not pay enough attention to the value of flexibility when deciding upon strategies. Particularly, the value of the *deferral option* – the option to postpone an investment – might have been overlooked. Given the fact that a deferral option lowers the NPV of a project, overlooking this option means the NPV is being overestimated. This results in overinvestment in reduction capacity.

Naturally, the valuation of the deferral option will affect an investment policy only if it represents sufficient value. Chao and Wilson (1993) have calculated the value of the deferral option at US$85 per emission right. It shows that this option can play a significant role in the decision-making process regarding investment policies. Furthermore, the deferral option is useful only with investment projects that have a relatively low NPV: projects that are just at-the-money. Then the added value of deferral compared with direct investment is highest.[11] Assuming that projects are more often just at-the-money than well in-the-money, the deferral option is an important factor in a large number of projects.

Insley (2002) concludes that investment behaviour of electricity producers under the US Acid Rain Program possibly does comply with proposed policies using "real option" techniques. He demonstrates that differing policies in the case of investment in a scrubber, in an otherwise identical market, could be caused by differing expectations concerning volatility of emission prices. Also the willingness to take risks plays a part. Ben-David *et al* (2000) have tested this willingness in an experimental setting. Their paper states that market parties avoid risks in an uncertain market environment (caused by volatility of market price). Yet the experiment shows that participants are in fact prepared to take risks, by postponing investments and opting for a "wait-and-see" strategy.

Nevertheless, it is clear that companies under the SO_2 regime, particularly at the starting phase, have made decisions that were not optimal from a financial point of view. In the early 1990s many companies followed the self-sufficiency policy, not necessarily for financial reasons but because of unfamiliarity with the new system (see Burtraw, 2000). Companies have since gone through a learning process and, bit by bit, have started to make more solid financial decisions. By looking at past experiences with the US SO_2 system, participants of the proposed CO_2 system can learn to go through this process more quickly and sooner. An important lesson in this case is that the deferral option deserves special attention. In case of the US Acid Rain Program, this could have resulted in more solid investment decisions and, to a certain extent, overinvesting might have been avoided.

1   The total number of electricity-producing units in the US in 1995 was 2,918, consisting of 263 Table A units and 2,655 other units. Of these other units 2,604 were included in Phase II; the remaining 651 units did not participate, for various reasons.

2   *Primary allocation* is the way emission rights are divided over participating entities at the beginning of a trade period. *Secondary allocation* is allocation as a result of emission trade between parties. Secondary allocation defines the actual economic efficiency of the trade system, whereas primary allocation mainly determines the costs for individual entities. This is part of the reason why the primary allocation method is regarded as controversial.

3   This method implicitly takes into account "early action" of participants, as opposed to allocation of rights based on historical emissions.

4   "lbs/MMBtu" means pounds SO_2 per million British thermal units.

5   Installations starting after 1985 do not obtain rights through "grandfathering".

6   Rights that will be auctioned become available by deducting part of the initially allocated rights. Proceeds will go to producers whose rights have been deducted.

7   This penalty of US$2,000 per tonne was in force in 1990; it is corrected yearly for inflation. In 2001 the fine was US$2,774 per tonne (EPA, 2002).

8   These amounts are respectively the minimum and maximum of the observed average monthly price of emission rights in 2001.

9   Scrubbers are installations that can "desulphurise" emission gases. They require substantial investments and guarantee long-term SO_2 reductions. Scrubbing is one of the two most important methods for autonomous emission reduction. The second method is *fuel switching* – switching to fuels that contain less sulphur, such as low-sulphur coal or natural gas. This method provides more flexibility than scrubbing.

10 Phaneuf and Requate (2002) make their point based on the assumption that banking and investing take place in one and the same period. Yet, when an emission constraint lies below the current emission level, the banked rights in period t correspond with surplus rights – investments as such – in period $t - 1$ or earlier.

11 The added value of deferral must be separated from its actual value. The added value equals the value of the option minus the standard NPV of the project. When a project is well "in-the-money" the added value of deferral is small (as opposed to the value of the deferral option!). After all, the risks in these projects are small, even when volatility of emission rights prices is high. Projects that are just "at-the-money" carry higher risks and the influence of the deferral option increases.

REFERENCES

Ben-David, S., et al, 2000, "Attitudes Toward Risk and Compliance in Emission Permit Markets", *Land Economics*, **76**, pp. 590–600.

Bohi, D. R., and D. Burtraw, 1997, "SO_2 Allowance Trading: How Experience and Expectation Measure up", "Resources for the Future" Discussion Paper 97-24.

Burtraw, D., 2000, "Innovation under the Tradable Sulphur Dioxide Emission Permits Program in the US Electricity Sector", "Resources for the Future" Discussion Paper 00-38.

Chao, H-P., and R. Wilson, 1993, "Option Value of Emission Allowances", *Journal of Regulatory Economics*, **5**, pp. 233–49.

Ellerman, A. D., 2000a, "From Autarkic to Market-based Compliance – Learning from our Mistakes", in R. F. Kosobud (ed), *Emission Trading – Environmental Policy's New Approach* (New York: John Wiley & Sons), pp. 190–203.

Ellerman, A. D., et al, 2000b, *Markets for Clean Air – the US Acid Rain Program* (Cambridge, UK: Cambridge University Press).

Environmental Protection Agency (EPA), 2002, EPA Acid Rain Program – 2001 Progress Report, EPA-430-R-02-009, Washington, DC: U.S. Environmental Protection Agency.

Gagelmann, F., and B. Hansjürgens, 2002, "Climate Protection Through Tradable Permits: the EU Proposal for a CO_2 Emissions Trading Programme in Europe", *European Environment*, **12**, pp. 185–202.

Insley, M. C., 2002, "On the Option to invest in Pollution Control under a Regime of Tradable Emission Allowances", Working Paper.

Insley, M., 2003, "On the Option to Invest in Pollution Control under a Regime of Tradable Emissions Allowances", *Canadian Journal of Economics*, **35(4)**, pp. 860–883.

Phaneuf, D., and T. Requate, 2002, "Incentives for Investment in Advanced Pollution Abatement Technology in Emission Permit Markets with Banking", *Environmental and Resource Economics*, **22**, pp. 369–390.

Rose, K. J., 2000, "Electric Industry Restructuring and the SO_2 Trading Program: A Look Ahead by Looking Back", in Kosobud, R. F., (ed), *Emissions Trading – Environmental Policy's New Approach* (New York: John Wiley & Sons), pp. 209–215.

Schennach, S.M., 2000, "The Economics of Pollution Permit Banking in the Context of Title IV of the 1990 Clean Air Amendments", *Journal of Environmental Economics and Management*, **40(3)**, pp. 189–210.

Schmalensee, R., et al, 1998, "An Interim Evaluation of Sulfur Dioxide Emissions Trading", *Journal of Economic Perspectives*, **12**, pp. 53–68.

Swift, B., 2001, "How Environmental Laws Work: An Analysis of the Utility Sector's Response to Regulation of Nitrogen Oxides and Sulfur Dioxide Under the Clean Air Act", *Tulane Environmental Law Journal*, **14**, pp. 309–424.

12

Investment Case Study: Valuation with Real Options

Cyriel de Jong; Kasper Walet

Erasmus University Rotterdam;
Maycroft Consultancy Services

Consequences of emission trade systems for participants are far-reaching. Companies need to develop a strategy covering all aspects of emission trading: they need to set up a monitoring system and control procedures, develop a view on future market developments and incorporate emission costs and benefits in their accounting and risk management practice. Most importantly, and even long before emission trading becomes operational, emission trading affects investment decisions. This is because current investment policies determine emission of greenhouse gases for a longer period. The emissions therefore represent a direct cost for the company and are an integral part of any investment strategy.

This chapter focuses on the investment issues that will arise with polluting energy companies under the emission trade system. Insight into the issues is needed, as up until now electricity producers (outside the US) have never been faced with market-dictated charging of emissions. Importantly, volatility of emission rights requires flexible investment options, much more so compared with previous operational policy instruments. The real-option valuation framework is well suited to deal with uncertainties and will be central to the analysis in this chapter.[1]

INVESTMENT DECISIONS

As explained in Chapter 10, when making an investment decision on reduction capacity, one needs to consider which part of the already existing static efficiency can be replaced by dynamic efficiency. Static efficiency is attained when emission rights are redistributed at short notice via trade. Dynamic efficiency can be achieved – or is aimed for – in the long term, when entities correct their *actual emission level*, for example, in order to avoid having to buy emission rights or realising a surplus that can be sold.

Investment decisions always take place in a dynamic environment, where there is uncertainty about future market circumstances. The standard net present value (NPV) method is a much-used way to judge various investment projects. However, this method is based on some implicit assumptions that projects in practice do not always comply with, especially the assumption that either an investment can be reversed free of charge, or – if the investment is final – the decision has a "now-or-never" character: if the decision not to invest has been made, the possibility of investing ends altogether, even in the coming periods (see Dixit and Pindyck, 1994). Incorporating this deferral option, as well as the abandonment option, the NPV can be adjusted (see Equation 4 in Chapter 10). The project generates value – and thus should be executed – if the overall NPV is positive.

In the case description in Chapter 10, the values for the two major real options – the option to abandon a project and the option to defer a project – were explicitly given. Of course, this is a simplification of the reality. In practice, these values need to be estimated and depend on a number of market variables, project variables and assumptions.

To illustrate the framework of investment decisions demonstrated earlier, and especially the influence of banking and real options, an example case will be worked out below. In this example we calculate the NPV of a relatively simple investment project. Although imaginary values are applied, the results do provide clear insights into the effect of banking and real options, as well as the extent to which various other variables influence the NPV of an investment project.

Case description

This case describes the situation of a European power generator, which is liable under the emission trading system from 2005 onwards.

From the start of 2004 it faces an investment opportunity that will reduce its emissions by 48,000 tonnes annually. The investment costs are equal to €6 million in 2004, but the investment may be postponed until 2009 at the latest.[2] If the project is deferred, the initial investment amount will increase with the risk-free interest rate equal to 4% per annum. The economic life span of the project is 20 years, which means that the emissions reductions are achieved in all the 20 years following the investment. After the decision to invest has been taken, it will take a year to implement. So, if the investment decision is taken in 2004 the first emission reductions will be realised in 2005.

The abatement costs to realise the emissions reductions are determined by the project variables. However, the revenues are mainly based on the expected price development of emissions allowances in the coming years. These revenues can be direct revenues from the sales of the emission rights if the power producer already meets its emission target. Alternatively, the revenues can be avoided costs from buying emission rights in the market to meet its target. Finally, the revenues can be a combination of both actual sales revenues and avoided costs.

For this case scenario we set the expected price for the right to emit one tonne of CO_2 in 2005 at €12.50. In 2008, at the start of the first Kyoto Compliance Period, we expect a price of €16.00 per tonne of CO_2. In 2013, at the start of the second Kyoto Compliance Period, the expected price is €13.00 per tonne of CO_2. For the other years the price equals the price of the previous year, increased by the risk-free interest rate of 4% (using continuous discounting). So, the expected price in 2006 will be: €12.50 $\times$ $e^{0.04}$ = €13.01. See Figure 1.

Note that the price increase from €13.54 to €16.00 is at odds with an efficiently working market as outlined in Chapter 10. Unless we assume very high-risk premia, extreme jumps in forward prices are not sustainable, because companies will respond to this expected price increase by banking before 2008, which in turn will make prices converge. This forward arbitrage drives the convergence process, and results in no or limited benefit of banking to individual companies. However, we maintain the jump in this case to illustrate the impact of banking.

In an efficiently working market, banking will have little benefit for purely financial reasons. Nevertheless, there may be reasons for

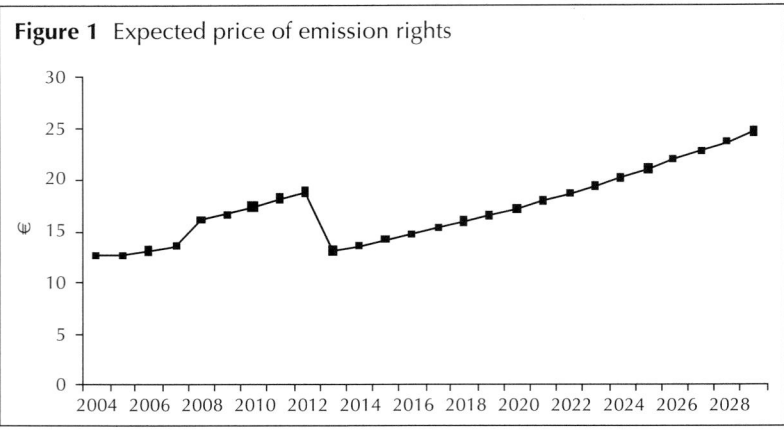

Figure 1 Expected price of emission rights

individual companies to bank. First, banking will mostly be applied to avoid trading costs. Second, companies may bank allowances if they have a preference to comply with emission targets in-house, for example to support an environmentally friendly corporate image. The latter effect should not be underestimated if we consider the results of the US Acid Rain Program, in which only a few companies heavily relied on (external) emissions trading.

Through the emission reduction a cost saving or sales revenue is realised each year. Its NPV is calculated by taking into account the *weighted average cost of capital* (WACC). In this case we use a WACC of 10%, which includes a premium above the risk-free rate, because the investment revenues are risky and the company's financing costs are always above the risk-free rate.

Finally, we need to produce a realistic estimate of the volatility of the emission price to quantify the real option value. In this case we use a volatility of 15% unless stated otherwise. The level of 15% might be somewhat on the low side compared with the 24% volatility in the market for SO_2 allowances.[3] On the other hand, in a comparable investment case, Dixit and Pindyck (1994) apply a somewhat lower volatility of 12% and we do not want to overestimate the value of the deferral option.

In the above case scenario we assume that the emission reduction project does not involve any switch of fuel. In this context, one could think in particular of an investment that improves the efficiency of an existing power plant. As a result, the scenario is relatively general and could easily be translated to other types of industry (where fuel switching does not represent a meaningful abatement option). We suppose furthermore that the company can forecast a reliable estimate of the number of hours the power station will use: the efficiency improvement determines the emission reduction per energy unit produced; combining this with the number of production hours leads to the 48,000 tonnes emission reductions. At the end of this chapter, we will discuss the approach to a solution when these two assumptions are relaxed, allowing for fuel price uncertainty and production uncertainty.

VALUATION
The NPV calculations are all carried out in a spreadsheet. The calculation of the NPV without deferral option is rather straightforward, so we will limit the amount of explanation for this situation. Calculations that incorporate the deferral option are much more complicated, although they could still be carried out in a spreadsheet. The relative complexity arises from the many steps that we need to go through, and the different actions that the investor may take in response to different price scenarios. This will be explained below.

Valuation without deferral option
If the deferral option is neglected, we can rely on Equation (1) and (3) of Chapter 10 in the situations excluding and including banking respectively. Without the banking opportunity the calculation of the NPV reads as follows:

$$NPV = \sum_t \frac{Q_t \cdot P_t^*}{e^{r \cdot t}} - I$$

$$NPV = \left(\sum_{t=1}^{20} \frac{48,000 \cdot P_t^*}{e^{0.10 \cdot t}} \right) - 6,000,000$$

$$NPV = 48,000 \cdot \left(\frac{12.50}{e^{0.10 \cdot 1}} + \frac{13.01}{e^{0.10 \cdot 2}} + \frac{13.54}{e^{0.10 \cdot 3}} + \frac{16.00}{e^{0.10 \cdot 4}} + \cdots + \frac{24.65}{e^{0.10 \cdot 25}} \right)$$
$$- 6,000,000$$

$$NPV = 62,014$$

In this case the NPV of the project is simply the difference between the revenues from the emission reduction during the life span of the project minus the investment costs, while taking into account the financing costs.

Next, we incorporate the possibility to bank. Then we need to determine first of all in what periods it would be optimal to bank our emission rights and when to sell them in the future. It is optimal to bank when the expected increase in the emissions price exceeds our financing costs (WACC = 10%). This is clearly the case when we bank in 2007 and sell in 2008 (expected increase is 17%), but also when we bank in 2006 and sell in 2008 (expected increase in emissions price is 10.34% per year). We incorporate the mutation in the emission bank in the calculation of the NPV as follows (Equation (3) in Chapter 10).

$$NPV = \sum_t \frac{(Q_t - \Delta S_t) \cdot P_t^*}{e^{r \cdot t}} - I$$

$$NPV = \left(\sum_{t=1}^{20} \frac{(48,000 - \Delta S_t) \cdot P_t^*}{e^{0.10 \cdot i}} \right) - 6,000,000$$

$$NPV = \left(\frac{48,000 \cdot 12.50}{e^{0.10 \cdot 1}} + \frac{144,000 \cdot 16.00}{e^{0.10 \cdot 4}} + \frac{48,000 \cdot 16.65}{e^{0.10 \cdot 5}} \right.$$
$$\left. + \cdots + \frac{48,000 \cdot 24.65}{e^{0.10 \cdot 25}} \right) - 6,000,000$$

$$NPV = 98,828$$

Banking offers a company some flexibility to optimise the revenues of emission reductions, by selling allowances (or avoiding having to buy allowances) in years with a relatively high price. Due to arbitrageurs in the market, the value of the banking is however limited. In this case, banking increases the value of the project by less than €37,000, but in practice arbitrageurs will reduce this profit. The spreadsheet calculations, up to 2010, are given in Figure 2.

Valuation with deferral option

If we include the deferral option in our decision-making process, we have to find a way to value this option. For our case scenario the binomial option price model can be used. The binomial model describes the development in time of a certain variable – in this case the emission allowances price – in a tree. In this tree it is assumed that prices can either go up or go down in each period

Figure 2 Overview of calculations of NPV

Base data

Risk-free rate	4%	
WACC	10%	
Emission reduction	48,000	tonnes/yr
Economic lifetime	20	year
Today	2004	

Year	2004	2005	2006	2007	2008	2009	2010
Emission in price (P)	€12.50	€12.50	€13.01	€13.54	€16.00	€16.65	€17.33
(Increase in price)		0%	4%	4%	17%	4%	4%
Initial investment	€6,000,000	€6,244,865	€6,499,722	€6,764,981	€7,041,065	€7,328,417	

NPV without banking

Year	2004	2005	2006	2007	2008	2009	2010
Initial investment	−€6,000,000						
Reduction * P		€600,000	€624,486	€649,972	€768,000	€799,343	€831,964
Present value		€542,902	€511,286	€481,511	€514,806	€484,826	€456,592

NPV	€62,014

NPV with banking

Year	2004	2005	2006	2007	2008	2009	2010
Intial investment	−€6000,000						
(Reduction − mutation) * P		€600,000	€0	€0	€2,304,000	€799,343	€831,964
Emission bank begin		0	0	48,000	96,000	0	0
Mutation		0	48,000	48,000	−96,000	0	0
Emission bank end		0	48,000	96,000	0	0	0
Present value		€542,902	€0	€0	€1,544,417	€484,826	€456,592

NPV	€98,828

225

of time. Time steps can be daily, weekly, monthly or yearly, depending on the desired accuracy of the calculations. In general, the smaller the time steps, the larger the accuracy. For ease of exposition we take relatively large time steps of one year in this case.

The binomial price tree can subsequently be used to analyse optimal decisions to determine the value of the project. In each node of the tree, we calculate the *remaining* value of the project: one value if we exercise our investment option and one value if we postpone investment. Other things being equal, these remaining project values will be higher when emission prices are higher, because the emission reductions represent a higher value. Similarly, remaining project's values will be lower when we approach the end of the economic lifetime, because fewer reductions remain to be realised.

On the basis of the remaining project values in the different nodes of the binomial tree, we can derive an optimal decision path: working backwards through the tree (so, assuming we take optimal actions in the future) we determine at what prices and on what dates it is optimal to invest. So, this decision path determines the timing and circumstances under which the investment will take place.[4]

This explanation may sound rather abstract for people unfamiliar with option-pricing theory. An example (for the situation *without* banking) of the first two periods of the binomial tree will probably give some more insight. The necessary basic data are listed in Figure 2, the binomial tree in Figure 3. Below we show the different steps that ultimately lead to the calculation of the value of the investment project.

(i) The NPV of an investment depends on the price development of the emission allowances over time. First of all, we have to establish the (expected) allowance price for the consecutive periods. The allowance price in, respectively, an *"up"* state ($P_{up,t+1}$: modelled price increase) and a *"down"* state ($P_{down,t+1}$: modelled price decline) of the binomial model can be derived from the price in the previous period (P_t) as follows (see Hull, 2001):

$$\begin{cases} P_{up,t+1} = P_t \cdot e^{\mu_t + \sigma} \\ P_{down,t+1} = P_t \cdot e^{\mu_t - \sigma} \end{cases}$$

We can simplify this analysis by counting the number of times an up-tick has occurred up to time t. Therefore, we define $P_{u,t}$ as the price at time t when the price has gone up u times, and gone down $t - u$ times. With this in mind, we translate the equation above to:

$$\begin{cases} P_{u+1,t+1} = P_{u,t} \cdot e^{\mu_t + \sigma} \\ P_{u,t+1} = P_{u,t} \cdot e^{\mu_t - \sigma} \end{cases} \quad (0 \leq u \leq t)$$

The average (percentage) change of the allowance price at time t is defined by μ_t (equal to 4% in most years) and the volatility is equal to σ (equal to 15% in our case). Figure 3 shows how the price process can be modelled in a spreadsheet (up to the year 2010).

The table should be interpreted as follows. In 2005, the price can either be €14.52 or €10.76. If the price is €14.52 in 2005, then it can either move up to €17.56 or move down to €13.01 in 2006; if the price is €10.76 in 2005, then it can either move up to €13.01 or move down to €9.64 in 2006. Continuing this, for example from a price of €26.12 in 2009, in 2010 the price is either €31.58 or €23.40. Of course, this binomial structure is a simplification of reality, but it is a convenient way to model the price uncertainty. It can be extended to a finer grid, assuming for example monthly price movements. Since the tree then grows much larger (12 possible prices in 2005, up to 72 possible prices in 2010), for demonstration purposes we keep the analysis a bit simpler here.

The last row of Figure 3 contains the expected price in the different years. This expected price is obtained as a weighted average of the possible prices in that year. These weights are not completely

Figure 3 Binomial tree price process of emissions prices

Year	2004	2005	2006	2007	2008	2009	2010
Emission price (P)	€12.50	€14.52	€17.56	€21.24	€29.15	€35.25	€42.63
		€10.76	€13.01	€15.73	€21.60	€26.12	€31.58
			€9.64	€11.65	€16.00	€19.35	€23.40
				€8.63	€11.85	€14.33	€17.33
					€8.78	€10.62	€12.84
						€7.87	€9.51
							€7.05
	€12.50	€12.50	€13.01	€13.54	€16.00	€16.65	€17.33

227

equal, but are derived in two stages. First, we establish the probability of an up-tick (q) and the probability of a down-tick in price ($1-q$). It can be shown (see Hull, 2001) that the probability q should equal 46.3%, using the following formula:

$$q = \frac{e^{\sigma} - 1}{e^{2\sigma} - 1}$$

For example, with the up-price being €14.52 and the down-price being €10.76, this ensures that the weighted average price in 2005 equals €12.50.

Next, we take into account that different orders of up- and down-ticks lead to the same price in a certain year. For example, the (middle) price of €13.01 in 2006 is possible if prices were €14.52 in 2005, then dropped to €13.01, but also when prices were €10.76, then moved up to €13.01. So, there are often multiple price trajectories (in this case two) that lead to the same price. Combining the probabilities of up- and down-ticks with the number of possible trajectories to arrive at a certain price, we obtain the probabilities of future prices, as shown in Figure 4.

Combining the information from Figures 3 and 4, we can see for example that there is a probability of 1.0% that the price goes as high as €42.63 in 2010.

(ii) The yearly revenues of the investment equal the product of the emissions price and the annual emissions reduction. The annual emissions reduction is 48,000 tonnes; the emissions prices are uncertain and given in Figure 3. For example, if we invest before 2007 and prices have gone up each year, revenues in 2007 are

Figure 4 Probabilities of future prices in the binomial tree of Figure 3

Year	2004	2005	2006	2007	2008	2009	2010
Probability of price	100.0%	46.3%	21.4%	9.9%	4.6%	2.1%	1.0%
		53.7%	49.7%	34.5%	21.3%	12.3%	6.8%
			28.9%	40.1%	37.1%	28.6%	19.8%
				15.5%	28.7%	33.2%	30.7%
					8.3%	19.3%	26.8%
						4.5%	12.4%
							2.4%
	100.0%	100.0%	100.0%	100.0%	100.0%	100.0%	100.0%

Figure 5 Yearly revenues for the years 2005–10 for the emission prices in Figure 3

Year	2004	2005	2006	2007	2008	2009	2010
Revenues per year		€697,101	€842,969	€1,019,359	€1,399,387	€1,692,208	€2,046,302
		€516,425	€624,486	€755,160	€1,036,692	€1,253,619	€1,515,938
			€462,631	€559,436	€768,000	€928,704	€1,123,035
				€414,441	€568,948	€688,001	€831,964
					€421,487	€509,683	€616,334
						€377,583	€456,592
							€338,252
	€0.00	€600,000.00	€624,486.46	€649,972.24	€768,000.00	€799,342.68	€831,964.47

$48,000 \times €21.24 = €1,019,359$. We calculate these revenues for each possible future price.

(iii) The revenues calculated in (ii) can be realised from the first year until the twentieth year after the investment, because of the lead time of one year. For example, when we decide to invest in 2004, the project yields revenues from 2005 until 2024. In general, when investing in year t the first revenues will be realised in year $t + 1$, up to year $t + 20$. We obtain the present value of total expected revenues by summing the revenues from year $t + 1$ to year $t + 20$, discounted back to year t at the WACC of 10%.

The expected revenues in a certain year depend on the emission price in that year. For example, if we had invested in 2006 and the emission price in 2007 were €21.24, then expected discounted revenues over the years 2007–26 equalled €11,109,011, whereas at a price of €15.73 in 2007 they equalled only €8,229,757. This difference is logical, because the higher next year's price, not only the larger the first revenue, but also the higher we expect prices in the coming 20 years and thus the overall revenues. The discounted future revenues are shown in Figure 6 (for the first year in which they are realised).

(iv) The NPV of the investment in year t equals the future expected revenues minus the investment cost. For example, when we invest in 2004, future – to 2005 discounted – revenues are either €7,783,786 or €5,766,366 (see Figure 6) with respective probabilities of 46.3% and 53.7%. When we discount these numbers back to 2004 and deduct the investment of €6,000,000 in 2004, we obtain a project value of €62,014. Please note that this is the same number as we obtained earlier, since it is the NPV if we invest directly in 2004, so ignoring any flexibility. The NPVs for the other years are derived likewise (see Figure 7).

(v) The next step is to compare the value of direct investment with the value of deferring the investment and determining an optimal action (invest, defer or cancel project). We can calculate the NPV of the deferral option in previous years by means of so-called *backward valuation*. We need to work backwards rather than forwards, because the value of deferral depends on our actions in the future years. So, first we establish what we do in the future and then we know what is best to do today: we are working backwards in the tree structure of the binomial model. We derive the value of

Figure 6 Expected future revenues of investment for emission prices in Figure 3

Year	2004	2005	2006	2007	2008	2009	2010
Present value		€7,783,780	€9,303,002	€11,109,011	€13,252,980	€15,580,202	€18,267,729
		€5,766,366	€6,891,833	€8,229,757	€9,818,049	€11,542,097	€13,533,067
(expected revenues			€5,105,596	€6,096,754	€7,273,390	€8,550,596	€10,025,542
from year t onwards				€4,516,587	€5,388,260	€6,334,437	€7,427,105
when invested in					€3,991,721	€4,692,667	€5,502,134
year t − 1)						€3,476,413	€4,076,081
							€3,019,635

Figure 7 NPV when invested in 2004-9, with prices in Figure 3

Year	2004	2005	2006	2007	2008	2009
NPV	€62,014	**€1,000,321**	€2,151,984	€ 3,556,450	€ 5,092,808	€ 6,898,505
when investing		−€877,499	**−€90,381**	**€881,323**	€ 1,947,929	€ 3,211,146
			−€1,751,565	**−€1,100,459**	**−€381,854**	€479,484
(present value t + 1-/-				−€2,568,600	**−€2,107,800**	**−€1,544,182**
initial investment)					−€3,386,413	**−€3,043,350**
						−€4,153,961

231

the deferral option assuming that from now on the optimal choices are made, ie, to invest, defer or cancel. This means that we will always choose the option that maximises the NPV.

Note first that we assumed that 2009 is the last date that we may invest, so the value of deferral is €0 in 2009. Similar to a US-style financial option, our option to invest expires in that year. The optimal choice in 2009 is to invest if the NPV of the investment project is positive (this will be determined by the price of emission allowances at that moment in time). In case of a negative NPV, the project will definitely not become operational.

One year before expiration of our investment option, the first actual backward valuation will take place. We calculate the NPV of the deferral option in 2008 assuming that we take an optimal decision in 2009. The NPV of the deferral option in 2008 is equal to the discounted values of the optimal decisions (deferral or investment) in 2009 multiplied by the respective probabilities q (46.3%) and $1 - q$ (53.7%). For example, if the emission price equals €21.60 in 2008, then directly investing yields a value of €1,947,929 (second table in Figure 8). If we defer investment for one more period, then the NPV is either €3,211,146 or €479,484 (second table in Figure 8), depending on whether emission prices move to €26.12 or €19.35 (Figure 3). Weighting and discounting these continuation values yields a deferral value of €1,577,194. This is less than the value of direct investment of €1,947,929, so with a price of €21.60 it is optimal to invest directly in 2008, assuming we did not invest before.

We repeat this procedure for all prices and all previous years. This finally leads to the NPV of the deferral option in 2004. Figure 8 shows the calculations of the deferral option (first table), the NPV assuming optimal actions (second table) and the optimal actions (third table).

In this example the decision in 2004 should be to wait, as the NPV of deferral (€557,476) is larger than the NPV of investing (€62,014). In general, in Figure 8 the bold numbers indicate that it is optimal to invest. We see that the "hurdle price" above which it is optimal to invest has in fact shifted upwards compared with the price at which the NPV of direct investment becomes positive. Put differently, we want to have more certainty before deciding to invest, because future prices might go down, turning an earlier "profitable" investment into a loss.

Figure 8 Derivation of optimal actions and project values in 2004–9 with prices in Figure 3

Year	2004	2005	2006	2007	2008	2009
NPV deferral option	€557,476	€1,106,386 €194,119	€1,932,486 €422,942 €35,158	€3,078,851 €912,899 €83,998 €0	€4,448,912 €1,577,194 €200,688 €0 €0	€0 €0 €0 €0 €0 €0

Year	0	1	2	3	4	5
NPV with optimal choice	€557,476	€1,106,386 €194,119	€2,151,984 €422,942 €35,158	€3,556,450 €912,899 €83,998 €0	€5,092,808 €1,947,929 €200,688 €0 €0	€6,898,505 €3,211,146 €479,484 €0 €0 €0

Year	0	1	2	3	4	5
Invest?	WAIT	WAIT WAIT	INVEST WAIT WAIT	INVEST WAIT WAIT CANCEL	INVEST INVEST WAIT CANCEL CANCEL	INVEST INVEST INVEST CANCEL CANCEL CANCEL

233

Table 1 Project values under the assumptions of banking and deferral

		Deferral option	
		No	Yes
Banking	No	€62,014	€557,476 WAIT
	Yes	€98,828	

If banking is also taken into account, the case becomes more complex. However, as we outlined earlier, the financial value of banking for individual companies will be limited, because arbitrageurs will quickly destroy any banking profits in a properly functioning market. Therefore, banking can safely be ignored in investment decisions.

The table above summarises the value of the investment opportunity under the alternative assumptions of banking and deferral. The difference between €557,476 and €62,014 is the pure deferral option value of €495,462.

The example clearly shows the consequences if the deferral option is not – or not sufficiently – recognised. When investing directly, the NPV of the project (excluding banking) is €62,014. So, on first sight the optimal decision is to invest in the project. However, deferral of the project has a higher value and therefore the optimal decision is to postpone.

Sensitivity analysis
The example is based on a number of assumptions that do not necessarily need to be correct and are at least uncertain. It is insightful to analyse how the project value and the optimal decisions change in response to changes in our assumptions.

We start by analysing at what emission prices in 2005 it becomes optimal to invest and call these price levels "hurdle rates". These hurdle rates are derived under the logical assumption that expected percentage price changes in the years after 2005 remain constant (so there is a parallel shift in the forward price curve). In the case study, we assumed an expected emission price of €12.50 in 2005.

Table 2 Investment hurdles and corresponding NPV under the assumptions of banking and deferral

			Deferral option	
			No	Yes
Banking	No	Price	€12.37	€15.29
		NPV	€0	€1,415,056
	Yes	Price	€12.30	
		NPV	€0	

This level was just enough to make the NPV (ignoring the option to defer) positive. More precisely, the hurdle rate at which the project just gets a positive NPV is €12.37 if we exclude banking and €12.30 if we include banking (see Table 2).

The project has a positive NPV at a price of €12.50, but it is optimal to postpone investment until later years. We calculated that waiting is optimal up to an expected price of €15.29. At that point, the direct revenues from the investment outweigh the benefits of waiting for even better market circumstances. The NPV at this price equals €1,415,056 (see Table 2).

The relation between the two NPVs (excluding and including the option to defer) is depicted in Figure 9. The light grey line depicts the classical call option value. When the expected emission price is above the hurdle rate of €15.29, the option is deep in-the-money, which means in this case that we should invest directly. However, when the emission price is low, we are not obliged to invest and rather wait for better prices. The value of the project never falls below zero, although at a price below €8 the project as a whole can safely be cancelled altogether: below an expected price of €8 in 2005, the probability is negligible that prices will rise sufficiently in the future to make the project economical. In other words, below €8 the project is so far out-of-the-money, that it has no value.

Again, similar to options in financial markets, the option to wait increases in value when there is more uncertainty about future emission prices. This relationship arises because, on the one hand, adverse price movements can be avoided if we wait to invest; on the other hand, we can fully benefit from positive price movements if

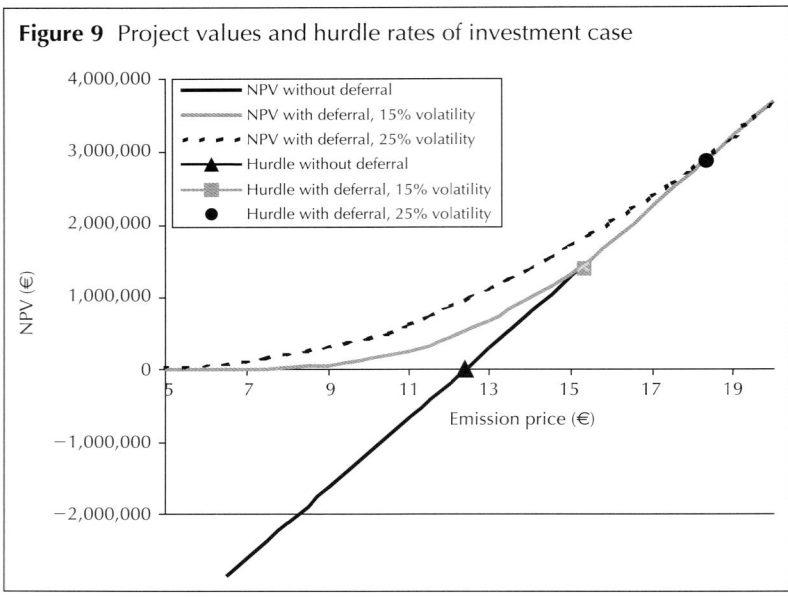

Figure 9 Project values and hurdle rates of investment case

we invest later. If the volatility in emission prices is higher than 15%, the value of the project increases and we observe an outward shift of the value curve in Figure 9. The figure shows that a higher volatility not only increases the project value, but also makes it optimal to wait even longer before investment takes place. With a volatility rise from 15% to 25%, the value of the project nearly doubles from €557,476 to €992,082. At the same time, the hurdle rate above which investment is economical reaches a level of €18.31 (where it was €15.29).

We can extend the analysis to determine in general how the volatility influences the investment decision. In Figure 10 the project values for different volatility levels are shown. It appears that there is a close to linear relation between the two variables. We obtain a similar linear relation between volatility levels and investment hurdles. Unfortunately, this strong dependence of optimal decisions on our assumption of volatility complicates the decision making. Volatility is a notoriously hard statistic to estimate, especially in a market that has yet to start. At the same time, it has a strong impact on what is optimal. However, ignoring volatility altogether is certainly worse.

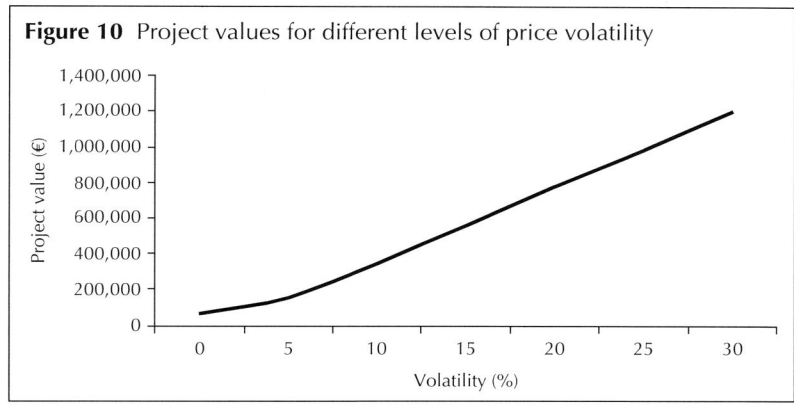

Figure 10 Project values for different levels of price volatility

Finally, it is insightful to analyse how changes in the investment costs impact the project. The investment costs have their analogue in the exercise price of financial options. So, the lower the investment costs (ie, the exercise price), the further the project is in-the-money, the more valuable the project and so the sooner it should be decided to actually carry the project out. Higher investment costs negatively impact the value of the project, both with and without taking the deferral option into account. However, the gap between the two widens as well, so the pure option value (defined as the value with deferral option minus the value without deferral option) is an upward-sloping function of investment costs (Figure 11). In other words, the larger the initial investment, the more important it is that we can postpone direct investment.

Power production – incorporating power and fuel prices
In the industrialised countries, by burning fossil fuels, the power sector emits around one-third of greenhouse gases. Power producers form also the majority of the European installations that will be affected by an emission cap. Consequently, this sector will be responsible for the bulk of reductions in CO_2. The pivotal role of the power sector has raised questions about who is eventually to pay for the rise in energy production costs. Will it be the sector itself? Or will the sector be able to pass prices on to end users, either the energy-intensive (large) industries or the smaller end users, or both? Rising power production costs will not have an

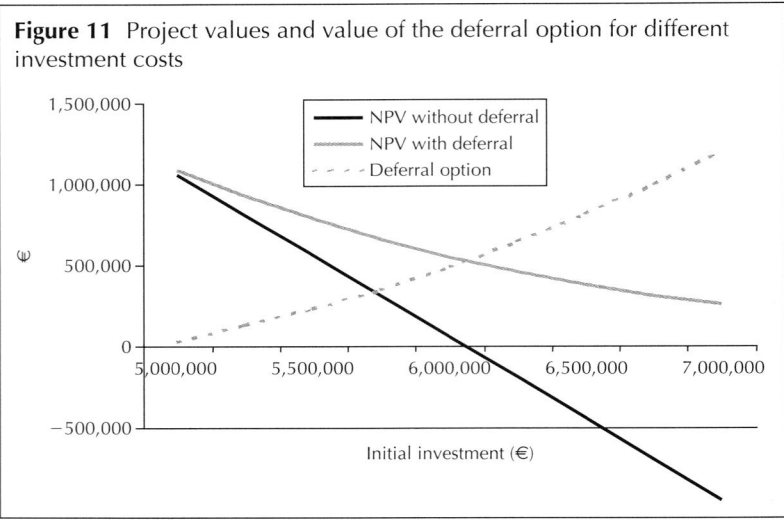

Figure 11 Project values and value of the deferral option for different investment costs

equal impact on each power generator. Depending on their fuel mix, their abatement curves and their national allocations, some companies are likely winners, others likely losers. Lower emission levels of natural gas and (to a lesser extent) gas oil and fuel oil will result in a shift towards these fuel types. With the important share in the use of these fuels, the demand changes in the power sector are likely to incite a change in relative prices between fuel types: gas prices may go up and coal prices may go down.

All these variables (power prices, fuel prices, emission prices) have a strong impact on the future profitability of current investments, and are all very uncertain. Instead of ignoring this uncertainty, it is paramount to incorporate it into any investment decision analysis. In the case so far we assumed that the investment in emission reduction did not alter the exposure towards fuel prices (no change in fuel mix, which is realistic if the investment is in efficiency enhancement) nor towards power prices (overall production capacity remained the same). The concept of "spark spread including emission" offers an elegant way to extent this analysis.

A generator's choice can be summarised by the choice of transforming fuel into power or not. Stated otherwise, a generator has the option to capture the gross profit margin on its assets or not. A plant can thus be thought of as a call option to exercise this gross profit margin, often referred to as spark spread: the difference between the prices at which power can be sold, minus the fuel costs for generating the power. The magnitude of the spark spread at time t of a gas-fired plant depends on the current market prices for power (P_t) and fuel (G_t) as well as the conversion efficiency of the plant, denoted by the heat rate (h):

$$\text{Spark Spread}_t = P_t - h \cdot G_t$$

The spark spread should include the major variable costs for producing power, which have traditionally been the fuel costs.[5] With the advent of emission trading, a second cost component is introduced: the price of emission rights (E_t). If we denote the CO_2 content of the fuel by c, then the spark spread including emissions becomes:

$$\text{Emission Spark Spread}_t = P_t - h \cdot (G_t + c \cdot E_t)$$

For example, if we take the following numbers –

market price for (base load) power	$P_t = 35 \ \text{€/MWh}$
fuel costs	$G_t = 3 \ \text{€/GJ}$
heat rate	$h = 8 \ \text{GJ/MWh}$
CO_2 content of the fuel	$c = 0.06 \ \text{tonne/GJ}$
price of emission rights	$E_t = 7.50 \ \text{€/tonne}$

– then the spark spread without emission costs equals $35 - 8 \times 3 = 11 \ \text{€/MWh}$, whereas the spark spread including emission costs is $8 \times 0.06 \times 7.50 = 3.60 \ \text{€/MWh}$ lower ($7.40 \ \text{€/MWh}$). So, the spark spread and thus the plant's gross profit margin do not only fluctuate because of power and fuel prices, but also because of emission price fluctuations.

The uncertainty in all of these variables should be taken into account when investing in new power production, when investing in fuel switching, when optimising any production decision and when analysing the risks of current production capacity. Unfortunately, this is not a straightforward problem to solve. The earlier described framework of a binomial tree is insufficient, because it contains only one decision variable (emission costs). In practice, either the decision tree has to be extended with two more variables (creating a complex three-dimensional tree) or scenario analysis and simulations need to be combined to model the uncertain future. The latter (simulations) is the more general. The framework presented in Longstaff and

Schwartz (2001) is very useful for this kind of application and is extensively used for complex option valuations in financial markets. Recently, their least-squares simulation method has also been successfully implemented to related real option problems in the gas and power sector, in particular for the valuation of swing options and gas storage. The details of such an approach are quite technical and beyond the scope of this book, but the interested reader may find a useful example in De Jong and Walet (2003a).

CONCLUSIONS

With the advent of emission trading, emissions become an integral part of investment decisions. Traditional investment analysis needs to be augmented with emission costs: the absolute level as well as its volatility. In the power-production sector, depending on the type of investment, the uncertain price behaviour of power and fuels may also have to be incorporated to make better investment decisions.

The case scenario shows the influence of emission price uncertainty on the investment decision process. From this we learn that banking and the option to defer an investment have opposite influences on the decision to invest. Banking will more easily lead to making the investment, though the effect is very limited, since banking profits will quickly vanish due to arbitrageurs in the market. On the other hand, the deferral option makes a project more valuable, but leads to a more hesitant attitude towards direct investments. The deferral option is especially valuable when a project is close to at-the-money, so when direct investment is on the edge of being economical or not.

The case also highlights the sensitivity of optimal decisions on model variables, especially the expected price level and the price volatility of emission rights. Widely varying expectations from market participants about future prices underline the difficult task of investment decision makers. In general, however, this uncertainty is an extra reason for an approach that explicitly takes this uncertainty into account.

In addition to these hard financial factors, some "soft" issues may play a role in the "make-or-buy" decision, for example the preservation of a "green" corporate image. This may make companies reluctant to pollute more than their allocated rights. However, companies should be aware that an internal strategy may involve considerable costs, because postponing reductions and buying rights externally instead may be cheaper and ensures flexibility for the future. At the same time, an external solution increases the number of buyers in the market, which is important for a proper functioning of emission trading. So, both for an individual company and the environment as a whole, what seems optimal at first sight may be far from optimal after thorough analysis.

1   Real options, just like financial options, give an owner the right, but not the obligation, to take action. Unlike financial options, they require ownership of real assets (see Dixit and Pindyck, 1994).
2   One could assume that the investment opportunity remains after 2009 as well. However, at that time better alternatives (cheaper/more effective) will normally be available, making the current investment opportunity no longer a viable option.
3   Calculation of the 24% volatility is based on the monthly price data in the period August 1994–December 2002, published by Cantor Fitzgerald.
4   Typically, a so-called risk-neutral valuation is used in such option calculations. This would be appropriate in financial markets with sufficient liquidity in hedging instruments. In our case, however, this is impossible due to the fact that there are insufficient hedging opportunities caused by a still illiquid futures market in emission rights. Frequent delta hedging with futures or forwards is therefore impossible. Hence, we use a traditional discounting approach.
5   Other variable costs such as variable maintenance and staff are relatively minor for a typical power plant.

REFERENCES

Cox, J., S. Ross, and M. Rubinstein, 1979, "Option Pricing: A Simplified Approach", *Journal of Financial Economics* **7**, pp. 229–63.

De Jong, C., and K. Walet, 2003a, "To Store or Not to Store", *Energy Risk* (formerly *Energy Power Risk Management*), pp. S8–S11, October.

De Jong, C., and K. Walet, 2003b, "Managing Emissions Risk", Maycroft Research Report.

Dixit, A. K., and R. S. Pindyck, 1994, *Investment under Uncertainty* (Princeton, NJ: Princeton University Press).

Hull, J. C., 2002, *Options, Futures and Other Derivatives*, 4th edition (New York: Prentice Hall).

Longstaff, F. A., and E. S. Schwartz, 2001, "Valuing American Options by Simulation: A Simple Least-square Approach", *Review of Financial Studies* **14**, pp. 113–47.

Section 4

Trading Experiences and Outlooks

Introduction

Cyriel de Jong; Kasper Walet

Erasmus University Rotterdam; Maycroft Consultancy Services

After the regulation, implementation and investment issues discussed in the previous sections, this section describes developments in the emissions markets: what have we observed so far and what are we going to observe in the future? It contains vital knowledge and experience from experts in the many countries around the globe involved in emissions trading.

Emissions trading has nowhere been implemented overnight and simulations have been an important part in the preparation process, for example preceding the EU Emissions Trading Scheme (EU ETS, see Chapter 13). Although the EU ETS has received considerable attention in previous chapters, Chapter 14 contains new information and discusses the largest greenhouse gas trading scheme in a comprehensive manner. Chapter 15 is similarly comprehensive on the UK ETS, a scheme that is already operational at the time of writing, and of which the functioning is in question.

Canada and Japan (Chapter 16) are often overlooked emissions markets, but will host trading in immense volumes of allowances, which will no doubt affect trading elsewhere. Many emission reductions are believed to be available cheaply in some of the central and Eastern European countries, so these countries also play a pivotal role (Chapter 17). On the other side of the globe, both New Zealand and Australia have taken on a leading role in the discussions surrounding greenhouse gas reduction, and have also taken important measures to achieve reductions, but their governments have no plans for a trading scheme in the near future

(Chapter 18). Whether this stance will hold for long remains to be seen and is not universally supported throughout Australia and New Zealand, as highlighted by the regional trading scheme in New South Wales (Australia).

In a sense, the penultimate chapter synthesises all the frameworks and analysis in the previous chapters. It discusses the universal focus of attention: prices for emission allowances. The chapter describes and weighs the factors that drive the price formation process in the EU ETS, but the resulting lessons are no less valid elsewhere.

All the attention to emissions trading implementation issues may cloud the opinion of sceptics, including researchers, politicians and business managers in the United States. These people may make a justified critique of the "universal" interpretation of global warming in general and emissions trading in particular. We leave it up to the reader to consider the opinions in the final chapter. So, this last chapter is not meant to be cynical, but serves as encouragement to remain critical at all times.

13

Lessons from Trading Simulations

John Scowcroft, Vasco de Janeiro

EURELECTRIC

Greenhouse gas emissions trading is one of three mechanisms envisaged by the Kyoto Protocol. To explore, gain experience and boost understanding of the issues at play in setting up a greenhouse gas emissions trading market, and to further develop the assessment of this type of market in a realistic setting, the European electricity industry, represented by EURELECTRIC, took part in a series of trading simulations. These Greenhouse Gas and Electricity Trading Simulations, called GETS 1, GETS 2 and GETS 3, were organised in 1999, 2000 and 2002. Companies from the electricity sector, and from other sectors such as cement, pulp and paper, chemicals, steel, oil, gas, glass and brokerage, participated on a voluntary basis through the payment of a fee.[1]

GETS 1 and GETS 2 were conceptually similar, pioneering, hands-on simulations on greenhouse gas emissions and electricity trading and were like no other simulations.[2] In these simulations, participants established virtual companies, traded emissions and electricity in a trading platform and simulated realistic scenarios. GETS 3 was fundamentally different from the previous simulations. It was model-based, did not interact with participants, and sought to look at the implications of various design options for emissions trading schemes at a time when the EU institutions were discussing the proposal for a directive on emissions trading. None of the simulations attempted to predict the price of CO_2 allowances, but essentially encouraged learning by undertaking exercises that allowed participants to become

247

familiar with emissions trading and to make valuable recommendations to policymakers.

GETS 3 (2002) was model-based and thus did not involve active participants. Its goal was to address key factors in developing the right policy framework, and therefore falls outside the scope of this chapter. Through GETS 1 (1999) and GETS 2 (2000), participants obtained practical experience that has proved useful in current trading systems. Moreover, they observed investment behaviour and trading strategies that are relevant for companies who have faced or may face emissions caps. Consequently, we will discuss GETS 1 and 2 in detail below.

GETS 1

In March 1999, 19 European electricity companies decided to engage in a practical emission and electricity trading simulation (see GETS 1, 1999). The goals of this exercise were:

❏ to try to simulate the effects of a CO_2 constraint on power generation when CO_2 emissions and electricity can be traded;
❏ to learn how electricity and emissions trading could be integrated into a company's activity; and
❏ to draw practical lessons for the design of emissions trading under the Kyoto Protocol.

The participants did not play on behalf of their companies, but *via* so-called virtual companies, which did not necessarily bear any resemblance to their parent companies. In total, 16 virtual companies were established. Companies were free to choose any profile they wished for their virtual companies. Each virtual company was defined for the year 2000 by its level of electricity production, its plant types and capacity, and its level of CO_2 emissions, which was used as the reference for its emission constraints. This information was shared among all virtual companies.

Modalities

The simulation period lasted eight weeks, covering the period 2000–12. Each week represented either one or two years of activity. First and foremost, virtual companies had to supply a fixed amount of electricity, based on their initial production level in 2000. At the beginning of each trading session, the level of electricity demand was announced to each virtual company.

To obtain a simulation that would generate realistic results, some real-world constraints were imposed on the activities of the virtual companies, especially on their investments. For instance, new capacity could only come on line after a certain lead time, specific to the chosen technology and a virtual company could start operating a combined-cycle gas turbine only if it had invested in the plant three "years" before. Furthermore, the capital cost and the minimum size for each technology were set. This was meant to avoid price differences across regions that would result only from different assumptions on capital cost.

Virtual companies were given limits on their CO_2 emissions, based on their level in 2000, for two consecutive periods, 2005–7 and 2008–12. At a level of 5% the reduction in the second period was higher than the 2% reduction in the first period. These targets were expressed as averages over the commitment period, and not as annual targets, in a way that is similar to the Kyoto Protocol commitment period. The purpose of the first budget period was to set companies on track with their 2008–12 commitments, along the lines of the "demonstrable progress by 2005" mentioned in the Protocol. From a learning perspective, it was also useful to give participants two opportunities to achieve an emission objective, each with a different time horizon.

CO_2 and electricity trading

Electricity demand could be met by either domestic production or electricity imports, through electricity trading. Virtual companies could reduce their emissions internally or acquire permits in the market. Banking – ie, the opportunity to carry over extra reductions from the first to the second period – was allowed. A "grace period" was introduced after each commitment period to allow noncomplying participants to acquire CO_2 emission units from participants with banked units. Failure to comply with either of the period's commitment levels obliged the failing company to reduce its emissions even more in the next budget period, by an amount equal to its extra emissions in the previous budget period. This also triggered a financial penalty equal to 150% of the highest observed price.

Electricity was traded on a spot market only, whereas CO_2 was traded for both the first and the second budget period from 2001–2. In technical terms, CO_2 contracts for the first and second budget period were futures contracts, with 2007 and 2012 maturity dates. Starting 2008, a spot market for CO_2 was introduced, on which units banked from the first budget period were traded.

Each week (corresponding to a one- or two-year period), the simulation functioned as follows:

❑ an announcement of electricity supply assumptions to all virtual companies;
❑ communication of investment decisions by virtual companies, compiled and communicated to all virtual companies;
❑ a two-hour trading session for CO_2 and electricity;
❑ confirmation of trades to each virtual companies by the exchange;
❑ a report on electricity supply, electricity trade, CO_2 emissions and CO_2 trades sent by virtual companies for audit; and
❑ audit of electricity and CO_2 results for each company.

Power generation: investment patterns and capacity management

As agreed beforehand, over the simulation period, electricity demand grew by 24%. For those companies that complied with their CO_2 emission objectives, this represented a 26% reduction in the CO_2 intensity of their power generation. This could not be achieved without significant investment in new power plants emitting less-CO_2. Therefore the vast majority of new capacity installed during the period was based on natural gas, either through a coal-to-gas conversion, or through the installation of co-generation and combined cycle gas turbines. The last two options, when substituting for coal, reduced CO_2 emissions for a lower cost than a simple coal-to-gas conversion, which delivered almost no improvement in plant efficiency. As a result, shown in Figure 1, there was a dramatic decline in coal-based power generation.

Smaller investments were recorded in wind- and biomass-based generation, even though they represented large percentage increases during the period (95% and 23% respectively). One company invested in a coal plant that came on line in 2010, as it was

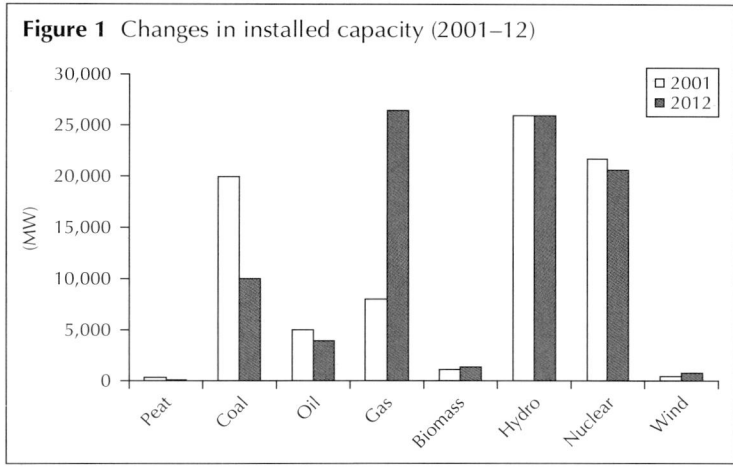

Figure 1 Changes in installed capacity (2001–12)

expected that electricity prices might rise faster than those of CO_2 emission allowances. This did not turn out to be the case in the simulation, at least not to the point where such investment generated significant profits. No new capacity was installed after 2011. This feature of the simulation deserves a note of caution. No emission objectives were specified beyond 2012; there was therefore no incentive to invest in capacity that was less CO_2-intensive beyond that date. In fact, further reductions beyond 2012 may have affected the choice of technology earlier. The absence of a subsequent commitment period also affected trading and compliance strategies. This reflects the current political situation where no emission reduction targets have been defined for the period post-2012.

The investment behaviour observed in the simulation largely reflected the constraint on emissions and the assumptions on the capital cost of various technologies adopted for this game. In the real world, capital cost may vary for a given technology from one country to the next, as well as the cost of generated power, eg, for wind or biomass.

Other means of CO_2 abatement were available to participants, in addition to straight investment in less CO_2-intensive capacity. Those virtual companies who relied on hydro and nuclear resources often increased the use of existing available resources, as these were not necessarily used at their full potential in the base year. Indeed, no new investment was made in these technologies during the simulation. As for other low-CO_2-emitting sources (natural gas, biomass and wind), virtual companies increased the number of hours of operation. When combined with the results on new capacity, virtual companies managed their installed capacity to minimise CO_2 reductions. The use of gas, biomass, wind and nuclear increased over the simulation. While the number of hours of use of peat and oil plants also increased, the total capacity of these plant types was reduced. In all, these technologies contributed a lower share of total power supply in 2012 than in 2001. The low operating hours of coal plants in 2012 is also consistent with the CO_2 objective applied to the virtual companies.

In brief, virtual companies combined new investment in less CO_2-emitting capacity (gas, but also renewable sources) with an increased use of available capacity in order to meet their emission constraints, while supplying increasing amounts of electricity over the period. For practical reasons, DSM and other energy efficiency measures were not introduced as options to reduce emissions in the simulation. This would have required much more detailed assumptions about the potential and cost of such options on a company-by-company basis.

GETS 2

After completion of the first simulations, GETS 2 was set up to study the usefulness of this type of market in a more realistic setting. To test various assumptions and parameters, three different simulations were run. Comparing the results of the three simulations provided data for comparisons between various assumptions such as modes of allowance allocation.

Figure 2 shows the general design of GETS 2. It kept some of the key principles of the previous simulations. For example, it did not attempt to determine a price for CO_2, hence the use of both virtual economic conditions and virtual companies. Similarly, only direct emissions (on the company's production sites) were accounted for and, therefore, traded. Accordingly, the electricity consumers, introduced in GETS 2, were not responsible for the emissions related to the generation of the electricity they were consuming.

However, GETS 2 was different in a number of respects. In GETS 1, primary energy prices were assumed to remain constant. In GETS 2, prices of primary energy and raw materials changed

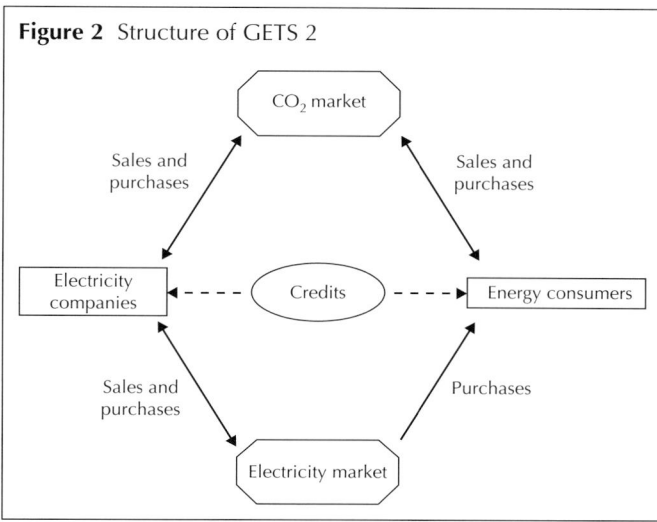

Figure 2 Structure of GETS 2

annually. As a result, some participants had to adapt their strategy to changes in these prices. GETS 2 also extended the power sector with some key energy consumers (and/or generators of electricity for their own needs).

The 40 companies that took part in GETS included five companies from the gas and oil-refining industry; three companies from the materials sector (eg, cement, glass); one steel company; two chemical companies; one company from the paper industry; and two financial institutions (as traders). Overall, with almost twice as many members in GETS 2 as in GETS 1, as well as many participants adopting widely differing strategies, the simulation saw a spectacular rise in the volume of transactions and many economic optimisations. The diversity of companies' profiles was a major aspect of the design of the simulation. In particular, the virtual companies had different marginal costs of CO_2 emission reductions, a precondition for a meaningful emissions trading market.

The introduction of the clean development mechanism (CDM), demand-side management (DSM) and the introduction of a futures market for electricity were also responsible for this liquidity increase. At the same time, they allowed for more realistic strategies.

In the previous simulations, a uniform CO_2 emission constraint had been applied to all companies. Allowances were allocated free of charge in line with a "grandfathering" methodology. In GETS 2, the three simulations provided an opportunity to test three different initial allocation methods:

❏ allocation based on grandfathering;
❏ allocation based on a benchmark, taking into account differences in the intensity of CO_2 emissions and therefore partly taking into account the early action of some participants; and
❏ allocation based partly (50%) on grandfathering and partly (50%) on auctions.

An important improvement was the extension of the emission objectives beyond 2012. Their absence had triggered a "wall effect" in GETS 1, when companies had little or no incentive to put together long-term strategies (extending beyond the horizon represented by the end of the simulation). However, this extension in GETS 2 did not completely prevent the occurrence of a similar phenomenon towards the end of the session, but just dampened its effect. For the three simulations, there were three commitment periods: from 2005 to 2007 (2% reduction compared with reference year 1999); from 2008 to 2010 (5% reduction); and from 2011 to 2015 (8% reduction). Over these three commitment periods the participants had to cover their emissions, on average, by holding a sufficient number of allowances.

LESSONS FROM GETS 1 AND GETS 2
In GETS 1, most – 15 out of 16 – virtual companies traded CO_2 actively (see Figure 3), even though most of them complied through internal reductions. For these participants, trading provided the opportunity to manage their extra CO_2 allowances as an asset, either to be used as banking from one period to the next, or to generate revenues in order to minimise the cost of meeting their CO_2 emission reductions.

The simulation clearly showed that trading could help participants to better manage their CO_2 emission objectives together with their core activity. Through the price signal generated by the market, participants were in a position to decide whether it is more economical to reduce emissions internally or to rely on the acquisition of allowances in order to comply. However, another striking lesson from the simulation was that trading did not guarantee compliance by all participating sources. It is worth noting that neither of the two

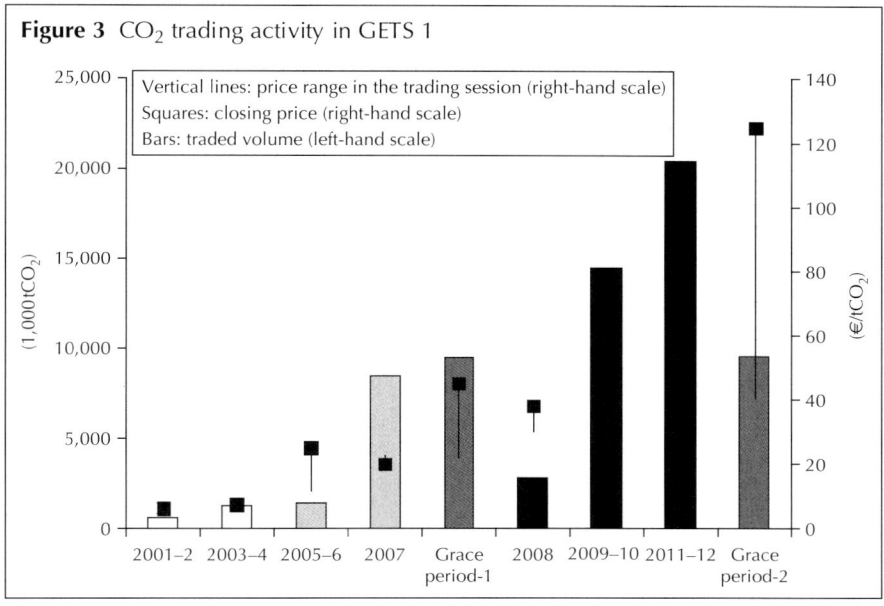

Figure 3 CO_2 trading activity in GETS 1

Vertical lines: price range in the trading session (right-hand scale)
Squares: closing price (right-hand scale)
Bars: traded volume (left-hand scale)

virtual companies in noncompliance had sold CO_2 allowances, a risk that is sometimes envisioned in the literature on emissions trading. The fictitious nature of the simulations, without real money at stake, may partly have contributed to the noncompliance of these two companies, but could occur in real-world markets as well. It is only through the formulation of expectations on future production needs and emission levels that a robust compliance strategy can be established. Trading is but one element in that picture. Nevertheless, emissions trading in the simulations enabled companies that were unable to comply to offset an important share of their surplus emissions. Overall compliance would have been greatly hampered without the ability to acquire CO_2 allowances from other participants.

Companies relied to a great extent on the ability to bank emission allowances generated in the first period, either to comply in the next period, or to sell for revenues, when market prices were favourable. Banking made it possible to benefit from additional reductions, on top of the ability to trade them immediately.

GETS 2 confirmed that, although the economic conditions were fictitious, the use of market mechanisms could help industrial companies to reduce their greenhouse gas emissions under optimal economic conditions. The three simulations of GETS 2 led to a number of other interesting results.

Despite a slightly longer-term horizon than in the previous simulations, a "wall effect" reappeared consistently in all three simulations. This revealed the requirement for a long-term horizon. This wall effect consisted of uneconomic behaviour and abnormal transactions, patterns and prices. Although this is a limitation of the simulation, and we have to consider the first two commitment periods for significant results, this was also a message to policy-makers that industry, especially the electricity sector, needs long-term horizons in order to optimise its strategic decisions.

During all simulations of GETS 2 (GETS 2.1, GETS 2.2 and GETS 2.3), global compliance was reached for each commitment period. This meant that, collectively, industrial companies suc-ceeded in generating emissions reductions beyond the objectives set by regulatory authorities. The setting up of a carbon market and investment in CDM and DSM schemes helped minimise the overall economic cost of reductions. Figure 4 shows the carbon efficiency, ie, emissions per unit of energy consumption, achieved throughout the simulations.

Global compliance was obtained with all of the allocation methods tested (eg, grandfathering, benchmarking and auctioning). However, the various methods impacted differently on individual companies.

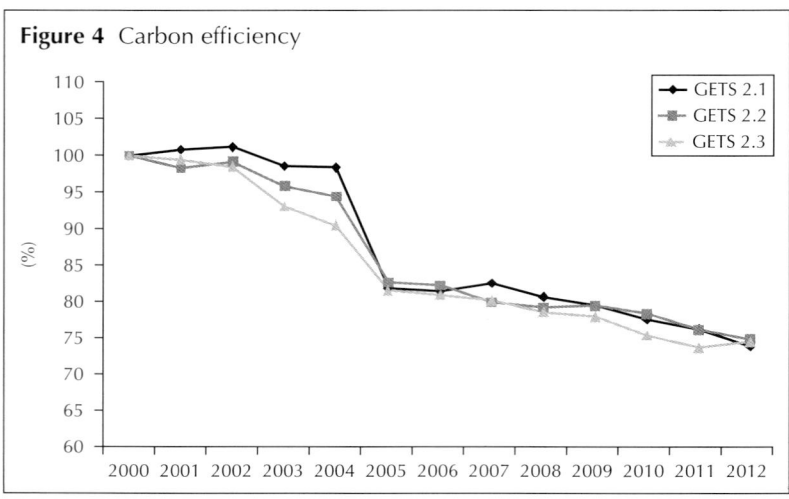

Figure 4 Carbon efficiency

Depending on the method of allocation, certain companies found themselves structurally needing to buy carbon, while others became structurally in surplus. Allocation methods are always inequitable to companies or sectors; changing allocation methods make allocation inequitable in different ways.

Market transactions did not take the place of environmental investment, including shifting from coal to gas, capital expenditure in renewable energy, improvement of industrial processes. Rather, they allowed the participants to optimise the timing of their investments (see Figure 5). Within a carbon market, CO_2 becomes one of the key criteria for running a business and therefore its price and availability will be integrated in every strategic decision. A carbon market coupled with other energy markets makes it possible to obtain a clear and objective price signal, allowing industrial companies to determine a cost of energy, "carbon included". This cost, related to the various market prices (eg, kWh, other fuels and raw materials) plays an important role and allows economic optimisation strategies to be designed.

CDM and DSM proved to be a useful addition compared with GETS 1. As the simulations developed, the participants made increasing use of credits obtained through such projects to reach compliance. The offer of credits remained comparable over the three simulations. It should be noted that these credits introduced additional emissions reductions achieved outside the simulation. These

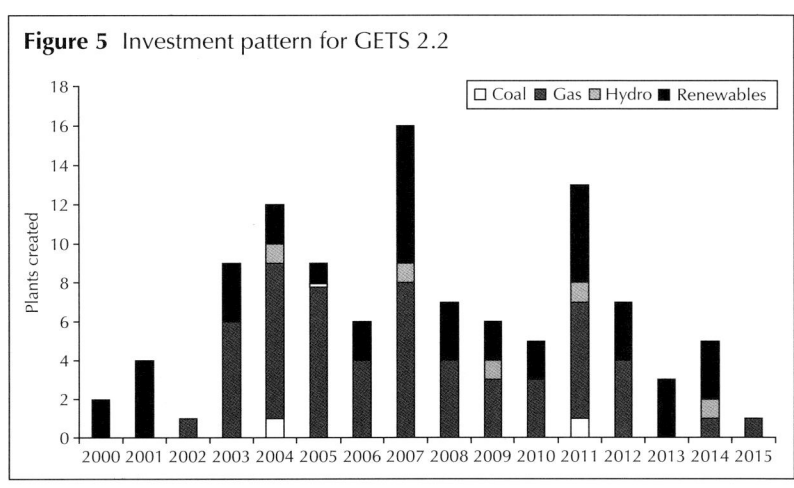

Figure 5 Investment pattern for GETS 2.2

credits were "commoditised" products, bearing levels of risk that were known to investors.

Another key result of the simulation was a significant transfer from coal- and oil-based generation towards gas-fired generation. The market share of nuclear and hydropower remained stable, and, while new renewable energy sources grew, they remained marginal. For renewable energies, a carbon market – on its own – clearly did not provide enough incentive to promote a significant expansion in their use. The introduction of Green Certificates in the simulation was considered, but it was decided not to proceed for reasons of complexity, for lack of time and because it might have confused other results.

CONCLUSIONS

What separates GETS from other simulations is its breadth and depth, which conferred on the simulations a remarkable realism. This enabled us to draw invaluable lessons that contributed to the clarification of many issues on emissions trading not only for policymakers but for the industry also.

The key lessons from the simulations are the following:

❑ companies learned quickly how to trade.
❑ emissions reductions were achieved through investment. The emissions trading market allowed companies to integrate fully environmental goals into business strategies and decision making.
❑ a carbon market makes it possible to obtain a clear and objective price signal, allowing companies to determine the cost of energy, "carbon included". This enabled economic optimisation strategies to be designed.
❑ industry needs long-term emission-reduction objectives in order to optimise its strategic decisions, otherwise uneconomic behaviour and abnormal transactions, patterns and prices may occur.
❑ different allocation methods triggered significant impact on companies. Depending on the method of allocation, certain companies found themselves structurally needing to buy carbon, while others became structurally in surplus.

At the time of writing, we are analysing the feasibility of undertaking GETS 4 (2004), which would assess the impacts of future world greenhouse gas emissions reduction and trading schemes to 2012 and beyond. The major difference from previous GETS studies is that participants from outside Europe will be sought, in particular from North America, Australia, Canada and Japan. This reflects the global nature of the schemes that will potentially be set up, possible linkages between them and the need to produce realistic scenarios based on the best available information.

1   The following companies participated in at least one of the simulations: Atofina, BP, British Energy, Copenhagen Energy, DEI, Edison, Electrabel, Electricidade de Portugal, Electricity Association, Electricité de France, Elf Trading, Elforsk, Elsam, E2, EnBw, Endesa, Enel, EnergieNed, E.ON, ESB, Essent Sustainable Energy, Finergy, Gaz de France, Goteborg Energi, HEW, Hidroelectrica del Cantabrico, Holderbank, Iberdrola, IndustriKraft Midt Norge, Innogy, Lafarge, MVV Energie, National Power, Natsource, Polish Electricity Association, Powergen, Rede Eléctrica Nacional, Roche, RWE, Saint Gobain, SCA, Société Générale, Swedish District Heating Association, Total Fina Elf, TXU Europe, Unesa, Union Fenosa, Usinor, Vattenfall, VEO.
2   With the exception of IEA's "Trading CO_2 and Electricity in the Baltic Sea Region", November 2002, which was based on GETS 1.

REFERENCES

GETS 1, 1999, "Greenhouse Gas and Electricity Trading Simulation", Unipede/EUR-ELECTRIC, International Energy Agency, ParisBourse SA, October.

GETS 2, 2000, "Greenhouse Gas and Electricity Trading Simulation", Union of the Electricity Industry, EURELECTRIC, Euronext, PricewaterhouseCoopers, November.

GETS 3, 2002, "Greenhouse Gas and Electricity Trading Simulation", Union of the Electricity Industry, EURELECTRIC, ERM, March.

GETS 3bis, 2002, "Greenhouse Gas and Electricity Trading Simulation", Union of the Electricity Industry, EURELECTRIC, ERM, December.

GETS 4, 2004, "Greenhouse Gas and Electricity Trading Simulation", Union of the Electricity Industry – EURELECTRIC, ERM, concept paper, March.

14

The European Emissions Trading System

Cyriel de Jong; Kasper Walet

Erasmus University Rotterdam; Maycroft Consultancy Services

The European Union ratified the Kyoto Protocol on 31 May 2002. Its commitment to emission reduction is so firm that it has even decided to commit to the agreed emission reduction of 8% in the period 2008–12 compared with 1990 levels, even without Kyoto's coming into force. To meet this goal, within the EU the first multinational trade system for greenhouse gas (GHG) emission is currently being devised. On 9 December 2002, the 15 EU countries' ministers accepted a proposal, followed by the approval of the European Parliament. The system will become operational in 2005, starting with an initial phase that lasts until the end of 2007.[1]

The legal framework of the EU Emissions Trading System (EU ETS) was presented in Chapter 3; here, we discuss the developments in the European emissions market. In particular, we focus on developments and implications for the power sector. In the industrialised countries, by burning fossil fuels, the power sector emits around one-third of GHGs. Power producers form the majority of the European installations that will be affected by an emission cap. Consequently, this sector will be responsible for the bulk of reductions and therefore impacts on many other sectors within the EU.

EMISSIONS TRADING

The 15 EU member states have redistributed their collective Kyoto reduction target among themselves in an attempt to achieve emission reductions flexibly and cost-effectively. This is done

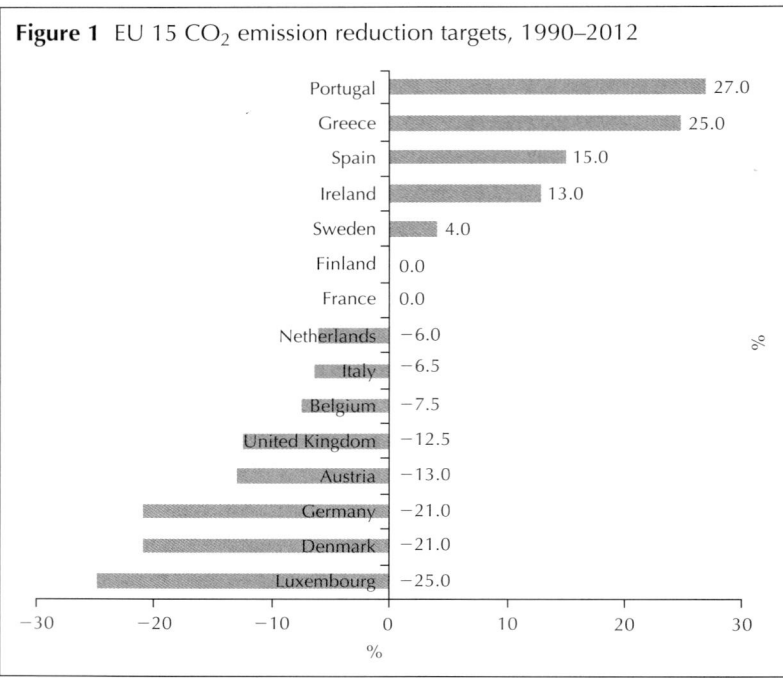

Figure 1 EU 15 CO$_2$ emission reduction targets, 1990–2012

Portugal	27.0
Greece	25.0
Spain	15.0
Ireland	13.0
Sweden	4.0
Finland	0.0
France	0.0
Netherlands	−6.0
Italy	−6.5
Belgium	−7.5
United Kingdom	−12.5
Austria	−13.0
Germany	−21.0
Denmark	−21.0
Luxembourg	−25.0

according to the Burden Sharing Agreement of June 1998, which takes individual economic circumstances into consideration. For example, the economies of Spain, Portugal, Greece and Ireland started from a less developed level in 1990 and so are allowed to increase emissions between 13 and 27%. Apart from Luxembourg, the greatest emissions reductions will have to be realised in Denmark and Germany, the largest polluter among the EU15 in absolute terms. Emission reductions for Germany were thought to be (and partly are) relatively easy to achieve, because of the industry collapse in former East Germany.

The EU will employ one of the major mechanisms suggested by the Kyoto Protocol – emissions trading – to meet its emissions reduction target. It will host the world's first multinational trade system for GHG emissions covering the current 25 EU member states, including the 10 accession countries, mostly from Central and Eastern Europe (Cyprus, the Czech Republic, Estonia, Hungary, Latvia, Lithuania, Malta, Poland, Slovakia and Slovenia). Emissions trading starts with an initial phase running from 2005 to the end of 2007. Thereafter, the scheme will run in periods of five years, the first period coinciding with the first Kyoto period (2008–12). From 2008 onwards, if Kyoto comes into force, the EU must meet the Protocol's targets, and international trading with countries outside the EU is expected to start. Therefore, what happens in the EU after 2007 depends largely on Kyoto's coming into force as well as the experiences from the initial phase.

The EU ETS Directive states that project-based mechanisms, including Joint Implementation (JI) and the Clean Development Mechanism (CDM), are important goals for both reducing global GHG emissions and increasing the cost-effective functioning of the EU ETS. In accordance with the relevant provisions of the Kyoto Protocol and Marrakech Accords, the use of the mechanisms should be supplemental to domestic action and domestic action will thus constitute a significant element of the effort made. The EU Commission has drafted a document commonly referred to as the "Linking Directive" with the intention of creating a bridge between these project-based mechanisms and the EU ETS. The Linking Directive aims to determine the extent to which CDM and JI credits can be used within the scheme.

Characteristics of the trading system

The policy framework for emissions trading was set by the EU Emissions Trading Directive of October 2003. It established a so-called "cap-and-trade" system, whereby individual installations receive absolute emission allowances. Gagelmann and Hansjürgens (2002) have distinguished five factors, which together determine the functioning of an emission trade system: (i) the range of the system, (ii) determination of the total emission level, (iii) primary allocation method of emission rights, (iv) market forces and (v) monitoring. We shall use these five factors to discuss the characteristics of the trade system within the EU.

1. Range of the system

The European Union has opted for a "downstream" approach, similar to the US SO_2 system. This means that it will not be the fuels that will be liable under the system, but instead the end users of these CO_2-emitting fuels. The EU Emissions Trading

Directive as adopted by the European Council in June 2003 covers the following industries:

❑ power generation;
❑ oil refining;
❑ coke ovens;
❑ metal industry;
❑ production of cement and lime;
❑ production of building materials and ceramics;
❑ glass fibre production; and
❑ production of paper, cardboard and pulp.

Initially, the system will apply only to CO_2 emission; at a later stage, possibly from 2008, the remaining GHGs mentioned in the Kyoto Protocol will also be involved. The EU expects that around 46% of the CO_2 emissions in the EU will be produced by the 10,000-plus installations that fall under the emission trading regime. Since CO_2 emissions represent the bulk of all GHG emissions, this corresponds to around 38% of the total estimated emission of the six Kyoto GHGs in 2010.

2. Determination of the total emission level
The EU proposal uses a cap-and-trade system with absolute emission allowances. In the first phase, these allowances will not be redistributed among installations by the European Commission, but by participating countries themselves. The countries must submit a National Allocation Plan (NAP) to the European Commission, which will then either accept or reject the plan. The plan must meet the criteria mentioned in Appendix III of the proposal. With regard to stipulation of the absolute emission allowance, the following criteria apply:

❑ The total number of emission rights to be allocated must be consistent with the commitment of the member state as described in the Kyoto Protocol. Sectors and companies must proportionally cover the Kyoto target (the rest of the target must be covered by emission sources that do not participate in the trade system).
❑ The total number of emission rights to be allocated should be in line with actual and expected emission trends.

The NAPs contain detailed information about the installations participating in the EU ETS and the caps they receive. The NAP can be implemented in various ways, but all EU member states must take a number of considerations into account.

3. Primary allocation method of emission rights

Based on political considerations – some parties strongly oppose an auction – the EU proposal recommends a free-allocation system for the first period (2005–7). In the second period (2008–12) member states are given the opportunity to auction rights, up to 10% of their allocated total.

The free-allocation programme can be implemented in various ways. Participants can choose the method they prefer and must write this down in their allocation plan. Individual EU member states must consider, amongst other things, the following in the design of their NAP (as mentioned in Appendix III of the proposal).

❑ Allocation plans should not encourage unfair competition.

❑ A unit cannot obtain more rights than necessary to cover its emissions. This could contradict the aforementioned "early action" principle, which states that companies that have already lowered their emissions should not be "punished" by receiving fewer rights than their more polluting counterparts. Furthermore, the fact that units cannot obtain more rights than they actually need to cover their emissions could frustrate emission rights trading due to a fundamental shortage of supply. After all, in a well-functioning market the supply of rights is created by (i) certain entities receiving more rights than needed to cover their emission and (ii) entities building up an emission rights surplus if they successfully apply cost-efficient autonomous reduction. The above criteria would make the supply of rights via point (i) disappear, implying that the supply of rights at the start of a trade period would be close to zero.

❑ Attention must be paid to "early action" (emission reduction measures taken before the year that is used as a basis for the calculation). Attention must also be paid to technical possibilities of emission reductions by specific companies and sectors.

❑ A NAP must be consistent with other legislative and policy instruments within the EU. Although (obligatory and/or subsidised) investments in renewable energy can be perceived as "early action", electricity producers do not receive emission rights for this kind of effort. Generating electricity from renewable sources already gives benefits such as governmental allowances and granted green certificates. The European Commission does not want to create another benefit in the shape of the allocation of rights for avoided emission.

Both for countries as a whole and individual companies, the outcome of the NAP may have considerable financial consequences. Extra allowances represent direct value; consequently, lobbying for favourable treatment from individual companies or sectors is intense. In Germany this has already led to heated debates between the environment minister and the economics minister Wolfgang Clement. The latter pleads for higher caps than envisioned by the former in the draft German NAP. At the time of writing, the outcome of this debate, with important consequences for the development of emission prices, is yet uncertain.

4. Market forces

The participation of more than 10,000 installations from various sectors seems to guarantee the presence of a sufficient number of market parties. The question is whether this sufficient supply and demand is secured on a continuous basis: it often happens that one company owns several installations. Reallocation of rights will first take place via internal trade, so the European Commission expects that internal trade will dominate the first period (2005–7).[2] What limits initial liquidity, furthermore, is that only a certain number of allocated rights will be traded, namely those rights that the selling party does not need to use in order to cover its own emission target.[3] Nevertheless, satisfactory supply and demand – and therefore liquidity – are expected to be present in the future trade system, even though it may take a few years. Experiences with the US SO_2 system and the RECLAIM programme in Southern California indicate this (see Chapters 4 and 11). Even with a much smaller number of participants, a liquid market did arise in both cases.

With regard to market restrictions, banking will be allowed in the first period (2005–7) and following five-year periods (2008–12, and so on). Only during the transition from the first to the second phase (2007–8) can individual member states impose restraints. Moreover, it is essential to create a system of plain and transparent rules to promote the free trade of emission rights with as few obstacles as possible. In particular, it is important to look at the EU ETS in relation to current relevant communal and national legislation. For instance, it is yet uncertain whether an existing measure regarding energy efficiency will still be valid. If it is, installations will be faced with permanent efficiency requirements, which will restrict emission trade possibilities.

5. Monitoring

In the proposed EU ETS, an independent authority will monitor the system. Each member state may decide whether this will be a public or private institution. Participating companies must report their yearly emission to this authority, after which verification follows. If a report turns out to be unsatisfactory, the participant can be temporarily excluded until the report has been revised. Apart from the monitoring of individual participants, a balanced administration of purchase and sale of rights is necessary – the EU system suggests a central register in which all trade activities and present emission rights are recorded per member. Chapter 6 discusses monitoring and verification in more detail.

During the first phase of the scheme, an excess emissions penalty of €40 per tonne of emitted CO_2e will be levied on all installations who fail to surrender the required number of allowances. A higher penalty of €100 per excess tonne emitted of CO_2e will be levied during the second and subsequent phases.

In addition to the fines in each phase, any installation that fails to meet its target will have to "make good" the next year – it will have to surrender enough allowances to cover its shortfall from the previous year in addition to the allowances required for the current year. For example, if Installation A emits 100 tonnes of CO_2e in 2005, but surrenders only 95 allowances at the end of the year, it will have to pay a fine of €200, and purchase five additional EU allowances to surrender in 2006.

EMISSIONS IN EUROPE

By January 2003, all EU member states as well as all accession countries had ratified the Kyoto Protocol. Nevertheless, actual emission reductions since 1990 have been limited.

Denmark was already a good environmental performer pre-ratification and in this sense, a rare exception. It placed restrictions on conventional thermal generators and promoted biofuels and wind power, which cut CO_2 emissions by a third in the power sector. Nevertheless, with an ambitious target of -21%, even Denmark is still far from meeting its target.

At first sight, some other countries seem to be on track towards commitment, but the biggest 1990s emissions reductions, seen in the UK and Germany, were one-offs. Germany is the EU's biggest polluter by a wide margin and reduced CO_2 emissions by 10% between 1990 and 2000. In general, however, the reductions in Germany were achieved incidentally, as a side effect of the collapse of heavy industries in the "Ost-Länder". Another large polluter, the UK, saw CO_2 emissions drop by 19%. The reductions in the UK are mainly due to the replacement of several coal-fired power plants with gas-fired plants, with the twofold aim of making production more flexible and less polluting. The gas-fired plants drove older and less efficient coal-fired plants almost completely from the market, providing a convincing case for the benefits of fuel switching. Further progress will be more expensive and will create political challenges for both countries.

If a country reduces emissions by the same percentage each year, ultimately meeting its emissions reduction goals under the Kyoto Protocol, the emissions trend can be labelled the "target path". In 2001, only five member states (France, Germany, Luxembourg, Sweden and the UK) were near or below their target path. The remaining ten countries are well above their targets. The countries that are allowed to increase their emissions appear to be furthest away from their target path. In particular, Portugal, Spain and Ireland saw emissions rise even faster than allowed under the EU Burden Sharing Agreement. Ireland's emissions, for example, stood 31% higher in 2001 than in 1990; this is well above the 13% increase Ireland is allowed between 1990 and 2008–12.

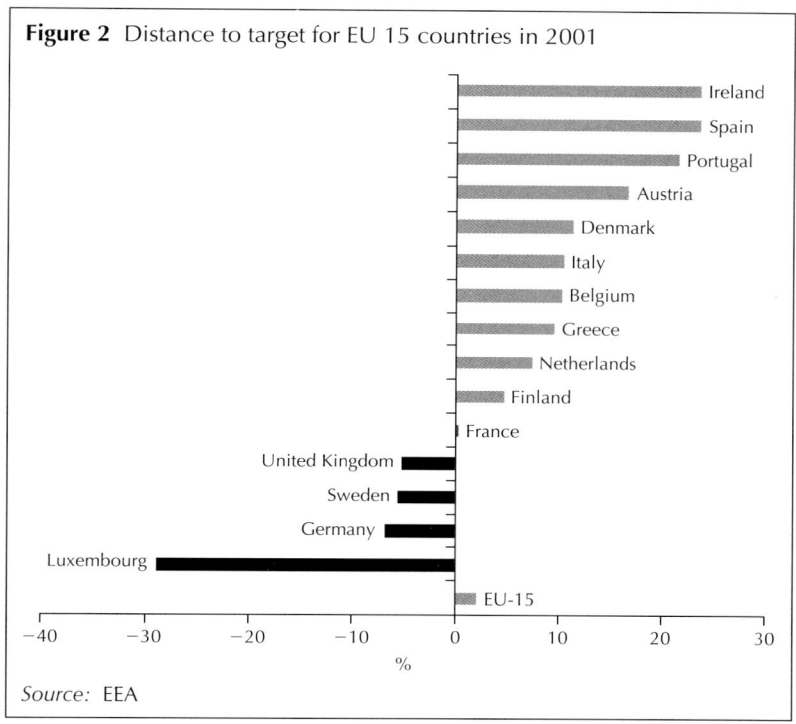

Figure 2 Distance to target for EU 15 countries in 2001

Source: EEA

EMISSIONS IN THE POWER SECTOR

Between 1990 and 2001 GHG emissions in the EU decreased by 2.3% (according to the European Environment Agency). The decrease occurred in most sectors, but many efforts were offset by a rise in transport emissions (see Figure 3). Increased transport flows and the political difficulties in association with transport emissions accounted for this negative development. Despite the decrease of 2.3%, much more progress is required within the EU: half the available time span has passed, and only about a quarter of emissions have been reduced. Looking ahead, a combination of gradually rising energy demand, closures of ageing nuclear plants, slow renewables build-up and continued support for coal, motorists and other heavy polluters could seriously jeopardise the EU's chances of hitting its target.

European policymakers could focus on major polluters such as power producers (in absolute terms) to reduce European CO_2

269

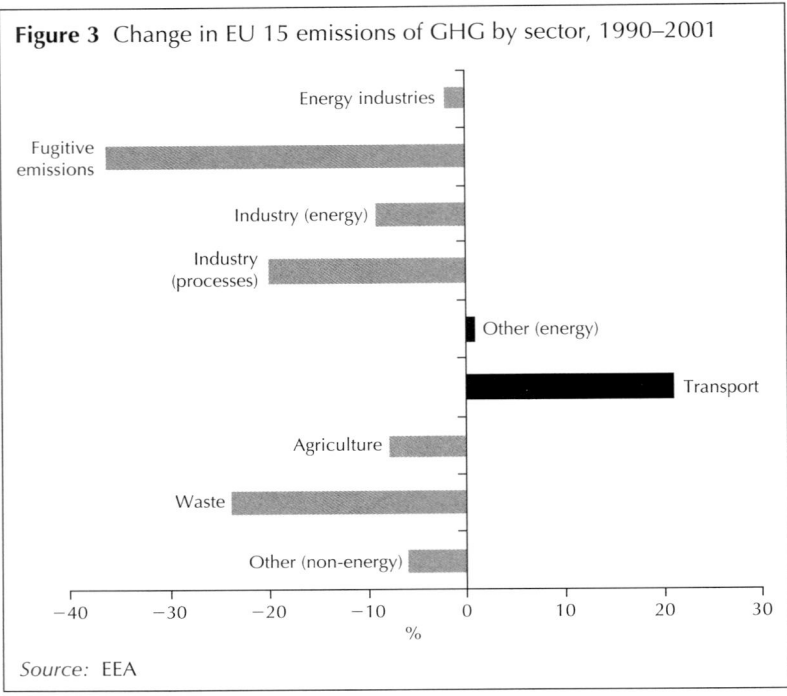

Figure 3 Change in EU 15 emissions of GHG by sector, 1990–2001

Source: EEA

emissions, but major polluters would be right to raise the issue of fairness. The UK, for example, is a strong performer in relative terms. Its conventional thermal sector produces fewer emissions per MWh than all other nations where conventional thermal power plays a central role in the power system. This is due to higher conversion efficiency rates. Spain, Ireland and Portugal may run small systems in the European context, but in relative terms they are poor performers and should be prime targets of any environmental policy based on fairness.

In 2002 the level of CO_2 emissions from Europe's major power companies was somewhat higher than the year before, according to a report published by PricewaterhouseCoopers and Enerpresse in 2003. This overall increase was mainly due to some temporary influences. In particular, a drought hit hydropower in the Iberian Peninsula and forced generators to depend more heavily on coal, resulting in a rise of CO_2 emissions. In general, however, the energy sector has been successful in decoupling energy output from emissions increases. This decoupling of energy output growth and emission growth occurred in all member states and shows the reduction potential in the energy industry. Even though the sector accounts for just over a quarter of total emissions, it will take on the largest share of future emission savings. According to the European Environment Agency (EEA), policies and measures in the energy sector account for the majority of the total expected savings (62% of savings from existing domestic measures and 58% of savings from additional domestic policies and measures).

Renewable energies (including hydro, wind, solar and biomass) do not produce GHG emissions. The same is true for nuclear energy, which makes it an attractive alternative for meeting emissions caps. However, the Kyoto Protocol contains a clause stating that emissions should not be reduced by building new nuclear plants. This is an obvious and important requirement for other environmental reasons. Therefore, reductions should naturally come from renewable, more efficient energies, and cleaner fossil fuels.

Although all fossil fuels produce emissions, lignite and hard coal are the dirtiest. In the future, the dirtiest fuels will have to be replaced by renewable energies and cleaner fuels (notably oil and natural gas). Typical emissions rates per energy output (MWh) are far lower for these fossil fuels than for lignite and coal, as shown in Table 1. Fuel switching alone can thus account for at least a one-third reduction. However, state subsidies to local lignite and coal producers in several European countries will often prevent switching from coal-fired to gas-fired plants. For example, total support to the German coal- and lignite-mining industry in 2001 – employing more than 50,000 – was €4.5 billion. And even natural gas, an environmental winner wherever it replaces coal and lignite, occasionally faces some pressure when it replaces nuclear plants or displaces

Table 1 Levels of CO_2 emissions (in kg CO_2/GJ) from various fossil fuels

Lignite	102.0
Hard coal	91.3
Heavy fuel oil	78.5
Gas oil	73.3
Natural gas	55.9

renewable investments. An example is the Nordic countries, where plans to build gas-fired power plants are constantly postponed due to environmental concerns despite the high efficiency rates of natural gas.

To calculate emissions per MWh it is necessary to combine the above statistics with the efficiency rate of a power plant. For example, with an efficiency rate of 50%, two units of fuel are needed to produce one unit of power. For hard coal, this would mean an emission of 182.6 kg CO_2/GJ, whereas for natural gas it would mean 111.8 CO_2/GJ power. Emissions can thus be reduced by increasing the efficiency or by burning cleaner fuels.

IMPACT ON THE POWER SECTOR

Producers claim the EU ETS will add sharply to generation costs. However, since emission rights are given away for nothing in the initial 2005–7 period, energy companies can even benefit from the EU ETS. The electricity industry is actually tipped by several experts to be a likely winner. The sector can compensate for the costs of carbon constraints through higher prices, and some reports have estimated that the power price in Europe will increase by as much as 60 per cent as a result of the EU ETS. Most have predicted windfall profits for the electricity industry. The investment bank Credit Suisse First Boston (CSFB), for example, in a study published in March 2003, expects an increase of 8–20% in average long-term power prices (see Table 1). In the short term, the impact on power prices may be larger, because the replacement of plants takes time. As a result, for countries where coal is the marginal fuel in the short term the increase in power prices might reflect the increase in coal-fired power. CSFB estimates the emission cost component per MWh in a coal-fired plant at 0.9 times the price of emissions rights. The emission caps thus result in additional costs of €9/MWh and €18/MWh for emissions prices of €10 and €20 respectively. In markets where coal is often the marginal fuel, the emission costs will be reflected in higher wholesale prices. Germany is a typical example of how power producers could benefit from the emissions trading scheme: emissions rights are obtained free, whereas additional costs are passed on to the end users, especially in view of the low historical price levels.

Table 2 Estimated percentage increase in wholesale power prices, 2006–10

Country	2006 Low*	2006 High*	2010 Low*	2010 High*
Belgium	7	19	8	20
Germany	22	57	21	55
Italy	14	36	8	20
Portugal	3	9	8	20
Spain	3	7	8	20
United Kingdom	16	40	14	28

*Low: based on CO_2e trading at €7.5/tonne. High: based on CO_2e trading at €20.0/tonne.
Source: CSFB/DrKW

Of course, the situation is different in markets where coal is not the typical marginal fuel. A typical combined-cycle gas turbine plant emits around 0.35 tonnes of CO_2 per MWh, which is around a third of a typical coal-fired plant. In countries with relatively clean power production, gas is often the marginal fuel. Reducing emissions will then be difficult and the rise in power prices may not compensate for the overall sector's emissions costs.

It is important to note that most estimates of the impact of the EU ETS on power prices were made at a time when price expectations hovered between €10 and €25 per tonne CO_2e. With prices decreasing since the beginning of 2004 to a level of around €7.5 per tonne, actual energy price increases are expected to be in the lower range of the expectations. Of course, whether sharp increases in power prices would ever be politically acceptable remains to be seen. Large energy price increases would seriously hamper the economic competitiveness of the European industry and are unlikely to be considered acceptable.

CONCLUSIONS
The EU was quick to embrace the Kyoto Protocol. It has imposed on itself a leading role in achieving emission reductions worldwide. The EU ETS will therefore be monitored closely not only in the EU itself, but also in other countries such as Russia, the US and Australia. Success of the European system is almost a necessary condition if the Kyoto Protocol is ever to be a success.

Individual captive companies struggle with much more basic concerns. What will be the NAPs? What will be expected emission prices? How to prepare? Furthermore, non-energy companies face an additional concern: what will be the impact on their energy costs? It will take time before all of these questions can be answered, but it is certain that structural changes are going to be required.

1 There were 15 EU member states at the time of ratification.

2 The benefit of internal compared with external trade is the fact that transaction costs are lower. Also, the issue of *intercompany pricing* comes up. By manipulating the internal transaction price of emission rights, companies with branches in different countries could assign their profits in the country with the lowest tax rates. To prevent this, the CO_2 trade system needs to make use of legislation that already exists covering the testing of internal prices by economic value. This means that internal transaction prices must follow external market prices.

3 Speculative trade is likely to come up during the course of the system. This type of trade adds to the liquidity of the market.

REFERENCE

Gagelmann, F., and B. Hansjürgens, 2002, "Climate protection through tradable permits: the EU proposal for a CO_2 emissions trading program in Europe", *European Environment*, **12**, pp. 185–202.

15

Learning by Doing? Experiences from the UK Emissions Trading Scheme

Frauke Roeser; Tim Jackson

Enviros Consulting Ltd; University of Surrey

In April 2002 the UK became the first country to introduce a fully fledged industry-wide emissions trading scheme (UK ETS) as one of a number of tools designed to achieve its domestic and Kyoto targets. Under Kyoto the UK has agreed to reduce greenhouse gas emissions by 12.5% over 1990 levels between 2008 and 2012. In addition, the UK government has set a much more ambitious internal target of a 20% reduction in carbon dioxide emissions by 2010 (see DETR, 2000). This target has been reiterated and exceeded in the recent Energy White Paper (see DTI, 2003) by a further commitment to reduce carbon emissions by 60% by 2050 in line with recommendations of the International Panel on Climate Change (IPCC). Emissions trading is expected to play a critical role in achieving this move to a low-carbon economy as efficiently and with as little disruption to industry as possible.

This important environmental objective, however, was not the scheme's sole purpose. According to the UK government, a key reason for the UK ETS was to provide a learning experience for UK business ahead of any international or global emissions trading schemes that are going to be developed within the framework of the Kyoto Protocol. As a first mover in GHG emissions trading, the UK also hoped to be able to influence other emerging schemes and to establish London as a centre of expertise for global emissions trading (see DETR, 2000).

The UK ETS will now overlap with, and in fact be superseded by, the European Union's Emissions Trading Scheme (EU ETS), which is due to start in 2005. Transition into the wider EU ETS will require fundamental adjustments to the existing UK policy framework. Two years into the UK scheme and on the eve of European-wide emissions trading, it is therefore interesting to ask how the UK scheme has fared against its objectives and to identify the lessons that can be and have been learned from it.

Starting with an outline of the UK ETS and developments in the UK market to date, this chapter will assess the effectiveness of the UK ETS in creating an efficient and environmentally credible carbon market. We will look at participants and at trading activity in the UK carbon allowance market to gain an insight into the performance of the UK ETS against its objectives. Finally, the chapter contains an outlook into future policy developments in view of the new EU ETS, including a commentary on the UK's National Allocation Plan (UK NAP). The chapter centres principally on the theme of learning. Its wider aims are to provide an assessment and overview of a new climate-change policy tool that is set to become the status quo and that requires business to adapt to a new way of dealing with one of the greatest challenges of our time.

THE UK EMISSIONS TRADING SCHEME

Fundamentally, one can distinguish between two types of trading scheme: the so-called "cap-and-trade" system and the "credit-based" trading regime. In the former, companies operate under an absolute emissions limit and may sell excess reductions to the market. The latter is based on relative reduction targets and measures emissions credits from a given baseline against business-as-usual scenarios or a set standard. Credit-based trading has the advantage of allowing companies to account for business growth. However, it is environmentally less robust as it does not limit emissions in absolute terms. Given that credits are based on counterfactual evidence, it also poses serious monitoring and verification challenges (for example, see Begg, 2001).

The UK scheme combines these two types of trading scheme in rather a unique way and is indeed a hybrid of the two. There are two kinds of participant. The first type is the "direct" participant who effectively operates under a cap-and-trade system with absolute reduction targets. The second type of participant, the "agreement" participant, has output-related or relative reduction targets

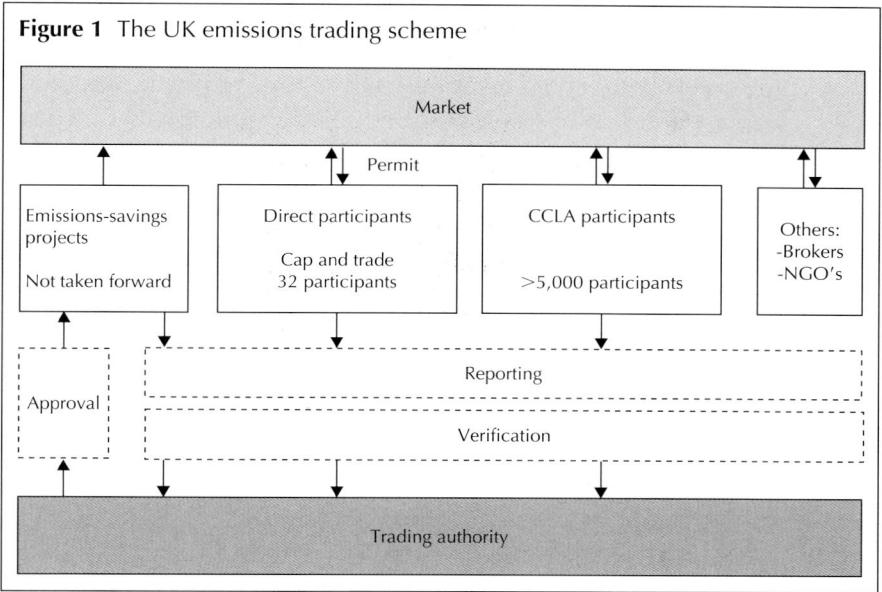

Figure 1 The UK emissions trading scheme

following the baseline and credit approach.[1] A third entry route into the scheme, based on emissions allowance credits for approved abatement projects, was originally planned but never finalised.

Figure 1 shows participants and trading routes in the UK ETS.

The UK ETS covers CO_2 and the basket of greenhouse gases as listed in the Kyoto Protocol.[2] It is a voluntary downstream trading system targeted at energy end users. The direct-entry route is open to all companies operating in the UK. Certain emissions sources, such as most transport activities, methane emissions from landfill and emissions from power generation (as upstream emissions) are excluded. Direct participants have adopted a voluntary five-year emissions reduction target, which is divided into five equal annual reduction targets. These reduction targets were determined via an auction, which took place in February 2002. The UK government set aside incentive payments of £215 million in total for the five-year period. Upon achievement of the annual reduction target, which is calculated from a baseline made up of average annual emissions over three years until 2000, the participant will receive the auctioned (taxable) incentive payment of £53.37 per tCO_2e reduced. Any excess in emissions reductions may be traded on the market. Equally, shortfalls to meet the annual target may be purchased from the market. The incentive payment is not linked to market price projections but is the result of the so-called descending-clock auction process. In this type of auction the bidding process starts at a given price and is progressively reduced for each bidding round until the total number of submitted reductions equals the amount of incentive money available.

The second part of the scheme, the agreement route, is open to companies from industry sectors that are covered by Part A of the Integrated Pollution Prevention and Control (IPPC) Regulations. These typically energy-intensive sectors have negotiated an 80% reduction in the Climate Change Levy upon achievement of certain energy efficiency targets.[3] Reductions or improvements in excess of the agreed target are converted into credits, which may be traded on the market. Companies operating under a Climate Change Levy Agreement (CCLA) may also buy emissions allowances to achieve their targets. Trading for agreement participants is regulated by a gateway, which is supposed to ensure that "weaker" credits from relative targets will not dilute the absolute emissions reductions achieved by direct participants (see DETR, 2001).

According to the policymakers, the UK ETS is an evolutionary scheme. The first trading period will run for five years until 2007. This will now coincide with the first trading period of the EU ETS, which starts in 2005 and has triggered a review of the UK scheme's current structure and procedures.

PARTICIPANTS IN THE UK ETS

The success of an emissions trading scheme depends on its ability to create an efficient market, which will enable companies to realise emissions reductions cost-effectively. Crucial for the environmental effectiveness of an ETS is how far it is able to internalise the cost of emitting carbon, thus providing an incentive to reduce emissions beyond legally required limits and to develop alternative abatement technologies and strategies. In short, an effective, environmentally credible carbon market requires sufficient players with diverse abatement potentials and stringent targets. Confidence in the market will depend on strict monitoring and control systems as well as transparency and ability to judge activities in the market (see Bartlam, 2001).

Table 1 Targets of FTSE 100 participants in the UK ETS*

Company	Total emissions 2001	Target reduction by 2006	Target reduction as % of total emissions
Barclays	269,880	10,000	3.71
BP	83,700,000	353,500	0.42
British Airways	17,396,000	125,000	0.72
Land Securities	46,380	1,381	2.98
Marks & Spencer	424,798	2,060	0.48
Rolls-Royce	888,000	27,000	3.04
Shell	100,358,000	438,750	0.44
Tesco	no absolute emissions data disclosed	74,000	

*Based on published reports 2001/2002.

With 32 direct participants the core UK market is relatively small. As participation is voluntary, generally only companies with decreasing emissions have taken on absolute targets. A survey of direct UK ETS participants conducted in 2003 (see Enviros, 2003) showed that only 6% of direct participants experienced rising emissions trends when considering participation in the UK ETS. Many of those with declining emissions trajectories attributed these trends to market conditions rather than active abatement.

In addition, targets are relatively low compared with overall emissions. Table 1 shows total emissions compared with UK ETS five-year targets of the FTSE 100-listed participants in the scheme.[4] Targets over five years represent a maximum of 3.7% of total emissions. However, in most cases targets do not even amount to 1% of the total climate change impact of the respective company.

Under UK ETS rules, participants were allowed to choose not only the emissions source they wanted to enter into the scheme but also the scope. Many companies therefore chose to enter only a fraction of their overall emissions or indeed emissions from one particular site only. This significantly reduces the number of participants with an ability to steer or influence the market. Eight companies account for approximately 85% of the total target and only ten companies have targets over $100,000\,tCO_2$.

Looking at the list of direct participants in Table 2, it is fair to say that the majority operate in less energy-intensive sectors. Very few

Table 2 Direct participants in the UK ETS and auction results

Participant	Sector	Emission reduction target 2006 in tCO_2e	Total incentive payment, £1,000s	Gases other than CO_2
Ineos Fluor	Chemicals	805,635	43,000	HFC$_S$
Dupont	Chemicals	500,000	26,685	N$_2$O
Shell UK	Oil and Gas	438,750	23,416	Methane
Rhodia Organique Fine	Chemicals	430,000	22,949	HFC$_S$
UK Coal Mining	Mining	400,000	21,348	Methane
British Petroleum	Oil and Gas	353,500	18,866	Methane
First Hydro	Electricity	285,000	15,210	–
Lafarge	Cement	250,000	13,343	–
British Airways	Aviation	125,000	6,671	–
British Sugar	Food	100,000	5,337	–
Asda Stores	Retail	80,000	4,270	HFC$_S$
Tesco Stores	Retail	74,000	3,949	HFC$_S$
Imerys Minerals	Minerals	37,000	1,975	–
Rolls-Royce	Manufacturing	27,000	1,441	–
Dalkia Utilities Services	Group/ESCO	22,400	1,195	–
Ford Motor Co	Manufacturing	12,500	667	–
Dana UK Holdings	Manufacturing	12,247	654	–
Battle McCarthy Carbon Club	Group	11,528	615	–
Barclays Bank	Services	10,000	534	–
Dalkia Energy	Group/ESCO	10,000	534	–
GKN UK	Defence	10,000	534	–
Somerfield Stores	Retail	6,000	320	–
Royal Ordnance	Defence	5,000	294	–
Motorola	Manufacturing	5,000	267	–

			HFC_S
General Domestic Appliances	Manufacturing	4,525	241
Budweiser Stag Brewing	Food and Drink	4,303	230
Marks & Spencer	Retail	2,060	110
Quantum Gas Management*	Group/ESCO	1,500	80
Land Securities	Property	1,381	74
Kirklees Metropolitan Council	Local authority	1,000	53
The Natural History Museum	Museum	1,000	53
Lend Lease Real Estate Investment Services	Property	977	52
Mitsubishi Corporation	Manufacturing	250	13
EGNI	ESCO	111	6
Wates Group*	Property	9	0.5

*Wates Group and Quantum Gas Management have since withdrawn from the scheme.
Source: Roeser and Jackson (2003)

of the largest industrial carbon dioxide emitters, which are cement, iron or steel manufacturing, brick and lime manufacturing, chemicals, and the fuel industry (see See, 2001), are actually represented in the direct part of the scheme. Companies from these sectors that have entered the UK ETS with absolute targets typically do not include energy-related greenhouse gas emissions. For example, the three chemical companies have entered only process emissions; similarly targets of oil and gas and mining companies are based on methane rather than the CO_2 emissions related to energy use. In fact, around 75% of emissions reductions in the absolute sector come from non-CO_2 sources. One can observe a correlation between size of target and emission source. Large reductions tend to relate to non-CO_2 gases, whereas energy-related CO_2 reduction targets populate the bottom end of the table. This may suggest that CO_2 reductions are either harder to achieve or at least are associated with much greater risk.

Most energy-intensive sectors are represented in the agreement sector, which is environmentally much weaker, because it is (mostly) based on relative reduction targets and therefore, in principle, allows for a net increase in emissions overall. With over 5,000 participants under 44 individually negotiated sector agreements, the relative sector now makes up the largest part of the scheme, quite contrary to policymakers' original intentions. There is little transparency in the relative sector, because targets are confidential, due to commercial sensitivities. In addition, overall progress is difficult to measure because base years are very diverse and range from 1990 to 1999. One could even argue that, due to the trading restriction imposed by the gateway, the agreement sector cannot really be regarded as a fully fledged emissions trading mechanism. All in all, this suggests that, while the agreement sector has turned into the pillar of the UK ETS, its real contribution to an effective carbon market and value as a learning experience is rather limited.

HOW HAS THE UK MARKET DEVELOPED?

Given the above parameters, it becomes apparent that the UK scheme does not fulfil the basic conditions for the establishment of an efficient and environmentally effective carbon market. The limited scope of the scheme, low number of direct participants and low reduction targets led to significant supply and demand imbalances, which had a bearing on trading activity and price developments.

Around 400 trading accounts had been opened in the registry by October 2002 and at the end of 2002 nearly 1.2 million allowances had been transferred through 150 to 250 trades. At the end of the first compliance period in April 2003, more than 2,000 trades of a total of 7.2 $mtCO_2e$ had been registered, ranging from 1 to 220,000 tCO_2e in volume (see Environmental Data Services, 2003). Alongside, a support industry of broking firms, verifiers and consultants has emerged since the inception of the scheme. While these figures may suggest a buoyant and dynamic carbon market, the trading reality has been more sedate.

The majority of trades, indeed 80%, occurred during the reconciliation period from January to March 2003 and many of the registered trades appear to have been intracompany transfers (see Enviros, 2003). Eight hundred and sixty-six of the approximately 5,000 agreement participants used the market, with 743 purchasing allowances to meet their sectoral targets and 123 selling overachievements. The majority of the overachievements were ring-fenced for future compliance periods (see DEFRA, 2003).

Direct participants generated very little trading activity, as targets were too low to create any demand. In fact, in Year 1, direct participants achieved emissions reductions of 3.85 $mtCO_2e$, exceeding their first-year target nearly five times. An additional 4 $mtCO_2e$ from overcompliance in the agreement sector contributed to the oversupply and depressed market prices.

Figure 2 gives a schematic overview of the development of carbon allowance prices in the UK.

Starting at around £5 per tonne of CO_2e, prices were continuously pushed up to above £12 per tCO_2e in September 2002. A drop occurred in November 2002 as companies felt secure about achieving the first compliance target, and since the first compliance period in February–March 2003, prices have remained very low, hovering at around £2 per tCO_2e.

The unbalanced price curve suggests that the early boom in trading activity was compliance-driven rather than based on rational economic assessment. Many agreement participants in particular bought allowances for fear of noncompliance, thus losing the

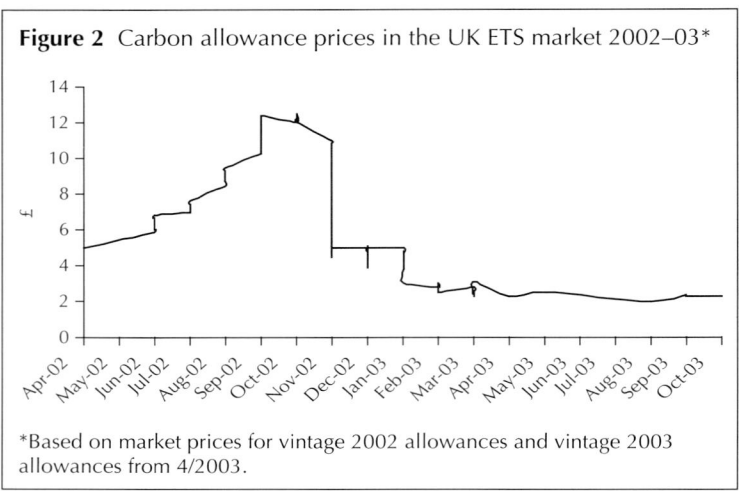

Figure 2 Carbon allowance prices in the UK ETS market 2002–03*

*Based on market prices for vintage 2002 allowances and vintage 2003 allowances from 4/2003.

significant climate-change levy rebate. Very few participants actually adopted trading strategies based on the concept of marginal costs. In order to benefit from flexibility mechanisms, companies need to establish their position in the market. This is done via the marginal abatement cost analysis, which determines the cost of reducing an additional unit of CO_2e. Depending on the marginal cost, companies then decide whether to abate or trade, thereby improving cost efficiency.

The price curve in Figure 2 reflects the insecurity of participants in the market and their inability to determine their trading position in order to achieve the dynamic efficiency benefits that trading schemes are supposed to generate. Since February 2003, the market has become stagnant with very little trading activity occurring. Many companies have already achieved future targets or have ring-fenced earlier overcompliance for future compliance periods, resulting in a lack of demand for allowances. This situation is exacerbated by the policy insecurity surrounding the introduction of the EU ETS and the potential consequences for the UK scheme.

REAL EMISSIONS REDUCTIONS OR HOT AIR?
From an environmental perspective the UK ETS has two objectives. First, there is the short-term aim to generate carbon emissions

reductions to contribute to the UK's national and international climate change commitments. Second, and one could argue, more importantly, the UK ETS was to provide a framework to stimulate long-term carbon emissions reductions that will put the UK economy on a path to a low-carbon future.

The Department for Environment Food and Rural Affairs (DEFRA) has been keen to emphasise the success of the UK ETS in generating emissions reductions of 3.85 mtCO$_2$e from direct participants and 4 mtCO$_2$e in the agreement sector in 2002 (see See, 2001). One has to question, however, the additionality of such reductions and therefore the value the UK ETS has provided in relation to UK environmental policy objectives.

There have been serious allegations of "hot-air" trading, particularly in the case of the participating chemicals companies, and of non-additional emissions reductions, which merely represent business-as-usual scenarios. In fact, at least 50% of claimed reductions in the direct sector are alleged to fall in this category (see Environmental Data Services, 2002).

The three chemicals companies, Ineos Fluor, DuPont and Rhodia, that are at the heart of the allegations are set to receive a substantial part of the overall incentive payments, amounting to a total of over £90 million. These companies account for 43% of the targeted absolute emissions reductions in the direct sector. And indeed, as the published data from the first compliance period showed, the majority of emissions reductions in the direct sector in Year 1 were achieved by Ineos Fluor and Dupont, who realised a combined reduction surplus of over 2.3 mtCO$_2$ (see Table 3). DEFRA and the companies involved have denied the allegations. However, they have so far failed to provide data to substantiate their positions.

The investigation into individual targets and incentive payments has certainly brought the environmental integrity of the UK ETS into serious dispute. There is a high risk that many participants have essentially become "free riders" on the incentive scheme. In addition, the difference between very low market prices resulting from the continuous oversupply and the incentive payment of £53.37 per tCO$_2$e means that companies with absolute targets face virtually no risk.

Table 3 UK ETS – targets and performance

Direct participant	Baseline emissions tCO$_2$e	2002 Allocation (baseline minus target)	2002 Actual emissions tCO$_2$e	2003 Allocation
Asda Stores	526,110	510,110	416,194	494,110
Barclays Bank	75,229	73,477	64,124	71,725
Battle McCarthy Carbon Club	141,894	139,722	140,324	137,550
British Petroleum	6,757,799	6,687,099	6,198,700	6,616,399
British Airways	1,011,785	986,785	850,448	961,785
British Sugar	579,367	559,367	486,646	539,367
Budweiser Stag Brewing	4,303	3,442	321	2,581
Dalkia Energy	24,077	22,102	23,560	20,127
Dalkia Utilities Services	59,513	55,033	50,121	50,553
Dana UK Holdings	37,306	35,194	27,333	33,082
Dupont	2,626,226	2,526,226	1,276,767	2,426,226
EGNI	–	–	–	–
First Hydro	1,370,410	1,313,410	1,147,311	1,256,410
Ford Motor Co	250,257	247,757	218,444	245,257
General Domestic Appliances	43,149	42,244	33,054	41,339
GKN (UK)	102,382	100,382	82,048	98,382
Imerys Minerals	358,124	351,003	352,506	343,882
Ineos Fluor	1,861,863	1,700,736	645,972	1,539,609
Kirklees Metropolitan Council	8,622	8,422	8,816	8,222
Lafarge plc	3,215,657	3,168,032	3,066,635	3,120,407
Land Securities	25,643	25,390	23,691	25,137
Lend Lease Real Estate	8,890	8,695	8,644	8,500
Marks & Spencer	13,892	13,480	10,902	13,068
Mitsubishi Corporation	1,134	1,084	862	1,034

Motorola	19,551	18,551	13,686	17,551
Natural History Museum	9,119	8,919	10,192	8,719
Rhodia Organique Fine	2,098,275	2,012,275	1,469,118	1,926,275
Rolls-Royce	315,203	310,167	268,232	305,131
Royal Ordnance	21,400	20,300	21,534	19,200
Shell UK	3,805,909	3,719,788	3,915,327	3,633,667
Somerfield Stores	380,367	379,222	384,046	378,077
Tesco Stores	271,155	256,355	211,983	241,555
UK Coal Mining	4,513,722	4,441,534	4,492,965	4,369,346
Totals	**30,538,333**	**29,746,303**	**25,920,506**	**28,954,273**

Source: DEFRA, 2003; EGNI data not available at the time

CREATING A MARKET TO STIMULATE THE SHIFT TO A LOW-CARBON FUTURE?

The rationale behind emissions trading is to create scarcity to provide an incentive for innovation and abatement action. Ironically, the UK ETS not only failed to create scarcity but also generated abundance and oversupply. The voluntary approach and exclusion of key industry sectors in the direct part of the scheme resulted in very low participation. In addition, participants were provided with a very high degree of choice and flexibility regarding the emissions sources they wanted to include in the scheme. Targets of direct participants were relatively low, which is illustrated by the significant overachievement in meeting targets and the fact that 22 of the 32 direct participants had already exceeded their second-year target in the first year. Table 3 shows achievements against targets in Year 1 of all direct participants.

The targets of companies in the agreement sector lack stringency by their nature and therefore contributed little to achieving sufficient scarcity in the market. The consequences of this weak regulatory framework are an inefficient market, which suffers from continuous oversupply and low market prices. Prices are indeed so low that the market incentive for companies to undertake abatement action has virtually been removed.

Contrary to the overarching intention of carbon-reduction policies, the UK ETS fails to internalise the social and environmental cost of emitting carbon. Participating companies do not have to pay for emissions allowances. In fact, the incentive bonus actually reverses the concept of cost internalisation and thus fails to provide a signal to industry that a fundamental change in the economy – away from fossil fuels and towards low-carbon energy sources – must occur. This is further exacerbated by the focus of the core part of the scheme on gases other than CO_2.

In addition, the scheme fails to include the majority of emissions sources in the UK, such as the transport sector, the domestic sector and, most importantly, electricity generation – sectors that hold the key to a low-carbon economy.

LEARNING BY DOING?

It is certainly the case that the UK ETS has provided the 32 direct participants and the 5,000-plus "agreement" companies with an opportunity to experience emissions trading at first hand. However, one must also ask how valuable and effective this learning experience has been – for participants, for policymakers, and in terms of value for taxpayers' money.

The UK ETS failed to establish an efficient and fluid carbon market. Another shortcoming of the UK ETS is its apparent failure to educate participants in the principles of emissions trading. The trading that occurred in the UK ETS has in most cases not been the result of proper assessments of a company's trading position but rather has been based on *ad hoc* decisions. It follows that the UK ETS market has not been used by participants as a tool to increase flexibility in carbon abatement but as a means to attain the significant Climate Change Levy rebate, to recoup a share of the incentive payment or to achieve publicity benefits. Qualitative research into the motivation of direct participants to enter the UK ETS showed that the learning experience was in most cases secondary, if a motivating factor at all.[5]

This suggests that the real learning value derived from the UK ETS for participating companies has been limited. While companies have become more familiar with this new policy tool, the depth of understanding of the concept of emissions trading and the degree to which the learning experience has penetrated organisations appears small.

The real learning benefits have been experienced by policymakers and regulatory bodies and by the peripheral emissions trading industry that has emerged in the UK. This certainly bears some wider economic value, but it is debatable whether this merited the significant costs associated with the establishment of the UK ETS.

INTERFACES WITH EU EMISSIONS TRADING

The EU scheme represents a much stronger framework and is fundamentally in conflict with existing UK ETS rules (see Sorrel, 2003). In contrast to the UK Scheme, the EU ETS is a mandatory cap-and-trade scheme that covers upstream emissions from electricity generation as well as process related CO_2 emissions (see European Commission, 2003). Non CO_2 emissions have been excluded at least from the first phase largely on the grounds of monitoring uncertainties.

Across the 15 member states and 10 accession and candidate countries, more than 12,000 installations (see European Commission, 2004) are expected to be subject to EU ETS, with around 1,500 installations in the UK. Effectively, each installation under the EU ETS will receive an annual emissions allowance. The directive also provides the alternative to opt out of the first phase of the EU ETS for companies or industry sectors that can demonstrate equivalent emissions abatement measures. Opt-out will be subject to approval by the European Commission.

THE UK NAP

The allowance and principles behind the allocation is determined by each member state in the so-called National Allocation Plans (NAPs). NAPs are the most complex and politically controversial part of the trading scheme, because they effectively set the future price of carbon and may have a bearing on competitiveness. The UK government released its draft NAP in January 2004 (see DEFRA/DTI, 2004). The overall cap set by the UK government for the first phase is relatively weak and only requires additional reductions from the power sector. In the second phase the overall cap is expected to be much more stringent in order to ensure that the domestic CO_2 reduction target will be achieved. Overall, the UK government hopes that emissions trading will generate 5.5 mt of CO_2 reductions by 2010.

Allocation of allowances is based on a two-tier approach. In the first step, allowances are allocated to the five affected industry sectors, based on projected energy use and emissions, minus a contribution to a reserve for new entrants (again calculated based on growth projections for each sector). The allocation to the power sector, which includes power stations and offshore generation as well as all commercial and manufacturing sites with large combustion installations, is further reduced to reflect the emission reductions expected from the sector.

In a second step, the total sector allowances are distributed to individual installations within each sector based on the share of historical emissions. The share is calculated by averaging annual emissions between 1998 and 2002 disregarding the year with lowest emissions.

Table 4 summarises the provisional allocation of allowances, as of March 2004.

Table 4 Proposed allocation, Draft UK NAP

Activity	Number of installations	Allocation for 2005–07	
		mtCO$_2$	% of total
Power stations	92	438.7	61
Iron and steel	15	65.8	9
Refineries	16	54.3	8
Cement	17	28	4
Lime	9	7.4	1
Bricks/ceramics	111	9.2	1
Glass	30	5.3	1
Pulp and paper	98	13.9	2
Offshore	135	41.4	6
Food and drink	130	11.1	1.5
Chemicals	93	22.8	3
Nonferrous	9	8	1
Other combustion	112	8.5	1
Total	**867**	**714.4**	

Source: ENDS Report, 348 (see Environmental Data Services, 2004)

A reserve has been created for new entrants to ensure that new-comers will also benefit from free allocation of allowances in the first phase of the scheme. A proportion of this new-entry reserve of 5.6% of total allowances each year will be ring-fenced for new com-bined-heat-and-power plants.

It is important to point out that UK companies under the EU ETS who are also part of the UK ETS – both direct and agreement par-ticipants – may apply to opt out of the first phase of the scheme. The opt-out will be subject to approval by the European Commission and may require more stringent targets for the agree-ment sector to be set (see Environmental Data Services, 2004).

WHAT DOES THIS MEAN FOR THE UK MARKET?
The already complex UK climate-change policy mix, including the UK ETS, the CCL and CCLAs, will be further complicated with the introduction of the EU ETS. Particular complications arise for com-panies that are regulated by both EU and UK emissions trading.

Only 13 of the total 32 direct participants will be covered by the EU ETS. Those that decide not to opt out are expected to be allowed to keep their incentive payments subject to state aid approval and will operate under both schemes until 2007, the end of the UK ETS.

Most of the energy-intensive agreement participants, on the other hand, fall under the EU ETS Directive. Due to the fact that UK market prices for carbon are significantly lower than EU prices, it is expected that only installations that are confident of achieving their targets will decide to transfer into the EU ETS to benefit from selling overcompliance at a higher price.[6] On the other hand, companies that face tougher targets will remain in the UK ETS to benefit from low carbon prices. In order to remove one of the incentives for opt-out, the UK government decided to grant the 80% CCL rebate also to EU ETS participants.

While the decisions surrounding opt-out may prove complicated for individual companies, the real problems for companies subject to both UK and EU ETS regulations are the differences in approach. Not only may different emissions sources at site level be subject to different reporting requirements, but also in many cases agreement sector targets will have to be split between the EU trading scheme and remaining climate-change agreement targets (for emissions relating to electricity use). The current output-related targets will also have to be converted into absolute targets under the EU ETS, leaving many companies and sites with a set of different targets and compliance regimes to adhere to. The Chemical Industries Association has already complained to government about the excessive administrative burden that companies face (see European Commission, 2004). An additional burden arises as CCLA targets on which allowances for EU ETS are based will have to be renegotiated and adjusted by the end of 2004.

It is apparent from this discussion alone that the introduction of the EU ETS is posing a huge challenge for participants as well as regulators. It may be that the potential learning benefits of early trading in the UK are outweighed by the additional organisational burden that the overlap of the two schemes puts on all involved.

The UK scheme did not inform the EU ETS, as UK government had hoped and intended. Rules and principles of the EU ETS are in many ways fundamentally different and, as a consequence, UK ETS allowances will not be fungible in the EU market. This means that the two carbon allowance markets are not directly linked and in principle will not influence one another. However, an indirect link through participants regulated under both markets will remain until banked allowances from direct participants to the

Table 5 Possible gross financial impacts on EU ETS facilities*

% Shortfall from target in 2010		Value in 2010 (£million/year)		
		5%	10%	20%
Power generation (coal)	1,200 MW	3.7	7.3	14.6
Power generation (gas)	1,200 MW	1.9	3.9	7.8
Oil refinery	60 mb/yr	1.3	2.5	5.0
Pulp & paper	400,000 t/yr	0.2	0.4	0.9
Cement	2,000 t/d	0.8	1.6	3.2
Brick	6 m/yr	0.01	0.02	0.04
Steel	1 m/yr	0.5	1.0	2.0

*Based on estimates by Enviros Consulting, 2004.

UK ETS are invalidated at the end of the Kyoto commitment period 2008–12. This means that companies operating in both schemes can effectively use the UK allowance market to achieve EU ETS absolute targets. Since the environmental credibility of UK allowances must be seriously doubted, there is a risk that some of the UK hot air will be indirectly traded into the EU market.

It is difficult to predict how the EU market will develop over time. This will depend on the stringency of the final NAPs and on linkages between the EU ETS and other Kyoto mechanisms, such as Joint Implementation and the Clean Development Mechanism. What is clear is that the financial impact and managerial challenges imposed on companies are likely to be significant. Table 5 estimates the gross financial impacts of purchasing allowances to cover shortfalls in a company's carbon budget of 5%, 10% and 20% in 2010. The figures assume a market price of £10/tonne CO_2 over the life of the scheme and a linear increase in the accumulated shortfall from 2005 to 2010. If a facility were to exceed its target by the same percentage difference, the negative costs would be converted to positive cashflows.

CONCLUDING REMARKS
The UK ETS has certainly given participating companies an insight into how a carbon allowance market might operate. The concept of environmental markets is now much more familiar in the UK, however, it is doubtful whether the general familiarity with this new policy tool can be translated into a competitive trading advantage

for UK companies in the wider European market. One could argue that the potential opt-out from the first phase of the EU scheme constitutes an advantage for UK ETS participants. This advantage, however, will be at the cost of the effectiveness of the EU market and wider climate-change policy targets. It may also place UK companies at a disadvantage in terms of the development of the EU market – a reverse of the original intention to promote "prime mover" advantage.

The learning experience was limited. Furthermore, only 13 companies of the original core of the UK ETS will be regulated under EU ETS rules, and only eight of these had actually entered emissions sources that will be covered under EU rules. For many "agreement" companies who will be subject to the EU ETS, rather than easing the transition into a market based policy environment, compliance has become much more complex and will most likely require additional management time.

The learning experience has been most beneficial for policymakers and the evolving support industries in the UK, who have had a head start in negotiating and preparing for the introduction of the EU scheme. Initial consultations and continuing negotiations and modification to the UK ETS have been very resource-intensive. It is possible that the significant public funds that have flowed into this policy trial could have been used more effectively, both in terms of benefiting the environment and informing UK business. It could be argued that waiting for the introduction of the stronger EU ETS and using the time in the run-up for capacity building and educating market players would have been more prudent than the course pursued. It might have even provided UK business with a real competitive advantage.

1   Agreement participants and so-called because they are companies who have already entered into carbon-reduction agreements under the Climate Change Levy scheme.
2   The basket of greenhouse gases comprises methane, nitrous oxide, hydrofluorocarbons, perfluorocarbons and sulphur hexafluoride.
3   The Climate Change Levy (CCL) is a downstream energy tax levied on energy users. It was introduced in the UK in its final form in March 2000. Renewables are exempt from the CCL; and energy-intensive industries (defined in terms of sites conforming to IPPC regulations) are eligible for up to 80% reductions in the CCL in exchange for negotiated climate change levy agreements (CCLAs) to improve energy efficiency.
4   These FTSE 100 list and emissions profiles (April 2002) were based on published data.
5   The Climate Change Levy (CCL) is a downstream energy tax levied on energy users. It was introduced in the UK in its final form in March 2000. Renewables are exempt from the CCL;

and energy-intensive industries (defined in terms of sites conforming to IPPC regulations) are eligible for up to 80% reductions in the CCL in exchange for negotiated climate change levy agreements (CCLA) to improve energy efficiency.

6   EU market prices are currently at around €13 per tCO_2.

REFERENCES

Bartlam, M., 2001, "Liquidity Matters", Paper for the Finance Liaison Group of the UK Emissions Trading Group, URL: http://www.uketg.com.

Begg, K., T. Jackson, P.-E. Morthorst, and S. Parkinson, 2001, "The Baseline Question – Dealing with the Problem of Counterfactuality", in T. Jackson, K. Begg, and S. Parkinson (eds), *Flexibility in Climate Policy – Making the Kyoto Mechanisms Work* (London: Earthscan).

DEFRA, 2003, "UK Emissions Trading Scheme off to a Flying Start", Press Release, 12 May.

DEFRA/DTI, 2004, "Department for Environment, Food and Rural Affairs/Department of Trade and Industry consultation paper on the UK Draft National Allocation Plan", London.

DETR (Department of the Environment, Transport and the Regions), 2000, "Climate Change: The UK Programme", London.

DETR, 2001, "Framework Document for the UK Emissions Trading Scheme", London.

DTI (Department of Trade and Industry), 2003, "Our Energy Future – Creating a Low Carbon Economy", London, 2003.

Environmental Data Services, 2002, "Hot Air Blows Gaping Hole in Emissions Trading Scheme", ENDS Report 329.

Environmental Data Services, 2003, "Oversupply Cripples UK Emissions Market", ENDS Report 340.

Environmental Data Services, 2004, "Carving up the Carbon Cake: UK Takes Lead with Allocation Plan", ENDS Report 348.

Enviros Consulting Ltd, 2003, "A Qualitative Study of the Direct Entry UK Emissions Trading Scheme", London.

European Commission, 2003, "Establishing a Scheme for Greenhouse Gas Emissions Allowance Trading", Directive 2003/87/EC.

European Commission, 2004, Memo 04/44, URL: http://europa.eu.int.

Roeser, F., and T. Jackson, 2003, "Early Experiences with Emissions Trading in the UK", *Greener Management International,* **17**, pp. 43–54.

See, M., 2001, *Greenhouse Gas Emissions: Global Business Aspects* (Berlin: Springer Verlag).

Sorrel, S., 2003, "Back to the Drawing Board: Implications of the EU Emissions Trading Directive for UK Climate Policy", Science Policy Research Unit, University of Sussex, UK.

Tietenberg, T., 1985, *Emissions Trading: An Exercise in Reforming Pollution Policy* (Washington, DC: Resources in the Future).

Tolley, G. S., and B. K. Edwards, 1997, "Slippage Factors in Emissions Trading", in R. F. Kosoboud, and J. M. Zimmerman (eds), *Market-Based Approaches to Environmental Policy: Regulatory Innovations to the Fore*, pp. 187–97, (New York: Van Nostrand Reinhold).

16

Overview of GHG Markets: Japan and Canada

Dirk Forrister, Makoto Katagiri, Doug Russell

Natsource

As countries advance their preparations of policies to implement the Kyoto Protocol, the trading market for greenhouse gas (GHG) emissions is gradually emerging. Although the Protocol will come into force only if Russia ratifies, many countries recognise the need to establish policies soon in order to ensure that Kyoto's required emissions reductions can be achieved cost-effectively. Delay could be costly, so they believe early action is prudent.

At the centre of their preparatory efforts are emissions market considerations. These new markets are recognised as the keys to success in meeting Kyoto targets in a way that maintains international competitiveness.

The global market is likely to be shaped by primary demand from three main areas – Europe, Japan and Canada. While Europe is providing the strongest near-term market drivers in GHG markets, it will be important to anticipate the growing role that Japan and Canada will play in galvanising the international market in the years leading up to the Kyoto period.

In fact, in early transactions of candidate Clean Development Mechanism (CDM) and Joint Implementation (JI) credits, private companies provided much of the demand. Even in the first broad national emissions trading programme in the UK, the first trades involved a Japanese buyer and seller represented by a trader in Canada.

This chapter discusses the policies that are emerging in Japan and Canada, providing the domestic infrastructure for interaction with the global market. As this infrastructure is in its early stages, the details are subject to change. However, the broad outlines and main drivers have been moving in a consistent direction that favours broad use of the Kyoto Mechanisms.

JAPAN
Introduction
As host of the Kyoto negotiations, Japan recognised the importance of demonstrating leadership on the climate change issue and accepted a challenging target. It agreed to reduce emissions to 6% below 1990 levels. Yet, since the 1990s, national GHG emissions have continued to increase every year. At present, its emissions have grown to around 5% above 1990 levels – making its distance to the Kyoto target a challenging 11–12%.

At first blush, Japan's target might appear less ambitious than other national targets (EU member states agreed to reduce to 8% below). But, given that Japan has one of the most energy-efficient economies in the world, it is approaching the international emissions trading market as a likely net buyer – perhaps the largest in the world. Japan's plans from 2002 were to increase its nuclear capacity as a large part of its Kyoto strategy, with 13 to 20 new nuclear plants envisioned, along with a set of voluntary agreements. Its emissions scenarios are illustrated in Figure 1, which reflects the government's projections of emissions with and without nuclear expansion (Cases A and B) compared with projections of emissions with further policies (Cases C and D) added to the two nuclear expansion cases.

Japan has been in the midst of an unprecedented recession marked by chronic stagflation and high unemployment. Even with its economic stagnation, Japan's GHG emissions have continued to rise and are forecasted to continue rising over the next decade. This has been due, in a large measure, to increases in energy use related to consumer use of electronic equipment and the increased use of fossil fuel to generate power. The nuclear expansion plans are not likely to be fulfilled – rather than 13 to 20 new plants, only five are now likely. Even the existing nuclear fleet has performed below expectations, which in turn has led to the use of more natural gas and coal.

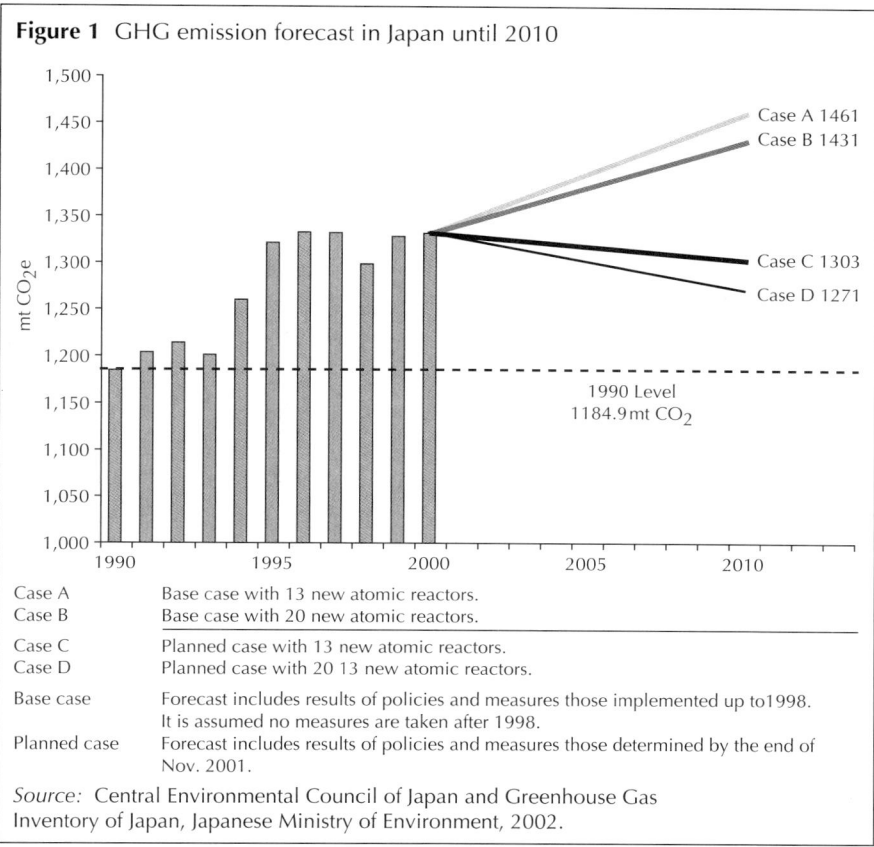

Figure 1 GHG emission forecast in Japan until 2010

Case A	Base case with 13 new atomic reactors.
Case B	Base case with 20 new atomic reactors.
Case C	Planned case with 13 new atomic reactors.
Case D	Planned case with 20 13 new atomic reactors.
Base case	Forecast includes results of policies and measures those implemented up to1998. It is assumed no measures are taken after 1998.
Planned case	Forecast includes results of policies and measures those determined by the end of Nov. 2001.

Source: Central Environmental Council of Japan and Greenhouse Gas Inventory of Japan, Japanese Ministry of Environment, 2002.

In emissions terms, the net result of these circumstances is that Japan cannot achieve the Kyoto target with purely domestic activities, so the access to a liquid international market is critical to the Protocol's future success.

Initial policy drivers

GHG markets are driven by policies that establish the supply and demand parameters. In Japan, these drivers are in very early stages of formation.

In March 2002, the government of Japan announced the "New Guideline for Measures to Prevent Global Warming", outlining steps to achieve the country's Kyoto emission reduction commitment. Japan announced the intention to undertake assessment and review of the progress of measures being taken at regular intervals, and it pledged to take additional measures step by step as necessary. While the 2002 plan did not set forth operational details in the "Guideline", it is commonly understood that use of the Kyoto Mechanisms – including the CDM and JI – would be a key feature in meeting its commitments in the future.

The Japanese government adopted a series of voluntary programmes as the foundation of its plan. To date, the government has not imposed mandatory emission reduction targets on any sector. Approximately 40 key industrial sectors made voluntary emission reduction commitments. The commitments were predominantly to reduce emissions per unit of output – which is different from the "cap-and-trade" model of the EU Emissions Trading Directive. The Japanese government will review progress in late 2004 and then will establish targets if such voluntary action is determined to be insufficient to achieve the country's Kyoto target.

The voluntary targets were established through Japan's primary industrial association, the Japanese Federation of Economic Organisations (JFEO). The targets aim to return national emissions to 1990 levels by 2010.

PANEL 1 FIVE SAMPLE JAPANESE VOLUNTARY GHG REDUCTION TARGETS, BY SECTOR

1. **Electricity generation**: agreed to achieve 20% reduction by 2010 from 1990 levels of CO_2 emissions per unit of output.
2. **Oil**: seeks to reduce the amount of fuel used for transportation on both land and sea by 9%, relative to 1990 levels. The sector will also attempt to reduce oil consumption by 1 million kilolitres per year through increased use of co-generation, and it will study of the possibility of further reducing the annual rate by 1%.
3. **Steel**: aims to reduce energy consumption in 2010 by approximately 10% compared with 1990 levels and aims to promote other energy-efficiency measures.
4. **Automobile manufacturers**: committed to increasing vehicle fuel efficiency and to maintain at 1990 levels the amount of energy used in manufacturing.
5. **Chemicals**: agreed to reduce energy input per unit of output in 2010 to 90% of 1990 levels.

Policy results

In analysing the performance of Japan's climate change policies, there are three areas on which to focus:

❑ *Environment*: Will the plan achieve the emission targets?
❑ *Competitiveness*: To what extent do the policies hamper competitiveness?
❑ *Efficiency*: Is the approach efficient, fair and equitable in terms of who pays?

These features will now be analysed briefly.

Environment

The initial set of policies and voluntary commitments have not succeeded in reducing emissions as much as originally intended, and alone they are not likely to enable Japan to meet its Kyoto commitment. As noted earlier, Japan's emissions have continued to grow, even with these policies and even with its economic sluggishness. Mitsubishi Research Institute, for example, estimates that industry is expected to reduce emissions by 7%, but it is on track to reduce them by only 1.3% (see Aoyagi, 2004). More will be needed, but this was expected.

Japan's strategy was to institute this initial set of measures, after which it would assess whether additional policies would be required. This assessment would be conducted by 2005, in order to allow time to implement any new programmes.

Already, the Ministry of Environment has sounded its concerns that stronger policies are needed, and it floated a proposal for a carbon tax. Other ministries appear more interested in the use of an emissions trading programme. As a general rule, Japanese companies would prefer to achieve a given carbon target with an emissions trading regime instead of a carbon tax, even if it means taking a cap (assuming the level of the tax would be set to achieve the same level of reductions).

Competitiveness

In light of the US's decision not to ratify Kyoto, Japan preferred to make as much progress as possible by voluntary and incentive-based approaches before instituting regulatory controls on industry. Japanese industry supported this approach, because it allowed them the required time and flexibility to make reductions in a cost-effective way.

Although some of Japan's voluntary initiatives appear to be fairly comprehensive, many industrial companies are concerned that deeper reductions will be required of them. Japanese industrials and trading houses are already engaging in CDM transactions, believing that the demand for CERs will grow in Japan. This is their strategy for hedging the risks of future controls.

The government of Japan is working closely with the Keidanran, a major association of businesses, to determine a workable path forward. The member companies advocate a continuation of voluntary commitments with access to global emissions markets, but they are deeply worried about the competitiveness impacts of a cap-and-trade or carbon tax regime. This is particularly acute in the regional economy, where Australia has opted out of the Kyoto Protocol and the large developing countries in the region have no binding emissions limits. Japan's biggest trade competitors in the region include China, India, Malaysia and Indonesia, among others.

Efficiency

Most analysts believe that starting early ("early action") and making gradual emissions improvements is a more efficient approach than waiting to adopt controls then making improvements hastily. In some measure, Japan's response puts this decision making in the hands of industry. However, many in industry are reluctant to take significant action unless they are confident that the early action will be recognised, as the baselines for regulation are set. At present, Japan has not offered such clarity, but industry has been satisfied with the voluntary approach. While it would be hard to argue that the voluntary approaches are inefficient, the true test will be how well Japanese industry is prepared to adapt to the stringency of the Kyoto regime in future years. For certain companies, there are encouraging signs, as their emissions market activity indicates that they are preparing early; for other companies, there are less encouraging signs – as they are making little progress.

An additional aspect of efficiency relates to whether the Japanese government's plans for Kyoto implementation spreads the burden equitably across various emitting sectors – industrial, transport, energy production and residential. At this stage, it is difficult to make firm judgements, since the actions taken in all of these sectors are fairly mild.

Finally, some governments have determined that their most efficient approach is to purchase reductions on the market to compensate for emissions growth in the residential and transport arenas (for example, the Netherlands, Finland, Denmark, Austria and Canada, among others, are taking this approach). Other governments, such as the UK, Germany and France, seem to believe that it is more efficient for their governments to apply targets to energy and industrial companies that will trade in the international markets, rather than governments entering the markets as purchasers. In large measure, it appears that Japan will follow a hybrid approach, with some government financial support for companies active in creating or purchasing CERs. In market terms, it is difficult to envision government purchasers becoming as efficient as private entities in market engagement – so we would expect Japan's approach to offer a more efficient performance over time than the systems with direct national purchasing.

Most Japanese companies believe that the approach taken thus far is fair, in terms of expectations on various sectors and among industrial groups. As noted, it generally follows an approach where the large emitters and manufacturers pay the dominant share of the burden rather than take on the complications of addressing individual consumers – but they, of course, pass on the costs to customers in the prices of their products. Power producers, for example, take the responsibility for addressing their direct emissions, while car manufacturers are expected to improve efficiency of vehicle fleets. This approach is gaining wide acceptance internationally, as Europe and Canada follow much similar approaches.

Emissions market activity

Although Japan does not yet have binding regulatory frameworks, many companies are beginning to engage in transactions, consider investment in carbon funds and collaborate with the government in pilot projects.

Transactions

Japan's private sector recognises that use of the Kyoto Mechanisms can be an efficient mechanism to reduce GHG emissions. Based on

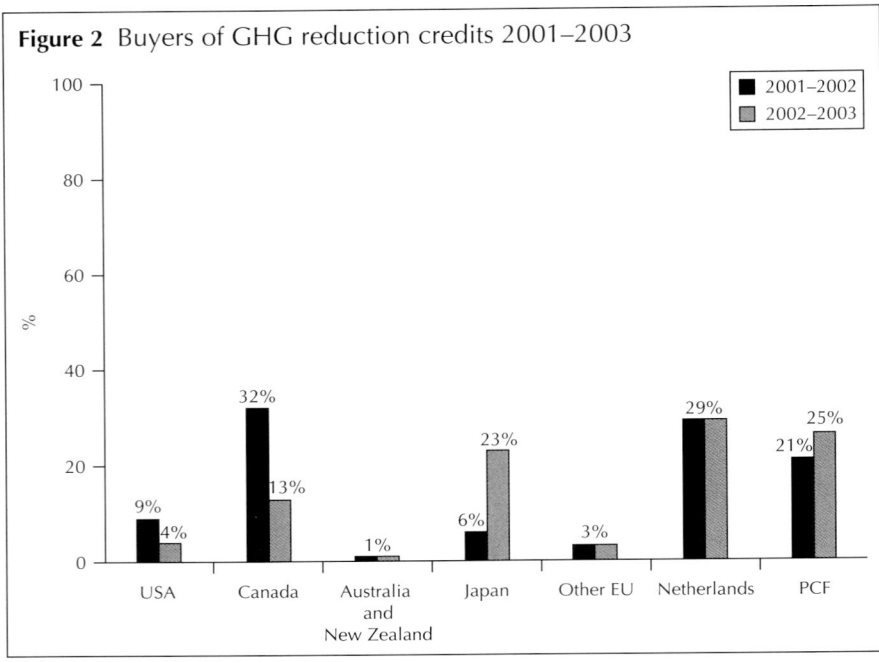

Figure 2 Buyers of GHG reduction credits 2001–2003

this recognition, industry sectors and/or companies are trying to obtain reductions through IET, JI and CDM.

In the annual market review by World Bank Carbon Group (2003), Natsource found that last year Japanese buyers represented the highest growth in purchases of any geographical region – a volume just slightly below the level of World Bank's Prototype Carbon Fund and Dutch government purchases (see Figure 2; see also World Bank Carbon Group, 2003).

With the government's encouragement, progressive companies in Japan are already buying CERs or are buying Verified Emissions Reductions (VERs) that they believe will ultimately qualify as either CERs or ERUs. For example:

❑ Toyota Tsusho Corporation purchased VERs from a project called "Production of Fire Wood Charcoal and Charcoal for Pig Iron Production in Brazil". This project may ultimately generate CDM credits for carbon sequestration resulting from eucalyptus plantations, where the wood will be used as a source of charcoal

in pig-iron making (charcoal releases less CO_2 into the atmosphere than coal).
❏ Mitsubishi Corporation agreed to purchase CERs from a small hydropower generation project, in Chacabuquito, Chile, one of the earliest projects supported by the World Bank Prototype Carbon Fund (PCF).

Carbon funds

Beyond individual purchases, there is also growing interest in Japan's purchasing of CERs and ERUs through carbon funds. A number of private companies participated, for example, in the World Bank's PCF: Chubu Electric, Chugoku Electric, Japan Bank for International Cooperation (JBIC), Kyushu Electric, Mitsubishi, Shikoku Electric, Tohoku Electric, Tokyo Electric Power.

More recently, the JBIC and the Development Bank of Japan (DBJ) announced the establishment of the Japan Carbon Fund. With anticipated value of US$100 million, the Fund started its development phase in spring 2004, with the aim of being launched by summer 2004. The Fund will give Japanese industry the opportunity of purchasing GHG reductions through a portfolio.

Pilot projects and other market support

The government of Japan has launched a suite of initiatives designed to assist Japanese companies interested in engaging in GHG transactions (see Kuratomi, 2004). Japanese government agencies will provide funding for feasibility studies for energy savings, alternative energy, forestry or other GHG mitigation projects in developing countries or transition countries. It will also fund model projects in these areas. For example, this support includes:

❏ 2.4 billion yen (€17.5 m) in grants for CDM/JI projects developed and operated by Japanese private companies. These grants may comprise up to 25% of project expenditures for preliminary examinations, initial investments in plant/construction, and verification of emission reductions (ERs), which are expected to go into the national registry and be owned by the sponsor. For this programme, projects with lower ER costs get priority consideration.
❏ A loan programme, including export loans, overseas investment loans for Japanese companies and untied loans for CDM/JI projects.

❑ An exploration by the Japanese governmental insurance body, Nippon Export and Investment Insurance, into how to provide foreign trade insurance to cover losses incurred by violation or repeal of the contract from the CDM/JI host governments.

❑ Several programmes by Japan's Ministry of Economy, Trade and Industry (METI) to fund capacity building efforts in developing countries. These programmes aim to ease the way for such countries to host emission-reduction projects that involve Japanese companies. Some assistance has been provided for host countries and local companies to join Japanese companies in preparing project design documents required for the CDM project approval process.

To date, the Japanese government has stopped short of subsidising the actual purchase of emission reductions. The government does not want to be perceived as subsidising its private sector to buy reductions.

Policy and market outlook

In view of the actual increase in GHG emission levels, many observers expect that the Japanese government will introduce further regulatory measures in the beginning of 2005. Discussions have begun on three possible scenarios:

❑ an "environmental tax" or "carbon tax";
❑ emission regulations on each industrial group or company with a trading regime; and
❑ a mix of the above.

As these policies become clearer, the Japanese private sector may be further induced to use the Kyoto Mechanisms in order to be internationally competitive and environmentally responsible.

CANADA
Introduction

Canada agreed to reduce its emissions to 6% below 1990 levels in the Kyoto Protocol. It ratified the Protocol in late 2002, pledging to meet its target without harming its competitiveness with the US and without placing undue burden on one sector of the economy or region of the country. Achieving this target will be a significant challenge, since its GHG emissions have grown 18.5% between 1990 and 2001 with continued projected growth through the Kyoto Period. It appears to be on a trajectory to exceed its Kyoto Target by nearly 30%.

Since the Kyoto Protocol was agreed, Canadian companies grew to be among the world's most active in formulating and executing strategies to reduce GHG emissions. These strategies often involved efforts to advance market-based policy solutions through partici- pation in voluntary GHG trades. Companies such as TransAlta and Ontario Power Generation pioneered such voluntary trades. TransAlta, for example, has invested in a wide-ranging set of emissions credit purchases, including landfill methane capture in Canada, the US and New Zealand and renewable energy projects in Canada and Europe. These companies and others also experi- mented with collective purchasing in the Greenhouse Gas Emissions Management Consortia, which entered into innovative project contracts in the areas of aggregating energy conservation and emissions reductions from a CO_2 pipeline project in the USA.

In recent months, companies engaged in fewer transactions, as domestic policy debates continued without final resolution. Late in 2003, a new prime minister, Paul Martin, came to power and con- firmed the ruling party's support for the Kyoto Protocol. At the

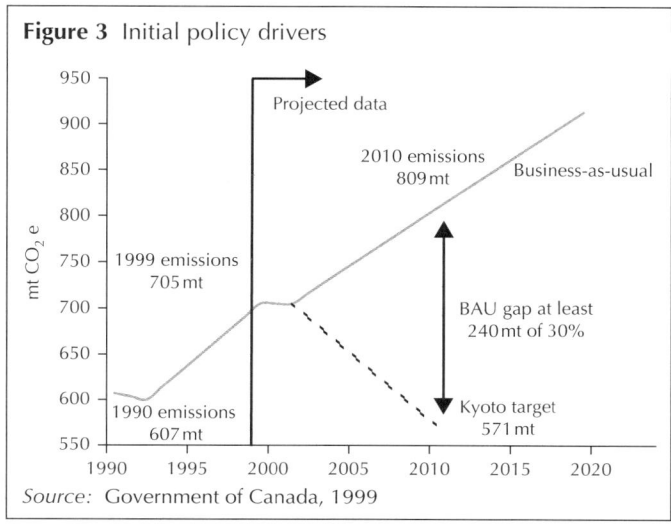

Figure 3 Initial policy drivers

Source: Government of Canada, 1999

same time, he also stated that Canada's current plan is not robust enough to fully bridge Canada's Kyoto gap, thereby casting additional uncertainty on how the goal will eventually be met.

In 1999, Canada announced projections showing that its emissions would grow from 705 million tonnes in 1999 to 809 million tonnes by 2010 in a business-as-usual scenario. Compared with its 1990 baseline emissions of 607 million tonnes, this represented a gap of 240 million tonnes, or about 30%. No comprehensive update has been published since that time, although individual sectoral projections used to formulate Canada's Climate Change Action Plan of 2002 were consistent with the 1999 projections. Further updates are likely in 2005, and early informal indications are that the gap may grow to something larger than 240 million tonnes per year during the Kyoto commitment period of 2008–12.

In late 2002, the government formulated a framework for action to close its forecast emissions gap of 240 mt CO_2e between Canada's actual and forecast emissions (see Figure 4). This framework is known as the Climate Change Plan for Canada.

The Plan seeks to achieve a total of 240 million tonnes in emissions reductions in five areas:

❏ 80 million tonnes through a set of domestic actions, announced in 2000 and funded by the federal budget of 2000 (these actions include tax incentives, technology investments, public education and outreach and community-based actions);
❏ 55 mt of reductions through a domestic emissions trading programme for approximately 670 companies in nine sectors of the economy (the domestic trading system is designed to reduce large industrial emissions from a business-as-usual projection of 334 million tonnes in 2010 to an actual figure of 279 million tonnes, or approximately 15% below business-as-usual estimates);[1]
❏ 35 million tonnes from directed domestic programmes funded in part by the federal government and delivered in partnership with the provincial, territorial and municipal governments;
❏ at least 10 million tonnes in international purchases of CDM, JI and international emissions trades of Kyoto Assigned Amount Units; and
❏ 60 million tonnes of reductions that will be specified at a future date.

In addition to these programmes, Canada is considering the implementation of a requirement for a 25% improvement in fleet efficiency of vehicle producers in Canada and has announced a "one-tonne challenge" aimed at inspiring energy conservation by each of its 32 million citizens.

Analysis

In analysing the performance of Canada's climate change policies, as with our earlier analysis of Japan, there are three areas to consider:

❑ *environment*: will the plan achieve the emission targets?
❑ *competitiveness*: to what extent do the policies hamper competitiveness?
❑ *efficiency*: is the approach efficient, fair and equitable in terms of who pays?

These features are analysed briefly as follows:

Environment

Canada has already acknowledged that further policies will be required to address a minimum of 60 million tonnes of additional reductions. But many observers are concerned that optimistic assumptions in the 2002 plan will lead to an even greater shortfall. If, as illustrated in Figure 4, there is a shortfall in programmes already under way, the domestic offset programmes and the future policies of roughly 10% (or 25 million tonnes compared with the 240-million-tonne gap), then Canada will need to turn to international markets for a minimum of 35 million tonnes of reductions. This number is probably very conservative, particularly if the next release of emissions projections for the country increases the size of the annual Kyoto gap more than the current 240 million tonnes. Should the gap increase, the amount of international purchases required to meet Canada's Kyoto target could approach 100 million tonnes annually.

Competitiveness

The government intends to incorporate several provisions in its domestic emissions trading system to protect Canadian competitiveness. In contrast to the European emission trading system,

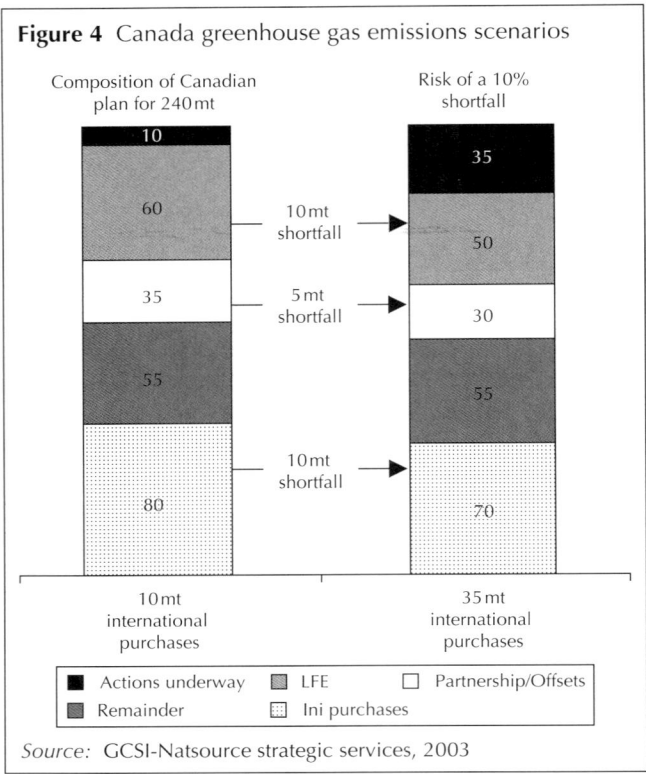

Figure 4 Canada greenhouse gas emissions scenarios

Composition of Canadian plan for 240 mt

Risk of a 10% shortfall

10 mt shortfall →

5 mt shortfall →

10 mt shortfall →

10 mt international purchases

35 mt international purchases

| ■ Actions underway | ▨ LFE | ☐ Partnership/Offsets |
| ▦ Remainder | ⠿ Ini purchases | |

Source: GCSI-Natsource strategic services, 2003

which places absolute limitations on regulated entities' emissions, the Canadian system will be based on emissions intensity targets (ie, emissions per unit of production). This allows for the organic growth of each sector, and the possibility that a corporation could be in compliance with the requirements of the domestic trading system, but still see an increase in its absolute emissions. Should that be the case, the federal government will need to make up the difference in order to meet its Kyoto target.

Second, the Canadian government has committed to ease the burden by capping the cost of compliance at C$15 per tonne. This cap provides regulated companies with cost certainty. The government has also assured regulated companies that they will have unlimited access to the Kyoto mechanisms for compliance. In order to assure that domestic reductions from non-covered sectors are given equal access to the market, Canada also intends to develop a domestic offset programme. Developing a mechanism to credit companies for their technology research and development investments, and allowing for banking could potentially provide further flexibility.

Efficiency

It is difficult to judge the efficiency of Canada's approach until more details emerge, such as emissions limits on specific facilities. Certainly, the use of a domestic emissions trading market should ensure that corporations can comply by using the most cost-effective approaches. More importantly, Canada plans to provide liberal access to international markets, and it supports use of carbon sinks (forestry, agricultural and geologic) and trading of credits for reductions in any of the six varities of GHGs covered by the Kyoto Protocols, which should also encourage an economically efficient outcome.

However, during the course of the ratification debate, a rallying cry was for a "made in Canada" approach that could result in a preference for achieving a measure of reductions purely in Canada. Depending on whether and how such a preference is implemented, it could result in dramatically less economically efficient performance or a failure to meet the Kyoto target.

Key features of the trading system are under negotiation at present, framed in a set of discussion papers (commonly referred to as "non-papers", reflecting the fact that they are floated for public comment and are not yet official government policy). Together, these outline an initial policy framework. Industry and other stakeholders were invited to submit comments on the "non-papers" that have been released to date.[2] Once this phase of the process is complete, the government plans to draft and introduce the legislation required to implement the trading system. Introduction of the draft legislation to Canada's Parliament is likely in 2005, with the requisite Bills, regulations and regulatory context in place by the end of 2006. The government is aiming to have the entire administration infrastructure completed by 2007 in time for a January 2008 launch.

Emissions market activity

The Canadian National Action Plan proposed that Canada participate in the international market for emission permits. It seeks to do so in close collaboration with the private sector. Although

Canadian companies were a major force for several of the early years of the international GHG market's formation, Japanese companies surpassed them in 2003 as being the more active buyers. As the domestic plan and related policies firm up, the Canadian participation in the global market should rebound.

Transactions

Anticipating the important role emissions trading would play in the future, Canadian companies have participated in several emissions trading pilot programmes in recent years to gain experience in transacting in emissions markets. These included the Ontario pilot Emission Reduction Trading in 1996, the Greenhouse Gas Emission Reduction Trading pilot in 1998 and the pilot Emissions Removals, Reduction and Learning Initiative in 2002.[3] These trading systems primarily focused on reductions in Canada, so their validity in the Kyoto period will depend on whether credits to reward early action become available.

On the positive side, these programmes established rules defining tradable ERs and procedures for external review of proposed trades in order to ensure their environmental integrity. These rules were tested in practice, and the lessons learned have helped to prepare Canadian companies for the future GHG trading markets.

In addition, as noted earlier, major power companies such as TransAlta and Ontario Power Generation adopted significant GHG purchasing initiatives. With these initiatives, the power companies wanted to gain experience and hedge the risk of complying with uncertain – but potentially expensive – emission reduction policies.

Some GHG emissions reductions purchased by Canadian companies involved projects located in the US. Many of these purchases involved products that would be used to meet pre-Kyoto voluntary commitments and/or voluntary pilot programme targets. Throughout the middle of 2001, emissions reductions not intended for compliance with Kyoto's binding emissions regulations traded for approximately US$0.60 to US$1.50 per tonne CO_2e. However, emissions reduction credits that could potentially be certified in the future for Kyoto compliance traded at higher prices, approximately US$1.65 to US$3.00 per tonne CO_2e (see Shell Canada Ltd and Natsource LLC, 2003).

As for the reductions purchased for Kyoto compliance, prices paid reflect the associated risks in these early projects. Corporate buyers made their purchase decisions in light of the uncertainties surrounding the question of whether the Kyoto Protocol would come into force, the undefined CDM process, the credit ratings of the project developers and the country risk involved. As more policy certainty appears and stronger project developers emerge, higher prices are likely to emerge.

While most of the Canadian companies' early transactions involved outright purchases or forward streams of reductions, some involved financial derivatives such as call options, which granted buyers the right, but not the obligation to purchase a specific quantity of ERs at a fixed price in the future. They also tested numerous "first-of-a-kind" transactions using different technologies or new trading structures. As such, the transactions were considered both instrument to hedge exposure to future greenhouse gas control programmes as well as learning-by-doing experiences.

Carbon funds and international capacity building
The Canadian government has invested C$15 million in the World Bank's PCF as one avenue for obtaining emissions reductions that might be useful in meeting its Kyoto commitment.

The Canadian government recognises that its private sector and the government itself will need to access the international market if Canada is to meet its Kyoto commitments. As part of its international efforts on climate change, in 2000 the government announced a C$100 million investment in the Canadian Climate Change Development Fund. This fund aims to build capacity in developing countries to address climate change. The funding is delivered by the Canadian International Development Agency in partnership with Canadian entities and local developing country partners. Some of the funding is being used to stimulate capacity building for CDM project development, but because of restrictions on the use of Overseas Development Assistance (ODA) for direct investment in CDM projects, the C$100 million investment is viewed as a way to establish relationships and build capacity for future Canadian CDM investments.

Canada has also invested C$20 million to facilitate private sector participation in CDM/JI projects through its CDM/JI office housed in the Department of Foreign Affairs and International Trade. In addition, the government has stated its intent to purchase a minimum of 10 mt directly of mainly project-based emission reductions in the international market as an element of its compliance strategy. As noted earlier, it is likely that this number will swell to a minimum of 35 million tonnes and perhaps as high as 100 million tonnes.

With the PCF and other market building initiatives, Canada recognises the importance of preparing a path forward on the CDM. This will prepare the way for Canadian companies to take advantage of the international market opportunities. But as with any groundbreaking effort, there is no guarantee that the associated emissions reductions will ultimately be certified for compliance with Kyoto.

In addition to the aforementioned government initiatives, a set of Canadian and Japanese companies retained Natsource to design a carbon purchasing initiative, known as the Greenhouse Gas-Credit Aggregation Pool. It would apply industry-standard risk management strategies to the purchase and management of a diverse portfolio of emissions reductions from CDM and JI projects. With a targeted investment of US$200 million, this pool is now under consideration by a number of Canadian companies, as well as European and Japanese entities. It is seen as a way of hedging exposure to the climate policies in a more cost effective way than individual companies can accomplish.

Future policy development

As noted earlier, future policy in Canada will emerge in part from decisions made in the design of its domestic emissions trading system for large final emitters. The remainder of this section contains a brief description of the design discussion papers for the trading system.

Allocation and credit for early action

The first discussion paper outlines the government's initial thinking on two defining issues for the emissions market: allocation and credit for early action. Although this paper was issued in 2003, negotiations continue between the government and industrial sectors, with a view to incorporating these discussions in the legislative framework to be introduced to the Canadian Parliament in early 2005. Much of the discussion has focused on the potential ways that the allocation system may deal with competitiveness issues. It states that the issue of competitiveness:

❑ should be addressed at the sector level and not at the company level – this means that the government will not try to protect individual companies with favourable allocations, but will rather apply allocations to the sector overall;

❑ will be considered a financial concept and will reflect a company's ability to cost-effectively purchase compliance instruments in the market as well as make internal reductions; this means that the government will not simply let the companies default in achieving emissions targets, but it will try to remedy the international competitiveness concerns with ample access to international reductions and, if all else fails, the government will provide access to credits at a capped value of C$15; and

❑ should take into account the normal useful life of facilities in determining competitive distress; this means that the government understands that old facilities are sometimes shut down in the normal course of business, and that it will not expect the GHG controls instituted to lead to premature shutdown of industrial facilities.

Regarding early action, the allocation discussion paper identifies a set of criteria to be considered in compensating companies who would be placed at a competitive disadvantage as a result of early actions they have taken to reduce GHG emissions beyond business-as-usual.[4] It will evaluate:

❑ whether the company achieved a minimum threshold emissions intensity improvement in excess of its sector's average intensity improvement from 1992 beyond business-as-usual;

❑ whether the reductions resulted from direct company activities – for example, no compensation will be awarded for indirect emissions reductions (ie, reduced electricity usage leads to indirect emissions reductions, while power generation is direct);

❑ whether the investment resulted in a financial disadvantage; a company would need to show that real costs were imposed beyond business-as-usual investment;

❑ whether the company is a world leader in terms of its emissions intensity; and

❑ whether a visible discontinuity in its emissions intensity performance occurred – ie, the company seeking compensation would need to demonstrate that the early-action activities resulted in a sharp decline of emissions intensity following their implementation.

Any compensation for early action will need to be taken from the total 55 million tonnes allocation for the large final emitters, so the criteria being proposed for such compensation are purposefully strict. It is doubtful that more than ten Canadian companies will be able to successfully negotiate a separate covenant with the federal government with provisions for target adjustments to compensate for their early actions.

Domestic offsets
A second discussion paper outlines the key elements of how the domestic offsets system might operate. The paper has generated significant volumes of comments from all sectors of the economy, and, like the allocation and early-action issue described above, it is likely that discussions will continue for the remainder of 2004 with the results being incorporated in the draft legislation for 2005.

Domestic offsets are hailed as a way of encouraging a "made in Canada" approach to meeting Kyoto objectives through domestic action and are seen as means of encouraging GHG emissions reduction activities from sectors of the economy not covered by the domestic emissions trading system. Like the aforementioned paper on compensation for early action, the initial domestic offset paper submitted by the federal government is quite restrictive in the activities that would be eligible for generating credits. The system as proposed would draw on the criteria being developed in the international arena for the creation of CERs under the CDM.

In its current configuration, for projects to be eligible to generate credits, the following criteria would need to be met.

❑ Only GHG reductions/removals that will be captured in Canada's GHG inventory for Kyoto Protocol reporting would be eligible.
❑ Only GHG reductions and removals that occur in the first commitment period would be eligible.

❏ Domestic offsets would be credited only if they result in real emissions reductions. A GHG reduction/removal is real if it reduces the concentration of GHGs in the atmosphere (all GHGs must be accounted for), and is the result of a specific and identifiable project net of leakage that is measurable and directly attributable to the project within the project boundaries.

❏ Reductions have to be measurable and verifiable. A reduction/removal is measurable if the level of GHG emissions/removals in the baseline (eg, business-as-usual projection, "before-project" or other baseline), and the actual level of GHG emissions/removals with the project in place, can be quantified with an acceptable level of confidence. A GHG reduction/removal is verifiable if the quantification methodology is sound, clear and replicable, and the raw data required to verify/audit the calculation are available.

❏ A GHG reduction/removal would count only if it were surplus. To be considered surplus, the activity cannot be required (eg, by existing federal/provincial regulation/operating certificate), and is in excess of the level that is required or that might reasonably be expected to be achieved from receipt of another government climate change measure.

❏ The activity is eligible only if it is unique. A GHG reduction/removal is unique if it is used only once (eg, a GHG reduction/removal cannot be reported as an improvement in the seller's GHG inventory and traded to another entity for use in meeting a compliance obligation).

❏ Clear ownership must be established. The entity (investor/owner) creating offsets must have secure and transparent ownership rights to the GHG reductions/removals.

Covenants and legislative backstop

A third discussion paper focuses on the structure of covenants with certain industry sectors. In particular, it discussed how large emitters that do not enter covenants could be legally forced to reduce emissions. This is the so-called regulatory "backstop". The paper describes a "sectoral model with company-specific covenants". In such a model, sector associations would facilitate negotiation of sectoral targets that are applied to each company based on a common formula. Then companies would either accept the targets agreed in sector-level negotiations or seek to negotiate their own target in a company-specific covenant with the government.

For example, the government indicated that it would consider negotiating company-specific emission targets to address issues of capital structures (ie, capital stock turnover, timing of breakthrough technology) or to account for early action as noted earlier. These are critical issues for industry, since most would prefer to time GHG emissions control to normal cycles of the replacement of facilities ("capital stock turnover"). For some industries, there are breakthrough technologies on the horizon that will not be commercially available for another 10 to 15 years, so it may make more economic sense to delay instituting internal controls until such technologies are ready. In such cases, international emissions market purchases offer a bridge until these breakthrough technologies are available.

As with most serious emissions trading policies, penalties for noncompliance with covenant obligations would be imposed. The covenants paper anticipates that compliance will be assessed annually, and penalties are likely to be financial in nature.

Market outlook

Throughout policy discussions leading up to the Kyoto Protocol – and later during the development of the domestic emissions trading system – Canadian companies showed strong support for emissions trading. They also urged flexibility in allowing reductions of any of the six GHGs and use of carbon sequestration (including forestry projects). Some have also sought the flexibility to demonstrate compliance at the consolidated corporate level rather than on a facility-by-facility basis. Features of the domestic emissions trading system outlined to date suggest that the government will likely agree to all these elements of cost-saving flexibility.

As a result of the remaining gap in reaching the national target, the Canadian government expects to be a significant player in the GHG market. Of course, this depends on the success of its domestic implementation plan. Details of the magnitude of the government's participation and associated costs are not yet available, but, as discussed earlier, they could range from a minimum of 35 million tonnes per tonne from 2008–12 to as much as 100 million tonnes per year. Decisions on how much to buy and when to buy it are not likely to be made until 2005, following initial reaction to the tabling of legislation associated with the domestic trading system and following results of further consultations with business, the provinces and other stakeholders.

Perhaps the biggest unsolved issue is the magnitude of individual installation targets for emission reductions: what allocations will emitters receive? Companies have urged that targets not penalise the use of new technology and clean energy used in the production process. It also remains to be seen how the government will implement the price cap. For example, government officials have indicated that companies must justify why their emissions management strategy failed to perform under the price cap in order to gain benefit of it. What that justification must entail and the criteria under which requests would be reviewed are not yet defined.

As these issues are resolved and policies are set, market activity is likely to pick up. The government must make the allocations decisions in order to create the basic supply and demand, but, given the emissions growth in virtually every industrial category, many Canadian companies are likely to be short.

GHG emissions trading has been embraced by both the government of Canada and influential companies throughout the country. This deep support suggests that, for the foreseeable future, Canada will continue to look to emissions trading as central to its response to the threat of global climate change. The government has signalled that it intends to honour its Kyoto commitments, whether or not the Protocol itself comes into force. However, many industrial companies are sceptical that the Canadian government would maintain a strict adherence to its Kyoto target, if prices rose high enough to breach the C$15 level of the price cap and created a significant budget outlay for the government to cover the emissions gap. In this case, it is likely that the government would retreat to a more achievable target, perhaps over a longer period of time. In addition, and regardless of whether the Kyoto Protocol enters into force, Canada will keep a close watch on the evolution of state and federal climate change measures in the US. A Kyoto failure would open the door to a more integrated North American approach – something that many corporations in Canada would likely welcome with open arms.

1 The 670 companies are referred to as "large final emitters". They operate in the following sectors: thermal power generation, oil and gas production and transmission, mining, pulp and paper, chemical production, iron and steel production, smelting and refining, cement and lime, glass and glass containers.

2 Three of the five "non-papers" have already been released and are discussed in the remainder of this chapter. These include papers on: (1) allocation and credit for early action; (2) covenants and a legislative "backstop"; and (3) a system of domestic offsets. The two papers still to be released will discuss: (4) measurement and verification; and (5) issues to consider in the implementation of a C\$15 per tonne cost cap.

3 http://www.gert.org and http://www.cleanaircanada.org.

4 Early action is likely to be interpreted as actions taken between 1992 (when Canada signed and ratified the UN Framework Convention on Climate Change) and 2002, the year in which Canada ratified the Kyoto Protocol.

REFERENCES

Aoyagi, T., 2004, "Climate Policy: What's Going On in Japan", Mitsubishi Research Institute (Point Carbon, Carbon Market Insights Conference, Amsterdam), April 2004.

Kuratomi, M., 2004, "Promoting Measures for Overseas GHG Emissions Reduction Projects by Japanese Government", Development Bank of Japan (London Representative Office), January.

Lecocq, F., and K. Capoor, World Bank Carbon Group's PCF Plus Research, 2003, "State and Trends of the Carbon Market 2003, based on data and insights provided in Natsource Market Intelligence Report.

Shell Canada Ltd and Natsource LLC, 2003, "Greenhouse Gas Trading in Canada", IETA Annual Conference.

Vickers, P., 2003, "Roles in the Marketplace: Natsource Greenhouse Gas Credit Aggregation Pool", IETA Annual Conference, October 2004.

17

A Region of Plenty? Understanding Central and Eastern Europe's Place in the Global Carbon Market

Camilla Taylor

Vertis Environmental Finance

In emissions trading circles, Central and Eastern Europe (CEE) is often synonymous with "seller". The Kyoto climate policy framework, historic economic conditions and features of the region's industry and infrastructure make emissions trading appear a tremendous opportunity. The region will easily meet and exceed its first commitment period of Kyoto targets and also has an abundance of relatively low-cost emission-reduction opportunities. However, it remains to be seen whether the evolving carbon market and future international policy frameworks will enable the region to realise its potential.

The European Union's mandatory Emissions Trading Scheme (EU ETS), initiated by but autonomous of Kyoto, will cover large EU heat, power and industry installations from 2005, and is playing the lead role in shaping the framework and standards of an international carbon market. Decisions made on the strictness of EU ETS targets and the use of international credits for EU ETS compliance have influenced and will continue to influence the size of potential carbon credit flows from CEE countries. Given the potential of carbon revenues to influence the outcome of project investment decisions, it is essential that effective regulatory frameworks and incentives be created.

This chapter explains the background to the CEE's unique role in the international carbon market. It outlines the rationale behind the view that the region should be a net supplier of emission reductions, gives some account of the region's emissions trading activity to date and suggests why commonly held expectations about the region's role in the global carbon market may not be immediately fulfilled.

The barriers to the supply of carbon credits from CEE may be divided into several areas. Two are related to the European trading framework: including generous Western European National Allocation Plans, which would dampen demand for CEE emission reductions, and overlap and conflict between Joint Implementation (JI) projects and the EU ETS. The other two are related to the international carbon market: uncertainty over Kyoto ratification and the tradability of Kyoto compliance instruments, and the competition between CEE and developing countries as suppliers of carbon credits.

A region of two halves

In many respects the CEE region may be divided in two, and this has led to the evolution of two distinct emissions trading markets. In May 2004, ten years after initial enlargement discussions, eight Central European countries joined the EU: Estonia, Czech Republic, Hungary, Latvia, Lithuania, Poland, Slovakia and Slovenia. These new member countries are now subject to EU legislation (including the EU ETS), and must adopt the EU's central body of laws, the *Acquis Communautaire*. Following decades of opaque politics and volatile economic circumstances, the outlook for these countries is improving. Healthy economic growth forecasts and increasing transparency are boosting confidence, and investment is accelerating eastward.[1]

The remaining countries of Eastern Europe include two second-wave EU candidates, Bulgaria and Romania, as well as the successor states to Yugoslavia. Russia, Belarus and Ukraine also share some of the important features of CEE countries described in the next section. With the notable exception of Russia (and Croatia), these countries have ratified the Kyoto Protocol and may host JI projects – the Kyoto project mechanism being designed precisely with these transition economies in mind.

In 1997, CEE countries participated actively in the negotiation of the Kyoto Protocol. At the time, the region was emerging from a period of major economic restructuring and recession, during which industrial production, energy demand and greenhouse gas emissions plummeted. CEE countries made their affirmative participation in the Protocol contingent on international recognition of the region's unfavourable economic circumstances – they negotiated for a base year and targets that acknowledged the reasons behind the "unintentional" emissions reductions of the 1990s and allowed room for economic reinvigoration. The CEE countries are classified (with the EU, Japan, Canada, etc) as Annex I parties to the Protocol, and must reduce emissions to 8% below base year levels (1990 or in some cases earlier, see Table 1), with the exception of Hungary and Poland, which negotiated 6% reduction targets. CEE targets were agreed independently of the EU and do not fall under the EU's internal Burden Sharing Agreement.

CEE SURPLUS AND THE EMISSIONS INTENSITY MOUNTAIN

The first feature of CEE countries that leads to the expectation that the region will be an important supplier of carbon credits is the 36% decline in total GHG emissions witnessed between Kyoto base years and 2001 (see European Commission, 2003). Thus, even in the context of expected growth in emissions, the CEE region holds a substantial surplus of Kyoto "currency" – Assigned Amount Units (AAUs) – that could be traded between governments and used for compliance with national Kyoto targets during 2008–12 (see Table 1). To date there have been few AAU transactions, partly due to the perceived stigma of purchasing "hot air", created as an indirect consequence of economic recession rather than dedicated emission reduction measures.

If structured carefully, AAU sales in CEE could provide a straightforward, sovereign-backed and (Kyoto risk aside) low-risk source of finance. Furthermore, they could provide much-needed motivation for emissions reductions in sectors excluded from the EU ETS (such as energy efficiency). CEE countries have been exploring ways to improve the appeal of AAU trading, and Slovakia conducted the first government-backed trade in 2003 with the Japanese trading firm Sumitomo. The funds raised must be used to develop projects whose emissions reductions will be at least equal to the number of AAUs sold.

The future prevalence of AAU transactions is explicitly linked to the successful implementation of a global climate regime that

Table 1 Comparison of EU new member and candidate country Kyoto targets with projected emissions in 2010[2]

New member or candidate country	Base year	Kyoto target $mtCO_2$ eq.	Actual 2001 emissions $mtCO_2$ eq.	Projected 2010 emissions, with existing policy measures $mtCO_2$ eq.	Difference between targets and 2010 projections $mtCO_2$ eq.
Bulgaria	1988	145.1	77.7	133.7	11.4
Czech Republic	1990	176.7	148.0	131.7	45.0
Estonia	1990	40.0	19.4	18.9	21.1
Hungary	1985–87	96.4	84.3	95.6	0.8
Latvia	1990	26.7	11.4	12.8	13.9
Lithuania	1990	47.4	20.2	n/a	–
Poland	1988	531.4	382.8	394.0	137.4
Romania	1989	243.6	148.3	n/a	–
Slovakia	1990	66.4	50.1	53.2	13.2
Slovenia	1986	18.3	20.2	22.1	–3.8
Total (minus Lithuania and Romania)		1101.1	793.9	862.0	239.1

Source: European Commission (2003)

recognises these instruments and targets. Most immediately, it depends on whether the Kyoto Protocol enters into force. It will also depend on whether AAUs may be used for compliance by companies in regional trading schemes (particularly in Japan and Canada), and whether an internationally acceptable compromise can be reached for the trading of "greened" or project-backed AAUs.

The second feature supporting the expectation of supply from CEE countries is the relatively low cost of achieving emission reductions (ie, marginal abatement cost) compared with other developed countries. This cost is related to the emissions intensity of the economy (emissions per unit of GDP, see Figure 1). The higher the emissions associated with the production of a unit of GDP (taking into account the economy's level of industrialisation), the less efficient the heat and power, energy supply infrastructure and industrial sectors are likely to be. With such high emissions intensities, the economies of CEE should have an abundance of low- or even negative-cost emission reduction opportunities in the region, compared with Western Europe. Figure 1 shows the emissions intensity of the CEE economies, compared with the EU average.

Figure 2, which plots emissions intensity against GDP per capita, illustrates the trajectories of change required to move to a low-carbon economy. The CEE region occupies the upper part of the

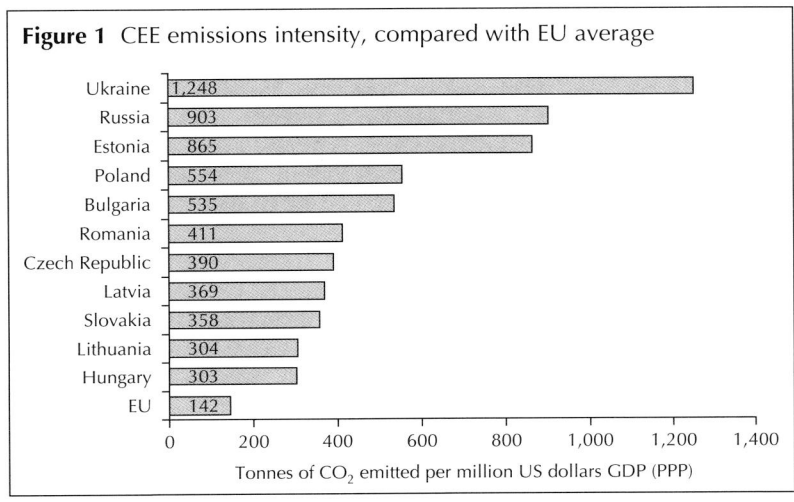

Figure 1 CEE emissions intensity, compared with EU average

Ukraine 1,248
Russia 903
Estonia 865
Poland 554
Bulgaria 535
Romania 411
Czech Republic 390
Latvia 369
Slovakia 358
Lithuania 304
Hungary 303
EU 142

Tonnes of CO_2 emitted per million US dollars GDP (PPP)

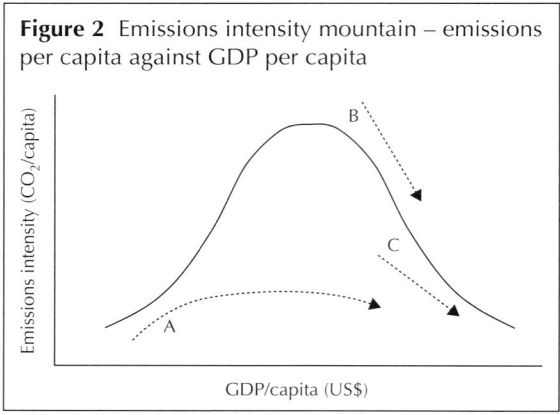

Figure 2 Emissions intensity mountain – emissions per capita against GDP per capita

curve, with the challenge to decouple emissions intensity and economic growth and move down the mountain according to trajectory "B". Technology upgrades, fuel switches and efficiency measures exist to enable this transition. Measurable progress is being made following the spate of privatisation and growing pressure from EU directives on emissions trading, renewable energy, combined heat and power (CHP) and large combustion plant emissions.

Figure 2 also illustrates the optimistic but desirable trajectory of developing countries – "A" – who, it is hoped, may shortcut the highly emissions-intensive stage of economic development by decoupling economic growth from increasing emissions. The challenge for these countries is to develop low-carbon energy, industry and transport sectors now, increasing GDP but avoiding the peak of the curve. Western European countries, as Figure 1 illustrates, occupy the lower right-hand side of the curve.

Descending the mountain

As the economies of CEE begin to grow again after the deep recession of the early to mid-1990s, the region faces a major challenge in decoupling GDP growth from emissions increases. A move from the predominance of fossil fuels to the widespread use of cleaner fuels and technologies will require major political commitment to resist vested interests and may even provoke social disquiet – among

Polish coal miners, for example. Much of the existing industrial plant is ageing but operational, and infrastructure would require major investment and overhaul. Moreover, many CEE countries are planning enlargement of their heat and power sectors and are in the process of commissioning further fossil-fuel-intensive industrial facilities whose useful lives will extend into the 2030s.

Trading emission rights has great potential to facilitate the flow of finance and motivation to owners of least-cost emission-reduction opportunities, provided certain conditions are met. The balance of overall targets – supply and demand – must create some scarcity or the market's basic environmental goal cannot be met; transaction costs of participation must be low enough to encourage participation and create liquidity; and emissions rights must be made available to those sectors of the economy that have the potential to reduce emissions.

As described in other chapters in this book, the international community and the EU have developed a network of policies that exist to drive emissions reductions in different regions of the world and in different sectors. The interrelationship of these frameworks will be fundamental to the ability of the CEE region to participate in, and benefit from, the international carbon market. The following sections of this chapter assess the importance of the EU ETS and allocation, the future role of JI projects and the impact of the international carbon market on CEE's prospects for moving down trajectory "B" (Figure 2), fulfilling its supply potential.

THE EU ETS CONQUEST

From 1 January 2005 the new member countries will participate in the EU ETS. The scheme effectively ensures that a large portion of potential Central European emissions reductions are secured for use for compliance by companies in the EU rather than being exported through the Kyoto framework to other Annex I countries to meet national targets. The mandatory nature and relatively well-developed framework of the scheme provide a promising opportunity for accession companies in the trading sector to raise finance for emission reduction projects. Many of these projects could also be candidates for JI finance, but stand to benefit from ETS due to the earlier start date (2005 rather than 2008) and the substantially lower transaction costs of a forward sale under the EU ETS compared with the paperwork and bureaucracy of JI. For example, there is no requirement to demonstrate additionality or produce project documentation in the ETS. Furthermore, new member country trading-sector projects prefinanced through the sale of future ETS allowances from 2005–7 could also, in the absence of certainty of their second phase ETS allocation (2008–12), raise finance through the JI mechanism as allowed by the Linking Directive (detailed below).

Phase-one ETS transactions have already taken place in both Hungary and Slovakia. In Hungary a chemicals manufacturer forward sold 20,000 EUAs (European Union allowances) to be delivered in 2006 and 2007, to raise finance for a biomass fuel switch project at its combustion facility. The transaction was closed at the beginning of 2004, when prices were around €12.50/EUA and the chemical company received a substantial portion of upfront payment.

However, even with inviting prices per EU allowance, the ability of the trading scheme to drive emissions reductions in CEE is also dependent on the trading sector's awareness of the opportunity. Governments and advisers have an important role to assist CEE companies in incorporating EU ETS into their investment decisions and financial planning at board level, rather than simply thinking of the scheme as a task for the environmental compliance officer.

The scheme presents further financial and risk management challenges beyond identifying and acting on the opportunity. Forward transactions to raise finance for emission reduction projects will require a more sophisticated credit risk assessment than simple spot market transactions for compliance trading. Counterparty credentials of Central European companies will be scrutinised by Western European traders' credit teams; there may be a role for a bank or intermediary to step in to guarantee and perhaps aggregate smaller projects. Companies will need to become familiar with trading contracts and, until there is more certainty in the market, counterparties will need to negotiate over terms such as the sharing of risk in the event of either country's late or failed implementation of the scheme.

Surplus and soft allocation

The most important impact of the EU ETS on the future supply of credits from Central Europe will become clear following the terms of EU allowance allocation, both within the CEE region and elsewhere in Europe. The European Commission's allocation criteria block the conversion of the CEE region's Kyoto surplus into EU allowances. Thus, CEE facilities may receive only the allowances they are likely to need for 2005–7 operations, with CEE governments unable to convert their "hot air" into something more accessible and valuable to their companies. Other than the possible surplus allocated as credit for efficiency measures implemented prior to the start of the scheme, the CEE's EU allowance supply potential will be limited, and will depend on the quantity of abatement projects that actually take place during 2005–7. Given that the sectors covered by the scheme usually have long-lived assets demanding high capital investment on replacement or refurbishment, there will also be a time lag to project implementation.

This raises the further question of whether the CEE's least costly reduction opportunities will reside in the sectors covered by EU ETS. The high energy intensity of Central Europe is partly a consequence of ageing infrastructure, poor distribution and insulation, and inadequate energy demand-side management, involving energy assets that are not covered by the EU ETS on account of their type and size. The best way to motivate such reductions may be through low transaction cost project-backed AAU deals, which at present are unpopular with buyers. Furthermore, the ownership structure of CEE energy and the industry sector may restrict supply of EU allowances; most of the largest emitters either belong to multinational companies or the State, of which the former should reconcile their net position across Europe before trading and the latter may be reluctant to trade actively at all.

The stringency of Western European allocation plans will also have an important role in defining the potential for carbon finance in the accession countries. Strict allocation (in line with their typically poor progress towards Kyoto) would increase the demand for EUAs among EU15 companies, raising the price of allowances and driving the creation of supply from CEE. Given the distance of many of the EU15 from their Kyoto targets, comfortable allocation plans designed to protect the private sector would require these governments to devise strict domestic climate policies for sectors not covered by the EU ETS (eg, transport and domestic energy efficiency) or to initiate procurement of Kyoto project credits to make up their national shortfall, as the Dutch government have done. If these governments do not pass on their burden to their private sectors through strict allocation, new member companies stand to lose, the EU ETS is their easiest means of monetising their carbon asset and without some demand from the participants of the EU ETS, projects that could create EU allowances will not take place.

JI VERSUS ETS

The JI mechanism has suffered from several conflicts. As the Kyoto project mechanism targeted for Annex I transition economies, it has been held back, particularly in Eastern Europe, by a lack of investor confidence and the required governmental support to establish the necessary institutions. In addition, accession and the EU ETS both impact the ability of companies to use the JI mechanism as a means to finance projects.

On joining Europe, new member country JI projects must go beyond the high environmental standards of the EU *Acquis Communautaire* before they will be eligible for carbon credits. First, this will erode the potential of the region to produce ERUs since many projects will cease to be 'additional', as required by the Kyoto Protocol – instead, the *Acquis* will require them to take place. Second, prior to agreement of the Linking Directive on the 20th April 2004, there was an expectation that many JI projects in the accession countries would be barred due to their indirect impact on the EU ETS trading sector, leading to double counting of emission reductions. For example, energy efficiency and renewable energy projects, which displace emissions from fossil fuel generation (thereby creating surplus emission rights for power generators within the European trading scheme) were not expected to be eligible to receive JI credits in 2008–12. This expectation contributed to the supposition that JI was all but dead in the new member countries.

However, the recent negotiation and approval of the Linking Directive could provide a means to boost the supply of emission reductions from the region. The Directive provides a mechanism for new member governments to approve and credit JI projects both within and outside of the trading sector, but it does so in competition with the distribution of EU allowances to the trading sector. The mechanism is expected to work as follows: companies within the trading sector may receive ERUs from 2008–12 (which they may sell forward), but an equivalent number of EU allowances will be deducted from their 2008–12 allocation in phase two of the EU ETS. Companies outside the trading sector, whose JI emission reductions lead to displacement of trading sector emissions (as described above) may also receive ERUs, but an equivalent number of EU allowances will be deducted from the total available to the trading sector. At the end of 2006 when 2008–12 National Allocation Plans are published, accession governments must describe how they will allocate EU allowances in 2008–12, taking into account ERUs promised to JI projects, whilst also meeting the strict allocation criteria.

Thus the Linking Directive provides a mechanism to aid the prospects for JI projects in the accession countries, but uncertainties remain that could stifle project development, at least in the short term. Companies who will be in the expanded trading sector from 2008 (it is expected that the EU ETS will enlarge to include chemical and aluminium sectors and all six greenhouse gases) are unlikely to forward sell ERUs unless they have assurance that their 2008–12 allocation, minus deducted allowances, will be at least sufficient to cover their project's actual emissions (ie, they will not need to buy back allowances they sold forward). This could be achieved through host country assurance during the project development process, but is at the discretion of individual new member country governments. Furthermore, by agreeing to allow JI projects, such as wind farms, outside the trading sector, governments risk upsetting their trading sector companies, from whom they must deduct corresponding allowances.

Although the level of future JI activity is currently hard to predict, there are several examples of successful projects that have already benefited from the JI mechanism and received up front finance. The Hungarian AES Borsod Power Plant raised €3.1 million, to help finance a coal-to-biomass fuel switch, through the forward sale of 700,000 Emission Reduction Units (ERUs) that will be created between 2008 and 2012 as a result of the project. The "business-as-usual" scenario was shut down. The reductions were sold to the Dutch government through its second ERU Procurement Tender (ERUPT 2).

Until 2004, most of the demand for ERUs had been from the Dutch programme and the World Bank. Now a variety of public and private buyers are willing to sign purchase contracts ranging from full sharing of Kyoto and project risk, to non-project-specific contracts to deliver ERUs (or their compliance equivalent) regardless. In addition to having compliance value in the EU ETS from 2008 (following confirmation of the Linking Directive), ERUs are expected to be valid for use under evolving Canadian and Japanese emissions trading programmes.

OPENING THE EU CARBON MARKET

The EU trading scheme will open its doors to credits from CDM projects from 2005, and JI projects from 2008. Companies will be able to use credits from JI and CDM for compliance with their EU ETS targets. AAUs, however, are not likely to be allowed. EU ETS buyers can select among these instruments to purchase the least-risk, least-cost unit of compliance. Prior to the discussions of "linking", Central Europe's EU allowances were expected to have an important role to play in meeting any demand. Now they will have to compete on price and terms with international project emission reductions. This will exacerbate the problems for CEE discussed in the previous section.

CEE JI projects will also have to compete with CDM projects in developing countries. Under Kyoto, CDM projects may theoretically create emission reductions from the year 2000 and projects will usually be credited for at least 10 years, whereas JI projects may receive credits only from 2008–12, giving comparable CDM projects lower relative transaction costs as a percentage of carbon revenue. The approval process for the creation of a CDM carbon credit is much more developed than for JI (through the CDM Executive Board), although there is the potential for JI host governments to develop their own independent project approval process. In short, this combination of market and political factors is making CEE an undeservedly less attractive source of supply in the global carbon market.

CONCLUSIONS

Ever since the Kyoto protocol enshrined the concept of international carbon trading in its various forms, the market has looked to CEE as a supplier for its combination of Kyoto quota surplus and plentiful low-cost emission-reduction project opportunities. As eight CEE countries enter the EU, despite attractive growth forecasts and improving investment climates, the prospects for the region to perform this role are uncertain.

The EU ETS and the recent Linking Directive present promising opportunities for CEE companies to monetise their carbon assets. However, a combination of lag-time to completion of abatement projects, unfamiliarity with the trading mechanisms, and institutional uncertainty cast doubt on CEE's ability to make immediate and optimal use of these frameworks. In addition, undemanding allocation plans in the EU15, designed to protect industry, will undermine the demand side of market for CEE EU allowances and ERUs. This would force EU15 governments to achieve their Kyoto targets through sovereign purchases of carbon credits on the international market for Kyoto instruments, a market in which developing countries may be more competitive suppliers.

Thus, at least for the short term, the CEE region is a political casualty of market inefficiency caused by the policy uncertainty surrounding the Kyoto Protocol and the somewhat isolated development of the EU ETS in its wake. There is cause for optimism, however: climate change policy is a long-term challenge whose market instruments have yet to mature, and, when countries and companies begin to feel the pain of emission reduction targets, there will be pressure to iron out these inconsistencies to take full advantage of an integrated global carbon market – one in which CEE will retain a distinct advantage.

1   3–6% per year according to *The Economist* of 20 November 2003.
2   Data derived from European Commission Report COM(2003)735.

REFERENCE

European Commission, 2003, COM(2003)735.

Market Experience and Outlook: Australia and New Zealand

Brett Janissen

The Allen Consulting Group

Like many other industrialised countries, Australia and New Zealand have agreed to take a leading role in combating climate change and its effects. Australia was among the first nations to ratify the United Nations Framework Convention on Climate Change (UNFCCC), committing itself to this treaty in December 1992. New Zealand's ratification came in September of the following year.

Since that time both nations have been active participants in the negotiations surrounding the Kyoto Protocol – the instrument whose primary function is to establish an action framework for putting the principles and objectives of the UNFCCC into effect. In parallel with their involvement in the international greenhouse negotiations, both nations have developed domestic policies to identify emission reduction measures. For both nations, emissions trading has loomed large in policy thinking; and trading instruments with a sectoral or localised focus form part of the current suite of measures. But a national emissions trading system for greenhouse gases (GHGs) does not feature in the near-term planning of either nation.

Instead, Australia and New Zealand have indicated a preference for other measures in the composition of GHG policy packages aimed at achieving the national emission targets accepted in the context of the Kyoto Protocol. These policy packages will affect the business environment in both these countries – particularly for emission-intensive and internationally oriented firms. Business planners and investors also need to consider a further GHG policy dimension that sets these two countries apart. New Zealand has taken a legally binding commitment to achieve its greenhouse target through ratification of the Kyoto Protocol; Australia's position is that it continues to accept its target – but currently does not see ratification as in the national interest.

An overview of the greenhouse policy and emissions trading positions of Australia and New Zealand is provided in the following sections, together with concluding remarks on the policy outlook for these countries and associated issues.

AUSTRALIAN GREENHOUSE PERSPECTIVES

Australia fought hard in the Kyoto Protocol negotiations for a national emissions target that reflected its circumstances as an efficient producer and exporter of energy-related and agriculture products. Its abundant coal reserves and comparative advantage in the production of land-intensive activities such as grains and livestock have established Australia as a supplier of these commodities, and closely aligned products, to the world. Australia's reliance on those activities makes its economy more vulnerable to GHG emission constraints than most. In addition, strong growth projections for the Australian economy mean that emissions are growing rapidly away from 1990 base-year levels. Figure 1 illustrates this trend, with Australia's economic and emission growth over the 1990s significantly exceeding that of the EU, USA and New Zealand. Growth in GDP and emissions is also expected to remain strong over the coming decade. Under these conditions, returning to 1990 emission levels would represent a greater task for Australia than most other industrialised economies.

In view of these factors, it was agreed that Australia's emission target (or quota) for the 2008–12 period would be equivalent to an annual average of 108% of 1990 emission levels. Australia was also able to benefit from a provision allowing emissions from land clearing to be factored into the 1990 base-year emissions calculation. Based on these provisions (and most recent National Greenhouse Gas Inventory estimates), Australia's 1990 emissions for Kyoto Protocol purposes were equivalent to 543.1 million tonnes of carbon dioxide ($mtCO_2e$), giving a notional allocation of over 2.9 billion Assigned Amount Units (AAUs) for the 2008–12 commitment period. This amount, of course, can be further

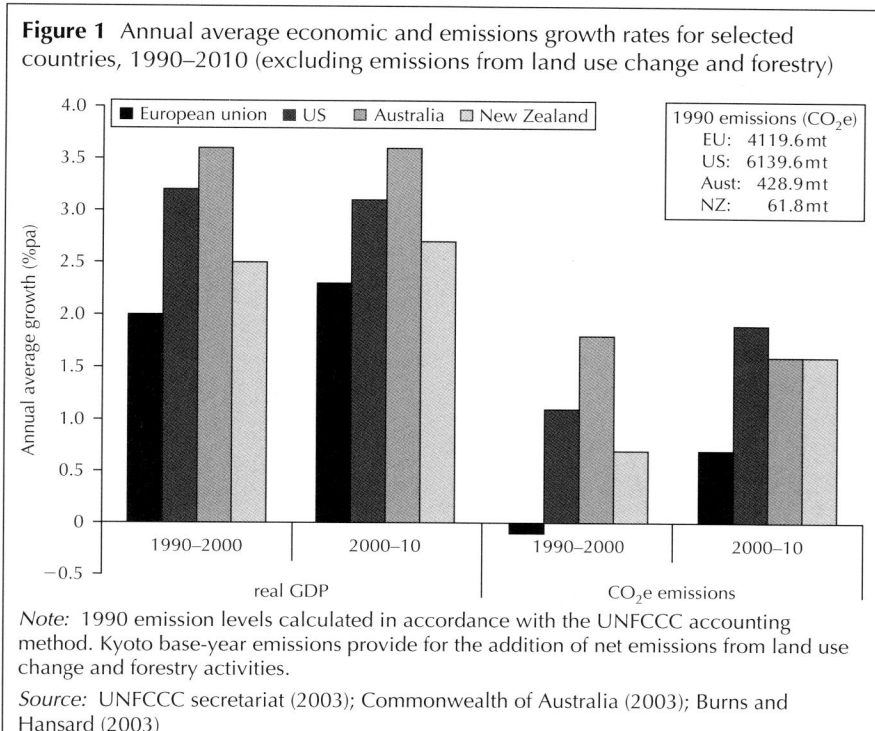

Figure 1 Annual average economic and emissions growth rates for selected countries, 1990–2010 (excluding emissions from land use change and forestry)

Note: 1990 emission levels calculated in accordance with the UNFCCC accounting method. Kyoto base-year emissions provide for the addition of net emissions from land use change and forestry activities.

Source: UNFCCC secretariat (2003); Commonwealth of Australia (2003); Burns and Hansard (2003)

supplemented through international quota transfers, sequestration credits arising from cultivation of new forests and investment in abatement in developing countries.

Supported by a range of programmes aimed at reducing GHG emissions, the Australian government publicly acknowledges that it is "within striking distance" of its Kyoto target. Indeed, based on national emission trends, Australia is likely to reach its target level of 108% of 1990 emissions in the closing years of the current decade. The task for Australia would be to maintain this level, on average, for five years beginning 1 January 2008. A variety of measures are being directed towards that outcome. Most recent projections of emissions growth and performance of existing greenhouse measures suggest a need to further reduce Australia's emissions by about 13 $mtCO_2e$ per annum during the commitment period in order to achieve the Kyoto target.

Commonwealth perspectives on the Protocol and emissions trading

Despite these efforts, and its announced proximity to its Kyoto target, the Australian government's current position is that it does not consider ratification of the Kyoto Protocol to be in the national interest. In July 2002, the environment minister, David Kemp, announced that Australia will retain its Kyoto target but does not intend to ratify the Protocol and take on the legally binding commitments that ratifying implies (see Kemp, 2002).[1] This reflects concerns about coverage of the Kyoto Protocol – in particular, the absence of the US, and lack of a clear pathway to acceptance of emission constraints by developing countries (some of which are close competitors with Australia in world resource markets).

In a recent speech at the Ninth Conference of Parties (COP9) in Milan, the environment minister signalled the need for participation by at least the 12 largest emitting nations to provide a "sustainable basis for effective action" (see Kemp, 2003).[2] In the absence of such commitments, or the clear promise of them, the federal government appears reluctant to take further actions that might threaten further investment in Australia's energy-intensive industries.

However, while the federal government has adopted a rather conservative stance on GHG emissions, there is growing momentum at the level of Australian state and territory governments for further action. Under the Australian constitution, these jurisdictions have significant scope to make laws and regulations affecting commercial and environmental activities within their borders – though they do not have the power to introduce a carbon tax. This option resides exclusively with the federal government.

Emissions trading has been under review for some time within Australia. At both a Commonwealth and state level there is recognition that an efficient response to GHG will require a mechanism that has the capacity to cover a wide range of emission types and activities, encourages new technology and innovation and readily adapts to change within a dynamic and growing economy. Emissions trading is seen as having the potential to deliver on these requirements, and to do so in a way that is more amenable to the needs and preferences of industry. Emissions trading can avoid some of the political stigma that often attaches to a new tax, can link readily into existing asset markets and leave the way clear for business participation in international emissions trading if this gathers momentum.

The leading Commonwealth government agency on GHG policy, the Australian Greenhouse Office (AGO), has been active in analysing and promoting the consideration of a national trading system for Australia for GHG emissions. During 1999, it released a series of four reports that detailed a range of design and implementation issues associated with emissions trading in Australia. In 2000, with ministerial endorsement, it released a consultation paper seeking industry views on a potential crediting arrangement for abatement action. Under this arrangement "credits" earned would be exchanged for tradable emission permits and linked, via a national trading system, to commitments under the Kyoto Protocol.[3]

The AGO has also been active in canvassing industry views on Australia's greenhouse policy stance, and attitudes towards emissions trading. Towards the end of 2002, in response to an announcement by the Commonwealth government that it would be developing a long-term GHG strategy for Australia, the AGO helped arrange the "Government–Business Climate Change Dialogue" and facilitated five industry working groups, established to provide a business perspective on greenhouse policy options. Reports from these working groups were put forward for consideration by ministers in the first quarter of 2003.[4]

Not surprisingly, there was a marked preference within industry for greenhouse measures of a voluntary or subsidy nature. Few participants favoured an explicit price on GHG emissions – introduced through either a taxation instrument or an emissions constraint, supported by a trading mechanism. There has been no official announcement of the government's response to business views on the content of a long-term policy package, or on the role that emissions trading might play in Australia's GHG future.

However, the AGO has been recently winding down its emissions trading design activities. In response to questioning by a parliamentary committee in November 2003, the chief executive of the AGO conceded that work on emissions trading had ceased, and staff from that work area had either left or been redeployed to other activities in recent months (see Commonwealth of Australia, 2003).[5]

The resource allocation decisions of this key government agency are likely to give a strong indication of the policy priorities and preferences of the Australian government. Even though there has been no official announcement, emissions trading appears to be off the current Australian federal greenhouse policy agenda.

However, a handful of more tightly focused policy measures have been established federally that comprise a trading or price-based element. State and territory government legislators are also moving to introduce trading arrangements – and address the structural adjustment and transparency issues associated with a carbon price that the Commonwealth government appears so anxious to avoid.

Market-based initiatives at Commonwealth and state level

The Australian government operates a number of greenhouse programmes that comprise trading and price-based elements. Chief among these are the:

❏ Mandatory Renewable Energy Target (MRET)

   ❏ this programme sets a mandatory renewable energy sourcing target for electricity wholesalers, requiring them to purchase an additional 9,500 GWh of electricity from renewable sources by 2010 – and maintain this level until 2020. This is equivalent to an increase of around 60% in renewable electricity output over a 10-year period and should see renewables supplying about 12% of the national market by 2010. Incremental annual targets are set for the period 2001 to 2010. Compliance with sourcing obligations is achieved through the purchase and surrender of renewable energy certificates (RECs). These are earned by renewable energy generators connected to the electricity grid, at a rate of 1 REC per MWh of electricity supplied.

   ❏ performance to date has an active spot and forward market in RECs, with spot prices averaging around A$36–38, and forward prices moving out to around A$40 per REC. The programme has induced an increase in the pool electricity price of around A$0.97 per MWh to date (equivalent to an increase of about 2.4%), and is expected to add about A$1.44 to the price of electricity (about 3.6%) over the 2008–12 period (see Australian Greenhouse Office, 2003).[6] The emission intensity of electricity generation within Australia is around 1 tonne per MWh on average – largely reflecting the relative contribution of black and brown coal generators supplying the grid.

❏ Greenhouse Gas Abatement Program (GGAP)

  ❏ this programme uses a competitive tendering process to identify projects that will deliver low-cost abatement during the Kyoto commitment period, and beyond. With a total budget of around A$400 million, this programme has some features similar to the auction process undertaken as part of the UK voluntary emissions trading system. It is underpinned by a rigorous process to determine the emission baseline of participants, and applicants are asked to compete on price. Unlike the UK system, GGAP is being run over several rounds (three rounds of tenders have been invited to date), and it price discriminates rather than paying a uniform price for the abatement received. While the UK auction purchased the commitment of participants to defined quotas of tradable emission allowances, GGAP is focused on the purchase of abated tonnes and progression through a series of investment and performance milestones. GGAP was not designed to support an emissions trading element.

  ❏ to date, 15 projects have been announced under GGAP, along with a funding commitment of nearly A$145 million aimed at achieving 27.5 million tonnes of abatement over the 2008–12 commitment period. The projects range from support for generation based on waste coal methane, to support for installation of industrial combined heat and power plants, and efforts to change travel demand patterns. Successful bids under GGAP Round 3 are yet to be announced.

❏ Greenhouse Friendly Program (GFP)

  ❏ "Greenhouse Friendly" is a government-backed certification and labelling programme that deals in emission offsets. Products wishing to obtain certification under the programme must undergo a rigorous assessment process aimed at estimating the full life-cycle emissions associated with their manufacture, use and disposal – and fully offset these through additional abatement action. The programme improves the ability of business to market a greenhouse-neutral product to consumers and establishes rules for the estimation and verification of abatement "credits" that can be transferred from one firm to another as an emission offset. To date, participation in the GFP has involved the "partnering" of certified products and discrete abatement projects, on a contractual basis, in order to achieve the offsets required. This programme is a form of *de facto* voluntary trading (albeit based on transfer of abatement "credits"). It has the potential to mature into a registry-based market in which project partnering is replaced by an ability to buy and sell certified and individual abatement tonnes via a broker. Consumer demand for "Greenhouse Friendly" products and the costs of achieving and maintaining certification will ultimately determine the future of this fledgling programme.

❏ the first Greenhouse Friendly product (BP's premium-grade fuel) was launched late in 2001 and a handful of others have received, or are in the process of earning, certification – including a Greenhouse Friendly electricity product. Current estimates for the programme indicate emission savings of about 600,000 tonnes of CO_2e per annum.

Alongside these measures, there is growing interest within Australian states to employ market approaches in the realm of greenhouse policy.

New South Wales (NSW), Australia's most populous state, has recently implemented an emissions trading system for its electricity retail sector, aimed at achieving a significant reduction in the emission intensity of electricity consumed within the state. This initiative, the NSW Greenhouse Gas Abatement Scheme, became operative on 1 January 2003 and targets a reduction in the per capita emissions from electricity use in the state. An initial benchmark of 8.65 tonnes of CO_2e per capita is set for 2003, falling in annual increments to 7.27 tonnes CO_2e per capita in 2007, and remaining at that level to the end of 2012. Population estimates within the state allow the calculation of an effective emissions cap, and electricity generators with emission intensities below the average level recorded for the electricity pool, or those able to improve their emission performance, are eligible to create NSW Greenhouse Abatement Certificates (NGACs). These NGACs can be traded and used by electricity retailers to achieve compliance with the emissions target allocated to them in line with their share of the NSW electricity market. A modest noncompliance penalty of A$10.50 per tonne of CO_2e (effectively a price cap) has been designed into the system. To date, NGAC trading has been rather limited due to the complexities of the scheme and its relatively light constraint on emissions in the start-up phase.

Queensland, another large Australian State, has also announced the implementation of a gas-fired electricity target for its retailers. The Queensland 13% Gas Scheme will operate from 1 January 2005 to 31 December 2019, and requires those selling electricity to Queensland consumers to provide Gas Electricity Certificates (GECs), created by gas-fired electricity generators and denominated in megawatt-hours, equivalent to 13% of those electricity sales. The scheme is intended as a major driver of gas development and supply in Queensland, and supports the use of natural gas, coal mine gas and waste gas from petroleum refining for electricity generation. It is primarily designed to improve the economics of marginal gas-fired power plant currently under consideration, by effectively "locking in" current demand projections. As such it does not represent a significant extension of abatement effort – although it does ensure that an opportunity for enhancing Australia's supply of low-emission power generation is not lost.

There is also the prospect that Australian states may, through coordination of greenhouse policies and programmes within their jurisdictions, deliver a set of national programmes. Some state ministers have mooted this concept. This is an ambitious goal that would require an unprecedented degree of interjurisdictional cooperation – particularly in the absence of support at the federal level. Nevertheless, the initiative appears to be gathering momentum. A state-level working group with the aim of developing a national emissions trading system for GHGs has been established.

NEW ZEALAND GREENHOUSE PERSPECTIVES

New Zealand is a small developed nation whose economy (and emission profile) is strongly oriented towards agriculture. Its 1990 GHG emissions are estimated to be equivalent to around 62 $mtCO_2e$, with about half of New Zealand's emission profile associated with farming activities. Methane emissions from digestion in livestock (particularly sheep) account for a large share of this total. New Zealand also has extensive forest sinks. It expects its Kyoto forests to sequester around 105 mtCO$_2$e between 2008 and 2012 and for national emissions to rise by about 16 mt per annum above 1990 levels during this period, on a business-as-usual basis.[7] New Zealand ratified the Protocol in December 2002. With a target of 100% of 1990 emissions, there is a good prospect that New Zealand could be a net seller in the international emissions trading arrangements established under the Kyoto Protocol. As illustrated in Figure 1, New Zealand has recorded fairly modest growth in emissions beyond 1990.

Major greenhouse measures

New Zealand has announced a package of measures designed to achieve emission constraint within the economy, in support of its Kyoto objectives. These measures cover all sectors, but focus greater pressure on emissions from energy use and industrial production, which will be subject to an emissions levy possibly from 2007. The levy will be adjusted to reflect the international emissions price, but will be capped at NZ$25 per tCO$_2$e. Agriculture is exempt from a direct emissions charge (or other levy) for the first commitment period, provided producers achieve satisfactory levels of investment in abatement research within the sector (see Hodgson, 2002).[8]

The New Zealand government is not moving to introduce an emissions trading system – although it retains the option of doing so if the international trading regime proves functional and emission prices are reliably below NZ$25 per tonne. The government has assumed responsibility for carbon sink assets and liabilities, thereby also effectively quarantining private activity in this sector from carbon price and Kyoto rules governing land-use change. However, a mechanism has been put in place that allows investors in abatement projects to earn "emission credits". These credits are synonymous with AAUs under the Kyoto Protocol, and can be traded internationally by the project proponents. Four million "emission credits" have been committed by New Zealand to date to 15 private investors via this competitive tender mechanism. Details of abatement projects are being released as contracts are signed, but at least some bidders appear to have offered more than

1 tonne of abatement for an AAU equivalent – in line with the expected value of an AAU and the marginal abatement costs of the project.

Negotiated greenhouse agreements are also an important feature of New Zealand's policy package. These are available to firms and industries whose international competitiveness is considered to be at risk as a result of greenhouse imposts within the domestic economy. Firms can apply for an exemption (either full or partial) from the effects of the emissions levy if they face competition from producers in countries with less rigorous climate change policies and they:

❑ are energy-intensive (with energy representing at least 20% of their costs); or
❑ confront a profitability decline in excess of 10% as a result of the emissions levy; or
❑ would have their rate of return reduced below the internationally accepted industry norm.

The extent to which competition from Australian companies trigger these criteria is a question for New Zealand policymakers. Certainly, Australia – which continues to accept its Kyoto target but refuses to ratify the Protocol itself – is a major trading partner to that country.

Now that eligibility has been established for a negotiated greenhouse agreement, further negotiations between government and the enterprise or industry concerned will focus on moving production towards international best practice – adjusted for what is "technically and economically feasible for New Zealand" (see Hodgson, 2003).[9]

There is clearly considerable scope for latitude and subjectivity in the negotiated agreement approach being implemented in New Zealand. They offer a haven to businesses that face a significant liability under the forthcoming emissions charge – with the prospect of negotiating lower compliance costs and advantageous treatment relative to other New Zealand businesses. On the other hand, they represent an understandable attempt on the part of government to quarantine trade-exposed firms from costs that are not shared by their major competitors. This issue is often faced by governments in formulating trade and industry policy.

Domestic policies reflect domestic needs and circumstances. These are seldom matched across nations, and it is the totality of policies operating in a country that affects the relative competitiveness of trade-exposed firms, and their location decisions. A key difficulty with domestic greenhouse policies is that they generate little direct, immediate or measurable benefit for nations taking action in isolation. This is particularly true for small nations. In entering GHG negotiations with domestic firms, officials of the New Zealand government must strive for consistency across participants and balance the trade competitiveness needs of the companies concerned with the threat of adverse efficiency implications for the national economy.

CONCLUSIONS

The greenhouse policies of Australia and New Zealand reflect attitudes and perspectives common among other developed nations. Both nations seek to strike an appropriate balance between the need to address climate change and the costs and structural changes that such action might entail. The reluctance of significant emitter nations, such as the US, China and India, to take meaningful abatement action with the Kyoto Protocol as its centrepiece threatens to reduce the effectiveness of abatement action in other countries. In addition, economies that are greenhouse-intensive, by reason of geography, consumer demand or resource endowment, can face significant structural change as they move to cut emissions.

These are salient issues in the antipodes. How to remain faithful to the principles and objectives endorsed in the international greenhouse negotiations without disturbing, too much, current patterns of production and consumption in the domestic economy?

New Zealand and some Australian states are implementing price and trading instruments to achieve greenhouse and related policy objectives – but are building safety-net provisions into these schemes to attenuate adjustment pressures in particular areas. These jurisdictions are moving towards the acceptance of greenhouse constraints at a structural level within their economies, and developing transitional arrangements that can help industry accommodate this change and factor greenhouse considerations into future planning and investment.

Australia's federal government has adopted a more conservative greenhouse stance. Dissatisfaction with Kyoto participation, strong sectoral interests and adjustment uncertainties underpin a reluctance to embrace policies that would result in an explicit and pervasive carbon price within the economy – albeit at a modest level. Yet the long-term sustainability of the current greenhouse policy approach – typified by a web of voluntary, regulatory and subsidy measures – is questionable. Generally, these measures have been preferred by business as reflecting a more "tailored" approach to industry needs and capabilities. But there is growing recognition that this mixture of policies may be adding to fragmentation, complexity and uncertainty within the business operating environment, rather than laying a foundation for a cost-effective long-term greenhouse response.

An opposition win in the 2004 Australian federal election is likely to see a significant thawing in attitudes towards the Kyoto Protocol, and emissions trading. The federal opposition supports ratification of the Protocol and, in May 2004, also announced its support for development of a national emissions trading system for Australia. There is a growing sense of inevitability within the Australian business community about the need for a structural policy response to climate change. Unpalatable as it may be, there is also recognition that such a response is best achieved through an emissions pricing mechanism – supported by either a trading system or tax.

Key segments of Australian industry would not welcome an emissions constraint. But, if a long-term constraint must come, emissions trading is seen by many companies as the *least* worst mechanism for achieving it. For policymakers, the political acceptability of any new greenhouse measure is an important consideration – as is the capacity to control costs and adjustment pressures within the economy. These perspectives, and the interplay of short and long interests, are likely to be important drivers of greenhouse policy development in Australia over the coming periods.

---

1   Minister for the Environment and Heritage (Dr David Kemp) 2002, speech to Royal Institute of International Affairs, Chatham House, London, 15 July.
2   Minister for the Environment and Heritage (Dr David Kemp) 2003, "Australia's Domestic Climate Change Approach", speech to Renewable and Sustainable Energy Roundtable, Milan, 9 December 2003.

3   The emissions trading discussion papers and ministerial consultation paper on potential abatement crediting arrangements can be found on the Australian Greenhouse Office website: http://www.greenhouse.gov.au/emissionstrading.

4   Working group reports from the "Government–Business Climate Change Dialogue" are available at http://www.greenhouse.gov.au/dialogue.

5   See Commonwealth of Australia (2003), Senate Hansard, Environment, Communications, Information Technology and the Arts Legislation Committee – Budget Estimates Supplementary Hearings (Australian Greenhouse Office transcript), Tuesday 4 November 2003.

6   See Australian Greenhouse Office (2003), Renewable Opportunities – A Review of the Operation of the Renewable Energy (Electricity) Act 2000, AGO, Canberra September

7   See details on the New Zealand Climate Change Office website at: http://www.climate-change.govt.nz/resources/info-sheets.

8   Hodgson, Pete (convenor, Ministerial Group on Climate Change), "Government confirms key climate change policies, NZ Government media statement", 17 October 2002.

9   Hodgson, Pete (convenor, Ministerial Group on Climate Change), "Negotiated Greenhouse Agreements under way, NZ Government media statement", 16 April 2003.

REFERENCES

Australian Greenhouse Office, 2003, "Renewable Opportunities – A Review of the Operation of the Renewable Energy (Electricity) Act 2000", AGO, Canberra, September.

Burns, K., and A. Hansard, 2003, "Economic Implications of the Kyoto Protocol for New Zealand – Sensitivity Analysis", ABARE eReport 03.11, Canberra, May.

Commonwealth of Australia, 2003, "National Greenhouse Gas Inventory 2001", Australian Greenhouse Office, Canberra.

Commonwealth of Australia, 2003, "Senate Hansard, Environment, Communications, Information Technology and the Arts Legislation Committee – Budget Estimates Supplementary Hearings", Australian Greenhouse Office transcript, 4 November.

Hodgson, P., 2002, "Government confirms key climate change policies", NZ government media statement, 17 October.

Hodgson, P., 2003, "Negotiated Greenhouse Agreements under way", NZ government media statement, 16 April.

Kemp, D., 2002, speech to Royal Institute of International Affairs, Chatham House, London, 15 July.

Kemp, D., 2003, "Australia's Domestic Climate Change Approach", speech to Renewable and Sustainable Energy Roundtable, Milan, 9 December.

UNFCCC secretariat, 2003, "Report on the national greenhouse gas inventory data from Annex I parties for the period 1990–2001", FCCC/SBSTA/2003/14.

19

What Determines the Price of Carbon?

Atle Christer Christiansen,
Andreas Arvanitakis

Point Carbon

INTRODUCTION

Carbon dioxide (CO_2) is the new kid on the block in commodity trading. The gas that makes up part of the atmosphere, which plants breathe in and we breathe out, is being bought and sold as if it were a barrel of oil or a tonne of coal.

There is, however, a fundamental difference between trading in CO_2 and more traditional commodities: what people are selling is a *lack*, an *absence* of the gas in question. Typical sellers will produce or expect to produce less than they are allowed, so they may sell that unused right to emit to someone who emits more than their allocated amount.

While companies in the UK and Denmark have already gained early experience from trading carbon under *domestic* emissions trading schemes, the first *international* market is being established in the European Union (EU), with the official start of the EU emissions trading scheme (ETS) of January 1, 2005. However, the market is already on its feet, with the first trade between Shell and the Dutch energy company Nuon – on a forward basis, payment on delivery – conducted in February 2003.

Against that backdrop, the key question asked by market players, and the topic addressed in this chapter, is: What are the factors that will determine the price of carbon in the first period of the EU ETS from 2005 to 2007? The answer to this question will inform a company's trading strategy, risk strategy and, ultimately, its investment decisions. In brief, we argue that the way to forecast market developments and price trends is to monitor and assess the following three drivers:

❏ policy and regulatory issues;
❏ market fundamentals; and
❏ technical analysis.

In monitoring and analysing market and price developments, one also has to understand how the drivers interact, which drivers carry more weight in the market and – last, but not least – to what extent and under what circumstances they may impact carbon prices.

Before we examine the different price drivers and their potential impact on price developments in more detail, the next section aims to put the EU ETS into perspective by highlighting some experiences from other "emissions markets", such as the US SO_2 allowance trading scheme and the UK ETS.

PRICES AND LIQUIDITY: EXPERIENCES FROM OTHER EMISSION MARKETS

Even though the use of emissions trading as an instrument in environmental policy is largely unexplored territory in Europe, practical experience from SO_2 allowance trading in the US suggests that it could be an effective instrument in ensuring cost-effective compliance with reduction targets. In fact, policymakers within the EU relied extensively on the design of the US SO_2 scheme when hammering out the rules and guidelines for the EU ETS. Hence, and although the US SO_2 and European carbon markets are likely to differ in key respects, the US experience can provide important insights.

US SO_2 allowance market

Trading of SO_2 allowances in the US has been running since 1995, structured in two phases. Phase I began in 1995, limited to emissions from the largest, highest-emitting power-generating facilities. Phase II, which commenced in 2000, tightened the annual limits on the large plants, and set restrictions on smaller, cleaner plants and all new plants. As of 2002, the programme encompassed 3,208 electricity-generating units. Total emissions from the sources covered amounted to some 10.2 million tonnes in 2002 (almost 70% of nationwide emissions), a reduction by more than 7 million tonnes from 1980 levels. By 2010, the programme will lower the cap to 8.95 million tonnes of SO_2 emissions, a 50% reduction from 1980.

Table 1 highlights some key activity indicators for the period 1995–2002, showing, for instance, that the total number of transfers and market value increased considerably over the period. We have here distinguished between overall market activity, which includes reallocations within organisations and intra-utility transfers, and transfers that involve economically distinct organisations (intercompany transfers). Serving as an indication of increasing market activity, the number and volume of intercompany transfers has increased almost tenfold since the start of the scheme. In comparison, total transfer of allowances increased by about 30%. In order to estimate the financial value of the market, it is important to distinguish between *transfer* and *trades*. The former refers to allowances moving from one account to another (the "physical" market) while the latter (the financial market) includes financial instruments (forwards, futures, options). Estimates suggest that the financial size of the market is comparable to the physical, in which case the market value for intercompany trades stood at some US$3.4 billion in 2002.

UK ETS

The UK ETS officially came into operation on April 2, 2002, following the government incentive auction on March 11–12, 2002, when a total of 34 organisations entered as so-called "direct participants". The establishment of the scheme also provided an opportunity for about 6,000 companies under climate change agreements (CCAs), so-called "unit participants", to enter the UK ETS. Through the incentive auction, direct participants volunteered to take on absolute emissions reduction targets over the period 2002–6 in return for a financial incentive. The government made £215 million (approximately €310 million) available to encourage companies to join this scheme, which was allocated through a descending clock auction to companies bidding in an absolute cap or reduction in their greenhouse gas emissions (GHG) against a 1998–2000 baseline. At the final *clearing* price of £53.37 per tonne of CO_2 equivalent emission reductions (tCO_2e), 34 companies bid in

Table 1 Activity data for US SO_2 allowance trading 1995–2002

Year	Total number of allowances ($mtSO_2$)	Total transfer of allowances ($mtSO_2$)[1]	Intercompany transfers ($mtSO_2$)	Total number of transfers	Intercompany transfers	Average market price ($US\$/tSO_2$)	Total market value (billion US$)	Market value intercompany transfer (billion US$)
1995	8.70	16.70	1.90	613	329	127.9	2.14	0.24
1996	11.70	8.20	4.40	1074	578	83.3	0.68	0.37
1997	13.50	15.20	7.90	1429	810	100.5	1.53	0.79
1998	15.00	13.50	9.50	1.584	942	158.7	2.14	1.51
1999	16.60	18.70	6.20	2.832	1.743	195.8	3.66	1.21
2000	21.58	30.09	12.66	4.690	2.889	142.3	4.28	1.81
2001	19.93	22.24	12.60	4.900	2.330	185.3	4.12	2.33
2002	18.80	21.40	11.55	5.700	3.080	152.3	3.26	1.76

Source: US Environmental Protection Agency[2]

emission reductions that will total some 4 million tCO_2e by 2006. This is equivalent to a price of about £12.45/tCO_2e (approximately €18) after tax. Initially, the UK government intended to include projects from particular sectors within the UK. However, the project rules were put on ice when negotiations on the EU ETS started.

Following a period in which prices increased considerably from about £5 in May 2002 to more than £12 in October 2002, prices gradually dropped to a level of some £2–3/tCO_2e, and have been stable at this level since (see Figure 1). The early price increase was largely due to a combination of a lack of sellers and unit participants entering the scheme to hedge against the risk of high prices and the noncompliance with relative targets. Owing to a significant surplus of allowances from direct participants, and the fact that the next "true-up" period for unit participants is not due until 2005, the demand for allowances has essentially vanished. This, in turn, has caused a downward pressure on prices and market activity. With respect to trading volumes, Point Carbon has estimated that some 1.2 million tonnes of CO_2-equivalent emissions ($mtCO_2e$) was traded between companies in the first year of the UK ETS (2002), only to decrease to a meagre 0.3 $mtCO_2e$ in year 2003.

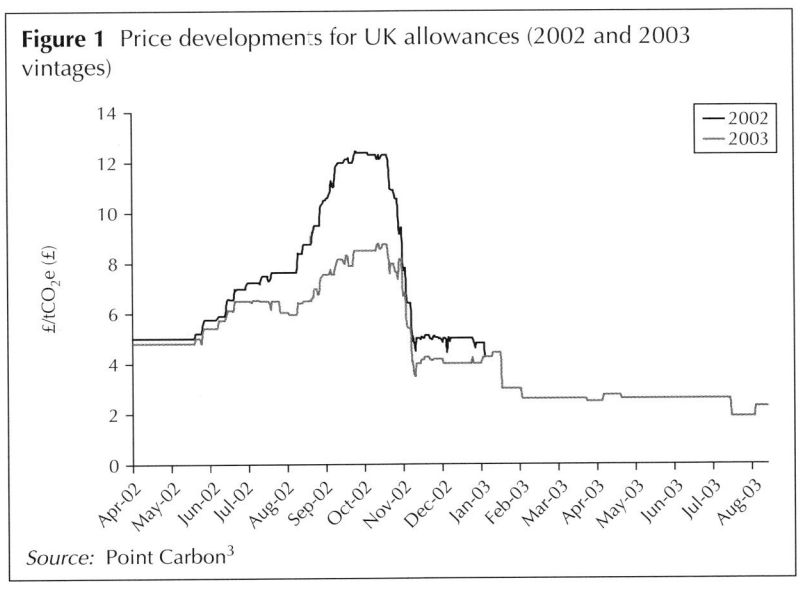

Figure 1 Price developments for UK allowances (2002 and 2003 vintages)

Source: Point Carbon[3]

EU ETS (2005–7)

In comparison, the total amount of allowances to be allocated in the EU ETS will be in the order of 2 billion tCO_2e, about 50 times the total quantity of allowances available in the US SO_2 allowance trading market in 2001. Estimates are that it will cover between 10,000 and 15,000 installations in the current and future EU member states (EU25). Point Carbon has estimated that traded volumes in the EU ETS amounted to some 600,000 tCO_2e in 2003, with prices increasing from about €5/tCO_2 in March/April to more than €13/tCO_2 towards year end (see Figure 2).[4] Most of the trades were on a forward basis, with payment on delivery. Traded volumes are expected to increase considerably in year 2004, as more clarity and information about key price determinants will become available (to be discussed further later).

Needless to say, it is difficult to have a firm opinion about the transferability of the US and UK experiences to the EU ETS, for several reasons. On the one hand, one could argue that differences in legal frameworks between member states (eg, legal status of allowance) and tax-related issues pertaining to cross-border trade could impair market *liquidity* in the EU compared with the US. The fact that borrowing allowances from next year's allocation is allowed in the first period of the EU ETS (2005–7) may also impede liquidity.

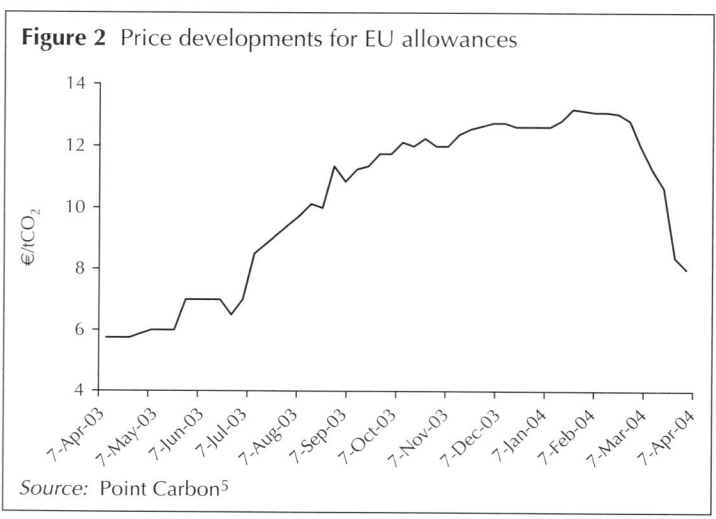

Figure 2 Price developments for EU allowances

Source: Point Carbon[5]

On the other hand, the range of options for emissions abatement and the opportunities to earn credits through project-based mechanisms such as the Clean Development Mechanism/Joint Implementation (CDM/JI) is much wider compared with the case of reducing SO_2 emissions, which could increase market depth and liquidity. One could also argue that liquidity should be higher than in the UK ETS, which has suffered strongly from structural deficiencies (oversupply) and a limited number of market players. Finally, weather is a factor that will cause fluctuations in emissions from the heat and power sector, for which the need to hedge against short positions and opportunities for speculative trading could increase volatility and liquidity (see 'The role of fundamentals').

Notwithstanding the above-mentioned caveats and prevailing uncertainties about the design of the EU ETS, one could draw upon the experience from the US SO_2 market and use, for instance, the ratio of *transferred* volumes between companies to the total volume of allowances ("turnover") as a proxy of liquidity for the EU ETS. Using the data shown in Table 1, we can see that turnover for inter-company transfers increased from about 10% in 1995, the first year of trading, to 70% in 1999, after which it has stabilised at around 50%. For the UK ETS, however, turnover in year 2002 was only around 2–3%.

Using a market turnover based on the US SO_2 scheme of 50% and a carbon price of €10/tCO_2, the financial value of the EU ETS would amount to €10 billion per year (2 billion $tCO_2 \times 0.5 \times 10$ €10/tCO_2). This would make the EU ETS the largest environmental market in the world. Based upon the UK experience, however, the financial value would be in the order of €0.5–0.6 billion per year.

POLICY AND REGULATORY ISSUES

Like other environmental markets, the "carbon market" is created through political decisions and has to be framed in law. Hence, and similar to other commodity markets such as oil, gas and power, decisions concerning framework conditions and operating guidelines could potentially have a key impact on market and price developments. Anyone aiming to analyse and forecast market and price developments, therefore, needs to understand the role and potential impact of policy choices. For the carbon market in particular, this means that market participants need to monitor and assess issues such as the national allocation plans (NAPs), the "linking" directive and banking, as well as the future status of the Kyoto Protocol.

Reduction targets and the national allocation plans

Since robust information about the NAPs has been limited thus far, market prices have not been affected much by fundamentals like CO_2 production trends or expected distance to targets. Once the NAPs are submitted to Brussels, it is the role of the European Commission (EC) as watchdog to "vet" them and make sure the carbon market is set on a level playing field. The EC has warned governments that they must create scarcity (establish short positions) for the market to work, but some doubt whether it has the political will to enforce this. Hence, until final decisions about the caps are taken (September 2004), policy and regulatory issues will play a key role in price developments.

In order to illustrate how the reduction targets to be set by the NAPs may affect the required reduction targets and relative positions (long or short), one may use historical emissions data for EU member states and compare with the targets set for each country under the Kyoto Protocol. Under the Kyoto Protocol, the EU as a whole committed itself to reduce greenhouse gas emissions by 8% compared with 1990 levels. This target was then distributed between member states according to the Burden Sharing Agreement (BSA), where different targets were set for each of the different member states (EU15) as shown in Table 2.

Hence, Luxembourg, Germany and Denmark were assigned the most "ambitious" targets, with reductions of 28%, 21% and 21% from 1990 levels, respectively. In comparison, countries like Spain, Greece and Portugal were allowed to increase their emissions, due to expected economic growth, by 15%, 25% and 27%, respectively.

By comparing emission levels in years 1990 and 2001, the latter representing the latest official emissions inventory, one may then calculate the distance to targets for each member state. As shown in Figure 3, only Sweden, Luxembourg and Greece had already reached their targets in 2001. In comparison, countries like Spain and Italy had emissions that stood some 50 and 70 $mtCO_2e$ above their BSA target. Hence, if emission levels were to remain constant at the level of 2001 in the period 2008–12, Spain and Italy would

Table 2 Total greenhouse gas emissions (mtCO$_2$e) in 1990 and 2001 and reduction targets for the period 2008–12 according to the EU BSA for current EU member states (EU15)

Member state	1990	2001	BSA (%)
Germany	1,216.2	993.5	−21.0
UK	747.2	657.2	−12.5
France	558.4	560.8	0.0
Italy	509.3	545.4	−6.5
Spain	289.9	382.8	15.0
Netherlands	211.1	219.7	−6.0
Belgium	141.2	150.2	−7.5
Greece	107.0	132.2	25.0
Austria	78.3	85.9	−13.0
Finland	77.2	80.9	0.0
Sweden	72.9	70.5	4.0
Denmark	69.5	69.4	−21.0
Portugal	61.4	83.8	27.0
Ireland	53.4	70.0	13.0
Luxembourg	10.9	6.1	−28.0
EU15	**4,204.0**	**4,108.3**	**−8**

Source: United Nations Framework Convention on Climate Change (UNFCCC)

have to reduce emissions by 50 and 70 mtCO$_2$e or purchase allowances or emission reductions from the market. Moreover, emission levels in the southern European countries are expected to increase further in coming years, for which the distance to target will increase even more in the absence of additional policy instruments.

Links to project-based mechanisms

Another key policy issue that may affect market prices is the link between the EU ETS and the project-based, "flexible" mechanisms established under the Kyoto Protocol. These mechanisms fall into two categories: JI, pertaining to investments in emission reduction projects in countries that have taken on a target under the Kyoto Protocol, and CDM, which applies to projects in developing countries.

The motivation for establishing a link between project-based mechanisms and the EU ETS is essentially threefold. First, it will provide incentives for European companies to become more

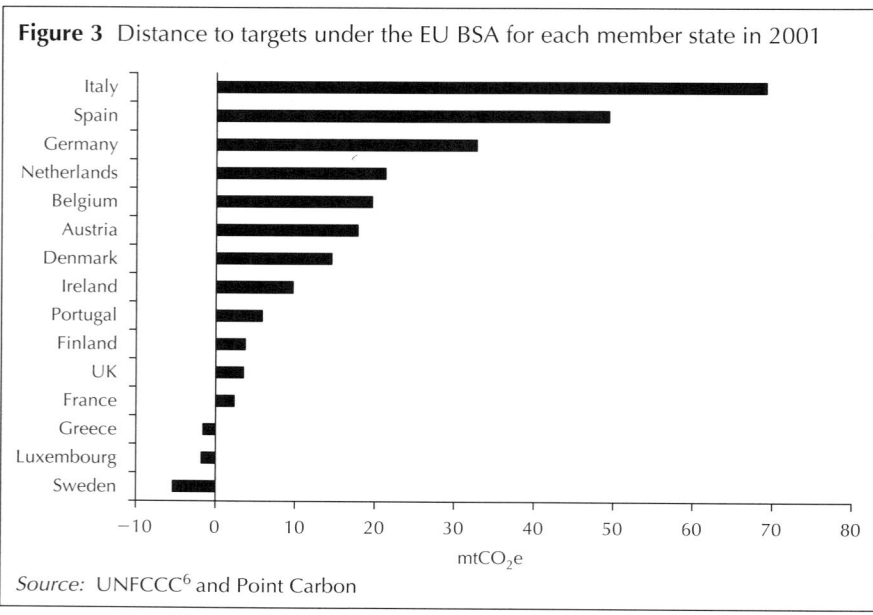

Figure 3 Distance to targets under the EU BSA for each member state in 2001

Source: UNFCCC[6] and Point Carbon

actively involved with the use of these mechanisms. Second, it would facilitate technology transfer to developing countries. Third, it would send a strong signal to countries that have not yet ratified to it that the EU is committed to the Kyoto Protocol.

In practice, a link would allow companies facing a cap under the EU ETS to invest in CDM projects or purchase emission credits (Certified Emissions Reductions – CERs) in the market and convert these into EU allowances (EUAs, the EU commodity), at parity. This could potentially boost the supply side of the EU ETS market, providing a bearish signal. Moreover, the price currently paid for emission reductions from CDM projects is lower than the price of EU allowances. The price paid for CDM/JI projects has thus far been in the order of US$4–6/tCO$_2$e, which generally has been set by sizable buyers like the Dutch procurement funds and the World Bank Prototype Carbon Fund.

However, experience so far suggests that the supply of CDM credits could be hampered due to difficulties with host-country approval and prevailing uncertainties about operational procedures. That said, analysis by Point Carbon suggests that the emergence of so-called "large-scale" CDM projects and new investment funds could increase supply, although total supply will probably be limited during the first phase of the EU ETS from 2005 to 2007. Nevertheless, volumes are still small compared with the estimated 2 billion tCO_2 that will be allocated to companies covered by the scheme.

Banking and borrowing

Another issue facing governments is whether or not to allow companies to transfer or "bank" any surplus allowances from Phase I (2005–7) into Phase II (2008–12) of the EU ETS.

If banking between phases is *not* allowed, prices towards the end of the first phase could be determined by a "true-up" logic, for which fundamentals could potentially play a key role. For instance, if the market proves to be fundamentally short (long) allowances, the price during the "true-up" period could increase (decrease). Conversely, if banking were allowed, prices would probably be affected by expectations of future prices and commitments. Even though one could argue that companies would foresee a possible shortage/surplus of allowances and embed this into their trading/hedging strategy, experiences from the US SO_2 market and the UK ETS market suggest that prices are in practice affected by "true-up".

Since companies will be issued allowances for the next calendar year two months prior to the date when they are required to submit allowances to cover their emissions for the previous year, they may decide to use allowances for the next year (borrow) for compliance. Allowing for borrowing could be seen as a relief-valve for companies, to the extent that extreme weather conditions could have a large impact on the balance for a single year. Whilst borrowing is seen as an opportunity for deferring action into the future, it could have a negative impact on liquidity. However, since this raises serious issues in relation to exposure and risk management, it remains to be seen whether and the extent to which companies will explore this option.

WHAT ABOUT KYOTO?

In the medium to long term, uncertainties with respect to the status of the Kyoto Protocol in general, and Russian ratification in particular, will affect market expectations and prices, at least in the long term. Owing to the economic restructuring in the early 1990s, Point Carbon's estimates suggest that Russian emissions have decreased by some 30% since 1990. Since Russia's target under the Kyoto Protocol is to stabilise emissions at the level of 1990, Russia has potentially vast volumes of allowances to sell into the market. Owing to the US repudiation of the Kyoto Protocol, there will probably be a vast surplus of allowances in the Kyoto period 2008–12, meaning that the market as a whole will be fundamentally long allowances. This, however, does not necessarily imply that prices will be low or even "collapse". Instead, it provides opportunities for Russia and other net sellers to affect prices by restricting supply or in other ways exercising market power. Analysis by Point Carbon suggests that Russia could earn up to US$10 billion by restricting supply.

Even though uncertainty prevails concerning if and when Russia will ratify, the coming into force of the Kyoto Protocol would send a very strong bullish signal to the market. This is simply because the price currently paid for credits from CDM and JI projects includes a significant premium to adjust for the risk that the Protocol might not come into force. Its arrival in the near term could also increase the likelihood that Canada and Japan will establish a link to the EU ETS through so-called "mutual recognition" of allowances. Since Japan and Canada are likely to be large net buyers of allowances and credits in the Kyoto period (2008–12), this would in itself provide a bullish signal by bringing into the scheme companies having to cover a sizeable short position.

The role of fundamentals

Market fundamentals, similar to other markets, concern demand and supply. The *supply* of allowances – the right to emit 1 tonne of CO_2 – will be fixed by governments through NAPs. In brief, governments in current and new member states will first determine the total quantity of allowances to be allocated (the "cap"), and then allocate the allowances to installations in energy-intensive industries (eg, production of iron and steel, building materials, pulp and paper) and the power and heat generation sectors. The *demand* for allowances is in turn a function of the level of CO_2 produced by the companies and installations covered by the scheme.

ESTIMATING AND FORECASTING CO_2 PRODUCTION

In order to monitor and forecast the demand side of the EU ETS, Point Carbon has developed a unique set of models that provide continuous updates and forecasts of CO_2 production for all sectors in each of the countries covered by the EU ETS. The models draw upon a wide variety of input data and structural information, including, for instance, detailed information about installations in the power and heat sectors (eg, installed capacity (MW), efficiency, availability).

In general, CO_2 production depends on a number of factors, such as weather data (temperature, rainfall, wind speed), fuel prices, carbon prices and economic growth. Among these factors, weather has a double effect: first, cold weather increases energy consumption and so CO_2 emissions through power and heat generation; second, rainfall and wind speeds will affect the share of power generated by non-emitting sources and thus emission levels. This is of course particularly important for countries and regions relying on hydro- and/or wind power to any significant extent.

The impact of weather

Consider for instance the Nordic Power Exchange area. During dry years, CO_2 emissions tend to soar along with the price of power, with Norway and Sweden drawing power from the pool at higher levels and coal-fired generation in Denmark and Finland ramping up. The Danish emissions profile is thus a good litmus test for the impact of weather.

As shown in Figure 4, annual emissions from power and heat generation in Denmark during the period 1990–2003 fluctuated from a low of about 24 $mtCO_2$ in 1990 to a high of 42 $mtCO_2$ in 1996, an exceptionally dry year, representing a swing of about 70% from the lowest to the highest level. According to the draft Danish NAP, the public power and heat sector will be allocated an average of 21.7 $mtCO_2$ annually in the first period, 2005–7. This is approximately 40% less than projected emissions over that period, and lower than any year during the 1990s. Hence, even under "normal" circumstances, not to mention what could happen if for instance 2005 proves to be another dry year like 1996, Danish power and heat producers will have to cover a potentially significant short position through the market.

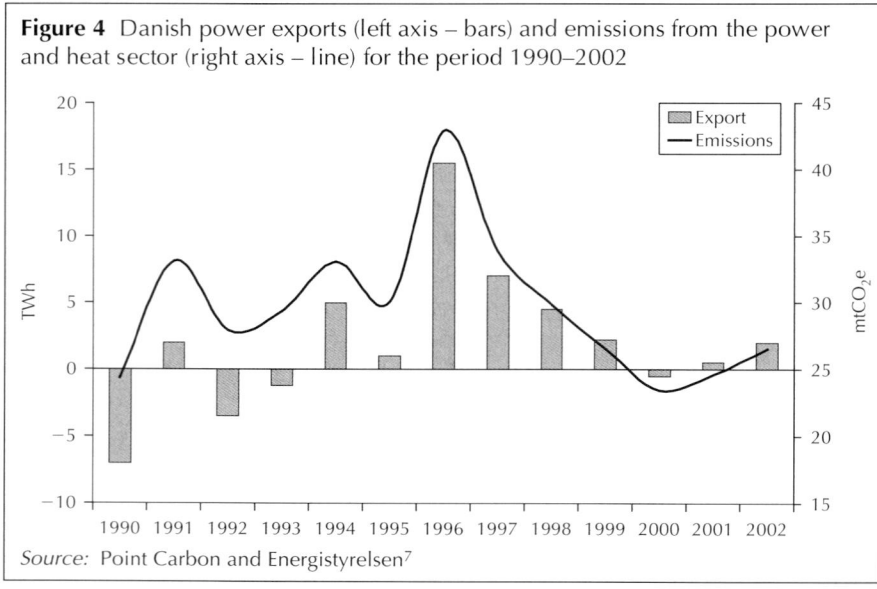

Figure 4 Danish power exports (left axis – bars) and emissions from the power and heat sector (right axis – line) for the period 1990–2002

Source: Point Carbon and Energistyrelsen[7]

Hence, the message is clear – weather can cause a swing for power producers and flip their position *vis-à-vis* its cap from short to long and back during a season. Similar to what is the case in the power markets, weather could thus become a key price driver in the short term and possibly increase volatility. For instance, the combination of a cold winter and a warm summer could cause power consumption and emissions to soar, which would provide a clear bullish signal.

Emissions-to-Cap

Another key fundamental parameter, emissions-to-cap (E-t-C), is calculated by subtracting the cap from emissions. Since electricity demand and emissions vary throughout the course of a calendar year, one needs to distribute the annual cap in representative portions across the year to obtain a "seasonally adjusted cap". The emission profile and seasonally adjusted cap will differ between countries. For instance, demand and emissions are typically higher during the winter than the summer in Northern Europe, while demand also tends to peak during summertime in Southern Europe due to the increased use of air conditioning. Calculating the

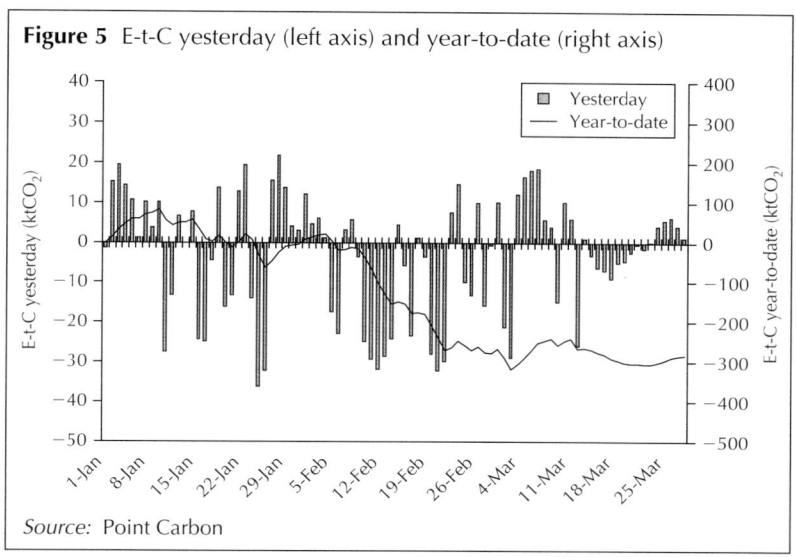

Figure 5 E-t-C yesterday (left axis) and year-to-date (right axis)

Source: Point Carbon

E-t-C then provides an indication of whether the market as a whole, a country or a sector produces more or less than the cap for the period in question. For the market as a whole, a positive (negative) value for E-t-C means that the market is fundamentally short (long) allowances, suggesting a bullish (bearish) signal.

An illustrative example is shown in Figure 5, using estimates of daily CO_2 production for the first three months of year 2004 and a (tentative) cap set at the level of emissions in year 2001 for the Danish power and heat sector. The figure first illustrates that E-t-C varies on a daily basis due to changes in, for instance, weather (as discussed above). Moreover, and interestingly, the accumulated E-t-C year-to-date (YTD) has switched from positive to negative, meaning that the relative position of the sector switched from short to long. To the extent that prices are affected by changes in fundamentals, the E-t-C provides strong buy (bullish) or sell (bearish) signals to the market.

Net carbon balance

As argued above, supply of credits from CDM projects (CERs) will also affect demand and supply. For that reason, Point Carbon has developed a tool to forecast the amount of CERs (supply) that is likely to be available in the market in the period 2005–7. The impact of CER supply is then determined by another metric, the Net Carbon Balance, which is obtained by subtracting the supply of CERs from the E-t-C for the market as a whole.

THE ROLE OF FUEL SWITCHING

While the marginal CO_2 abatement cost might in the long run direct investment towards abatement projects, fuel switching from coal to gas for power and heat production is probably the single most important measure in the short term. This is, first, because the public power and heat sector is the largest in terms of emissions for most of the current member states. As illustrated in Figure 6, public power and heat represent more than 70% of total emissions covered by the EU ETS in Denmark, Ireland and Greece, and about 60% in Germany and the UK, who represent the two single largest emitters.

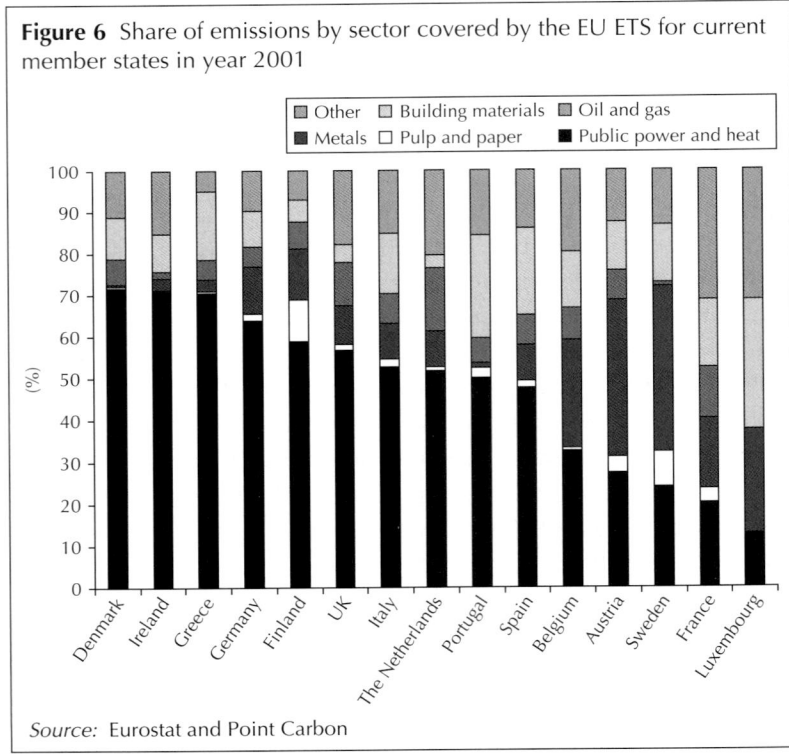

Figure 6 Share of emissions by sector covered by the EU ETS for current member states in year 2001

Source: Eurostat and Point Carbon

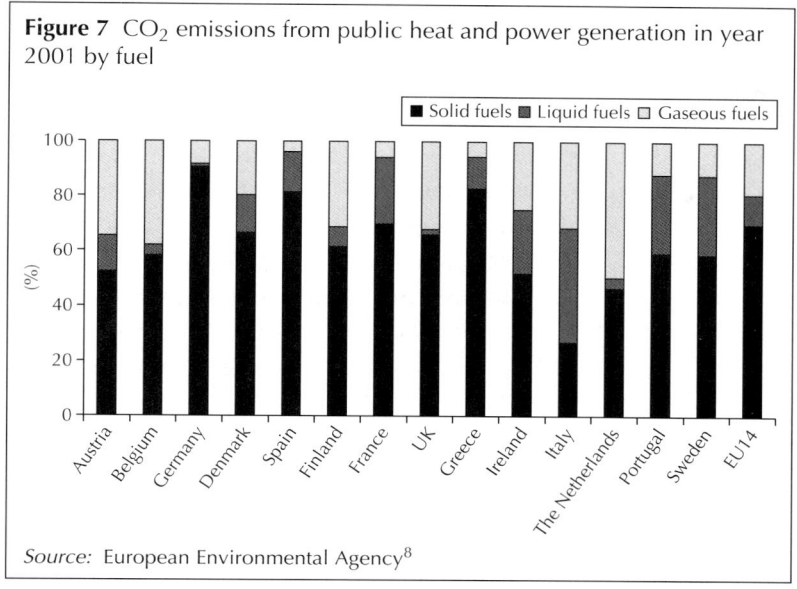

Figure 7 CO_2 emissions from public heat and power generation in year 2001 by fuel

Source: European Environmental Agency[8]

Second, and even though burning *any* fossil fuel creates CO_2 emissions, coal causes about twice that of natural gas per consumed unit. Figure 7 shows that solid fuels (hard coal, lignite) accounted for about 70% of total CO_2 emissions from public heat and power stations in the respective current member states (less Luxembourg, EU14) in year 2001. The figure also shows that the share of emissions by fuel varies between countries, depending on factors such as resource endowments, fuel prices and state subsidies/taxation. For instance, solid fuels accounted for almost 90% of emissions from thermal power stations in Germany, but only about 26% in Italy. In comparison, natural gas is an important fuel for countries such as the Netherlands, Austria, Belgium and the UK.

There is a considerable scope for switching from coal to natural gas and other liquefied fuels in several member states, most notably Germany and Spain. Hence, in order to forecast CO_2 emissions into the future, it is also important to monitor developments in fuel prices and assess their potential impact on fuel switching.

TECHNICAL INDICATORS

Like other commodity markets, technical analysis can be used to assess historical price movements and forecast future price trends.

In brief, this type of analysis focuses on the formation of charts and formulae to capture major and minor trends, identify buying/selling opportunities and assess the extent of trend reversals. In its simplest form, technical analysis assumes that the development of historical market prices reflects all existing information, both rational and irrational. In practice, this means that technical analysts do not study market information directly, but simply try to discover trends in historical price series instead.

Among the more common indicators are support and resistance levels, representing points where a chart experiences recurring upward or downward pressure. A support level is usually the low point in any chart pattern, whereas a resistance level is the high or the peak point of the pattern. These points are identified as support and resistance when they show a tendency to reappear. Once these levels are broken, they tend to become the opposite obstacle. Thus, in a rising market, a resistance level that is broken could serve as a support for the upward trend; whereas, in a falling market, once a support level is broken, it could turn into a resistance. It is usually best to buy/sell near support/resistance levels that are unlikely to be broken.

Looking at price developments in the EU market since spring 2003, the price bounced off the €12 per tonne mark towards the year end and early 2004. This could be seen as an indication of an early formation of a support line, as suggested in Figure 8. However, since liquidity and the robustness of the underlying

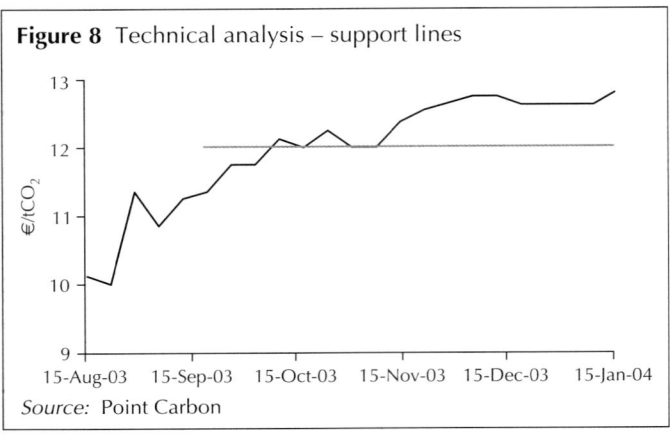

Figure 8 Technical analysis – support lines

Source: Point Carbon

price data are limited, one should not put too much emphasis on results from technical analysis at this early stage of market development. When market activity and liquidity picks up, technical analysis will allow market players to assess price trends and be informed about market developments, similar to other commodity markets.

CONCLUSIONS

In brief, this chapter has proposed and analysed three key drivers that are likely to have an impact on market prices in the EU ETS:

❑ policy and regulatory issues;
❑ market fundamentals; and
❑ technical indicators.

Similar to what is the case with other environmental markets, decisions concerning policy and regulatory issues could potentially have a key impact on market and prices. For instance, policymakers will determine the total supply of allowances for the first period of the EU ETS from 2005 to 2007 through the NAPs and that is not even the end of it! Halfway through the first phase, the whole process starts again – with negotiations for the new NAPs for the second period (2008–12). Doubtlessly this will also trigger renewed worry over Russia's next move and the imminent Kyoto Commitment Period throwing up yet more questions. In the longer term, countries such as the USA and Australia may decide to re-evaluate their stance in climate politics and enter into an agreement that would form the basis for a truly global emissions trading market.

Even though early movers in the EU emissions trading market have been operating in an environment dominated by political and regulatory risks, fundamentals will probably play an equally, if not more, important role. Among the key fundamentals in this market are CO_2 production, which in turn is a function of parameters such as weather, fuel prices and economic growth; E-t-C (is the market/sector short or long allowances?); and supply of credits from CDM projects.

Companies aiming to trade or hedge their risks actively in the carbon market need to understand the role and potential impact of these key drivers and the way(s) in which they might interact.

1 This number equals the allocated allowances for that year plus banked allowances from previous years.
2 See http://www.epa.gov.
3 See http://www.pointcarbon.com.
4 Prices are based upon Point Carbon's Carbon Market Indicator (CMI), which is an independent, broker-based methodology for assessing the European carbon dioxide emissions market.
   It is designed to indicate market values at a certain moment each week. For more information
   about the CMI, see http://www.pointcarbon.com.
5 Carbon Market Indicator: http://www.pointcarbon.com.
6 See http://www.unfccc.int.
7 See http://www.ens.dk.
8 See http://eea.eu.int/.

20

Climate Change and Climate Awareness: A Critical Note

Robert S. Dischel

Consulting Meteorologist

"It's not over til it's over."[1]

DESPITE WHAT SOME HAVE TOLD YOU, THE GLOBAL WARMING DEBATE IS NOT SETTLED*

The experts agree on only a few points in the debate over global warming. That the earth is warmer now than any time in the last millennium is *not* one of them (see Mann *et al*, 2003; Soon and Baliunas, 2003). The data show that there has been a real increase in temperature when averaged over the earth's surface, but only over the last century or so. Additionally, the temperature of the upper atmosphere, if it has warmed at all, has not warmed as much as the earth's surface (see Karl, Knight, Easterling and Quayle, 1995). No one has yet explained this apparent disparity in warming. The areas most in agreement among climate scientists are these:

❑ There is a planetary warming effect (the greenhouse effect) that occurs when water vapour, clouds, CO_2, methane, and more, are present in the atmosphere, trapping some space-directed heat.[2] The earth would be a much colder place without a greenhouse effect (about $-18°C$ or near $0°F$), so the greenhouse effect is good.[3]
❑ The atmospheric concentrations of CO_2, methane and maybe some other gases have increased over the last century as a result of human activity.

*A chapter questioning the premise of emissions trading may seem odd, but you might need this information if the debate continues.

❑ The global mean surface temperature has probably increased during the same period.

PANEL 1 THE EARTH IS WARMING AT AN ALARMING RATE – OR IS IT?

Whether you see the earth as warmer depends on your age

"Warming of the earth is really the surface of the earth while there is no evidence of warming of the atmosphere."[4]

There is wide agreement that the globally averaged surface temperature of the planet has increased about 0.6°C (1°F) over the 20th century, and that, globally, the 1990s was the warmest decade and 1998 the warmest year in the instrumental record.[5] The differences of opinion begin when the above quote is dissected, as scientists are inclined to do.

The top chart in Figure a is of the annual average temperature difference (the bars) from the average temperature for the 1861–2000 period at many recording stations around the world.[6] The continuous line through the data is the same but filtering out sub-decadal fluctuations (a moving average). The thin whiskers at the end of each bar are the 95% confidence limits on uncertainties.

The averaged surface temperature increased from the beginning of the 20th century to the present with one significant pause beginning in the mid-1940s. The temperature actually decreased for about three decades before resuming the trend up. This has posed two problems for the anthropogenic global warming argument:

1. during the three decades of cooling, the concentration of CO_2 continued to increase, and, at least for this period, the CO_2-temperature correlation degraded;
2. the computer models have not readily recreated this cooling feature and this causes concern about the models.

Another problem for the modellers is that the models had predicted a greater warming of the earth's atmosphere for the most recent decade greater than we have observed.[7] Also, observations of the upper atmosphere show little of the warming seen at the surface. This has been difficult to explain. The US National Research Council formed a panel with members from both sides of the anthropogenic global warming debate to explore these issues. This council's conclusions, as summarised by them, are:

"Many in the scientific community believe that a distinctive greenhouse-warming signature is evident in surface temperature data for the past few decades. Some, however, are puzzled by the fact that satellite temperature measurements indicate little, if any, warming of the lower to mid-troposphere (the layer extending from the surface up to about 8 km) since such satellite observations first became operational

---

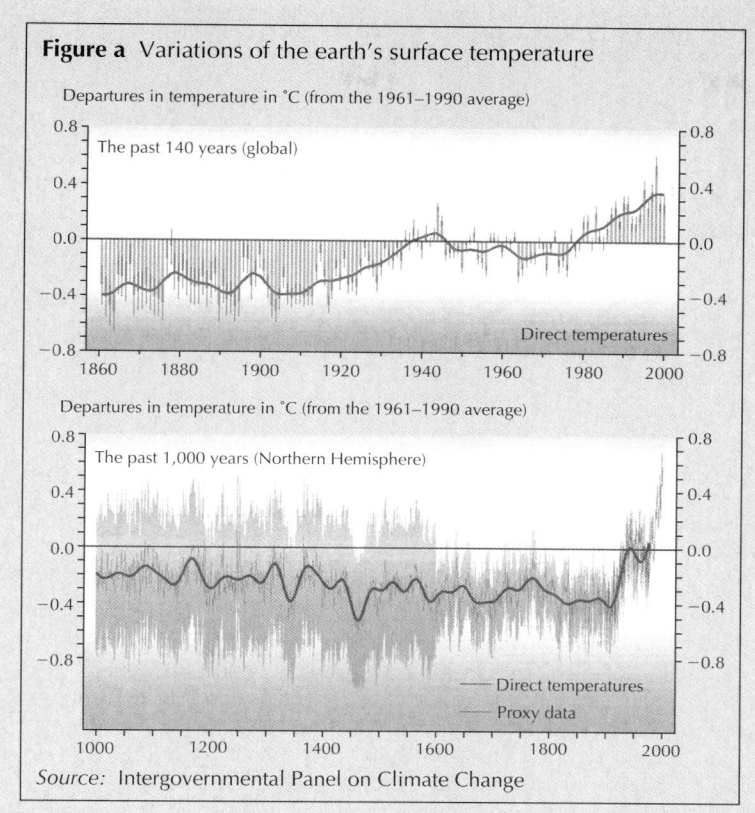

Figure a Variations of the earth's surface temperature

Departures in temperature in °C (from the 1961–1990 average)

The past 140 years (global)

Direct temperatures

Departures in temperature in °C (from the 1961–1990 average)

The past 1,000 years (Northern Hemisphere)

—— Direct temperatures
—— Proxy data

Source: Intergovernmental Panel on Climate Change

in 1979. The satellite measurements appear to be substantiated by independent trend estimates for this period based on radiosonde data. Some have interpreted this apparent discrepancy between surface and upper air observations as casting doubt on the overall reliability of the surface temperature record, whereas others have concluded that the satellite data (or the algorithms that are being used to convert them into temperatures) must be erroneous. It is also conceivable that temperatures at the earth's surface and aloft have not tracked each other perfectly because they have responded differently to natural and/or human-induced climate forcing during this particular 20-year period."[8]

Figure b is compiled from the recent three and a half centuries of the Central England temperature series and is the longest available instrumental record of temperature in the world.[9] Unfortunately, no measure of uncertainty is available, and it is a regional, not global temperature series.

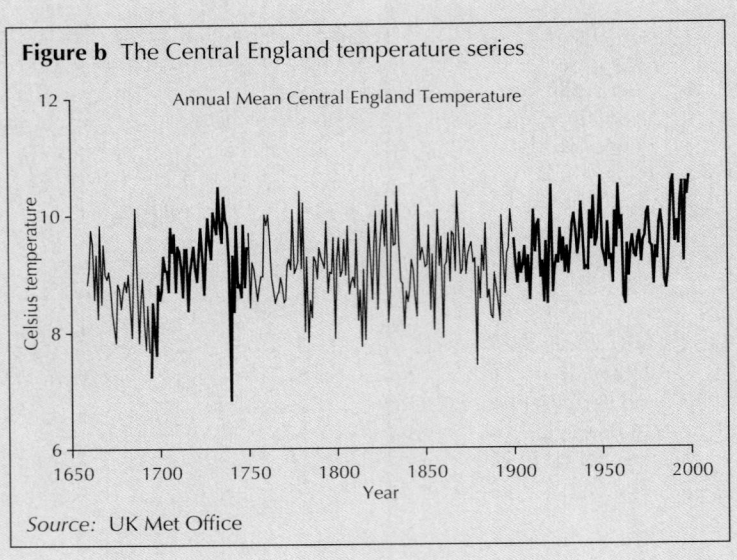

Figure b The Central England temperature series

Source: UK Met Office

The series in Figure b begins with a sharp cooling, seen as a drop of almost 2°C in annualised temperature. This is followed by an almost three-quarter century warming of about 3°C, from about 7.25°C to 10.5°C (the darkened line). In this warming period, the temperature rose from a point lower than those of the 20th century warming, to a point close to those of today – this earlier period in Central England witnessed a larger warming in a shorter time than that of the last century. It was abruptly terminated with a dazzling drop of 3.5°C in only a few years. Then temperatures recovered almost to the previous high, again, in only a few years. In terms of volatility, the warming, then precipitous cooling, then warming of the 18th century was more dramatic than the warming in the last century (also a darkened line).

The data in the top chart of Figure a is appended at the right of the lower chart in Figure a, to temperatures derived from non-instrumental sources (tree rings, corals, ice cores and lake sediments: proxy data). The thick continuous line is the 50-year moving average, and the grey region represents the 95% confidence limits.

Mann *et al* prepared the first version of the lower chart in Figure a, often called the "Hockey Stick" because of the long handle to the left and the sharp rise to the right. It is used to assert that temperatures today are warmer than anytime in the last 1,000 years. This is not demonstrated with certainty in the chart as the anomalies of the last decade are within the confidence limits in the middle of the millennium. This chart and the following assertion of the "warmest period in 1,000 years" are widely reproduced.[10]

Figure b shows some differences from the lower chart in Figure a. It is, however, only one of the many time series that have been used to construct a different view of temperatures for the last millennium.[11]

Most climate scientists believe that there was a century long warm period in Medieval times that was at least hemispheric in extent. A "little ice age" followed. Neither the warm period not the "Ice Age" appears in Figure a, and this led to a dispute on the accuracy of the data in Figure a, and how the investigators treated the data in the preparation of the chart.

There is a debate among scientists between two interpretations of proxy data for the last millennium. The alternative interpretation of proxy data from the last 1,000 years is consistent with descriptions of human events in historical times, particularly the medieval warm period and the little ice age.[12]

Since the last glacial epoch 11,000 years ago, there have been many warm and cool periods.

These three points are enough for some to conclude that humanity is altering the climate; but, for many others, this alone is not evidence enough to reach that conclusion. A correlation between CO_2 and temperature in the last century, no matter how strong or how weak, may be a warning of climate interference, but it is not demonstration of a cause and its effect.

Scientists have been able to point to retreating glaciers, longer growing seasons, changes in animal behaviour and much more as indicators of a planetary response to a warming climate. While these may be part of a *warning*, they are not proof of a *warming*, as some would have us believe.

Strong evidence of a warming is shown in the collective results of computer models of climate (the Coupled General Circulation Models, or GCMs). Many computer studies indicate that, if greenhouse gases (GHGs) increase, the temperature will continue to rise. Models estimate that the temperature might rise 1°C–2°C if concentrations of CO_2 should double.

Some scientists have challenged the computer model results, based on the difficulty of modelling some of the earth's features. Among these are the atmospheric concentration of water vapour (which is considered to be the most important GHG), clouds (also an important factor in the greenhouse effect) and the ocean circulation and heat storage (the ocean is where almost all of the incoming sunlight is absorbed).

Recently, two studies have been published that put the assumptions in models about water vapour and clouds further into question. In one, the investigators found new evidence of decreasing cloud cover with increasing sea surface temperature. They modelled this effect and found that it could be a negative feedback in the global climate – a temperature increase leads to a temperature decrease, just as the thermostat in a centrally heated home shuts down the heating when the home is warm enough (see Lindzen, Ming-Dah Chou and Hou, 2001[13]). In another study the investigators found less water in the tropical upper troposphere and their analysis suggests that assuming fixed relative humidity in climate models overestimates the greenhouse effect from water vapour.[14]

PANEL 2 CLIMATE PREDICTION AND GENERAL CIRCULATION MODELS

Researchers studying the earth's climate must understand the external forces on the earth and the exchanges within the earth system to explain past climate and to predict future climate. Figure a in this panel provides a schematic of exchanges on and within the earth system and helps to illustrate the processes central to our discussion.

Fundamental features of climate

Nature moves toward equilibrium and acts to relieve imbalances. While climate is usually explained in terms of weather statistics over long periods, we can also think of climate as the state of exchanges within the earth system as the system attempts to reach equilibrium (which it never really achieves).

The earth system is heated by solar radiation (sunlight) and cooled by terrestrial radiation directed to space (earthlight). For the purpose of our discussion of climate we can consider that nothing is added or removed from the system. (Meteors and molecular exchanges across the "top" of the atmosphere are important in other applications, but not for us.)

Sunlight, with only small variations, continuously heats the earth, more in the tropics and near the equator than it does elsewhere. Not only is there more ocean at these latitudes than elsewhere, but also the atmosphere is almost transparent to sunlight, allowing much of the sun's

Figure a A schematic of the earth-atmosphere-ocean system

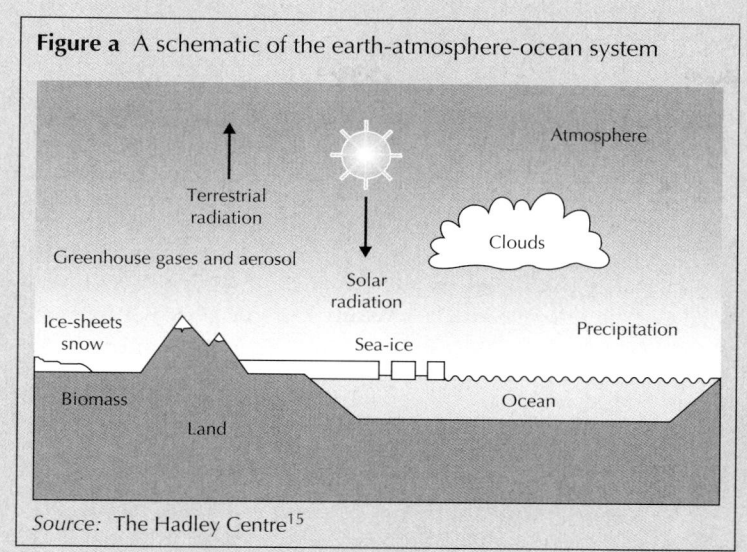

Source: The Hadley Centre[15]

energy to reach the earth's surface, and the ocean is also a better absorber of sunlight than other surface features (land and ice).

The greater heating of the ocean at lower latitudes causes temperature and density differences and currents flow in response. The tropical ocean also continuously heats the portions of the atmosphere lying just over it and evaporates water into it. This sets up horizontal temperature differences in the atmosphere causing winds and driving the atmospheric circulation. The rotation of the earth introduces significant complexities into the atmosphere and ocean circulations, but the end result is that the heat from the tropics is moved poleward in the great swirls of high and low pressure systems (which we respectively call fair weather and storms). The equator-to-pole temperature differences in both the atmosphere and ocean are much reduced from what they would be if there were no currents or winds.

The earth system radiates heat in the infrared portion of the spectrum of light from everywhere, and in energy levels that are related to temperature (higher temperature means more heat radiation). Some heat is redirected within the system and some is absorbed and reradiated by GHGs. Some of this radiation leaves the system as earthlight. The atmosphere would be almost transparent to spaceward directed infrared radiation but for reflecting and absorbing clouds and absorbing and reradiating GHGs.

It is the small difference between two large numbers (sunlight in and earthlight out) that determines whether the earth is warming or cooling (not daily or monthly, but over decades, centuries and millennia).

CLIMATE MODELS

Climate modellers set out to replicate the observed states of climate through time; they should be able to reproduce climates of the past at least as far back in time as they expect to project into the future ; only then can we have confidence in models. But that is not enough: the processes internal to the model must also fairly represent the observed processes in nature. If they did this, then we could have more confidence in their ability to make believable predictions.

The principal modellers tool is the Coupled Atmosphere-Ocean General Circulation Model (GCM). Within the GCM, the earth system is represented on a three-dimensional grid and at steps in time considered appropriate to the problem to be solved. The internal representation is by the Navier-Stokes equations (Newton's equations of motion and a variety of conservation equations), and parameterisations for real processes that are either difficult to replicate or are smaller than the grid of the model. Parameterisation is the "Achilles heel" of models.

Generally, models do well given that we are in an early stage of computer simulations of climate. There has been a stream of advances in the few decades of computerised numerical models of climate, and the rate of advance has been accelerated by a perceived urgency to better understand the climate effects of humanity.

Some of the most difficult problems in climate studies are also some of the most important processes yet to be modelled well. One of the most difficult is the hydrologic cycle: evaporation (mostly from the ocean), the take-up and transport of atmospheric water and water vapour, cloud formation and dissipation, and precipitation. Another is the quantification of cloud effects in the radiation budget: clouds reflect and absorb sunlight, and absorb and radiate infrared radiation. Some phenomena are smaller than the smallest scale in the models and must be parameterised, that is, expressed as empirical rules based on estimates (thunderstorms, for example).

Variability in the above processes make quantification of climate and climate prediction difficult. Also, water vapour is the most abundant and the most variable of the GHGs, and the purpose of the CO_2 model studies is to test the sensitivity of the climate to changes in CO_2 where these are small compared to naturally occurring water vapour variations.

Our knowledge of climate is limited by the intricacy of climate processes and this is a primary source of our uncertainty. We use computer models to help us integrate our understanding and to try out ideas and scenarios. We ask ourselves – "what will happen to the climate if the CO_2 concentrations double?" To answer the question we build computer models of climate in the hope of replicating at least some of the climate dynamics and to try out the scenarios. We use an

> incomplete set of observations (because we cannot measure the entire planet all the time) and are forced to make a variety of simplifying assumptions to represent the most difficult processes. We then numerically solve complicated equations.

A scientist, who is in the enhanced global warming "camp" and is a prominent climate modeller writes with his co-authors:

> There are many sources of uncertainty in the climate simulations and their interpretation. Principal among the uncertainties are climate sensitivity … and the simulated heat storage in the ocean (which depends upon the realism of the ocean circulation and mixing). It is possible to find other combinations of these 'parameters' that yield satisfactory agreement with observed climate change.[16]

Is it any wonder that scientists are uncertain of the future?

WILL RENEWED QUESTIONING OF GLOBAL WARMING LEAD TO QUESTIONING THE NEED TO TRADE CREDITS?

As a result of the reporting of the global warming debate, if the debate over global warming were held in a courtroom today, with lay citizens as the jury and the developed nations as the defendants, the majority verdict would certainly be guilty – guilty of disrespecting the climate and causing unintended consequences. The developed nations have already been convicted in the court of political opinion, and that court sentenced them to reduce emissions to the Kyoto limits.

Science always leaves room for doubt. In any case, science is not decided by consensus but by evidence, and the evidence to continue the debate is strong. Both sides – being convinced or not – have strong arguments in their favour.

"Climate change" is a redundant phrase, as climate has never been in a steady state: it evolves; it always has and always will. This is because climate, on all time scales, is the integration of many events, each with its own variability. There is no static state of climate, and perhaps not even a dynamic steady state where the sequence of events has a stationary average.

Some respected scientists continue to challenge the assertions of anthropogenic warming, so the issue is not settled. If they are able to reopen the issue in the court of public opinion, and the challenge they bring is seen to have merit (meaning the link between CO_2 and warming is thrown into question), what would be the implications for the Kyoto limits? What would then be the durability of an emissions trading market?

Surely, the decision to impose limits would not be immediately reversed. But would the discussions of the inadequacy to reverse climate change lead to a change in the requirements? The reality of the cost of meeting the limits weighs in as reluctance for some to move forward quickly and could provide support for a re-evaluation. Many admit that society may have altered the climate, even though the magnitude and mechanism of the change is still in debate. The likely outcome of the re-evaluation would be a modification of limitations and practices.

POLITICAL ACTION – DO SOMETHING BEFORE IT IS TOO LATE

A recent guide to the United Nations Framework Connection on Climate Change (UNFCCC) states, "While the world's climate has always varied naturally, the vast majority of scientists now believe that rising concentrations of GHGs in the earth's atmosphere … are overriding this natural variability and leading to potentially irreversible climate change" (see UNFCCC, 2002).

It is clear from this statement that the UNFCCC is operating only within the context of anthropogenic global warming. Importantly, the assertion that "the vast majority of scientists now believe" in the enhanced global warming is misleading, yet it has become a mantra for advocates of action. A more truthful phrase would have been, "many scientists believe". In the eyes of the UNFCCC, its main achievement is in having promoted recognition of global climate change and setting limits on "greenhouse gas concentrations in the atmosphere at a level that would prevent dangerous anthropogenic interference with the climate system" (see Chapter 1).

NASA SCIENTIST FANS THE EMBERS OF GLOBAL WARMING

Scientists had recognised the potential for anthropogenic warming of the planet for more than a century, but it was during the unusually hot and dry summer of 1988 that the wall between climate science and political agenda was struck hard and began to crumble. A US National Aeronautics and Space Agency (NASA) scientist, Dr James Hansen, testified before a US Senate committee that, based on computer model results he could say, with "ninety-nine percent confidence", that "the greenhouse effect has been detected, and it is changing our climate now" (See *Atlantic Monthly Online*, 2000). The resulting events developed very quickly.

(Hansen took much heat from the scientific community for reaching beyond what others thought was the state of knowledge. He has moderated his statement several times since 1988. For example, he has said more recently, in the *New York Times* of 19 August 2000, "The prospects for having a modest climate impact instead of a disastrous one are quite good, I think.")

The UNFCCC guide states,[17]

> Increasing scientific evidence of human interference with the climate system, coupled with growing public concern over global environmental issues, began to push climate into the political agenda in the mid-1980s. Recognizing the needs of policy makers for authoritative and up-to-date scientific information, the World Meteorological Organization and the UN Environment Programme (UNEP) established the Intergovernmental Panel on Climate Change (IPCC) in 1988.[18]

The IPCC's mandate is to assess the available scientific, technical and socioeconomic information in the field of climate change. The panel is the most prominent of all agencies studying climate change; it is in IPCC documents that most advocates of the anthropogenic global warming find support for their view. In a 1995 report (see Intergovernmental Panel on Climate Change, 1996) the IPCC concluded that human activity was likely influencing global climate:

> Our ability to quantify the human influence on global climate is currently limited because the expected signal is still emerging from the noise of natural variability, and because there are uncertainties in key factors. ... Nevertheless, the balance of evidence suggests that there is a discernible human influence on global climate.

These "uncertainties" of the first sentence were not as widely reported and quoted as the second. In particular, the phrase "the balance of evidence suggests that there is a discernible human influence" is significant because it was the strongest statement of human culpability from an organisation led by renowned scientists. It quickly became a familiar quote heard from global change advocates who insisted the debate over anthropogenic warming was now settled; it significantly increased people's conviction that humanity was at fault; it shifted the balance of influence in the global warming debate in favour of a need for action.

ONE ADMINISTRATION'S BALLOON IS ANOTHER'S FOOTBALL

The US National Assessment Synthesis Team (NAST) stated on the front of its report (2001), "Climate Change in the United States",

> Humanity's influence on the global climate will grow in the 21st century. Increasingly, there will be significant climate-related changes that will affect each one of us. We must begin now to consider our responses, as the actions taken today will affect the quality of life for us and future generations.

NAST delivered the report to the US Congressional Subcommittee on Global Change Research just before the Clinton administration left the White House. It is a significant statement from a scientific group, notable for the absence of any doubt about the future.

This statement (Hansen *et al*, 2000) is by a prominent climate scientist: "There is consensus among scientists that GHGs are to blame for global warming, and most scientists believe CO_2 is the main culprit."

The reader is cautioned to be alert whenever phrases such as "the vast majority believe" or "there is a consensus". The debate is very much continuing because many scientists are not convinced of a global crisis on the current evidence and are quite clear that alternative interpretations of the evidence are quite satisfactory. For a new concept to sweep away more conventional thought, the evidence needs to be overwhelming, and some believe the evidence of enhanced global warming is not.

CAN'T WE JUST GET ALONG?

Climate science is a young science and all evidence is a piece of a grand puzzle. The climate is a complex process involving interactions among air, land, water and ice, the understanding of which is more conceptual than quantitative. This leaves much room for a wide range of beliefs.

Among the advocates of immediate action to reduce emissions, there are those who sincerely believe we are endangering the climate. Many of these advocates are responsible scientists and other informed people who are genuinely concerned for the environment, and who, after carefully considering the evidence, think it important to be cautious about continued emissions. But, as thinking people, they would also consider the concern surrounding the certainty expressed by others.

We can find among the advocates the "activists", who, in the extreme, are those who promote, with no uncertainty, these four precepts:

❏ the world is warming at an alarming rate;
❏ emissions of GHGs from human activities, primarily CO_2, are the cause of global warming;
❏ there is enough evidence now to believe that humans are dangerously perturbing global climate; and
❏ we must act now to reduce emissions to preserve the current climate.

For a broader discussion of the activist position, see Essex and McKitrick's *Doctrine of Certainty*.[19]

Among those who prefer no reduction in emissions at this time, we might expect to find some businesses, politicians and others who could benefit from delayed action, regardless of the potential danger. We would also find those who have not been convinced by what (the "unruffled") they see as inadequate evidence for alarm: people who see no scientific problem, except for the perceived misuse of scientific results. The "unruffled" believe the following four precepts:

❏ the world is not warming anywhere at an alarming rate, and may not be warming at all;
❏ CO_2 is a minor GHG whose current increases may have no effect on the planet's heat budget;
❏ there is enough evidence of similar climate events in history to see the events causing anxiety today as fitting comfortably in the realm of "normal" events; and

❏ acting now to reduce emissions will be costly and ineffective and is misguided.

Most of us will find ourselves clustered somewhere along the spectrum bounded by these positions. Rather than "activist" and "unruffled" we might have chosen the terms "protagonist" and "antagonist". However, we see antagonists on both sides of the issue.

There are, of course, other important opinions. For example some believe that:

❏ the Kyoto limits are unworkable;
❏ if they could be met, it still would not alter the climate process; and
❏ it is too costly to try.

We might call those with this view the "non-activists" because we do not know their opinion on climate, but we do know their opinion on action. The US view towards climate change action has moved from an activist position under the Clinton administration to the non-activist position under the Bush administration.

Many in the energy industry would agree with this prominent scientist when he writes: "It is impractical to stop CO_2 from increasing in the near term, as fossil fuels are the engine of the global economy."[20]

The 2001 IPCC assessment (see IPCC Third Assessment Report) states,

> Global surface temperatures have increased about 0.6°C (plus or minus 0.2°C) since the late-19th century, and about 0.4°F (0.2 to 0.3°C) over the past 25 years (the period with the most credible data). The warming has not been globally uniform. Some areas (including parts of the southeastern U.S.) have, in fact, cooled over the last century. The recent warmth has been greatest over North America and Eurasia between 40 and 70°N. Warming, assisted by the record El Niño of 1997–1998, has continued right up to the present, with 2001 being the second warmest year on record after 1998.

Few dispute that these statistics point to real warming at the earth's surface. The disagreements occur over the interpretation and use of the data. People misuse this data if they disregard or trivialise the following:

❏ The warming of the last century was not continuous: from the 1940s through the mid-1970s, scientists observed a cooling at the earth's surface that has never been adequately explained, except as a natural climate variation (see Karl *et al*, 1995).[21] The catastrophists of the time worried about global cooling and a returning ice age; so far they have been wrong.

❑ Direct measurements of the temperature of the atmosphere from instruments carried aloft by balloons (radiosondes) show that the upper atmosphere is not warming at the same rate as is the earth's surface.

❑ Indirect measurement of atmospheric temperatures inferred from satellite instruments are consistent with the radiosonde observations.

❑ The details of the few instrumental records in mid-latitude Europe going back a few centuries to the time of Galileo show periods when warming was more rapid than it was in the last century (see Figure b in Panel 1).

❑ Many scientists believe that temperatures in medieval times were warmer than today. Among the wealth of anecdotal evidence is that this *climate optimum* allowed the Vikings to populate Greenland and explore the North American coast, and it was followed by the mini ice age that ended the Greenland occupation as the colony collapsed.

This quotation from the US National Climate Data Center (NCDC) of the National Oceanic Atmospheric Administration (NOAA), in explaining the need to measure the present against the past, puts it clearly:

> The last decade of the 20th Century was the warmest in the entire global instrumental record, starting in the mid-19th century. All 10 years rank among the 15 warmest, and include the 6 warmest years on record. This warmth is unusual for the past century, but what about in the context of past centuries or millennia? It is only through the reconstruction of past climate that we can truly evaluate the magnitude of this warming.[22]

TIME MAKES THE DIFFERENCE

The meteorological community describes the current condition of the atmosphere and its near-term evolution as weather. The community understands that its view of evolving weather is constrained by the amount of information it possesses, and believes that there are immeasurable events that will drive the atmosphere in ways that cannot at present be foreseen. This means that there is a limit to predictability – that weather is somewhat unpredictable. Meteorologists believe that this limit on weather predictability is somewhere between a few days to two weeks into the future. This depends on regional and global current weather patterns and on what is to be predicted.

Climate is more than the average state of the atmosphere. Climate is a complex and ever-changing event that is described by average conditions and departures from average of conditions. Global and regional climate depends on the states of the atmosphere, the ocean, ice cover on land and sea, land surfaces and the influences of living things (correspondingly, the atmosphere, hydrosphere, cryosphere, surface of the lithosphere, and biosphere). The interplay among these physical and biological "spheres", driven principally by the sun's energy, is the focus of climate and its variations. This interplay (called interactions or exchanges), from local to global scales, over periods of months to geological time, shapes the climate.

WEATHER OR CLIMATE: THE MEDIA'S ROLE
There is a difference between weather and climate. A drought in a normally humid region is not its climate unless the drought is prolonged for years or decades – but drought in a desert is its climate. Record rainfall in a normally arid region is not its climate, but rainfall of a few metres in Bangladesh during the monsoon season is normal and is its climate.

Retreating glaciers, thinning of sea ice, lower daily minimum temperatures and longer growing seasons might be indicators of local, regional or even global warming, as these are potentially the beginnings of a sustained shift. Changes in ocean temperatures bear close scrutiny as the ocean normally changes slowly and its impacts on the atmosphere are prolonged.

Record-breaking heat, cold, rainfall, snowfall, wind, hail, flooding, heat waves and storms are weather events. Extremely hot summers or cool summers, and extremely cold or warm winters are not the climate of temperate regions unless they persist over years or decades.

The media could offer clear and comprehensible reporting on science, but in reporting on global warming they have not always done so: too often they have presented alarming proclamations as evidence for global change, and this has supported political agendas and treaty decisions. And the media can quickly take the other side when a scientist discovers something like a colder Antarctic, which at a glance appears to contradict global warming, but, when understood in a broader context, may not.

Of course, it may be that some in the media fail to understand the difference between weather and climate. This might explain the blurring of the line between weather events and climate events. The disservice to the public is that some events are indeed climate-related, and the media often do not, or perhaps cannot, distinguish them from weather-related events. Confused reporting promotes a confused public.

Complex processes such as enhanced global warming are always difficult for a scientist to explain to a layperson, partly because the language of science is not often in the vernacular of the public, and because scientists include uncertainty in their thinking. Uncertainty, often required in science to remain truthful to the imperfect information, can seem undecided or unnecessarily cautious to a layperson. When media or political agendas filter out the uncertainty, the issues can be misrepresented. (Weather forecasts, for example, are statements of possibilities and probabilities that are filtered for the public.)

THE LAST WORDS

I have, I hope, demonstrated my belief that there is no *direct* connection between fossil fuel burning and climate change, and that asserting "developed nations caused a climate change" might be stretching the underlying science and facts. I believe that it is too soon, and the world's climate is too complex, to allow anyone to speak with certainty of CO_2 as the cause and global warming as the result.

I have criticised the popular view of anthropogenic global warming, not to argue that continuing to emit pollutants is acceptable, but to encourage caution in the views of the readers – especially in a politically affected arena such as the Kyoto limits. As the focus on climate matures, thinking evolves and new ideas replace old ones. Some scientists are reporting that methane as a GHG might be more important than CO_2, and that soot particles in the atmosphere may have reduced incoming sunlight by a surprising 10%. The particles reflect sunlight and are a catalyst for cloud production as they encourage the coalescence of water droplets. The decrease in sunlight was observed during the warmest decade in a century and a half. Looking again at the proposed "Iris effect" (see Lindzen, *et al*, 2001), we have to ask – What other surprises await us as we develop a deeper understanding of the interactions and inter-dependencies of climate?

Scientific articles raising doubt about our ability to reduce fossil fuel consumption are on the rise as the demand for power increases each decade. Awareness of the difficulty and cost of reducing emissions is also on the rise. The current paucity of alternatives to burning fossil fuels will not easily change: new technologies take decades to work their way into the economy. If you believe in anthropogenic global warming, then you must be troubled by the possibility of our not being able to reverse climate change.

No citizen of any country, developed or not, could reasonably assert that pollution is good for the environment or for health. What then must we do? We must begin to shift away from current power-generation practices; we must prepare for a possible shift in climate; we must adapt.

1   Yogi Berra, commenting on the New York Mets' chances of winning the 1973 National League East Pennants race. See Pepe, Phil, 1989, *The Wit and Wisdom of Yogi Berra* (Triumph Books, Chicago, 2002).

2   Naturally occurring greenhouse gases (GHG) are primarily water vapour, carbon dioxide, methane, nitrous oxide and ozone. Water vapour is the most abundant, most variable and most effective GHG. The principal anthropogenic GHGs are carbon dioxide, nitrous oxide, methane and chlorofluorocarbons.

3   Some people use the use term "greenhouse effect" to mean the enhanced greenhouse effect, where humanity has added GHGs to those that naturally occur and caused a climate change. We mean the naturally occurring greenhouse effect. We also distinguish between the general term "global warming", a rise in average temperature with no reference to cause, and "anthropogenic global warming", the postulated impact on climate from burning fossil fuels.

4   S. Fred Singer, "The Kyoto Protocol: A Post-Mortem," *The New Atlantis*, Number 4, Winter 2004, pp. 66–73.

5   IPCC Third Assessment Report: Climate Change 2001: The Scientific Basis, 2001. URL: http://www.ipcc.ch/pub/reports.htm

6   ibid.

7   "Inhaling a Decade of Hot Air Vapors" by Patrick Michaels The Washington Times Sunday, June 28, 1998 Dr. Michaels, climatologist and professor at the University of Virginia.

8   Panel on Reconciling Temperature Observations, National Research Council, 2000, Reconciling Observations of Global Temperature Change, National Academies Press. Mann, M.E., R. S. Bradley, and M.K. Hughes, 1999. Northern Hemisphere temperatures during the past millennium: Inferences, uncertainties, and limitations. *Geophysical Research Letters* **26**: 759–762.

9   The UK Met Office, Hadley Centre, URL: http://www.metoffice.com/research/hadleycentre/
    obsdata/CET.htm

10 Mann, M.E., R. S. Bradley, and M.K. Hughes, 1999. "Northern Hemisphere temperatures
    during the past millennium: Inferences, uncertainties, and limitations". *Geophysical Research
    Letters* **26**: 759–762.

11 IPCC Third Assessment Report: Climate Change 2001: The Scientific Basis, 2001. URL:
    http://www. ipcc.ch/pub/reports.htm

12 Soon, Willie and Baliunas, Sallie, 2003, "Proxy climatic and environmental changes of the
    past 1000 years". Climate Research vol. 23, pp. 89–110.

13 In this, they write, "This new mechanism would, in effect, constitute an adaptive infrared
    iris that opens and closes in order to control the Outgoing Longwave Radiation in response
    to changes in surface temperature in a manner similar to the way in which an eye's iris opens
    and closes in response to changing light levels."

14 Minschwaner, K., and A. E. Dessler, 2004, "Water Vapor Feedback in the Tropical Upper
    Troposphere: Model Results and Observations", *Journal of Climate*, **17**, 1272–82.

15 http://www.met-office.gov.uk/research/hadleycentre/models/climate_system.html

16 Hansen is head of the NASA Goddard Institute for Space Studies.

17 "A Guide to the Climate Change Convention and Its Kyoto Protocol," UNFCCC,
    Climate Change Secretariat, Bonn, Germany, 2002. URL: http://unfccc.int/resource/
    guideconvkp-p.pdf.

18 Summary for Policymakers: The Science of Climate Change – IPCC Working Group I, URL:
    http://www.ipcc.ch/pub/sarsum1.htm

19 In this, they say,
    "The Earth is Warming
    Warming has already been observed.
    Humans are causing it.
    All but a handful of scientists on the fringe believe it.
    Warming is bad.
    Action is required immediately.
    Any action is better than none.
    Uncertainty only covers the ulterior motives of individuals aiming to stop needed action.
    Those who defend uncertainty are bad people"

    Taken by Storm – The Troubled Science, Policy and Politics of Global Warming.

20 Hansen, J. E., 2001, "The Forcing Agents Underlying Climate Change", statement of
    Dr. James E. Hansen, Head, NASA Goddard Institute for Space Studies, before the United
    States Senate Committee on Commerce, Science and Transportation on May 1, 2001.

21 Here, they write, "The record in Karl (1995) shows a sharp rise in temperature during the
    1930s and a modest cooling trend from the 1950s to the 1970s, at which time the temperature
    rapidly increased …"

22 "A Paleo Perspective On Global Warming", 19 May 2000, NOAA Paleoclimatology Program,
    US National Climatic Data Center. URL: http://www.ngdc.noaa.gov/paleo/globalwarming/
    home.htm

REFERENCES

Atlantic Monthly Online, 2000, URL: http://www.theatlantic.com/issues/2000/07/
sarewitz.htm, July.

Essex, C., and R. McKitrick, 2002 "Taken by Storm: The Troubled Science, Policy and
Politics of Global Warming" (Toronto: Key Porter Books).

Hansen, J. E., 2001, "The Forcing Agents Underlying Climate Change", statement of Dr. James E. Hansen, Head, NASA Goddard Institute for Space Studies, before the United States Senate Committee on Commerce, Science and Transportation on May 1, 2001.

Hansen, J., et al, 2000, "Global Warming in the Twenty-First Century: An Alternative Scenario". (US) National Academy of Science, *USA,* **97**, pp. 9875–80.

Intergovernmental Panel on Climate Change, 1996, *Climate Change 1995: The Science of Climate Change* (Cambridge, UK: Cambridge University Press).

IPCC Third Assessment Report, "Climate Change 2001: The Scientific Basis", URL: http://www.ipcc.ch/pub/reports.htm.

IPCC Working Group I, "Summary for Policymakers: The Science of Climate Change", URL: http://www.ipcc.ch/pub/sarsum1.htm.

Karl, T. R., et al, 1995, "Trends in U.S. Climate during the Twentieth Century", *Consequences* **1(1)**.

Lindzen, R. S., M.-D. Chou, and A. Y. Hou, 2001, "Does the Earth Have an Adaptive Infrared Iris?", *Bulletin of the American Meteorological Society,* **82(3)**, pp. 417–32.

Mann, M. E., et al, 2003, "On Past Temperatures and Anomalous Late 20th Century Warmth", *Eos,* **84**, pp. 256–8.

Minschwaner, K., and A. E. Dessler, 2004, "Water Vapor Feedback in the Tropical Upper Troposphere: Model Results and Observations", *Journal of Climate,* **17**, 1272–82.

National Assessment Synthesis Team, 2001, "Climate Change Impacts on the United States: The Potential Consequences of Climate Variability", US Global Change Research Program, Available from Cambridge University Press and at URL: http://www.usgcrp.gov/usgcrp/Library/nationalassessment/00Intro.pdf.

Soon, W., and S. Baliunas, 2003, "Proxy Climatic and Environmental Changes of the Past 1000 years", *Climate Research,* **23**, pp. 89–110.

UNFCCC, 2002, "A Guide to the Climate Change Convention and Its Kyoto Protocol", Climate Change Secretariat, Bonn, Germany, URL: http://unfccc.int/resource/guideconvkp-p.pdf.

Index